The Quotable Saint

THE QUOTABLE SAINT

Rosemary Ellen Guiley

Checkmark Books®
An imprint of Facts On File, Inc.

The Quotable Saint

Checkmark Books
An imprint of Facts On File, Inc.
132 West 31st Street
New York NY 10001

Library of Congress Cataloging-in-Publication Data

The quotable saint / [compiled by] Rosemary Ellen Guiley.
p. cm.
Includes bibliographical references and index.
ISBN 0-8160-4375-2 (hc : alk. paper)—ISBN 0-8160-4376-0 (pbk. : alk. paper)
1. Christian life—Quotations, maxims, etc. 2. Christian saints—Quotations, maxims, etc. 3. Christian life—Catholic authors. I. Guiley, Rosemary.

BX2350.3.Q86 2002
230—dc21 2002023540

Checkmark Books are available at special discounts when purchased in bulk quantities for businesses, associations, institutions, or sales promotions. Please call our Special Sales Department in New York at (212) 967-8800 or (800) 322-8755.

You can find Facts On File on the World Wide Web at http://www.factsonfile.com

Cover design by Cathy Rincon

Printed in the United States of America

MP Hermitage 10 9 8 7 6 5 4 3 2 1

This book is printed on acid-free paper.

CONTENTS

PREFACE

The Quotable Saint is organized alphabetically by topic. Some of the long entries, such as CHRIST, GOD, and PRAYER, are subdivided into categories, and the subheadings are in alphabetical order. I did not alphabetize the saints by name within topics, in order to provide variety. However, if I used more than one quotation from a particular saint within the same topic, I grouped all those quotations together.

In choosing the material, I sought to provide a broad representation of works and saints, from well-known to lesser-known throughout the history of Christianity. I researched treatises, sermons, orations, books, journals, personal writing, autobiographies, biographies, and diaries of mystical experiences. My primary objective was to find nuggets of wisdom that would resonate with the interests and concerns of daily life in present times, so that this book would be useful, illuminating, and inspiring to the reader. Many lesser-known saints delivered magnificently in that respect, sometimes outshining their more famous associates. The writings of the saints of course reflect their roles and concerns of their own times. For example, many of the towering figures of early Christianity were focused on refuting heresies and establishing the theology of the church. Mystics were focused on their inner lives, and preachers and missionaries gave their full attention to exhorting people on virtues, vices, sin, and repentance. Some saints were very prolific, while others left behind few written works.

My general definition of saint was those individuals recognized by the church as canonized, beatified, and declared venerable. There are exceptions, such as the hermits, monks, and abbots known as Desert Fathers; the holy men whose writings are compiled in *The Philokalia;* and individuals considered saints by acclaim or martyrdom. I included Julian of Norwich, whose cause for beatification stalled because of lack of information about her personal life, but whose mystical work, *Revelations of Divine Love,* is significant.

The words of the saints make them come alive in a vivid way. I hope that through this book the reader can become better acquainted with them, so that they are no longer remote, exalted figures, but wise people we can envision meeting and talking with today.

INTRODUCTION

"Words are truly the images of the soul," Basil the Great once wrote in one of his letters. No better description can be made of the writings of the saints. For centuries, golden wisdom and inspiration have poured forth from those whose holiness has given them the exalted status of sainthood, either by popular acclaim or by official church recognition. In their lives and mystical experiences, in their religious studies and practices, the saints have looked into the depths of their souls and recorded what they found there.

The compilation of this book was a spiritual journey for me. For a long time, I have been reading and researching the saints as part of the broad net I have cast for my own spiritual study. After completing *The Encyclopedia of Saints*, a collection of biographical profiles of saints and their lives and works, it was natural to focus more closely on their personal works: their explanations of theology and dogma; their views on virtues and vices; their mystical views on God, Christ, Mary, creation, heaven and hell, the soul and the human condition; their poignant diaries and letters detailing their triumphs, fears, accomplishments, and sufferings; and their personal ecstasies and experiences in the presence of the divine. The result is *The Quotable Saint*, a distillation of the thoughts and insights of saints, which continue to illuminate and inspire us in daily life.

At times I felt weighed down by what seemed like an emphasis on sin, penance, and suffering. As I went deeper into the writings, I felt more and more uplifted. The message of the saints is not so much the consequences of sin, but the call to the right life: to embody the virtues and unite with God. Of course, they often had to write for the needs of their audiences, and sometimes people listen only when they hear of the potential dire consequences of their actions—or their failure to act.

For several years, I read nothing but works about the saints and by the saints. Toward the end of the research, I suddenly realized how profoundly this spiritual study had changed me—the way I think, my outlook, my behavior, my spiritual consciousness. One cannot immerse one's self in spiritual thought without being changed by it. If you take this book and read a little of it every day, and spend a few minutes meditating on the wisdom of the saints, you will experience significant inner changes, too. Those changes will in turn change your outer world for the better.

Contemplation of spiritual wisdom is essential for our well-being. "Every day keep turning over in your mind some thought which has deeply impressed you and fallen into your heart. Unless you exercise your powers of thought, the soul becomes numb," advised Theophan the Recluse, the Russian bishop who translated *The Philokalia* writings of the Eastern fathers and ascetics into Russian. Much of our reading and entertainment in daily life is soul-numbing. But the words of the saints stimulate soul-searching.

I cannot say that I have a favorite saint, or even several favorite saints, as a result of this research and contemplation. Each saint weaves a unique strand in a tapestry of grand design. I appreciate the intellectual thought of saints such as Augustine and Thomas Aquinas equally with the heart-centered mysticism expressed by the women visionaries such as Gertrude the Great, Hildegard of Bingen, and Julian of Norwich. Each has its place and its power.

I would give the titles "golden-mouthed," "honey-mouthed," and "golden-streamed" to many saints besides John Chrysostom, Bernard of Clairvaux, and John Damascene, respectively. I was quite taken with the writings of some other saints as well. For example, the *Divine Mercy in My Soul* of Faustina Kowalska moved me deeply. The sermons of Vincent Ferrer express a succinct and crisp wisdom. The writings of Josemaría Escrivá dispense a most practical advice. The letters of Paulinus of Nola about early Christianity are illuminating. Overall, I resonated profoundly with the mystical insights of the Desert Fathers and the Eastern saints, such as collected in *The Philokalia*. I highly recommend John Climacus's *The Ladder of Divine Ascent*.

A mystic and abbot of Sinai, John Climacus was regarded as one of the Eastern Fathers of the Church. After studying at the famous monastery at Mount Sinai, he retired to a cave and spent 20 years in near isolation, studying the lives of the saints and practicing severe austerities. He visited monks in Egypt. In 600 he became abbot of the Sinai monastery, and attracted many pilgrims. His surname, Climacus, comes from *The Ladder of Divine Ascent*; Climacus *(klimakos)* means "ladder." There are 30 chapters in the book, which correspond to the first 30 years of Jesus' life. They provide steps in the spiritual ladder of ascent to God. Each step describes a certain virtue or passion and the path that can lead from it. The book offers no formulae, but instructs that "the life you have is hidden with Christ in God." The stages of the spiritual life set forth by John are the break with the world; the practice of asceticism; the struggle against the passions; the practice of simplicity, humility, and discernment; and union with God.

John Climacus's work is but one of many by numerous other saints that have strong merit. The works of the saints are like jewels in a crown—they are all beautiful.

I also especially appreciated the visionary writings of women saints, among them—besides those already mentioned—Catherine of Siena, Catherine of Genoa, Teresa of Ávila, Mary of Agreda, Elisabeth of Schönau, Mechtilde of Magdeburg, Maria Maddalena de' Pazzi, and others. Women, shut out of the central authority of the church, often established their authority through direct experience.

The women visionaries reveal an essential part of the spiritual quest. No matter how much we read and study, each of us ultimately discovers Truth through our own direct experience and understanding.

In all, the wisdom of the saints helps us by providing shining lamps to light our way. The saints' wisdom is timeless. The same concerns, difficulties, struggles, insights, yearnings, aspirations, and triumphs that have engaged them over the centuries are found in the hearts and minds and lives of people today. Their wisdom transcends religious boundaries and speaks to all people, everywhere.

Reading the wisdom of the saints turns our thoughts to different and higher planes. Peter of Alcantara counseled in his *Treatise on Prayer & Meditation*, "Keep the thought of God continually before you, and walk always in his presence."

—Rosemary Ellen Guiley, Ph.D.

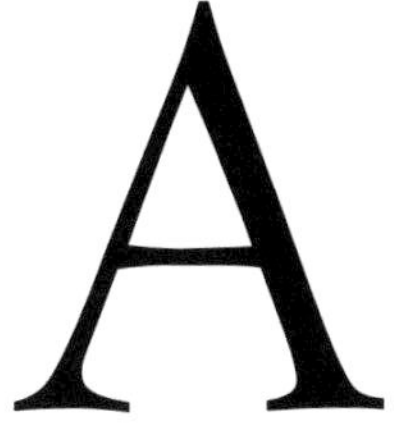

Abortion

The woman who destroys voluntarily a fetus incurs the pain of murder.

—Basil the Great, *letter to Amphilochios*

Abundance

God, my God, because you are mine, I lack nothing.

—Gertrude the Great, *Spiritual Exercises*

God feeds the fowls, and daily sustenance is furnished the sparrows, and to those creatures who have no sense of things Christian, do you think that to a servant of God, do you think that to one devoted to good works, do you think that to one dear to the Lord anything will be lacking?

—Cyprian of Carthage, *Works and Almsgiving*

Giving and receiving—this is the principle of the multiplication of goods. It holds good in agriculture, in teaching, in any sort of trade.

—John Chrysostom, *On the First Letter to the Corinthians*

Action

Action is worth nothing without prayer: prayer grows in value with sacrifice.

—Josemaría Escrivá, *The Way*

Never be men or women of long action and short prayer.

—Josemaría Escrivá, *The Way*

We cannot preach what we do not practice.

—Josemaría Escrivá, *The Forge*

Adoration

What an honor it is for your body to be spiritually sacrificed in the hour of your adoration before the Blessed Sacrament!

What a privilege for your soul to do here below what the angels and saints are doing in heaven so sweetly and gloriously although you have not their understanding nor their light but only the feeble light of faith.

—Louis de Montfort, *letter*

May your prayer always be a real and sincere act of adoration of God.

—Josemaría Escrivá, *The Forge*

Adultery

There is nothing polluted in the human frame except a man defile this with fornication and adultery.

—Cyril of Jerusalem, *Catecheses*

Never seek another woman's couch; never yearn for physical union with anyone else. Adultery is a grave matter: it is an outrage against nature.

—Ambrose, *Hexaemeron*

A man who has a spouse joined to him and in a legal marriage secretly pollutes the wife of his neighbor and, in her turn, a woman takes the husband of another woman. This is the worst iniquity and vast is the number of those who offend in this way. The earth is full of the uncleanness of fornication.

—Elisabeth of Schönau, *The Book of the Ways of God*

Ambition

Men in high places are driven by insatiable ambition to clutch at still greater prizes. And nowhere is there any final satisfaction, because nothing there can be defined as absolutely the best or the highest.

—Bernard of Clairvaux, *On Loving God*

The ambitious are not satisfied by the attainment of certain honors: their ambition and pride continually increase; and their inquietude, their envy, and their fears are multiplied.

—Alphonsus Liguori, *sermon*

Poor worldings! they labor and toil to acquire an increase of wealth and property; but never enjoy repose: the more they accumulate riches, the greater their disquietude and vexation.

—Alphonsus Liguori, *sermon*

Avoid the slippery dangers of exacting state service. Position has an inviting title, but it brings evil slavery and a wretched end. He who now delights in desiring it, later repents of having desired it. It is pleasant to mount the summit, but fearsome to descend from it; if you stumble, your fall from the top of the citadel will be worse.

—Paulinus of Nola, *letter*

Angels

Creation and Nature of Angels

Each angel is imprinted by the creative Word of God with the forms of all things, spiritual and corporeal.

—Thomas Aquinas, *Summa Theologica*

When God created the angels in heaven he established them in his grace.

—Francis de Sales, *Oeuvres*

In my opinion, an angel is characterized by the fact that he is not tricked into sinning.

—John Climacus, *The Ladder of Divine Ascent*

God loves in the Seraphim as charity, knows in the Cherubim as truth, is seated in the Thrones as equity, reigns in the Dominations as majesty, rules in the Principalities as principle, guards in the Powers as salvation, acts in the Virtues as strength, reveals in the Archangels as light, assists in the Angels as piety.

—Bernard of Clairvaux, *De Coinsideratione*

His holiness is so great that all the Powers and Virtues tremble before Him.

—Faustina Kowalska, *Divine Mercy in My Soul*

Cherubim means knowledge in abundance. They provide an everlasting protection for that which appeases God, namely, the calm of your heart, and they will cast a shadow of protection against all the attacks of malign spirits.

—John Cassian, *Conferences*

The angels were created in the empyrean heavens and in the state of grace by which they might be first to merit the reward of glory. For although they were in the midst of glory, the Divinity itself was not to be made manifest to them face to face and unveiled, until they should be merited such a favor by obeying the divine will.

—Mary of Agreda, *The Mystical City of God*

Those closest to God in heaven, the Seraphim, are called the fiery ones because more than the other angels they take their fervor and ardor from the intense fire of God.

—Robert Bellarmine, *The Mind's Ascent to God by the Ladder of Created Things*

If an angel is compared to the rational human soul, he can be rightly enough called a perfect soul just as a soul can be called an imperfect angel. . . . An angel is a complete and perfect spiritual substance; the human soul is a diminished and imperfect substance because it is the form of the body and, therefore, is part of man.

—Robert Bellarmine, *The Mind's Ascent to God by the Ladder of Created Things*

An angel by a single glance intuits an object and at the same moment sees its causes and effects and penetrates not only to its accidents but also to its substance. He sees not only physical objects but also spiritual ones.

—Robert Bellarmine, *The Mind's Ascent to God by the Ladder of Created Things*

Angels can without effort and without hands and instruments and in scarcely a moment of time mold a body for themselves so that intelligent men would judge it a human body seeing that it walks, speaks, eats, drinks, and can be touched, felt, and even washed.

—Robert Bellarmine, *The Mind's Ascent to God by the Ladder of Created Things*

The holy angels were created at the same time with heaven and earth and are like certain bright, spiritual stars so that they can be called the sons of God; when they saw heaven and earth come forth from nothing and stand on nothing and still rest most firmly on their own stability, they doubtless praised the omnipotence of the Craftsman with immense awe and rejoicing.

—Robert Bellarmine, *The Mind's Ascent to God by the Ladder of Created Things*

The angels cherish no envy or jealousy; they are full of true and burning charity.

—Robert Bellarmine, *The Mind's Ascent to God by the Ladder of Created Things*

Good angels, therefore, cannot mediate between miserable mortals and blessed immortals, for they themselves also are both blessed and immortal; but evil angels can mediate, because they are immortal like the one party, miserable like the other.

—Augustine, *The City of God*

The good angels, therefore, hold cheap all that knowledge of material and transitory things which the demons are so proud of possessing—not that they are ignorant of these things, but because of the love of God, whereby they are sanctified, is very dear to them, and because, in comparison of that not merely immaterial but also unchangeable and ineffable beauty, with the holy love of which they are inflamed, they despise all things which are beneath it, and all that is not it, that they may with every good thing that is in them enjoy that good which is the source of their goodness.

—Augustine, *The City of God*

Think how, when Christ reached heaven with the blessed Fathers, many thousands of them gathered in the first street; that of the Angels. These were the souls who, in this world, saved themselves by means of penance; each, seated on his throne, over which his name had already been written, and each placing his crown on his head. With the Choir of Archangels were those who saved their souls by spiritual works. Among the Principalities were those who had saved themselves by works of mercy. Among the Powers were those who saved themselves by great patience in adversity. Among the Virtues were those who saved themselves by patience bearing ill-will to no one. Among the Dominations were gathered the earthly Lords, Rulers and Judges, who had ruled those under them with great justice. Among the Thrones were those who, for love of Christ, had lived a life of great poverty. Among the cherubim were the contemplatives, who possessed divine wisdom in an eminent degree. Among the Seraphim were those who loved God with an ardent love.

—Vincent Ferrer, *sermon*

Angels that have fallen have acquired a noetic volition which is perpetually evil, while the good angels possess one that is perpetually good and has no need of a bridle.

—Gregory Palamas, *Topics of Natural and Theological Science and on the Moral and Ascetic Life: One Hundred and Fifty Texts*

God delineated all the beauty in the works of divine omnipotence in the first angel. God adorned him like the starry heavens—with all the stars and with the beauty of the greening of every kind of sparkling rock. And God called him Lucifer because that angel bore the light from the One who alone is eternal.

—Hildegard of Bingen, *Book of Divine Works*

For the angels owe both their spirits and lives to God. For all eternity they will behold God's fiery splendor. Out of this splendor they will glow like flames.

—Hildegard of Bingen, *Book of Divine Works*

God is the brightest of lights which can never be extinguished, and the choirs of angels radiate light from the Divinity. Angels are pure praise without any trace of a bodily deed.

—Hildegard of Bingen, *Book of Divine Works*

Duties and Activities of Angels

We have no right to claim that the Angels should obey us—but we can be absolutely sure that the Holy Angels hear us always.

—Josemaría Escrivá, *The Forge*

We should believe that the angelic spirits are especially present to us when we give ourselves in a special way to divine services, that is, when we enter a church and open our ears to sacred reading, or give our attention to psalm-singing, or apply ourselves to prayer, or celebrate the solemnity of mass.

—Bede the Venerable, *homily on the Gospels*

God is man's universal teacher and guardian, but his teaching to men is mediated by angels.

—Thomas Aquinas, *Summa Theologica*

I have great reverence for Saint Michael the Archangel; he had no example to follow in doing the will of God, and yet he fulfilled God's will faithfully.

—Faustina Kowalska, *Divine Mercy in My Soul*

I would fain be secure as the angels are secure, toiling not, but serving God without stay.

—Abbot John of Short Stature, *saying*

Thus God ordains, we think, that the angels should have the knowledge by which they constantly sing reverent hymns of praise and love for God. They have no other desire than to see God and sing God's praises.

—Hildegard of Bingen, *Book of Divine Works*

And just as the sun's rays indicate the sun, the angels reveal God by their hymns of praise. And just as the sun cannot exist without its light, the Godhead could not be if it were not for the angels' praise.

—Hildegard of Bingen, *Book of Divine Works*

The angels who shine like the stars feel sympathy for our human nature and place it before God's eyes just as if it were a book. They attend us. They speak to us in a reasonable way, just as God inspires them to do. In the sight of God they praise people who do good deeds but turn away from whose who are evil.

—Hildegard of Bingen, *Book of Divine Works*

At the orders of the Queen the angels frequently assisted the Apostles in their travels and tribulations and in the persecutions as well of the gentiles and the Jews, as of the demons, who continually excited evil-minded men against the preachers of the Gospel. The angels often visited them in visible shapes, conversing with them and consoling them in the name of the most blessed Mary. At other times they performed the same office interiorly without manifesting themselves; sometimes they freed them from prison; sometimes they warned them of dangers and snares; sometimes they accompanied them on their way or carried them from one place to another where they were to preach, or informed them of what they were to do according to the circumstances peculiar to certain places or peoples. Of all these things they also kept their blessed Lady informed; for She took care of all of them and labored with them more than all of them together.

—Mary of Agreda, *The Mystical City of God*

The reason why God, who is everywhere and can easily speak to the hearts of men by himself, should wish nonetheless to send angels seems to be so that men may understand that God has a care for human affairs and that he rules and directs everything, for men can easily persuade themselves that divine inspirations are their own reasonings and plans. But when they see and hear that angels are sent by God and that the things that the angels predict come true as they foretold, they cannot doubt that God oversees human affairs and especially directs and arranges those which relate to the eternal salvation of his elect.

—Robert Bellarmine, *The Mind's Ascent to God by the Ladder of Created Things*

It is rightly and truly said in Scripture that all the works of the angels and the inspirations they impart are also accomplished or granted by God. For ordinarily these works and inspirations are derived from God by means of the angels, and the angels also in turn give them one to another without delay. . . . Consequently, the nearer the higher spirits (and those that follow) are to God, the more purged and clarified they are by a more general purification; the last spirits receive a fainter and more remote illumination. Humans, the last to whom this loving contemplation of God is communicated, when God so desires, must receive it according to their own mode, in a very limited and painful way.

—John of the Cross, *The Dark Night of the Soul*

True visions ordinarily come from the good angel, even if Christ is represented, for he hardly ever appears in his own Person. If a person receives true visions from the good angel, God permits the bad angel to represent the false ones of the same kind. Thus an incautious person can be deceived, as many have been.

—John of the Cross, *The Dark Night of the Soul*

Fallen angels

Iniquity was found among them, and God cast them out because they rebelled against him. Imperfection was found among them not only before their confirmation in grace, but since then. For they were not made so entirely perfect that there does not remain in them a certain negative imperfection which, however, does not render them displeasing to God. Confirmed in grace, their imperfection can no longer cause them to fall from beatitude, nor cause them to commit any sin. Their imperfection lies in the fact that, although they enjoy the clear vision of God, they do not always clearly and fully recognize his will, so that while waiting to have a clearer knowledge, they do as perfectly as they are able what they judge to be most comfortable to the divine good pleasure, although at times there are different opinions among them.

—Francis de Sales, *Oeuvres*

The bad spirit knows well how to transform himself into an angel of light. Aware of the pious desires of the soul, he will begin by seconding them, but soon he will begin to lead it to his own ends. Thus at first he will feign to consent to your good and holy thoughts, and even applaud them, but by degrees he will draw you into his hidden snares and entangle you in his dark meshes.

—Ignatius of Loyola, *Spiritual Exercises*

Pride and nothing else caused an angel to fall from heaven. And so one may reasonably ask whether one may reach heaven by humility alone without the help of any other virtue.

—John Climacus, *The Ladder of Divine Ascent*

Guardian angels

Whenever you are in need of anything, or are facing difficulties, whether great or small, invoke your Guardian Angel, asking him to sort the matter out with Jesus, or to carry out the particular service you may require.

—Josemaría Escrivá, *The Forge*

Get into the habit of praying to the Guardian Angel of each person you are following up. Their Angel will help them to be good and faithful and cheerful, so that when the time comes they will be able to receive the eternal embrace of Love from God the Father, God the Son, God the Holy Spirit, and from the Blessed Virgin.

—Josemaría Escrivá, *The Forge*

Greetings, holy angel of God, guardian of my soul and body. Through the most dulcet heart of Jesus Christ, the Son of God, for love of him who created you and me, for love of him who commended me to you at baptism, take me into your most faithful fatherly care. May I, then, aided by you, pass through the torrent of this life along a spotless path until, with you, I come gladly to see that mellifluous face which you see: that merriest radiance of imperial divinity, dulcet beyond all sweetness.

—Gertrude the Great, *Spiritual Exercises*

The powers of Hell will assail the dying Christian; but his angel guardian will come to console him. His patrons, and St. Michael, who has been appointed by God to defend his faithful servants in their last combat with the devils, will come to his aid.

—Alphonsus Liguori, *sermon*

Humans and Angels

Since God often sends us his inspirations by means of his angels, we ought frequently to offer him our aspirations through the same channel. . . . Call on them and honor them frequently, and ask their help in all your affairs, temporal as well as spiritual.

—Francis de Sales, *The Devout Life*

Is there a greater happiness than to imitate on earth the choir of angels?

—Basil the Great, *letter to Gregory of Nazianzus*

We should show our affection for the angels, for one day they will be our coheirs just as here below they are our guardians and trustees appointed and set over us by the Father.

—Bernard of Clairvaux, *sermon*

Your tears were collected by the angels and were placed in a gold chalice, and you will find them when you present yourself before God.

—Padre Pio, *Send Me Your Guardian Angel*

So if we detect an angel by the effect he is producing, let us hasten to pray since our heavenly guardian has come to join us.

—John Climacus, *The Ladder of Divine Ascent*

Although the angels are superior to us in many ways, yet in some respects . . . they fall short of us with regard to being in the image of the Creator; for we, rather than they, have been created in God's image.

—Gregory Palamas, *Topics of Natural and Theological Science and on the Moral and Ascetic Life: One Hundred and Fifty Texts*

God gave to us human beings the place and honor of the fallen angels so that we might complete God's glory, which is something those angels had refused to do.

—Hildegard of Bingen, *Book of Divine Works*

We are not angels but have bodies, and it is madness for us to want to become angels while we are still on earth, and as much on earth as I was.

—Teresa of Ávila, *Life*

Our soul is also marked with nine levels when within it the following are arranged in orderly fashion: announcing, declaring, leading, ordering, strengthening, commanding, receiving, revealing and anointing. These correspond level by level to the nine choirs of angels. In the human soul the first three of these levels pertain to human nature; the next three, to effort and the last three, to grace. Having attained these, the soul, by entering into itself, enters the heavenly Jerusalem, where beholding the choirs of angels, it sees in them God, who dwells in them and performs all operations.

—Bonaventure, *The Soul's Journey Into God*

The Angels of God accompanied the faithful when the light of His truth only dawned in the world. And now that the day sprung from on high was visited, and exalted our nature to a union with the Divinity, will these beneficent beings be less associated or delighted to dwell with the soul that is panting for heavenly joys and longing to join in their eternal Alleluias? Oh, no, I will imagine them always surrounding me and in every moment will sing with them "Holy, holy, holy, Lord God of Hosts, heaven and earth are full of Thy glory!"

—Elizabeth Seton, *Collected Writings*

If you are willing to listen to the Lord of the angels, my soul, you will have no reason to envy the angels their lofty place or how they move at tremendous speeds without tiring. For you will not only be equal to the angels when you are freed from the body, but also, when you return to the body that Christ "has made like to the body of glory" (Philippians 3:21), you will possess together with your body heaven as your own home.

—Robert Bellarmine, *The Mind's Ascent to God by the Ladder of Created Things*

Let good men love their fellow citizens, the angels; let wicked men shudder at the power of the angels, servants of the wrath of almighty God, from whose hands no one can snatch them.

—Robert Bellarmine, *The Mind's Ascent to God by the Ladder of Created Things*

Let us be like the holy Angels now. If you wish to place your son in the court of a king or bishop, you will have to begin to teach him court manners beforehand. So it is with us; if one day we are to be in the Angelic Court, we must learn how, while we are still here, the manners of the Angels.

—Vincent Ferrer, *sermon*

Oh, that God who is loved by the seraphim, served by the angels, feared by the powers, and adored by the principalities, is offended by such a vile worm of the earth as man. Marvel at this, O ye heavens!

—Anthony Mary Claret, *autobiography*

If you remembered the presence of your Angel and the angels of your neighbors, you would avoid many of the foolish things which slip into your conversations.

—Josemaría Escrivá, *The Way*

For if you have chosen the life of angels, you have passed the confines of human nature and crossed over to the bodiless state.

—Basil the Great, *On Ascetic Discourse*

Anger

Above all everyone should in conversation try to avoid anger or bad temper, or showing he is annoyed with someone, and no one should hurt another in word or deed, or in any way.

—Vincent de Paul, *Common Rules or Constitutions of the Congregation of the Mission*

If an angry man were to raise the dead, because of his anger he would not please God.

—Abbot Agatho, *saying*

Never have I suffered to remain in my heart a thought that angered me.

—Abbot Silvanus, *saying*

I exhort you earnestly never to give way to anger; and never, under any pretext whatever, let it effect an entrance into your heart.

—Francis de Sales, *The Devout Life*

As a general thing, self-control and contempt for calumny and evil reports are more successful remedies than resentment, disputes and revenge.

—Francis de Sales, *The Devout Life*

Ah, my dear Lord, what melancholy company is that person who is a slave to anger!

—John Baptiste Marie Vianney, *sermon*

Anger never travels alone. It is always accompanied by plenty of other sins.

—John Baptiste Marie Vianney, *sermon*

Angry men betray themselves not knowingly, but because they can't hide things.

—Thomas Aquinas, *Summa Theologica*

Freedom from anger is a triumph over one's nature. It is the ability to be impervious to insults, and comes by hard work and the sweat of one's brow.

—John Climacus, *The Ladder of Divine Ascent*

The first step toward freedom from anger is to keep the lips silent when the heart is stirred; the next, to keep thoughts silent when the soul is upset; the last, to be totally calm when unclean winds are blowing.

—John Climacus, *The Ladder of Divine Ascent*

It is impossible to destroy wild beasts without arms. It is impossible to achieve freedom from anger without humility.

—John Climacus, *The Ladder of Divine Ascent*

The memory of insults is the residue of anger. It keeps sins alive, hates justice, ruins virtue, poisons the heart, rots the mind, defeats concentration, paralyzes prayer, puts love at a distance, and is a nail driven into the soul.

—John Climacus, *The Ladder of Divine Ascent*

All the days of their life, persons addicted to anger are unhappy, because they are always in a tempest.

—Alphonsus Liguori, *sermon*

When a person is indignant at some injury which he has received, you may, by exhorting him to patience, extinguish the fire; but, if you encourage revenge, you may kindle a great flame.

—Alphonsus Liguori, *sermon*

Nothing so converts anger into joy and gentleness as courage and mercy. Like a siege-engine, courage shatters enemies attacking the soul from without, mercy those attacking it from within.

—Gregory of Sinai, *The Philokalia*

If you have a dispute with someone, make peace with that person before the sun goes down.

—Benedict, *Rule*

He wants us to smother anger when it is still only a spark. If it grows to the full flame of its fury, it does not get checked without bloodshed.

—Peter Chrysologus, *sermon*

The full victory is to keep silent when another shouts, to make no reply when he provokes. Then you get the reward both for your patience and for your brother's correction, if insult is consigned to oblivion. But, when words follow upon words, fuel is supplied to a fire.

—Valerian, *homily*

If one of you should be cross with another because of some hasty word, the matter must at once be put right and you must betake yourself to earnest prayer.

—Teresa of Ávila, *The Way of Perfection*

We should make it a point never to do anything when we are "hot and bothered," but strive first of all to calm down, to hand ourselves over to the will of God and of the Immaculate and then to act with serenity so that we may not commit blunders.

—Maximilian M. Kolbe, *letter to friars in Japan, 1941*

Keep a guard on your anger and do not seek revenge for any injury that may be done to you.

—Vincent Ferrer, *sermon*

Conquer your rage with wise, rational thought. Offer it up as a sacrifice to God.

—John Chrysostom, *letter during exile*

But to a mind that is drunk with fury every right thing that is said appears wrong.

—Gregory the Great, *The Book of Pastoral Rule*

I will never get angry, but suffer in silence, and offer to God everything that gives me pain.

—Anthony Mary Claret, *autobiography*

Be slow to anger, quick to learn, also slow to speak, as St. James says, equally quick to listen.

—Columban, *letter, c. 610*

Say what you have just said, but in a different tone, without anger, and your argument will gain in strength and, above all, you won't offend God.

—Josemaría Escrivá, *The Way*

Don't recall to your memory anything your neighbor may have said in a moment of acrimony, whether he insulted you to your face, or spoke evil of you to another and that person has come and reported it to you. If you let yourself become angry, it is but a short step from anger to hatred.

—Maximus the Confessor, *Centuries on Charity*

Animals

Like me, creatures have received a being which is in some sort the efflux of his August perfections; but they have not, like me, the honor of being the living image of God, and made in his likeness.

—Ignatius of Loyola, *Spiritual Exercises*

All creatures were given to man to lead him to his proper end.

—Ignatius of Loyola, *Spiritual Exercises*

The love of the crow for its young is laudable! When they begin to fly, she follows them, gives them food, and for a very long time provides for their nourishment.

—Basil the Great, *homily on the Hexaemeron*

Anxiety

see WORRY

Appearance

It is not your outward appearance that you should beautify, but your soul, adorning it with good works. Although the body, to be precise, should be made beautiful, though in a measured way.

—Clement of Alexandria, *The Teacher*

Study to be neat, and let nothing about you be slovenly or disorderly. It is an affront to those with whom you associate to be unsuitably dressed, but avoid all conceits, vanities, finery and affectation. Adhere as far as possible to modesty and simplicity, which, doubtless, are the best ornaments of beauty, and the best atonement for its deficiency.

—Francis de Sales, *The Devout Life*

Let your dress be neither elegant nor slovenly, and let it not be noticeable by any strangeness that might attract the notice of passers-by and make people point their finger at you.

—Jerome, *letter to Eustochium, 384*

But let thine apparel be plain, not for adornment, but for necessary covering: not to minister to thy vanity, but to keep thee worth in winter, and to hide the unseemliness of the body: lest under pretense of hiding the unseemliness, thou fall into another kind of unseemliness by thy extravagant dress.

—Cyril of Jerusalem, *Catecheses*

Appetites

see DESIRES; LUST; PASSIONS

Arguing

Don't argue. Arguing seldom brings light, for the light is quenched by passion.

—Josemaría Escrivá, *The Way*

Arrogance

It is a greater thing to change one's disposition than to change one's dress. We part with arrogance less easily than with gold and jewels.

—Jerome, *letter to Oceanus*

Atonement

Atonement: this is the path that leads to Life.

—Josemaría Escrivá, *The Way*

Attachment

There are even spiritual souls who possess what they have with such attachment and take such pleasure in seeing and reflecting on what they do, that they commit a kind of idolatry, making and adoring as many idols as they have actions.

—Francis de Sales, *Oeuvres*

Righteousness is the natural and essential food of the soul, which can no more be satisfied by earthly treasures than the hunger of the body can be satisfied by air. If you should see a starving man standing with mouth open to the wind, inhaling draughts of air as if in hope of gratifying his hunger, you would think him lunatic. But it is no less foolish to imagine that the soul can be satisfied with worldly things which only inflate it without feeding it.

—Bernard of Clairvaux, *On Loving God*

If you truly love God and long to reach the kingdom that is to come, if you are truly pained by your failings and are mindful of punishment and of the eternal judgment, if you are truly afraid to die, then it will not be possible to have an attachment, or anxiety, or concern for money, for possessions, for family relationships, for worldly glory, for love and brotherhood, indeed for anything of earth.

—John Climacus, *The Ladder of Divine Ascent*

But how great soever a man's attachment to the things of this world may be, he must take leave of them at death. Naked he has entered into this world, and naked he shall depart from it.

—Alphonsus Liguori, *sermon*

For all visible things on earth which are lovable and desirable—riches, glory, wife, children, in a word everything of this world that is beautiful, sweet, and attractive—belong not to the soul but only to the body, and being temporary, will pass away as quickly as a shadow.

—Dimitri of Rostov, *The Inner Closet of the Heart*

He who through the power of the Spirit has extirpated his materialistic worldly proclivities in this life will hereafter live a divine and truly eternal life in communion with Christ.

—Gregory Palamas, *To the Most Reverend Nun Xenia*

Thus when the soul renounces its attachment to inferior things and cleaves through love to God and submits itself to him through acts and modes of virtue, it is illuminated and made beautiful by God and is raised to a higher level, obeying his counsels and exhortations; and by these means it regains the truly eternal life.

—Gregory Palamas, *Topics of Natural and Theological Science and on the Moral and Ascetic Life: One Hundred and Fifty Texts*

But as long as we have peace with the natures of this world we remain enemies of God and of his angels and all his saints.

—Anthony, *letter*

To die to the world is no light matter, but a business of the greatest difficulty and importance. Those find it most difficult who do not know the power of God's grace and have not tasted the sweetness of His love, but are carnal, not having the Spirit; all carnal objects become insipid when once we taste the divine sweetness.

—Robert Bellarmine, *The Art of Dying Well*

Therefore let him who desires to live well and to die well enter into the chamber of his heart and not deceive himself; but seriously and attentively consider over and over again whether he is in love with the pomps of this world, or with sins, which are the works of the Devil; and whether he gives them a place in his heart, and in his words and actions. And thus, either his good conscience will console him, or his evil conscience will lead him to penance.

—Robert Bellarmine, *The Art of Dying Well*

It ought to be kept in mind that attachment to a creature makes a person equal to that creature; the stronger the attachment, the closer is the likeness to the creature and the greater the equality, for love effects a likeness between the lover and the loved.

—John of the Cross, *The Ascent of Mount Carmel*

However, if we are overcome by sloth or by carelessness, if we give ourselves over to dangerous and useless chattering, if we are caught up in worldly cares and in profitless worries, there will follow in effect from this a harvest of tares to serve as a ministry of death to our hearts.

—John Cassian, *Conferences*

When a person is a beginner, he should go through and thoroughly examine all the corners of his soul to see whether he can find anything that he has fastened onto with pleasure, whether he suspects some creature (hiding) in some corner. Drive it out now! Before all else this must be the first thing, just as one teaches children first of all their ABCs.

—Henry Suso, *sermon*

It is not that prestige and worldly pleasure and other people are evil in themselves; what is evil is our attachment to them when by such attachment we disregard the sweet commandment of God.

—Catherine of Siena, *letter to a nobleman's wife*

He that is without a wife is solicitous for the things that belong to the lord, how he may please God. But he that is with a wife is solicitous for the things of the world.

—Paul, *1 Cor. 32–33*

Mind the things that are above, not the things that are of the earth.

—Cyprian of Carthage, *Jealousy and Envy*

Earthly wisdom of which St. James speaks, is love for the things of this world. Worldly men secretly subscribe to this wisdom when they set their own hearts on worldly possessions and strive to become rich.

—Louis de Montfort, *The Love of Eternal Wisdom*

Of what avail will it be to you if you are here in the body, and your heart is anxious about your earthly treasure?

—Basil the Great, *homily on the Hexaemeron*

Anyone who truly wants to follow God must be free from the bonds of attachment to this life. To do this we must make a complete break with our old way of life. Indeed, unless we avoid all obsession with the body and with the concerns of this world, we shall never succeed in pleasing God.

—Basil the Great, *The Greater Rules*

For a life which loves the world is dead to the soul.

—Paulinus of Nola, *letter*

However enjoyable these be, however alluring, let us avoid the earthly goods of others, that we may not lose our own eternal good.

—Columban, *sermon*

For the flesh dies when its wisdom passes over into the spirit, so that it no longer has a taste for the things of the flesh, but for the things of the spirit.

—Ambrose, *Concerning Repentance*

Concern for material things multiplies wheat and wine and contains in every part pleasure related to the stomach and banquets. They lie at the root of every material preoccupation and do not profit us at all.

—Gregory of Nyssa, *Commentary on the Inscriptions of the Psalms*

Be men and women of the world, but don't be worldly men and women.

—Josemaría Escrivá, *The Way*

You ask me to what you must avoid becoming attached: You must be attached to nothing, neither fortune, nor relations, nor directors, nor interior consolation; there must be nothing in the world which we are not ready to forgo without trouble if God asks it of us.

—Claude de la Colombière, *letter*

Authority

The constitution of the world comes from God, whereas the works of the world come from the evil one. So the authority comes from God, but the ambition to wield authority comes from the evil one.

Authority is not evil in itself, but a certain use of authority is. Although it does not come from the devil, authority is subject to the snares of the devil.

—Ambrose, *On the Gospel of St. Luke*

Avarice

see GREED

B

Baptism

Every soul purified through baptism and raised to the state of grace is thereby conceived through Christ and is born for His sake.

—Edith Stein, *Essays on Woman*

Baptism washes off those evils that were previously within us, whereas the sins committed after baptism are washed away by tears. The baptism received by us as children we have all defiled, but we cleanse it anew with our tears. If God in his love for the human race had not given us tears, those being saved would be few indeed and hard to find.

—John Climacus, *The Ladder of Divine Ascent*

At the moment that the soul receives holy baptism, original sin is taken away from her, and grace is infused into her, and that inclination to sin, which remains from the original corruption . . . is indeed a source of weakness, but the soul can keep the bridle on it if she choose.

—Catherine of Siena, *Dialogue*

If we beheld a soul after baptism with the eyes of faith, we would see angels taking their watch around it.

—Elizabeth Seton, *Collected Writings*

On the day on which the grace of holy baptism is received, a person gets two angels: one good and the other evil. A person is always attacked by one but defended and helped by the other.

—Elisabeth of Schönau, *Third Book of Visions*

The soul is regenerated in the sacred waters of baptism and thus becomes God's child.

—Maximilian M. Kolbe, *meditation, 1940*

Ah Jesus, fountain of life, make me drink a cup of the living water from you so that, having tasted you, I thirst for eternity for nothing other than you. Immerse me totally in the depth of your mercy. Baptize me in the spotlessness of your precious death. Make me new in the blood by which you have redeemed me. In the water from your holiest side, wash away every spot with which I have ever spotted my baptismal innocence. Fill me with your Spirit and possess me totally in purity in body and soul.

—Gertrude the Great, *Spiritual Exercises*

For just as baptism with water cleanses us of original sin and gives us grace, so in the blood we will wash away our sins and our unwillingness to suffer. There all wounds will be healed: not only will we cease to brood on them or seek revenge, but we will receive the fullness of grace to lead us along the right path.

—Catherine of Siena, *letter to Cardinal Iacopo Orsini, 1374*

Every baptized person should consider that it is in the womb of the Church where he is transformed from a child of Adam to a child of God.

—Vincent Ferrer, *sermon*

A baptized person dying in a state of innocence is exalted most highly, because he ascends at once to heaven, since such a one is received immediately into the glory of Paradise without passing through purgatory.

—Vincent Ferrer, *sermon*

Before baptism every Christian was a slave of the devil because he belonged to him. At baptism he has either personally or through his sponsors solemnly renounced Satan, his seductions and his works. He has chosen Jesus as his Master and sovereign Lord and undertaken to depend upon him as a slave of love.

—Louis de Montfort, *Treatise on True Devotion to the Blessed Virgin*

As far as the higher grace of baptism is concerned, in the heavens a mystery is celebrated and in hell Gehenna is extinguished; in the one the waters flow, in the other the fire grows cold; in the one we are submerged in the bath, in the other we are set free from the underworld.

—Maximus of Turin, *sermon*

In the baptism of Christ, both the heaven and the underworld are opened—the former so that the Holy Spirit might come, the latter so that the mercy of the Savior might penetrate. Lie is brought down from heaven, death is destroyed in the underworld.

—Maximus of Turin, *sermon*

The water cleanses the body, and the Spirit seals the soul; that we may draw near unto God, having our heart sprinkled by the Spirit and our body washed with pure water. When going down, therefore, into the water, think not of the bare element, but look for the salvation by the power of the Holy Ghost: for without both thou canst not possibly be made perfect.

—Cyril of Jerusalem, *Catecheses*

Baptism is the end of the Old Testament, and beginning of the New.

—Cyril of Jerusalem, *Catecheses*

For they to whom the rough garment of their sins still clings are found on the left hand, because they came not to the grace of God which is given through Christ at the new birth of Baptism: new birth I mean not of bodies, but the spiritual new birth of the soul.

—Cyril of Jerusalem, *Catecheses*

But if anyone wishes to know why the grace is given by water and not by a different element, let him take up the Divine Scriptures and he shall learn. For water is a grand thing, and the noblest of the four visible elements of the world.

—Cyril of Jerusalem, *Catecheses*

If any man receive not the Baptism, he hath not salvation; except only Martyrs, who even without the water receive the kingdom. For when the Savior, in redeeming the world by his Cross, was pierced in the side, He shed forth blood and water; that men, living in times of peace, might be baptized in water, and, in times of persecution, in their own blood.

—Cyril of Jerusalem, *Catecheses*

When you go down to the water to be baptized, you take with you your sins. But the grace which is called down upon you marks your soul in a new way. You go down dead because of your sins: you come up given new life by grace. For if you were planted in the likeness of the Savior's death, you were also thought worthy of resurrection.

—Cyril of Jerusalem, *Catecheses*

We should rejoice that we have become the temple of God by our baptism, according to the testimony of the Apostle, "for the temple of God, which you are, is holy." (1 Corinthians 3:17)

—Bede the Venerable, *homily on the Gospels*

Beauty

But once I had seen the Lord's great beauty, I could find no one who seemed handsome to me in comparison, and no one to occupy my thoughts.

—Teresa of Ávila, *Life*

For beauty is never without truth, nor truth without beauty.

—Francis de Sales, *Oeuvres*

Beauty is the interior adornment which is renewed day by day as the power and strength of Christ grows within the soul.

—Bernard of Clairvaux, *On the Canticle of Canticles*

Praise, hatred, and even love based on outward beauty comes from impure souls. Seek beauty of soul, and imitate the Bridegroom of the Church.

—John Chrysostom, *homily*

All the beauty of creatures compared to the infinite beauty of God is the height of ugliness.

—John of the Cross, *The Ascent of Mount Carmel*

The ugliness of the world—which is its contempt and its adversity—is a profitable sort of bitterness that heals the just. The world's beauty is its prosperity; and this is a flattering sort of sweetness, but false and seductive. . . . Therefore, in order to escape the ugliness of hell and to acquire the sweetness of heaven, it is necessary to go after the world's ugliness rather than its beauty.

—Bridget of Sweden, *Book of Questions*

If you see a person who's plump, who's in very good condition, who's tall and towers over others because of body length, don't admire them until you've thoroughly ascertained the state of their soul. It's not from external shapeliness but from the beauty which adorns the mind that we should call anyone blessed.

—John Chrysostom, *homily*

Now whatever is to be regarded as coming within the sphere of the beautiful becomes the character of God.

—Gregory of Nyssa, *The Great Catechism*

God does not judge of the beauty of His work by the charm of the eyes, and He does not form the same idea of beauty that we do. What He esteems beautiful is that which presents in its perfection all the fitness of art, and that which tends to the usefulness of its end. He, then, who proposed to Himself a manifest design in

His works, approved each one of them, as fulfilling its end in accordance with His creative purpose.

—Basil the Great, *homily on the Hexaemeron*

It is for us to seek to acquire beauty, so that the Bridegroom, the Word, may welcome us into his presence and say, "You are utterly fair, my love, and there is no flaw in you." (Song of Solomon 4:7)

—Basil the Great, *Commentary on Psalm 29*

By our nature we human beings aspire to what is beautiful and love it. But what is beautiful is also good. God is good. Everyone looks for the good, therefore everyone looks for God.

—Basil the Great, *The Greater Rules*

The flashes of divine transcend all speech and description; words cannot express them nor hearing receive them.

—Basil the Great, *The Greater Rules*

True beauty is unseen by human eyes, and grasped only by the soul and the mind when it has happened to illuminate one of the saints, and left behind a wound of unbearable yearning.

—Basil the Great, *The Greater Rules*

Look at the heavens: how beautiful they are! And look at the earth: how beautiful it is! Both heaven and earth radiate beauty.

—Augustine, *On Psalm 148*

Behavior

There is always the possibility of offending God when one is uncertain how to behave.

—Louise de Marillac, *Spiritual Writings*

The best means of being reserved is to think frequently that God sees you.

—Vincent de Paul, *Conferences to the Daughters of Charity*

For people cling tightly to that which they acquire with labor; but that which they acquire easily they quickly throw away, because it can be easily recovered.

—Gregory of Nazianzus, *theological oration*

Never think badly of anyone, not even if the words or conduct of the person in question give you good grounds for doing so.

—Josemaría Escrivá, *The Way*

When we are having a party we must be sensible. We must avoid licentious music and an excess of drink. Otherwise we will be prone to drunkenness and erotic exhibitions.

—Clement of Alexandria, *The Teacher*

If two people are engaged in conversation they should speak in measured tones. Yelling and shouting is what idiots do. Talking in a whisper so that the person cannot hear is the mark of a fool.

—Clement of Alexandria, *The Teacher*

If you are inclined to entertain and give dinner parties, there should be nothing immodest or excessive about them.

—John Chrysostom, *homily*

It is better to do less with patience, meekness and kindness, than to do more with precipitation, anger and impatience. When people see a person who does things in the latter fashion, they are scandalized and repulsed.

—Anthony Mary Claret, *autobiography*

Being

But you have something here to lift you up in wonder, for Being itself is first and last; it is eternal and most present; it is utterly simple and the greatest; it is most actual and most unchangeable; it is most perfect and most immense; it is supremely one and yet all-inclusive. If you wonder at this with a pure mind, you will be flooded with a greater light when you see further that it is last because it is first, it does all things for itself; and therefore it must necessarily be the ultimate end, the beginning and the consummation, the Alpha and the Omega.

—Bonaventure, *The Soul's Journey Into God*

Blasphemy

The remedy for temptations to blasphemy is to realize that no sort of temptation is more distressing than this, and yet none less dangerous. The cure is not to make much of these temptations. To experience them is no sin; sin lies in consenting to them and delighting in them; and there is nothing of that here, but rather the contrary. Consequently they must be regarded as a punishment rather than a fault.

—Peter of Alcantara, *Treatise on Prayer & Meditation*

The sin of blasphemy, then, is so enormous, that the saints themselves appear not to have courage to pray for a blasphemer.

—Alphonsus Liguori, *sermon*

For it will be of little profit to hear Mass daily, and to adore Christ in the Holy Mysteries, if, in the meantime, we impiously blaspheme God, or swear falsely by His holy name.

—Robert Bellarmine, *The Art of Dying Well*

Blasphemy is a word which connotes the hating and cursing of infinite beauty, which explains why this sin directly attacks God.

—John Baptiste Marie Vianney, *sermon*

We can say that blasphemy is truly the language of hell.

—John Baptiste Marie Vianney, *sermon*

We blaspheme when we perform actions which are directly opposed to the goodness of God—as when we despair of our salvation and yet are not willing to take the necessary steps to obtain it; as when we are angered because others receive more graces than we do. Take care never to allow yourself to fall into these kinds of sins because they are so very horrible!

—John Baptiste Marie Vianney, *sermon*

Be warned, my friends, that if blasphemy reigns in your homes, all therein will perish.

—John Baptiste Marie Vianney, *sermon*

If you have blasphemous thoughts, do not think that you are to blame. God knows what is in our hearts and he knows that ideas of this kind come not from us but from our enemies.

—John Climacus, *The Ladder of Divine Ascent*

Blessedness

Every sublime notion pertaining to God may, in my opinion, define blessedness. . . . Therefore, the definition of human blessedness is likeness to God.

—Gregory of Nyssa, *Commentary on the Inscriptions of the Psalms*

When our humanity will be united to the angels and when the divine battle-order lifts it out of its present turmoil, it will sing a victorious song of triumph at the bloody defeat of the enemy. Then every spirit will praise God's grace forever, continually magnifying his blessedness by further graces. This I call true blessedness.

—Gregory of Nyssa, *Commentary on the Inscriptions of the Psalms*

Body

For we who are slaves to Christ make our bodies serve and our minds govern, so that the flesh receives its orders and accompanies our will which is guided by Christ our Maker. The body derives steadfastness from the mind's courage, and the servant obeys in accordance with the disposition of the master.

—Paulinus of Nola, *letter*

The very reason you are given a body as well as a soul is to help you gain the favor of this outward and visible world; though at the same time you must also pray for insight into the invisible world as well, so that you may come short of nothing and the whole treasury of the Spirit may be yours.

—Ignatius of Antioch, *epistle to Polycarp*

Treat your body always as an enemy, for the flesh is an ungrateful and treacherous friend. The more you look after it, the more it hurts you.

—John Climacus, *The Ladder of Divine Ascent*

The soul indeed is molded by the doings of the body, conforming to it and taking shape from what it does.

—John Climacus, *The Ladder of Divine Ascent*

The body is made of earth; yet it is not something dead but alive and endowed with a living soul. Into this soul is breathed a spirit—the spirit of God, intended to know God, to reverence him, to seek and taste him, and to have its joy in him and nothing else.

—Theophan the Recluse, *letter*

Yet so long as body and soul have to live with one another, they will be locked in a powerful struggle. For the soul suffers whenever the flesh rejoices in sinning.

—Hildegard of Bingen, *Book of Divine Works*

So it is not the body that gives bliss to the soul, but the soul will give bliss to the body, because the soul will give of her abundance, and will re-clothe herself on the Last Day of Judgment, in the garments of her own flesh which she had quitted.

—Catherine of Siena, *Dialogue*

At the time of death, the soul only is reproved, but, at the General Judgment, the soul is reproved together with the body, because the body has been the companion and instrument of the soul—to do good and evil according to the free will pleased. Every work, good or bad, is done by means of the body.

—Catherine of Siena, *Dialogue*

My spirit is so pervaded with God that I feel it physically, and the body partakes of its joys.

—Faustina Kowalska, *Divine Mercy in My Soul*

For this body of ours has one fault: the more you indulge it, the more things it discovers to be essential to it. It is extraordinary how it likes being indulged.

—Teresa of Ávila, *The Way of Perfection*

Because of our bodies, we commit sin. The soul of itself is like the Angels in desiring perpetual contemplation; but the body drags it now to pride, now to avarice, now to sensuality, and so of the rest. . . . So the flesh must be rebuked and punished by affliction and fasts, since it is better for a father to correct his son or his daughter, than that they should go to prison. The body is the son and the flesh the daughter; and it is better for them to be corrected by you than by the prison warders of hell; that is, the demons.

—Vincent Ferrer, *sermon*

If any human's body were to see the Godhead, it would melt like wax before a fire; and the soul would rejoice with such great exultation that the body would be annihilated like a cinder.

—Bridget of Sweden, *Book of Questions*

We must hate our bodies with their vices and sins because the Lord says in the Gospel: All evils, vices and sins come from the heart.

—Francis of Assisi, *saying*

Let us chastise our body crucifying it with its vices, concupiscence and sins, because by living according to the flesh, the devil wishes to take away from us the love of Jesus Christ and eternal life and to lose himself in hell with everyone else.

—Francis of Assisi, *manuscript fragment*

Our bodies are so corrupt that they are referred to by the Holy Spirit as bodies of sin, as conceived and nourished in sin, and capable of any kind of sin.

—Louis de Montfort, *Treatise on True Devotion to the Blessed Virgin*

Do not believe anyone who maintains that our bodies have nothing to do with God. I might say in passing that people who regard the body as corrupt most often defile it with impure actions.

—Cyril of Jerusalem, *Catecheses*

Suffer none of those who say that this body is no work of God: for they who believe that the body is independent of God, and that the soul swells in it as in a strange vessel, readily abuse it to fornication.

—Cyril of Jerusalem, *Catecheses*

The body sins not of itself, but the soul through the body. The body is an instrument, and, as it were, a garment and robe of the soul: and if by this latter it be given over to fornication, it becomes defiled: but if it dwell with a holy soul, it becomes a temple of the Holy Ghost.

—Cyril of Jerusalem, *Catecheses*

There is nothing to be ashamed of in your body. If you are in control of its members, they are not in the slightest evil. Adam and Eve in paradise were naked at first and their bodies did not appear shameful or disgusting. Our limbs do not cause sin, but the wrong use of them does. The Creator of our bodies knew what he was doing.

—Cyril of Jerusalem, *Catecheses*

We should habituate ourselves to do good and nothing else. The body is insatiable; the more we give it the more it demands.

—Joseph Cafasso, *first panegyric on St. Joseph Cafasso by St. John Bosco*

As the soul extends throughout the whole body and no part of the latter lacks its share, so is it necessary that the flesh in turn, being inseparable from the soul—indeed, unable even to live without it—be wholly directed by the soul's will; and, as it is not possible for a body to live without a soul, neither can the body in that case have a will which is said to be foreign.

—Symeon the New Theologian, *Ethical Discourses*

For what is a body other than the juice of masticated food?

—Symeon the New Theologian, *Ethical Discourses*

Woman's soul is present and lives more intensely in all parts of the body; whereas, with men, the body has more pronouncedly the character of an instrument which serves them in their work and which is accompanied by a certain detachment.

—Edith Stein, *Essays on Woman*

The parts of our body involved in sexual union are not base, the embrace of the married couple is not base, nor are the words that talk about all this. The human organs, including the genitals, deserve respect and are not base. Their use is base, if we use them in a disordered way.

—Clement of Alexandria, *The Teacher*

Anyone who loves their body desires something that is not theirs, and if they can remove the disease of corruption from their heart they will find themselves fortified against every form of suffering because the body is death while life is immortal.

—Basil the Great, *letter*

Even as the body flourishes, so doth the soul become withered: and when the body is withered, then doth the soul put forth leaves. Insomuch as the body is cherished, so doth the soul wax lean: and when the body has grown lean, then doth soul wax fat.

—Abbot Daniel, *saying*

Calumniation

see SLANDER

Charity

So charity keeps us in faith and in hope. And faith and hope lead us in charity, and in the end everything will be charity.

—Julian of Norwich, *Showings*

When charity is deeply rooted in the soul it shows itself exteriorly: there is so gracious a way of refusing what we cannot give, that the refusal pleases as much as the gift.

—Thérèse of Lisieux, *The Story of a Soul*

True charity consists in bearing with all the defects of our neighbor, in not being surprised at his failings, and in being edified by his least virtues; Charity must not remain shut up in the depths of the heart, for *no man lighteth a candle and putteth it under a bushel, but upon a candlestick, that it may shine to all that are in the house.* (Matthew 5:15) It seems to me that this candle represents the Charity which ought to enlighten and make joyful, not only those who are dearest to me, but *all who are in the house.*

—Thérèse of Lisieux, *The Story of a Soul*

If it [charity] is hard to give to anyone who asks, it is very much harder to let what belongs to us be taken without asking for it back. I say that it is hard, but I should really say that it *seems* hard, for "the yoke of the Lord is sweet and his burden is light." The moment we accept it, we feel how light it is.

—Thérèse of Lisieux, *The Story of a Soul*

Let us be charitable and humble, both in our thoughts and words.

—Margaret Mary Alacoque, *Life and Writings of St. Margaret Mary*

While at prayer, I begged our Lord to make known to me by what means I could satisfy the desire that I had to love him. He gave me to understand, that one cannot better show one's love for him than by loving one's neighbor for love of him; and that I must work for the salvation of others, forgetting my own interest in order to espouse those of my neighbor, both in my prayers and in all the good I might be able to do by the mercy of God.

—Margaret Mary Alacoque, *Life and Writings of St. Margaret Mary*

When charity is united and joined to faith, it vivifies it. . . . Just as the soul cannot remain in the body without producing vital actions, so charity cannot be united to our faith without performing works conforming to it.

—Francis de Sales, *Oeuvres*

The waters of the most bitter afflictions cannot quench the fire of his charity toward us, so ardent is it. Even the persecutions of his enemies were not powerful enough to vanquish the incomparable solidity and constancy of the love with which he loved us. Such ought to be our love for the neighbor: firm, ardent, solid, and persevering.

—Francis de Sales, *Oeuvres*

The good man is like a tree planted by the water-side that will bring forth its fruit in due season, because when a soul is watered by charity, it brings forth good works seasonably and with discretion.

—Francis de Sales, *The Devout Life*

No, my dear brethren, even if you could perform miracles, you will never be saved if you have not charity. Not to have charity is not to know your religion; it is to have a religion of whim, mood, and inclination. Carry on, carry on, you are only hypocrites and outcasts! Without charity, you will never see God, you will never go to heaven!

—John Baptiste Marie Vianney, *sermon*

Alas, my dear brethren, the person who has no charity goes far afield for evil! If someone does him harm, you see him examining all his actions then. He judges them. He condemns them. He turns them all to evil and is always quite certain that he is right.

—John Baptiste Marie Vianney, *sermon*

Adore the infinite charity of God, who deigns to save men, notwithstanding their unworthiness and ingratitude.

—Ignatius of Loyola, *Spiritual Exercises*

Charity makes its own what belongs to our neighbors.

—Gertrude the Great, *Love, Peace and Joy*

Is there anything as beautiful and precious in the eyes of God as perfect charity? It is the fullness of the Law, as we have learned from our Master.

—Basil the Great, *letter to the Clerics of Colonia*

Since you can't do good for everybody, first care for those who by chance of place or time or any other circumstance are closest to you. When our Lord told us not to invite our friends, brothers and kinsmen to our banquet, but rather the poor and disabled, he was not forbidding us to invite kinsmen as such, but rather forbidding the kind of inviting that wants to be invited back, and stems from greed rather than charity.

—Thomas Aquinas, *Summa Theologica*

Charity is instilled into us and preserved in us by God, in the way the sun gives light. A single obstacle to the sun's rays cuts that light off, and a single obstacle to God's action in the soul cuts off charity.

—Thomas Aquinas, *Summa Theologica*

Nothing in the definition of charity can set a limit to its growth, for it is a sharing in the limitless charity of the Holy Spirit. Moreover, its agent of growth is God with unlimited power. And even on our side, each increase in charity produces an even greater increase in our capacity to grow—*our heart is enlarged.*

—Thomas Aquinas, *Summa Theologica*

Charity is friendship between God and man based on sharing eternal happiness: something we share not by nature but by *the free gift of God.* So charity is not born in us by nature, nor acquired by our natural powers, but is a created share in the Holy Spirit, the love of Father and Son, instilled into us by him.

—Thomas Aquinas, *Summa Theologica*

Whoever lives in charity participates in all the good that is done in the whole world; but since one man can certainly make satisfaction for another, he for whom some good work is done benefits in a special way.

—Thomas Aquinas, *letter on articles of faith*

What charity obliges us to love in our neighbor is this: that together we may attain to happiness.

—Thomas Aquinas, *On the Perfection of the Spiritual Life*

I would call his charity unspotted who never keeps anything of his own for himself. When a man keeps nothing of his own for himself, everything he has is God's and what is God's cannot be unclean. Therefore the unspotted law of God is charity, which seeks not what may benefit itself, but what may benefit many.

—Bernard of Clairvaux, *letter to Guy the Carthusian Prior*

Remember that the axis of perfection is charity; who lives centered in charity, lives in God, because God is charity, as the Apostles said.

—Padre Pio, *Spiritual Maxims*

The man of charity spreads his money about him, but the man who claims to possess both charity and money is a self-deceived fool.

—John Climacus, *The Ladder of Divine Ascent*

Be sure, too, to show to your neighbor the same love which God has shown towards you. If you are harsh to others, you will find God harsh to you. . . . He will pardon you many crimes for the one offense you forgive your neighbor; he will be long-suffering with you in return for a little patience shown toward others; he will reward you with abundant riches for the small alms you bestow. Strive earnestly, therefore, to keep the law of charity, for that is your life.

—John of Ávila, *letter to a disciple, 1563*

The charity of God is poured into our hearts by the Holy Ghost, who is given to us.

—Paul, *Rom. 5:5*

Let all that you do be done in charity.

—Paul, *1 Cor. 16:14*

Should it happen that, in a fit of passion, you have insulted a neighbor, charity requires that you use every means to allay his wounded feelings, and to remove from his heart all sentiments of rancor towards you. The best means for making reparation for the violation of charity, is to humble yourself to the person whom you have offended.

—Alphonsus Liguori, *sermon*

Many people say that charity and love are the same thing, and they are wrong. For charity is very different from love, since charity is a bond that binds us and generates in God, whereas love is a compendium of every virtue.

—Maria Maddalena de' Pazzi, *The Dialogues*

Let us, therefore, be rooted and grounded in charity so that with all the saints we may be able to comprehend what is the length of eternity, the breadth of liberality, the height of majesty and the depth of discerning wisdom.

—Bonaventure, *The Soul's Journey Into God*

Charity gives life to all the virtues.

—Catherine of Siena, *Dialogue*

For people lose everything they leave behind in this world; but they carry with them the rewards of charity and the alms which they gave, for which they will have a reward and a suitable remuneration from the Lord.

—Francis of Assisi, *letter to the faithful*

Let us, therefore, have charity and humility and give alms because it washes the stains of our sins from our clothes. For, although people lose everything they leave behind in this world, they, nevertheless, carry with them the rewards of charity and the alms they have given for which they will receive a reward and a fitting repayment from the Lord.

—Francis of Assisi, *admonition*

The most excellent virtue of charity is the mistress, the queen, the mother, the life and beauty of all the other virtues; charity governs, moves and directs them to their ultimate perfection, preserves them and makes them grow, enlightens them and beautifies them, gives them life and efficacy. If the other virtues confer each their measure of perfection on creatures, charity gives them perfection itself and brings them to their full complement.

—Mary of Agreda, *The Mystical City of God*

Without charity all is of small value, obscure, languid, lifeless and unprofitable, not being endowed either with the essence or the appurtenances of true vitality.

—Mary of Agreda, *The Mystical City of God*

We will call God our charity, not only because we receive it from the Lord, and because He communicates it to us, but because He himself is essential charity, and the overflow of this divine perfection, which we represent to ourselves as a form and attribute of his Divinity, redounds in our souls, transforming it more perfectly and abundantly than any other virtue.

—Mary of Agreda, *The Mystical City of God*

Charity begun is justice begun, advanced charity is advanced justice, great charity is great justice, perfect charity is perfect justice.

—Robert Bellarmine, *The Mind's Ascent to God by the Ladder of Created Things*

We ought therefore to do alms that we may be heard when we pray that our past sins may be forgiven, not that while we continue in them we may think to provide ourselves with a license for wickedness by alms-deeds.

—Augustine, *The City of God*

If I give, you're not saved; if the church makes an offering, you haven't blotted out your sins either. . . . Don't you know that God laid down laws about almsgiving not so much for the sake of the poor as for the sake of those very people who make an offering?

—John Chrysostom, *homily*

Charity is the bond of brotherhood, the foundation of peace, the steadfastness and firmness of unity; it is greater than both hope and faith; it excels both good works and suffering of the faith; and, as an eternal virtue, it will abide with us forever in the kingdom of heaven.

—Cyprian of Carthage, *The Good of Patience*

The angel [Raphael] reveals and makes manifest and confirms that our petitions are made efficacious by almsgiving; that by almsgiving life is redeemed from dangers; that by almsgiving souls are freed from death.

—Cyprian of Carthage, *Works and Almsgiving*

Have no fear when you bestow an alms; you are storing up for yourself a good reward for the day of necessity, for alms delivers from death and does not suffer one to go into darkness. Alms provide a great confidence for all who do it before the most high God.

—Cyprian of Carthage, *Works and Almsgiving*

For the law of Christ is Charity; since it has from Him bountifully bestowed on us its good things, and has patiently borne our evil things. We, therefore, then fulfil by imitation the law of Christ, when we both kindly bestow our good things, and piously endure the evil things of our friends.

—Gregory the Great, *The Book of Pastoral Rule*

Lord, grant me, I pray you, in the name of Jesus Christ, your Son, my God, the charity that does not fail, so that my lamp may always be lighted, never extinguished, and may burn for me and give light to others.

—Columban, *sermon*

Almsgiving is another kind of washing of souls, so that if perchance after baptism a person should commit a fault through human frailty he has but to be cleansed again by almsgiving, as the Lord says, "Give alms and behold! All things are clean for you." (Luke 11:41)

—Maximus of Turin, *sermon*

For without charity no virtue is pleasing to God.

—John of the Cross, *The Dark Night of the Soul*

Charity also empties and annihilates the affections and appetites of the will of whatever is not God and centers them on him alone. Thus charity prepares the will and unites it with God through love.

—John of the Cross, *The Dark Night of the Soul*

The fulfillment of every law, the totality of Christian virtue, according to St. Paul, consists in charity. A man raises himself toward God in proportion as he perfects himself in this heavenly virtue, and when this virtue is accompanied by its external fulfillment in a person, that person becomes a perfect Christian, a model of sanctity: "Love therefore is the fulfilling of the law." (Romans 13:10)

—John Bosco, *second panegyric on St. Joseph Cafasso*

You will become a saint if you have charity, if you manage to do the things which please others and do not offend God, though you find them hard to do.

—Josemaría Escrivá, *The Forge*

In charity true tranquillity and true gentleness exist, because charity is the Lord's yoke. If we bear this at the Lord's invitation we shall find rest for our souls, because the Lord's yoke is easy and the Lord's burden light.

—Aelred of Rievaulx, *Mirror of Charity*

But charity, which permits other virtues to be virtues, must exist in all virtues. It is most particularly rest for the weary, an inn for the traveler, full light at journey's end and the perfect crown for the victor.

—Aelred of Rievaulx, *Mirror of Charity*

If someone else is harboring ill-feeling against you, show yourself friendly towards him and also humble. Treat him well and you will set him free from his passion.

—Maximus the Confessor, *Centuries on Charity*

True charity is that by which we are commanded to love God with our whole heart, our whole soul, our whole strength, and our neighbor as ourself.

—Bede the Venerable, *homily on the Gospels*

Chastity

Every marriage should be set up so that it may work together with us for chastity.

—John Chrysostom, *sermon*

For God, being spirit, lives in that spirit and in that mind which seems to him undefiled, in which there is no adulterous thought, no stain of a polluted spirit, and no spot of sin.

—Columban, *Rule*

Examine the path of chastity and notice that it has the greenness of grass and the beauty of flowers on both sides. Make room for chastity not only in the flesh but also in the spirit, because chastity of the flesh is useless where incontinence of the spirit reigns—likewise with the other things that defile the soul.

—Elisabeth of Schönau, *The Book of the Ways of God*

Unchaste people . . . have blear-eyed souls: "For wisdom will not enter into a malicious soul." (Wisdom 1:4) Therefore, those who wish to enter into the secrets of scripture ought to preserve themselves in pure chastity.

—Vincent Ferrer, *sermon*

And He wishes all of us to be saved through Him and receive Him with our heart pure and our body chaste.

—Francis of Assisi, *admonition*

For chastity has made even angels. He who has preserved it is an angel; he who has lost it is a devil.

—Ambrose, *Concerning Virgins, to Marcellina, His Sister*

When you resolve firmly to lead a clean life, chastity will not be a burden to you: it will be a triumphant crown.

—Josemaría Escrivá, *The Way*

Chastity is the lily of the virtues. It renders men almost equal to the angels. Nought is beautiful save through purity, and the purity of men is chastity. We call chastity integrity, and its opposite corruption. In short, it is its own peculiar glory to be the white and beautiful virtue of both body and soul.

—Francis de Sales, *The Devout Life*

As to those who are married, it is quite true (although the mass of men cannot perceive it) that they stand greatly in need of chastity, for in them it lies not in total abstinence from carnal pleasures, but in self-control amidst the pleasures.

—Francis de Sales, *The Devout Life*

The various casualties of human life, besides long illnesses, often separate husbands and wives. Therefore, they need two kinds of chastity, one for absolute abstinence when thus separated, the other for moderation when they are together as usual.

—Francis de Sales, *The Devout Life*

By simple chastity we lend our body to God, still retaining the liberty to submit it to sensual pleasures; but by the vow of chastity we give it him as an absolute irrevocable gift, without reserving any power to recall it, thus happily rendering ourselves his slave, whose service is better than all royalty.

—Francis de Sales, *The Devout Life*

Do not associate with immodest persons, above all if they are impudent, as for the most part is the case; for just as the stag causes the sweet almond tree to become bitter by licking it, so these infected, stinking souls can scarcely speak to any one, either of one sex or the other, without injuring their purity: venom is in their eyes, and their breath is like the basilisk.

—Francis de Sales, *The Devout Life*

For His sake, for many years I have been at pains to live in chastity and restraint. I resist my evil passions. I apply myself to constant prayer. I am on the watch against temptations.

—Bernard of Clairvaux, *On the Canticle of Canticles*

Either we must speak as we dress, or dress as we speak. Why do we profess one thing and display another? The tongue talks of chastity, but the whole body reveals incontinence.

—Jerome, *letter to Furia, 394*

In temptations against chastity, the spiritual masters advise us, not so much to contend with the bad thought, as to turn the mind to some spiritual, or, at least, indifferent object. It is useful to combat other bad thoughts face to face, but not thoughts of impurity.

—Alphonsus Liguori, *sermon*

Children

If your children incur damnation at home with you, you, too, will be damned.

—John Baptiste Marie Vianney, *sermon*

If you do not bring up your children well, what *do* you do? It is the only thing you have to do; it is this that God requires of you, for this that he established Christian marriage; and it is on this that you will be judged.

—Claude de la Colombière, *sermon*

It is true that we love our children very much, more than anything else. But those who speak only gentle words to them are in fact loving the children they are afraid of hurting only a little. On the other hand, those who correct them strictly are hurting them today but doing them good for the future.

—Clement of Alexandria, *The Teacher*

It is a most grievous sin for people united in matrimony and blessed with children to neglect their children or their good upbringing, or to allow them to lack the necessities of life.

—Robert Bellarmine, *The Art of Dying Well*

The parents are naturally bound to instruct their children from their infancy in this knowledge of God and to direct them with solicitous care, so that they may at once see their ultimate end and seek it in their first acts of intellect and will. They should with great watchfulness withdraw them from the childishness and puerile trickishness to which depraved nature will incline them if left without direction. If the fathers and mothers would be solicitous to prevent these vanities and perverted habits of their children and would instruct them from their infancy in the knowledge of their God and Creator, then they would afterwards easily accustom them to know and adore Him.

—Mary of Agreda, *The Mystical City of God*

It happens to many boys, whether through having the misfortune of falling under the influence of bad company or through neglect of their parents, or because they neglect to profit from the good education they receive, that they lose the inestimable treasure of the innocence of childhood before knowing its value, and that they become slaves of the devil without even tasting the sweetness of being the children of God.

—John Bosco, *first panegyric on St. Joseph Cafasso*

If you desire children, you can get much better children now, a nobler childbirth and better help in your old age, if you give birth by spiritual labor.

—John Chrysostom, *sermon*

We have a great deposit in children; let us attend to them with great care.

—John Chrysostom, *homily*

Children have not been given to parents as a present, which they may dispose of as they please, but as a trust, for which, if lost through their negligence, they must render an account to God.

—Alphonsus Liguori, *sermon*

Hence, he who teaches his son to live well, shall die a happy and tranquil death.

—Alphonsus Liguori, *sermon*

Would to God that certain parents paid as much attention to their children as they do to their horses!

—Alphonsus Liguori, *sermon*

If you dissipate the goods which you possess, and leave your children in poverty, you do wrong, and are guilty of sin.

—Alphonsus Liguori, *sermon*

Impart to my childbearing something of thine own divine excellence, and by thy never-failing assistance, help me to bear this babe, the result of thy creative power, until the hour is ripe to bring the child to birth. Then O God, come to my aid, with thy whole hand support my weakness and receive the fruit of my womb, preserve the infant who is thine by creation until the sacrament of baptism lays him in the bosom of your bride, the Church, and makes him thine too by redemption.

—Francis de Sales, *prayer for an expectant mother, 1620*

Christ

Attributes and Adoration of Christ

He is the Way, the Truth, and the Life; that is, the Bridge which leads you to the height of Heaven.

—Catherine of Siena, *Dialogue*

Oh, Word, how beautiful you are! What do you give to the soul that is the first in this communication of yours? Oh, you give it the vision of yourself, your embrace, your fruition, Yourself, and everything that is suitable both in heaven and on earth.

—Maria Maddalena de' Pazzi, *The Dialogues*

We know that Christ alone performed all the great works which belong to our salvation, and no one but he; and just so, he alone acts now in the last end, that is to say he dwells here in us, and rules us, and cares for us in this life, and brings us to his bliss.

—Julian of Norwich, *Showings*

All the ends of the earth, all the kingdoms of the world would be of no profit to me; so far as I am concerned, to die in Jesus Christ is better than to be monarch of earth's widest bounds. He who died for us is all that I seek; He who rose again for us is my whole desire.

—Ignatius of Antioch, *epistle to the Romans*

Come, therefore, O Jesus Christ, minister of our spiritual circumcision, touch my lips, take away my iniquity, purge my affections, illuminate my mind, eliminate my imperfections, move my tongue and make my speech and action such that, for the glory of Thy Name, it may burst forth with the burning heat of Thy charity, mixed with the flame of Thy piety.

—Bernadine of Siena, *sermon*

Hail, my light and my salvation! May all in heaven, on earth, and in the depths give thanks to you. You have given me the extraordinary grace to know and consider what passes within my heart.

—Gertrude the Great, *The Herald of Divine Love*

You gave me a clearer knowledge of yourself. This knowledge awakened such love in me that now I wished to correct all my faults not for fear of your just anger but because of love alone.

—Gertrude the Great, *The Herald of Divine Love*

Whoever turns his face fully to the Mercy Seat and with faith, hope and love, devotion, admiration, exultation, appreciation, praise and joy behold him hanging upon the cross, such a one makes the Pasch, that is, the passover, with Christ.

—Bonaventure, *The Soul's Journey Into God*

Therefore, spurning the things that are seen, journeying through the world, let us seek the fountain of glory, the fountain of life, the fountain of living water, in the upper regions of the heavens, like rational and most wise fishes, that there we may drink the living water which springs up to eternal life.

—Columban, *sermon*

How lovely is the fount of living water, whose water does not fail, springing up to life eternal. O Lord, you are yourself that fountain ever and again to be desired, although ever and again to be consumed. Give this water always, Lord Christ, that it may be in us too a fountain of water that lives and springs up to eternal life.

—Columban, *sermon*

The Son of Man must be lifted up that all who believe in him will not perish but may have life everlasting.

—Vincent Ferrer, *sermon*

Christ was called the foundation-stone (1 Corinthians 3:11) because he bears everything and holds it together and props it up.

—John Chrysostom, *homily on "My Father's Working Still"*

He is called Light as being the Brightness of souls cleansed by word and life. For if ignorance and sin be darkness, knowledge and a godly life will be Light. . . . And He is called Life, because He is Light, and is the constituting and creating Power of every reasonable soul. For in Him we live and move and have our being, according to the double power of that Breathing into us; for we were all inspired by Him with breath, and as many of us were capable of it, and in so far as we open the mouth of our mind, with God the Holy Ghost.

—Gregory of Nazianzus, *theological oration*

Rest assured that the more you turn to Mary in your prayers, meditations, actions and sufferings, seeing her if not perhaps clearly and distinctly, at least in a general and indistinct way, the more surely you will discover Jesus. For he is far greater, more powerful, more active, and more mysterious when acting through Mary than he is in any other creature in the universe, or even in heaven.

—Louis de Montfort, *Treatise on True Devotion to the Blessed Virgin*

Blood of Christ

Oh, what a sweet smell was the fragrance of your blood! And what a great power you had when you shed it.

—Maria Maddalena de' Pazzi, *The Dialogues*

For if the Word of God had not poured out blood for the salvation of people, sin would have so restrained people that they would not be able to reach the joy of the heavenly city.

—Hildegard of Bingen, *Scivias*

The just man does not turn to admire his past virtues, because he neither can nor will hope in his virtues, but only in the Blood in which he has found mercy; and as he lived in the memory of that Blood, so in death he is inebriated and drowned in the same.

—Catherine of Siena, *Dialogue*

For with the Blood of this door—Thy truth—hast Thou washed our iniquities and destroyed the stain of Adam's sin. The Blood is ours, for Thou hast made it our bath, wherefore Thou canst not deny it to any one who truly asks for it. Give, then, the fruit of thy Blood to Thy creatures.

—Catherine of Siena, *Dialogue*

Imitation of Christ

First, have habitual desire to imitate Christ in all your deeds by bringing your life into conformity with his. You must then study his life in order to know how to imitate him and behave in events as he would.

—John of the Cross, *The Ascent of Mount Carmel*

The good Lord has worked and still works daily that we may achieve the glory of being fashioned as God, as long as we follow the example of our fashioning here in Christ.

—Paulinus of Nola, *letter*

For no one can begin anything good unless he begins it from Christ. He is the foundation of all that is good.

—Aelred of Rievaulx, *sermon*

If Christ is our life, then it follows that all our speech should be about him and that everything we do and think should be guided by his teaching, so that our soul should be formed in his image.

—Basil the Great, *letter*

Incarnation of God

The beloved of the love of God came through the fountain of life to nourish us back to life and to help us in our dangerous state. The Word is the deepest and sweetest love preparing us for repentance.

—Hildegard of Bingen, *Scivias*

The rational soul and flesh are united in one human nature; therefore, God and man are joined in the one nature of Christ.

None of the philosophers before the coming of Christ could by bending all effort to the task know as much about God and things necessary for eternal life as after the coming of Christ a little old woman knows through her faith.

—Thomas Aquinas, *On the Union of the Incarnate Word*

It was our sorry case that caused the Word to come down, our transgression that called out His love for us, so that He made haste to help us and to appear among us. It is we who were the cause of His taking human form, and for our salvation that in His great love He was both born and manifested in a human body.

—Athanasius, *On the Incarnation*

There were thus two things which the Savior did for us by becoming Man. He banished death from us and made us anew; and, invisible and imperceptible as in Himself He is, He became visible through His works and revealed Himself as the Word of the Father, the Ruler and King of the whole creation.

—Athanasius, *On the Incarnation*

If any honest Christian wants to know why He suffered death on the cross and not in some other way, we answer thus; in no other way was it expedient for us indeed the Lord offered for our sakes the one death that was supremely good. He had come to bear the curse that lay on us; and how could He "become a curse" (Galatians 3:13) otherwise than by accepting the accursed death? And that death is the cross, for it is written "Cursed is every one that hangeth on the tree." (Galatians 3:13)

—Athanasius, *On the Incarnation*

At the very moment Mary consented to become the Mother of God, several miraculous events took place. The Holy Spirit formed from the most pure blood of Mary's heart a little body which he fashioned into a perfect living being: God created the most perfect soul that ever could be created. Eternal Wisdom, the Son of God, drew the body and soul into union with that person. Here we have the great wonder of heaven and earth, the prodigious excess of the love of God. . . . God became man without ceasing to be God. This God-man is Jesus Christ and his name means Savior.

—Louis de Montfort, *The Love of Eternal Wisdom*

How beautiful, meek and charitable is Jesus, the incarnate Wisdom! Beautiful from all eternity, he is the splendor of his Father, the unspotted mirror and image of his goodness. He is more beautiful than the sun and brighter than light itself. He is beautiful in time, being formed by the Holy Spirit pure and faultless, fair and immaculate, and during his life he charmed the eyes and hearts of men and is not the glory of the angels. How loving and gentle he is with men, and especially with poor sinners whom he came upon earth to seek out in a visible manner, and whom he still seeks in an invisible manner every day.

—Louis de Montfort, *The Love of Eternal Wisdom*

Name of Jesus Christ

The Name of Jesus is the most sweet-tasting nourishment of contemplation, for it feeds and revives those souls that are famished and spiritually hungry.

—Bernadine of Siena, *sermon*

Wherever there is the Lord's name, everything will be well. . . . Wherever the

Name of the Lord is set up, all things prosper.

—John Chrysostom, *homily*

For where Christ is named, idolatry is destroyed and the fraud of evil spirits is exposed; indeed, no which spirit can endure that Name, but takes to flight on sound of it. This is the work of One who lives, not of one dead; and, more than that, it is the work of God.

—Athanasius, *On the Incarnation*

How shall we explain the worldwide light of faith, swift and flaming in its progress, except by the preaching of Jesus' Name? Is it not by the light of this Name that God has called us into his wonderful light, that irradiates our darkness and empowers us to see the light?

—Bernard of Clairvaux, sermon on the *Song of Songs*

With the name of Jesus lash your enemies, for there is no more powerful weapon in heaven or on earth.

—John Climacus, *The Ladder of Divine Ascent*

The Name of Jesus. Oh, how great is Your Name, O Lord! It is the strength of my soul. When my strength fails, and darkness invades my soul, Your Name is the sun whose rays give lights and also warmth, and under their influence the soul becomes more beautiful and radiant, taking its splendor from Your Name. When I hear the sweetest name of Jesus, my heartbeat grows stronger, and there are times when, hearing the Name of Jesus, I fall into a swoon. My spirit eagerly strains toward Him.

—Faustina Kowalska, *Divine Mercy in My Soul*

Jesus! A sweet name, a delightful name! A name that comforts sinners and offers blessed hope. A name that is a joyful cry from the heart, that is music to the ear and honey in the mouth.

—Anthony of Padua, *Sermones*

How sweet the name of Jesus sounds to the ear and the heart of a chosen soul! Sweet as honey to the lips, a delightful melody to the ears, thrilling joy to the heart.

—Louis de Montfort, *The Love of Eternal Wisdom*

See also: RESURRECTION

Communion

Communion is the life of your soul. If you were to eat only one meal each week, would you survive? It's the same thing with your soul: you must nourish your soul with the Holy Eucharist. There is a beautiful table set up in front of us, with great food on it. But sometimes we don't even bother to take it!

—Brother André, *Brother André According to Witnesses*

By the communion, Jesus is really united to our soul and to our body, and we are united to Jesus.

—Alphonsus Liguori, *sermon*

Two sorts of persons ought to communicate often: the perfect, to preserve perfection; and the imperfect, to arrive at perfection.

—Francis de Sales, *The Devout Life*

Thanksgiving after communion is also necessary. The prayer we make after communion is the most acceptable to God, and the most profitable to us.

—Alphonsus Liguori, *sermon*

What a source of grace there is in spiritual Communion! Practice it frequently and you'll have more presence of God and closer union with him in your life.

—Josemaría Escrivá, *The Way*

If you are sinful, repent so that you can communicate often. If you are imperfect, go often to Communion that you may amend your faults.

—Claude de la Colombière, *spiritual notes*

Compassion

Just as the Father is compassionate toward you in a threefold way, so ought you to show compassion towards others in three ways. The Father's compassion is gracious, spacious and precious. The Father's compassion is gracious, that is, grace-filled, because it purifies the soul of vice. . . . The Father's compassion is spacious because with the passage of time it extends itself to good works. . . The Father's compassion is precious in the joys of eternal life.

—Anthony of Padua, *Sermones*

For God has more compassion for the lowly and they are forgiven more easily, but the mighty will be punished mightily.

—Louis de Montfort, *The Love of Eternal Wisdom*

But you cannot be a neighbor unless you have compassion on him; for no one can be called a neighbor unless he have healed, not killed, another.

—Ambrose, *Concerning Repentance*

If we thus have compassion, we are not stained with the sins of others, but we gain the restoration of another to the increase of our own grace, so that our integrity remains as it was.

—Ambrose, *Concerning Repentance*

Conceit

Everything pursued in this life is reckoned as conceit and without substance: honor, dignity, a noble birth, pride, arrogance, wealth, and all the other things with which the webs of this life are concerned. Because of this, God's healing power is needed.

—Gregory of Nyssa, *Commentary on the Inscriptions of the Psalms*

How many people when they are coming to church think of nothing else except themselves and their clothes and styles. They enter the temple of the Lord saying from the depths of their hearts: "Have a good look at me." When we see such wrong dispositions, how can we help but shed tears?

—John Baptiste Marie Vianney, *sermon*

Beware of angling for compliments, lest you lose God's favor in exchange for people's praise.

—Jerome, *letter to Nepotian*

But many, as I have said, make the mistake of supposing they can come to understand spirituality without themselves being spiritual.

—Teresa of Ávila, *Life*

We must not follow the showy fashions of the world in our dress, our furniture or our dwellings. Neither must we indulge in sumptuous meals or other worldly habits and ways of living. . . . Putting this into practice is more necessary than is generally thought.

—Louis de Montfort, *The Love of Eternal Wisdom*

Concupiscence

see LUST; PASSIONS

Confession

By confession the sinner is loosed, not only from the guilt of sin, but from the eternal punishment due to it. . . . You see, then, that it is a very grave fault not to go to Confession for, perhaps, four or five years.

—Vincent Ferrer, *sermon*

Confession opens the door to Christ, for then the chamber of conscience is cleansed.

—Vincent Ferrer, *sermon*

Confession is of such efficacy that it blots all sins from the Book of Death and the memory of the devil.

—Vincent Ferrer, *sermon*

Confession is like a bridle that keeps the soul which reflects on it from committing sin, but anything left unconfessed we continue to do without fear as if in the dark.

—John Climacus, *The Ladder of Divine Ascent*

After we have offended God, the Devil labors to keep the mouth closed, and to prevent us from confessing our guilt.

—Alphonsus Liguori, *sermon*

For those who have sinned grievously, there is no means of salvation but the confession of their sins.

—Alphonsus Liguori, *sermon*

If you do not confess your sin, God himself, shall, for your confusion, publish not only the sin which you conceal, but also all your iniquities, in the presence of the angels and of the whole world.

—Alphonsus Liguori, *sermon*

It is useless to confess your sins, if afterwards you return to your former vices.

—Alphonsus Liguori, *sermon*

A soul does not benefit as it should from the sacrament of confession if it is not humble. Pride keeps it in darkness.

—Faustina Kowalska, *Divine Mercy in My Soul*

The Lord knows all things, but He waits for your words, not that He may punish, but that He may pardon. It is not His will that the devil should triumph over you and accuse you when you conceal your sins. Be beforehand with your accuser: if you accuse yourself, you will fear no accuser; if you report yourself, though you were dead you shall live.

—Ambrose, *Concerning Repentance*

Eggs warmed in dung hatch out. Unconfessed evil thoughts hatch evil actions.

—John Climacus, *The Ladder of Divine Ascent*

Always entertain a sincere hatred of the sins you confess, even though they be trifling, and a heartfelt resolution to amend.

—Francis de Sales, *The Devout Life*

Confidence

It is confidence, and confidence alone, that must lead us to Love.

—Thérèse of Lisieux, *letter to Sister Marie of the Sacred Heart*

He that prays with confidence, obtains whatever he asks.

—Alphonsus Liguori, *sermon*

Prayer nourishes our hope and confidence; for the more often we speak with another person, the more confidently we approach him.

—Robert Bellarmine, *The Art of Dying Well*

Don't flutter about like a hen, when you can soar to the heights of an eagle.

—Josemaría Escrivá, *The Way*

Cultivate thoughts of confidence as long as it pleases God to give them to you; they honor God far more than contrary thoughts. The more wretched we are, the more God is honored by the confidence we have in him.

—Claude de la Colombière, *letter*

If your confidence were as great as it ought to be, you would not worry about what may happen to you; you would place it all in God's hands, hoping that when he wants something of you he will let you know what it is.

—Claude de la Colombière, *letter*

Conscience

Keep your conscience pure; be careful not to fall; but if you do fall, hasten to rise again.

—Maximilian M. Kolbe, *text for the Assumption, 1940*

For purity of conscience, by which love of self is judged, is born of good works.

—Aelred of Rievaulx, *Mirror of Charity*

Those who possess the fear of God are the furthest from telling lies, because they have an honest judge, their own conscience.

—John Climacus, *The Ladder of Divine Ascent*

Now there are some people whose consciences are not decorated with flowers; rather, their hearts are strewn with dung.

—Henry Suso, *sermon*

Contemplation

But the believing soul longs and faints for God; she rests sweetly in the contemplation of him. She glories in the reproach of the cross, until the glory of his face should be revealed. Like the Bride, the dove of Christ, that is covered with silver wings, white with innocence and purity, she reposes in the thought of thine abundant kindness, Lord Jesus; and above all she longs for that day when in the joyful splendor of thy saints, gleaming with the radiance of the Beatific Vision, her feathers shall be like gold, resplendent with the joy of thy countenance.

—Bernard of Clairvaux, *On Loving God*

The light of holy contemplation enlarges and expands the mind in God until it stands above the world. In fact, the soul that sees Him rises even above itself, and as it is drawn upward in His light, all its inner powers unfold. Then when it looks downward from above, it sees how small everything really is that was beyond its grasp before.

—Gregory the Great, *The Dialogues*

In fact, as the Infinite God brings my unmoored soul into the heights of contemplation, I have lost touch with the earth. I am so awed that I forget I was ever on this earth! When the flight is at its highest, unfortunately, the soul must depart.

—Mechtilde of Magdeburg, *The Flowing Light of the Godhead*

For contemplation is nothing else than a secret and peaceful and loving inflow of God, which, if not hampered, fires the soul in the spirit of love.

—John of the Cross, *The Dark Night of the Soul*

Contemplation is mystical theology, which theologians called secret wisdom and which St. Thomas says is communicated and infused into the soul through love. This communication is secret and dark to the work of the intellect and the other faculties.

—John of the Cross, *The Dark Night of the Soul*

Contemplation, consequently, by which the intellect has a higher knowledge of God, is called mystical theology, meaning the secret wisdom of God. For this wisdom is secret to the very intellect that receives it.

—John of the Cross, *The Ascent of Mount Carmel*

Contemplation of God can be understood in more than one fashion. For God is not solely known by way of that astonished gaze at His ungraspable nature, something hidden thus far in the hope that comes with what has been promised us. He can also be sensed in the magnificence of His creation, in the spectacle of His justice, and in the help He extends each day to the running of the world.

—John Cassian, *Conferences*

Keep watch also over the senses, especially the eyes, the ears and the tongue, for through the lips the heart is scattered, and by eyes and ears it is filled with varied imaginings, and with much that disturbs the peace and repose of the soul. Hence it has been truly said that the contemplative soul should be as one deaf, blind and dumb, for the less he dissipates his energies abroad, the more will he be recollected within himself.

—Peter of Alcántara, *Treatise on Prayer & Meditation*

Do you know what cleansing properties there are in this living water, this heavenly water, this clear water, when it is unclouded, and free from mud, and comes down from Heaven? Once the soul has drunk of it I am convinced that it makes pure and clean of all its sins; for, as I have written, God does not allow us to drink of this water of perfect contemplation whenever we like: The choice is not ours; this Divine union is something quite supernatural, given that it may cleanse the soul and leave it pure and free from the mud and misery in which it has been plunged because of its sins.

—Teresa of Ávila, *The Way of Perfection*

On all the paths of truth, God must be contemplated.

—Elisabeth of Schönau, *The Book of the Ways of God*

If indeed there are disputes among you, and dissent, slander, murmuring, anger, hatred and jealousy, haughtiness, hunger for glory, idle talk, jesting, gluttony, sleepiness, impurity of the flesh, idleness and the like, in which the children of this world talk, where will be the space for divine contemplation?

—Elisabeth of Schönau, *The Book of the Ways of God*

Walk in the way of contemplation of the Lord with all the attention of your mind, with all humility and obedience and love and patience.

—Elisabeth of Schönau, *letter to the sisters in Dirstein*

Prayer and contemplation shut out the temptations of the devil.

—Vincent Ferrer, *sermon*

A single plant, a blade of grass is sufficient to occupy all your intelligence in the contemplation of the skill which produced it.

—Basil the Great, *homily on the Hexaemeron*

While it is acknowledged that good things in the present life have sadness, despondency, and pain as their accompaniment and consequence, yet the life and converse with God, and the contemplation of His unspeakable good things, go beyond all beatitude and transcend every glory, prosperity, joy, and ease. They are exalted above the honor and delight and enjoyment of everything which is supposed to be good in the present life.

—Symeon the New Theologian, *Ethical Discourses*

Contrition

see REPENTANCE

Copulation

see LUST; PASSIONS

Corruption

Never has the world been so corrupt as it is now, for never has it been so cunning, so wise in its own way, and so crafty. It cleverly makes use of the truth to foster untruth, virtue to justify vice, and the very maxims of Jesus Christ to endorse its own so that even those who are wisest in the sight of God are often deceived.

—Louis de Montfort, *The Love of Eternal Wisdom*

Courage

I look upon the courage which the Lord gave me to fight the devils as one of the greatest favors that He has bestowed upon me. It is very wrong for a soul to behave like a coward or to fear anything except offending God, since we have an all-powerful King and a Lord so mighty that He can do everything and make all men His subjects.

—Teresa of Ávila, *Life*

The Lord opens for us the gate of life if we are willing to struggle against the most unyielding devil.

—Elisabeth of Schönau, *First Book of Visions*

Courage can be learned by following the example of Job. Here was a man who suffered a complete reversal of fate and, having once been rich and the father of numerous children, was reduced in a single moment to poverty and childlessness. And yet he managed to remain completely unchanged, never ceasing to attend to the well-being of his soul and even showing no anger towards those friends of his who had come to console him but who ended up by insulting him and merely increasing his afflictions.

—Basil the Great, *letter to Gregory of Nyssa*

Covetousness

To strengthen his fraud, one man arms his falsehood by perjury, and another sometimes opposes someone else's lawsuits with a corrupted heart. Thus, through the vice of covetousness alone an estate is both gained and rent apart. Where is esteem for what Scripture says: "A false witness shall not be unpunished?"

—Valerian, *homily*

Covetousness is so great with some persons that chastity is put up for sale and finds a price for its own depravity. Thus money is eagerly weighed out for the corruption of a body, just as if something worthy were being purchased. Clearly unfortunate is that man who has more interest in covetousness than in his chastity.

—Valerian, *homily*

If a covetous eye is restrained, parricidal hatreds are not sown.

—Valerian, *homily*

Covetousness is a great evil; and it is not possible in a single letter to set forth those scriptures in which not robbery alone is declared to be a thing horrible and to be abhorred, but in general the grasping mind, and the disposition to meddle with what belongs to others, in order to satisfy the sordid love of gain. And all persons of that spirit are excommunicated from the Church of God.

—Gregory Thaumaturgus, *canonical epistle*

When we inveigh against someone's covetousness, let us call to mind whether we ourselves have never done anything covetously. . . . Covetousness is the root of all evils, and is working in our bodies like a serpent secretly under the earth.

—Ambrose, *Concerning Repentance*

Do not therefore covet praise which can make you a sinner; you will only collect contempt in the end if you do. It is better to love a good person who reproves you in his kindness.

—Augustine, *On Psalm 140*

Cowardice

If you see your way clearly, follow it. Why don't you shake off the cowardice that holds you back?

—Josemaría Escrivá, *The Way*

Creation

First of all God created the heavens and earth as a kind of all-embracing material substance with the potentiality of giving birth to all things. In this way he rightly rebuts those who wrongly think that matter preexisted on its own as an autonomous reality.

—Gregory Palamas, *Topics of Natural and Theological Science and on the Moral and Ascetic Life: One Hundred and Fifty Texts*

So great was the honor and providential care which God bestowed upon man that he brought the entire sensible world into being before him and for his sake.

—Gregory Palamas, *Topics of Natural and Theological Science and on the Moral and Ascetic Life: One Hundred and Fifty Texts*

All things in heaven and earth have been made subject to him; everything that breathes pays him homage; he comes to judge the living and the dead, and God will require His blood at the hands of any who refuse him allegiance.

—Polycarp of Smyrna, *epistle to the Philippians*

The plan by which God, as ruler of the universe, governs all things, is a law in the true sense. And since it is not a plan conceived in time we call it the eternal law. It is promulgated through God's eternal Word, though creatures bear its promulgation in time. . . . When God governs he is his own goal, and his own law, so the eternal law serves no other purpose than itself.

—Thomas Aquinas, *Summa Theologica*

God's management of the world does many things. There is one actual goal: the imitation of the highest good. But there are two general means by which God achieves that: he holds things in existence, maintaining the good in creation that imitates God's own goodness; and he stimulates and directs creatures to pursue good and so imitate God's causality.

—Thomas Aquinas, *Summa Theologica*

All things deriving from God are ordered to one another and to him. And that is what makes the unity of the world.

—Thomas Aquinas, *Summa Theologica*

By an all-powerful word God created heaven and earth. He brought forth being from non-being, since this word is efficacious, effecting what it says. By that word, it made that which is not to be that which is.

—Francis de Sales, *Oeuvres*

God spoke once, but his speech is continual and perpetual.

—Bernard of Clairvaux, *Sermones de diversis*

Everything which lives, chooses to live from God.

—Hildegard of Bingen, *Scivias*

Consider that God, your benefactor, is present in all creatures and in yourself. If you look at every step of the visible creation, in all you will meet God. He is in the elements, he gives them existence; in plants, he gives them life; in animals, he gives them sensation. He is in you; and, collecting all these degrees of being scattered through the rest of his creation, he unites them in you, and adds to them intelligence.

—Ignatius of Loyola, *Spiritual Exercises*

All things, which you [God] have created, are governed both inwardly and outwardly by your secret inspiration.

—Augustine, *Confessions*

For the shape of the world exists everlastingly in the knowledge of the true Love which is God: constantly circling, wonderful for human nature, and such that it is not consumed by age and cannot be increased by anything new. It neither remains just as God has created it, everlasting until the end of time.

—Hildegard of Bingen, *Book of Divine Works*

For he had created he world and clothed himself in human nature. Hence, all creatures are an indication of him, just as a coin displays the image of the ruler. God had created the world which God wished to prepare us as our home. Because God wished to attract us, God made us in God's own image and likeness. Hence, everything belongs to God.

—Hildegard of Bingen, *Book of Divine Works*

Everything in the world he has created for your service: sea and land, birds and fishes and animals, the plants and even the angels in heaven.

—Peter of Alcantara, *Treatise on Prayer & Meditation*

God works in all and sustains all by His sole will; in Him lies the preservation of all things or their annihilation, for without Him they would return to the non-existence, from which they were drawn. But since He has created the universe for his glory and for the glory of the incarnate Word, therefore He has from the beginning opened the paths and prearranged the ways by which the same Word should lower Himself to assume human flesh and to live among men, and by which they might ascend toward God, know Him, fear Him, seek Him, serve Him, love Him, praise Him and enjoy Him eternally.

—Mary of Agreda, *The Mystical City of God*

What for us is the word *to call* is the word *to create* for God. "He calls all things that are not" (Romans 4:17) and by his calling makes them exist.

—Robert Bellarmine, *The Mind's Ascent to God by the Ladder of Created Things*

There is nothing in this whole universe of beings from the first angel down to the last little worm and from the summit of heaven to the lowest depth which was not made by God's power.

—Robert Bellarmine, *The Mind's Ascent to God by the Ladder of Created Things*

The Most High alone by his infinite power established, conserves, and will conserve without interruption right into eternity spiritual beings, the angels and human souls, which are the most noble and sublime of all his works. In making these no creature had any part. Even if all creatures got together, they would never be able to make or destroy a single angel or a single soul.

—Robert Bellarmine, *The Mind's Ascent to God by the Ladder of Created Things*

The aim of creation, the end of man himself, is the love of God, Creator and Father—an ever greater love, the divinization of man, his return to God from whom he came, union with God, a fruitful love.

—Maximilian M. Kolbe, *meditation, 1940*

The most perfect figure is circular or spherical, because in this figure the beginning and the end are merged in one. . . . The perfection of the universe consists in this, that the beginning and end are merged in one. . . . The circle was perfected when the end, man, was united to the Beginning, God, through the Blessed Incarnation.

—Vincent Ferrer, *sermon*

The Word of the Father is Himself divine, that all things that are owe their being to His will and power, and that it is through Him that the Father gives order to creation, by Him that all things are moved, and through Him that they receive their being.

—Athanasius, *On the Incarnation*

For everyone agrees that the Universe is linked to one First Cause; that nothing in it owes its existence to itself, so as to be its own origin and cause; but that there is on the other hand a single uncreated eternal Essence, the same for ever, which transcends all our ideas of distance, conceived of as without increase or decrease, and beyond the scope of any definition; and that time and space with all their consequences, and anything previous to these that thought can grasp in the intelligible supramundane world, are all the productions of this Essence.

—Gregory of Nyssa, *On Infants' Early Death*

Now the world is good, and all its contents are seen to be wisely and skillfully ordered. All of them, therefore, are the works of the Word, of one who, while He lives and subsists, in that He is God's Word, has a will, too, in that He is absolutely good and wise and all else that connotes superiority.

—Gregory of Nyssa, *The Great Catechism*

For how could this Universe have come into being or been put together, unless God had called it into existence, and held it together? For every one who sees a beautifully made lute, and considers the skill with which it has been fitted together and arranged, or who hears its melody, would think of none but the lutemaker, or the luteplayer, and would recur to him in mind, though he might not know him by sight. And thus to us also is manifested That which made and moves and preserves all created things, even though He be not comprehended by the mind.

—Gregory of Nazianzus, *theological oration*

If it is said, "In the beginning God created," it is to teach us that at the will of God the world rose in less than an instant, and it is to convey this meaning more clearly that other interpreters have said: "God made summarily" that is to say all at once and in a moment.

—Basil the Great, *homily on the Hexaemeron*

For everything in the world He has prepared for our enjoyment; He does everything for our profit, and He has created this universe in such a way that some elements are servants, some provide challenges and some rule. So by our reason we men are masters over physical and animal nature.

—Paulinus of Nola, *letter*

The creation is beautiful and harmonious, and God has made it all just for your sake.

He has made it beautiful, grand, varied, rich. He has made it capable of satisfying all your needs, to nourish your body and also to develop the life of your soul by leading it towards the knowledge of himself—all this, for your sake.

—John Chrysostom, *On Providence*

Criticism

To criticize, to destroy, is not difficult; any unskilled laborer knows how to drive his pick into the noble and finely-hewn stone of a cathedral.

To construct: that is what requires the skill of a master.

—Josemaría Escrivá, *The Way*

Whenever you need to criticize, your criticism must seek to be positive, helpful, and constructive. It should never be made behind the back of the person concerned.

To act otherwise would be treacherous, sneaky, defamatory, slanderous even, as well as utterly ignoble.

—Josemaría Escrivá, *The Forge*

The Cross

The Cross will not crush you; if its weight makes you stagger, its power will also sustain you.

—Padre Pio, *Spiritual Maxims*

The prototype, the example on which one should reflect and model one's self is Jesus Christ. But Jesus chose the cross as his standard, so he wants all his followers to tread the path to Calvary, carrying the cross and then dying stretched out on it. Only this way do we reach salvation.

—Padre Pio, *letter to Maria Gargani, 1916*

God doesn't ask for the impossible, but he wants everyone to offer their good intentions, their day's work, and some prayers; that will help them a lot. The best Way of the Cross is when people accept willingly the crosses that are sent to them.

—Brother André, *Brother André According to Witnesses*

What is a soul living on earth without its cross? One must get a cross either from the devil or from the other creatures, because there is no greater cross than being without any cross.

—Maria Maddalena de' Pazzi, *The Dialogues*

The only way to protect oneself against the devil is by constant remembrance of God: this remembrance must be imprinted in the heart by the power of the Cross, thus rendering the mind firm and unyielding.

—Simeon the New Theologian, *The Art of Prayer*

You should venerate not only the icon of Christ, but also the similitude of his cross. For the cross is Christ's great sign and trophy of victory over the devil and all his hostile hosts; for this reason they tremble and flee when they see the figuration of the cross.

—Gregory Palamas, *A New Testament Decalogue*

Death blossomed in paradise but was slain on the cross.

—John Chrysostom, *homily*

You cannot better appreciate your worth than by looking into the mirror of the Cross of Christ; there you will learn how you are to deflate your pride, how you must mortify the desires of the flesh, how you are to pray to your Father for those who persecute you, and to commend your spirit into God's hands.

—Anthony of Padua, *Sermones*

For my part, I believe that love is the measure of our ability to bear crosses, whether great or small.

—Teresa of Ávila, *The Way of Perfection*

The cross signifies that a truly detached person should always be disposed, both outwardly and inwardly, to self-surrender in everything that God wants him to endure, no matter where it comes from; that he be inclined, dying to self, to accept it all for the praise of his heavenly Father.

—Henry Suso, *Little Book of Truth*

By the sign of the cross . . . all magic is stayed, all sorcery confounded, all the idols are abandoned and deserted, and all senseless pleasure ceases, as the eye of faith looks up from earth to heaven.

—Athanasius, *On the Incarnation*

In the very presence of the fraud of demons and the imposture of the oracles and the wonders of magic, let him use the sign of the cross which they all mock at, and but speak the Name of Christ, and he shall see how through Him demons are routed, oracles cease, and all magic and witchcraft is confounded.

—Athanasius, *On the Incarnation*

And demons, so far from continuing to impose on people by their deceits and oracle-givings and sorceries, are routed by the sign of the cross if they so much as try.

—Athanasius, *On the Incarnation*

The cross is a sure sign that he loves you. I can assure you of this, that the greatest proof that we are loved by God is when we are despised by the world and burdened with crosses, i.e., when we are made to endure the privation of things we could rightly claim; when our holiest wishes meet with opposition; when we are afflicted with distressing and hurtful insults; when we are subjected to persecution, to have our actions misinterpreted by good people and by those who are our best friends; and when we suffer illnesses which are particularly repugnant, etc.

—Louis de Montfort, *letter*

If Christians knew the value of the cross, they would walk a hundred miles to obtain it, because enclosed in the beloved cross is true wisdom and that is what I am looking for night and day more eagerly than ever.

—Louis de Montfort, *letter*

Through his dying upon it the Cross of ignominy became so glorious, its poverty and starkness so enriching, its sorrows so agreeable, its austerity so attractive, that it became as it were deified and an object adored by angels and by men. Jesus now requires that all his subjects adore it as they adore him.

—Louis de Montfort, *The Love of Eternal Wisdom*

One must be humble, little, self-disciplined, spiritual and despised by the world to learn the mystery of the Cross.

—Louis de Montfort, *The Love of Eternal Wisdom*

The Cross is precious because it enlightens the mind and gives it an understanding which no book in the world can give.

—Louis de Montfort, *The Love of Eternal Wisdom*

Wise and honest people living in the world, you do not understand the mysterious language of the Cross. You are too fond of sensual pleasures and you seek your comforts too much. You have too much regard for the things of this world and you are too afraid to be held up to scorn or looked down upon. In short, you are too opposed to the Cross of Jesus.

—Louis de Montfort, *The Love of Eternal Wisdom*

I believe that all my crosses come from God.

—Anthony Mary Claret, *autobiography*

Genuine love brings joy in its wake, a joy that has it roots in the shape of the Cross.

—Josemaría Escrivá, *The Forge*

The Cross symbolizes the life of an apostle of Christ. It brings a strength and a truth that delight both soul and body, though sometimes it is hard, and one can feel the weight.

—Josemaría Escrivá, *The Forge*

The Cross is not pain, or annoyance, or bitterness. It is the holy word on which Jesus Christ triumphs . . . and where we triumph, too, when we receive what he sends us with cheerful and generous hearts.

—Josemaría Escrivá, *The Forge*

The glory of the cross . . . has enlightened all those who were blinded by ignorance. It has set free all those who were slaves of sin. It has redeemed the whole human race.

—Cyril of Jerusalem, *Catecheses*

All those who are willing to be saved through the cross will find salvation there. But those who desire to be saved without it will perish miserably. There is no salvation except in this cross.

—Francis de Sales, *Oeuvres*

Culture

The human mind is designed to understand and enjoy works of culture. It cannot be developed fully if it does not come into contact with a multiplicity of cultural disciplines. And the individual human being cannot attain his destined calling if he is unable to discover the cultural domain suited to his talent.

—Edith Stein, *Essays on Woman*

Cursing

see SWEARING AND CURSING

D

Damnation

Either you will be religious or you will be damned. What is a religious person? This is nothing other than a person who fulfills his duties as a Christian.

—John Baptiste Marie Vianney, *sermon*

Lucifer promises things unworthy of you, uncertain, which will leave a void in your heart, which will only add to your disgusts and agitations, and which will soon pass away, and will end in everlasting punishments.

—Ignatius of Loyola, *Spiritual Exercises*

God's initial will is every man's salvation, but his justice may finally require some man's damnation.

—Thomas Aquinas, *Summa Theologica*

The unfortunate reprobate shall be continually employed in reflecting on the unhappy cause of their damnation. To us who live on Earth our past life appears but a moment—but a dream. Alas! what will the fifty or sixty years which they may have spent in this world appear to the damned, when they shall find themselves in the abyss of eternity, and when they shall have passed a hundred and a thousand millions of years in torments, and shall see that their miserable eternity is only beginning, and shall be forever in its commencement?

—Alphonsus Liguori, *sermon*

So great is the thirst of the damned, that if one of them were offered all the water on this Earth, he would exclaim: All this water is not sufficient to extinguish the burning thirst which I endure. But alas! the unhappy damned shall never have a single drop of water to refresh their tongues.

—Alphonsus Liguori, *sermon*

A false Christian is punished more than a pagan, and the deathless fire of divine justice consumes him more, that is, afflicts him more, and, in his affliction, he feels himself being consumed by the worm of conscience, though, in truth, he is not consumed, because the damned do not lose their being through any torment which they receive.

—Catherine of Siena, *Dialogue*

That dreadful thought of being rejected by God is the actual torture suffered by the damned.

—Faustina Kowalska, *Divine Mercy in My Soul*

Damnation is for the soul who wants to be damned; but for the one who desires salvation, there is the inexhaustible ocean of the Lord's mercy to draw from.

—Faustina Kowalska, *Divine Mercy in My Soul*

For there is no greater or worse death than when death never dies. But because the soul from its very nature, being created immortal, cannot be without some kind of life, its utmost death is alienation from the life of God in an eternity of punishment.

—Augustine, *The City of God*

I call upon you, my God, my mercy, who made me, and did not forget me, although I forgot you. I call you into my soul, which you prepare to accept you by the longing that you breathe into it. Do not desert me now when I call upon you, for before I called upon you, you went ahead and helped me, and repeatedly you urged me on by many different words, so that from afar I would hear you, and be converted, and call upon you as you called to me. For you have wiped away all my evil deserts, O Lord, so as not to return them to these hands of mine, whereby I fell away from you, and you went ahead and helped me in all my good deserts, so that you could restore them to your own hands, whereby you made me.

—Augustine, *Confessions*

Dark Night

God sought me out when I fled from him; he will not abandon me now that I seek him, or at least do not flee from him anymore.

—Claude de la Colombière, *retreat notes*

O may it be the Truth, the light of my heart, not my own darkness, that speaks to me. I fell away to those material things, and I became darkened over, but from there, even from there, I loved you. I went astray, but I did not forget you. "I heard your voice behind me," calling me to return, but because of the tumult of men hostile to peace, I scarcely heard it. But now, see, I return, burning and yearning for your fountain. Let no man forbid me! I will drink at this fountain, and I will live by it. Let me not be my own life: badly have I lived from myself: I was death to myself: in you I live again. Speak to me, speak with me. I have believed in your books, and their words are most full of mystery.

—Augustine, *Confessions*

There are those who tire of their spiritual exercises and fall into tepidity and so walk the ways of the Lord with sadness. When this befalls us, we must turn to the Lord looking for his compassion and allow him to tell us the things of Heaven. This will transport the sleepy and indolent soul.

—Bernard of Clairvaux, *On the Canticle of Canticles*

Dear Father, when will the sun shine in the heavens of my soul? Alas, I see myself astray in the deep dark night through which I am passing. But praise be to God, who never abandons anyone who hopes and places his trust in him!

—Padre Pio, *letter to Padre Agostino, 1916*

Don't be bewildered if the night becomes deeper and darker for you. Don't be frightened if you are unable to see, with the eyes of the body, the serene sky that surrounds your soul. But look above, elevating yourself about yourself, and you will see a light shining, that participates in the light of the eternal Sun.

—Padre Pio, *letter to Assunta di Tamaso, 1916*

Live in faith and hope, though it be in darkness, for in this darkness God protects the soul. Cast your care upon God for you are his and he will not forget you. Do not think that he is leaving you alone, for that would be wrong to him.

—John of the Cross, *letter to a Carmelite nun, c. 1589*

Since God puts a soul in this dark night in order to dry up and purge its sensory appetite, he does not allow it to find sweetness or delight in anything.

—John of the Cross, *The Dark Night of the Soul*

Death

After death

The sage passes from glory when death comes, the Christian proceeds to glory when he dies.

—Jerome, *letter*

May you see your Redeemer face to face, and standing evermore in his presence, gaze upon Eternal Truth revealed in all its beauty to the eyes of the saints. Finally, may you take your place among the ranks of the blessed, and enter into the sweetness of the Beatific Vision for ever and ever.

—Peter Damian, *letter to a dying friend, c. 1065*

Within a few short hours my soul will quit this earth, exile over, and battle won. I shall mount upwards and enter into our true home. There among God's elect I shall gaze upon what eye of man cannot imagine, hear undreamt-of harmonies, enjoy a happiness the heart cannot remotely comprehend. But first of all the grain of wheat must be ground, the bunch of grapes trodden in the wine-press. May I become pure bread and wine perfectly fit to serve the Master!

—Théophane Vénard, *letter to his family before his martyrdom, 1861*

The face of God that the angels desire to gaze upon, shall be seen in all its sweetness, lovableness, and desirability.

—Aelred of Rielvaux, *letter to his sister, 1160*

Physical death can well be called a new birth, because of the release from an onerous body and because one enters unencumbered into eternal blessedness.

—Henry Suso, *letter*

When I shall have departed to the grave, I pray the Lord to make my memory perish on the earth so that no one will think of me except those few faithful ones who will, as I hope, come to pray for my soul. I accept in penance for my sins all that will be said against me in the world after my death.

—Joseph Cafasso, *first panegyric on St. Joseph Cafasso by St. John Bosco*

Fear of death

It is not Death that will come to fetch me, it is the good God. Death is no phantom, no horrible specter, as represented in pictures. In the catechism it stated that *death is the separation of soul and body*, that is all! Well, I am not afraid of a separation which will unite me to the good God forever.

—Thérèse of Lisieux, *Counsels and Reminisces*

Our ancient Fathers teach that we must fear death without fearing it. What does this mean? It means that although we must fear it, it must not be with an excessive fear, but one accompanied by tranquillity; for Christians ought to walk under the standard of God's providence and be ready to embrace all the effects and events of this kind of providence, confident that it is quite able to take very good care of us.

—Francis de Sales, *Oeuvres*

Although there have been saints who desired and asked for death, we must not conclude from that that they were not also fearful of it. There is no one, no matter how holy, who does not justly fear it, the only possible exception being those who have had an extraordinary assurance of their salvation by very special revelations.

—Francis de Sales, *Oeuvres*

We must then fear this last passage, but without anxiety or inner disturbance. Let us rather have a fear which keeps us prepared and always ready to die well.

—Francis de Sales, *Oeuvres*

Fear of death is a property of nature due to disobedience, but terror of death is a sign of unrepented sins.

—John Climacus, *The Ladder of Divine Ascent*

Death scares only those who are still in a state of sin, not those who, like St. Paul, desire to die and be with Christ, or lament with Job that their days are prolonged, much as they long to depart.

—Philip Neri, *letter to his spiritual son, 1556*

Death is too ordinary a thing to seem any novelty, being a familiar guest in every house. Since his coming is expected and his errand not unknown, neither should his presence be feared nor his effects be lamented.

—Robert Southwell, *letter to a friend, 1591*

The man who for God's sake intrepidly spurns death and knows no fear is rightly raised to a friendship with God.

—Peter Chrysologus, *sermon*

Therefore, brethren, as the Lord said, let us not fear those who kill the body. For, they do not annihilate that life, but merely pull it down while they are changing it from temporary life into something everlasting.

—Peter Chrysologus, *sermon*

Hour of Death

O Jesus, sweetness of hearts and sweetness of minds, by the bitterness of the vinegar and gall which thou didst taste for us, grant me at the hour of my death worthily to receive thy body and blood, for the remedy and consolation of my soul.

—Bridget of Sweden, *Revelations*

At the moment of death shall I be content or discontent with my life?

—Pope John XXIII, *Journal of a Soul*

The sorrows of death compass me, and the pains of death take hold upon me, when I consider the uncertainty of that last passage, not knowing whether my hereafter will be terrible or blessed; for no man knoweth whether he be worthy of love or hatred.

—Sebastian Valfrè, *letter to his own soul, 1709*

As your soul departs from your body, may the shining cohort of angels hasten to greet you, the tribunal of apostles acquit you, the triumphant ranks of white-robed martyrs accompany you, the lily-bearing bands of glorious confessors surround you, the choirs of virgins bring up your train with rejoicing, and in blest tranquillity may the patriarchs receive you into their loving embrace. May our Lord Jesus appear before you gentle and eager of countenance and assign you a place amidst those who stand in his presence for evermore.

—Peter Damian, *letter to a dying friend, c. 1065*

At death, the Devil exerts all his powers to secure the soul that is about to leave this world; for he knows, from the symptoms of the disease, that he has but little time to gain her for eternity.

—Alphonsus Liguori, *sermon*

When a Christian is about to leave this world, his house is filled with devils, who united together in order to effect his ruin.

—Alphonsus Liguori, *sermon*

Dying, we are constantly protected by Christ, and by the touching of his grace we are raised to true trust in salvation.

—Julian of Norwich, *Showings*

The soul extracts itself from the body with a groan. Grieving, it shatters its seat. By removing itself from the body with distress, it allows the place of its dwelling to fall away with much trembling. It will then know the merits of its works by the just judgment of God.

—Hildegard of Bingen, *Scivias*

Among the absurd fallacies introduced by the demon into the world none is greater or more pernicious than the forgetfulness of the hour of death and of what is to happen at the court of the rigorous Judge.

—Mary of Agreda, *The Mystical City of God*

There is one thing that reveals itself to an undiscerning person at death and makes death difficult for him: When he considers the years gone by and that his life has been consumed by insignificant things, he discovers that he stands covered with guilt before God, and in his final hour he does not know what to do about it.

—Henry Suso, *letter*

And just think how good he will feel on our deathbed if we are able to say to her [Mary] in all sincerity, "O Immaculate, through your kindness I have consecrated my entire life to you. For you I worked and suffered and for you I am dying. I am yours!" What peace! What serene joy will flood our hearts because of our hope of seeing her presently!

—Maximilian M. Kolbe, *letter to newly invested brothers in Grodno, 1927*

O most efficacious death, ah, let my death be safe and carefree under your care. O life-giving death, ah, may I melt beneath your wings. O death, drop of life, ah, may the very dulcet spark of life you bring burn in me forever. O glorious death. O fruitful death. O death, the sum of my whole salvation, the lovable contract [leading] to my ransom, the firmest pact [leading] to my reconciliation. O triumphant death, dulcet and life-giving, in you shines forth for me such charity whose equal has not been found in heaven and on earth.

—Gertrude the Great, *Spiritual Exercises*

Ah, Jesus, very closest to my heart, always be with me in such a way that my heart may abide with you and your love may indivisibly persevere with me, and thus may my passing be blessed by you and may my spirit, set free from the shackle of the flesh, from then on rest in you.

—Gertrude the Great, *Spiritual Exercises*

O Mary, what a happy lot will be mine if I see thee at that dread hour appear by the side of my bed of death! This, I know, is a great grace, and great also is my unworthiness; but greater than all is thy mercy.

—Joseph Cafasso, *prayer*

Inevitability of Death

Our days glide by; death is at our door.

—Francis de Sales, *The Devout Life*

The dominion of God is immortal, like myself; it begins with time, and continues through eternity; death, which deprives men of all their rights, is unable to do anything against the rights of God.

—Ignatius of Loyola, *Spiritual Exercises*

I will lay me down in peace, and take my rest.

—Gregory of Nazianzus, *Funeral Oration on His Sister Gorgonia*

It is an indisputable truth that all of us one day will receive visit from our sister Death, as Saint Francis of Assisi called her. She sometimes represents herself in a sudden and unexpected manner. But we shall remain tranquil, or better undisturbed, if our tree has known how to yield its fruits. He who has worked well, departs when the day is ended.

—Pope John XXIII, *General audience, March 7, 1961*

Die when it pleases God you should, and if only his will be done in all things, all will be well.

—Sebastian Valfrè, *letter to an invalid, 1690*

I confess that I am bewildered and lose myself at the thought of divine goodness, a sea without shore and fathomless, of God who calls me to an eternal rest after such short and tiny labors—summons and calls me to heaven, to that supreme Good that I sought so negligently, and promises me the fruit of those tears that I sowed so sparingly.

—Aloysius Gonzaga, *letter to his mother, 1591*

To die is a matter of nature; it is necessary to perish. Our ancestors lived for us; we live for future men; no one lives for himself. . . . Before death arrives it does not exist, but, when it has come, one no longer knows that it has arrived. Therefore, do not grieve about the loss of something about which, once you have lost it, you will have no more grief.

—Peter Chrysologus, *sermon*

If the hour of death is painful, if it is bitter, it still must come sometimes. No one was ever excused from the hour of death.

—Henry Suso, *letter*

Of this at least I am certain, that no one has ever died who was not destined to die sometime.

—Augustine, *The City of God*

Judgment at Death

I ought to think about it [death] and remember the judgment that follows it, for whenever we do all in our power to keep ourselves in the state in which we would wish to be at that time, we will not fear the judgment when we are close to it, and death is sweeter to bear.

—Marguerite Bourgeoys, *Autographic Writings*

For death is not natural to us. We are condemned to die only because of sin. Since Adam's fall, all are subject to sin, and each will be judged in the state in which he dies. At that very moment, we know we must give an account of our whole life, and that we will be judged on what we have done. For that reason we dread death.

—Francis de Sales, *Oeuvres*

Consider that when the soul quits the body, it must go either to the left hand or to the right. Whither will yours go? Which will be its path? Even such as it has chosen while on earth.

—Francis de Sales, *The Devout Life*

Consider the distress a man experiences when he calls to mind the fate which awaits his soul and his body after death. For his body, he knows nought better is in store than a seven-foot grave, side by side with the other dead. For the soul, nothing sure, neither as to its future nor as to its fate.

—Peter of Alcantara, *Treatise on Prayer & Meditation*

Dead men have their sins still clinging to them, unless before their demise they purged them away through the intercession of their tears before God. Hell, armed with due punishments, awaits its prisoner.

—Valerian, *homily*

At death, when my sins known and unknown trouble me, I will take them all and cast them at Our Lord's feet to be consumed in the fire of his mercy. The greater they are, the worse they seem to me, the more willingly will I give them to him because the offering will be all the more worthy of his mercy.

—Claude de la Colombière, *retreat notes*

Preparation for Death

At least once daily, cast your mind ahead to the moment of death so that you can consider the events of each day in this light.

I can assure you that you will have a good experience of the peace this consideration brings.

—Josemaría Escrivá, *The Forge*

Oh, how happy we would be if every day of our life we would seriously reflect on the account we shall have to render. We would constantly keep ourselves in the same state in which we would wish to be at the hour of death. This would be a good means of living well and of being found without reproach on that last day.

—Francis de Sales, *Oeuvres*

We must neither desire nor ask for death, nor refuse it when it comes. And in this consists the summary of Christian perfection: to ask for nothing and to refuse nothing.

—Francis de Sales, *Oeuvres*

The general rule for a good death is to lead a good life.

—Francis de Sales, *Oeuvres*

It [death] is also a very useful thought to have every time we retire, as some do, by reminding ourselves that someday we will be lowered down into the grave.

—Francis de Sales, *Oeuvres*

But let us resolve to die, because it is something we must do, and with a peaceful, tranquil heart always keep ourselves in the same state in which we would wish to be found at the hour of death. It is the true means of preparing ourselves to die well. Doing this, we will reach eternity, and leaving these days of death, we will reach those of life. God grant us this grace.

—Francis de Sales, *Oeuvres*

Often fill your mind and thoughts of the great gentleness and mercy with which God our Savior welcomes souls at death, if they have spent their lives trusting him, and striven to serve and love him, each according to his calling.

—Francis de Sales, *letter to a penitent, 1617*

If we were required to die twice, we could jettison one death. But man dies once only, and upon his death depends his eternity. Where the tree falls, there it shall lie. If, at the hour of his death, someone is living in bad habit, the poor soul will fall on the side of hell. If, on the other hand, he is in the state of grace, it will take the road for heaven. Oh, happy road!

—John Baptiste Marie Vianney, *sermon*

Life is short. If you defer changing your ways until the hour of your death, you are blind, for you do not know either the time or the place where you will die, perhaps without any assistance. . . . If we desire a good death, we must lead a Christian life. And the way for us to prepare for a good death is to model our deaths upon the death of Jesus Christ.

—John Baptiste Marie Vianney, *sermon*

I keep myself ready and prepared for death every day, and for a good death, desiring nothing else but the Lord's will . . . living in this way, every day being ready and prepared for a good death, ends by filling my heart with a profound and serene sense of peace, even greater than I had before, surely a foretaste of heaven where our dear ones are awaiting us.

—Pope John XXIII, *letter to his sister Maria, January 8, 1955*

The man who has died to all things remembers death, but whoever holds ties with the world will not cease plotting against himself.

—John Climacus, *The Ladder of Divine Ascent*

When a man first comes to the use of reason, he should begin so to regulate his life that at death his days may all have been spent in preparation for worthily receiving the crown of glory. When he reaches maturer age, the forerunner of death, he must repent and make amends for any past negligence. This is the time to renew our courage and to exert ourselves to remedy the weaknesses of our youth and to devote ourselves with fervor to making ready for death.

—John of Ávila, *letter to a friend, 1565*

I do not regret this world; my soul thirsts for the waters of eternal life. My exile is over. I am approaching the soul of my true country; earth vanishes, heaven opens, I go to God.

—Théophane Vénard, *letter to his family before his martyrdom, 1861*

If we think well upon the miseries of this life, we shall rejoice at the joy of those who are already with God.

—Teresa of Ávila, *letter to her nephew, 1580*

Accustom yourself to repeat as your first words upon awaking, and your last words before sleep, the names of Jesus and Mary, so that God will give you grace to die with these holy Names on your lips and in your heart.

—John Eudes, *The Holy Name of Mary*

He who is prepared to die, regards death as a relief. . . . Happy then are they who die in the Lord: because they escape from pains and toils, and go to rest.

—Alphonsus Liguori, *sermon*

He that offers to God his death, makes an act of love the most perfect that it is possible for him to perform; because, by cheerfully embracing death to please God, at the time and in the manner which God ordains, he becomes like the martyrs, the entire merit of whose martyrdom consisted in suffering and dying to please God.

—Alphonsus Liguori, *sermon*

Death, my sister, if you do not open the gate to me, I cannot enter to enjoy my God.

—Alphonsus Liguori, *sermon*

God has concealed from us the day of our death, that we may spend all our days well.

—Alphonsus Liguori, *sermon*

To think of the necessity of preparing for a blessed death does not require sadness or a painful exercise of mind. On the contrary, considering through faith and hope in the merits of our Divine Redeemer, that we are His children and the purchase of His blood, we more naturally anticipate with joy the hour which will deliver us from the dangers we constantly experience.

—Elizabeth Seton, *Collected Writings*

Since death is nothing more than the end of life, it is certain that all who live well to the end, die well; nor can he die ill who has never lived ill. On the other hand, he who has never led a good life cannot die a good death.

—Robert Bellarmine, *The Art of Dying Well*

My God, I accept whatever kind of death it may please Thee to send me, with all the terrors, all the pains, all the sufferings that shall justly accompany it. Finally, I pray Thee to accept the destruction of my body as the last act of homage that I can offer to Thy Supreme Divine Majesty, in satisfaction for the offenses committed in the course of my life.

—Joseph Cafasso, *second panegyric on St. Joseph Cafasso by St. John Bosco*

TRIUMPH OVER DEATH

O Death, then dost thou realize that thou hast been destroyed by thine own law, when thou perceivest that God has subjected thee to thyself.

This body of mine who thou holdest cannot perish, and corruption hath no dominion over it.

All the infirmity of our flesh is stronger than thou art; the nature of the flesh is related by birth to God.

—Hilary of Poitiers, *hymn*

Death has become like a tyrant who has been completely conquered by the legitimate monarch; bound hand and foot the passers-by sneer at him, hitting him and abusing him, no longer afraid of his cruelty and rage, because of the king who has conquered him. So has death been conquered and branded for what it is by the Savior on the cross.

—Athanasius, *On the Incarnation*

Deceit

The world thrives on lies even twenty centuries after the Truth came among men.

—Josemaría Escrivá, *The Forge*

He who has forbidden us to use any deception can much less be a deceiver himself; untruth is the only thing impossible to God.

—Clement of Rome, *first epistle to the Corinthians*

Let your speech be gentle, frank, sincere, clear, simple and truthful. Avoid all duplicity, artifice and affectation; for although it is not expedient to tell everything which is true, it is at no time allowable to tell what is not.

—Francis de Sales, *The Devout Life*

A sincere excuse is of far more avail and more powerful than a lie.

—Francis de Sales, *The Devout Life*

Lying, duplicity and dissimilation are the sure signs of a low, groveling mind.

—Francis de Sales, *The Devout Life*

Wealth acquired by fraud or cunning will not only be of no profit but it will cause whatever you acquire legitimately to wither away and your days be shortened.

—John Baptiste Marie Vianney, *sermon*

A lie can never know the truth.

—Maria Maddalena de' Pazzi, *The Dialogues,*

I am positively certain that the devil will not deceive, nor will God permit him to deceive, a soul that puts no trust whatever in itself, that is fortified in the faith, and that is absolutely certain that it would suffer a thousand deaths for any single article of it.

—Teresa of Ávila, *Life*

For the Lord touched all parts of creation, and freed and undeceived them all from every deceit.

—Athanasius, *On the Incarnation*

I shall not tremble nor in God's cause shall I fear the tongues of men, who lie more often than they speak the truth.

—Columban, *letter*

Deeds

Deeds precede words, and in fact without deeds words profit nothing. . . . We are taught better by deeds than by words.

—Maximus of Turin, *sermon*

But the angels carry our finest deeds in an aroma of goodness into the divine presence, calling them to the attention of the Highest God. At the same time, our evil deeds, which follow a path different from that of God, are consigned to their lawful Judge.

—Hildegard of Bingen, *Book of Divine Works*

We were meant to consider all our deeds within our heart before carrying them out.

—Hildegard of Bingen, *Book of Divine Works*

Every good deed is rewarded, and every fault is punished.

—Catherine of Siena, *Dialogue*

Our best actions are usually tainted and spoiled by the evil that is rooted in us.

—Louis de Montfort, *Treatise on True Devotion to the Blessed Virgin*

If we are the temple of God, let us take great care and busy ourselves with good deeds, so that he may deign to come more often into this temple of his, and to make his dwelling place there.

—Bede the Venerable, *homily on the Gospels*

Let us be known by our works, by the sound education of children, by the good instructions we give them, by the edification of our neighbor, by Christian modesty, by detachment from all things, by our love for God's word and for virtue. It is not by their dress that men are known, but by their works.

—Marguerite Bourgeoys, *Autographic Writings*

True glory is that which is eternal and that, to achieve it, there is no need to perform outstanding deeds. Instead, one must remain hidden and perform one's good deeds so that the right hand knows not what the left hand does.

—Thérèse of Lisieux, *The Story of a Soul*

The noblest inspirations are worthless without good works.

—Thérèse of Lisieux, *The Story of a Soul*

Your crown shall be your good works.

—Mechtilde of Magdeburg, *The Flowing Light of the Godhead*

A good work of the soul is like an exceedingly beautiful bulwark in the sight of God and the angels, while a bad action resembles a house made of dung and full of filth.

—Hildegard of Bingen, *Book of Divine Works*

Cost what it may, O Lord, I pray You not to let me appear before You so empty-handed, since a man's reward must be proportionate to his works.

—Teresa of Ávila, *Life*

First of all, every time you begin a good work, you must pray to God most earnestly to bring it to perfection.

—Benedict, *Rule*

If we wish to dwell in God's tent, we will never arrive unless we run there by doing good deeds.

—Benedict, *Rule*

But yet there are many children in the house, and the number of offspring prevents you from applying yourself to good works. Still by this very fact you ought the more to do good works, since you are the father of many pledges.

—Cyprian of Carthage, *Works and Almsgiving*

And so, my most beloved brethren, let us whose fear is inclined toward God, and whose minds, after turning and trampling upon the world, are turned to heavenly and divine things to deserve well of the Lord, offer obedience with full faith, devoted minds, and continual good works.

—Cyprian of Carthage, *Works and Almsgiving*

Dead men cannot take effective action; their power of influence on others lasts only till the grave. Deeds and actions that energize others belong only to the living.

—Athanasius, *On the Incarnation*

For indeed we sin greatly if we love not the good deeds of others.

—Gregory the Great, *The Book of Pastoral Rule*

Deliverance

God delivers us from ourselves.

—John of the Cross, *letter*

Demonic possession

Out of the thousands whom I exorcised, I scarcely found one who was sure that he was possessed by the devil, because I knew that there were other causes for their condition, some physical, others moral. . . . I do not say that there are no people possessed by the devil, for I know there are, and I have known some of them personally, but what I do say is that they are few.

—Anthony Mary Claret, *autobiography*

There were certain people who had been converted and told me in all frankness that they were not possessed by the devil nor had any physical infirmities as a result of this, but they had illusions of being possessed by the Evil Spirit, which they kept up to attract the attention and compassion of other people in order to obtain help, and for a thousand other ends.

—Anthony Mary Claret, *autobiography*

God has given Mary such great power over the evil spirits that, as they have often been forced unwillingly to admit through the lips of possessed persons, they fear one of her pleadings for a soul more than the prayers of all the saints, and one of her threats more than all their other torments.

—Louis de Montfort, *Treatise on True Devotion to the Blessed Virgin*

Demons

Attacks by demons afflict us for three reasons: because we are sensual, because we are proud, or because the demons envy us. The last is a ground of rejoicing, the middle for pity, and where the first is concerned, the prospect is lifelong failure.

—John Climacus, *The Ladder of Divine Ascent*

Some hold that demons work against each other. But I do know that all of them work to destroy us.

—John Climacus, *The Ladder of Divine Ascent*

When grace does not dwell in man, demons curl like serpents in the depths of his heart, completely preventing the soul from desiring good; but when grace enters the soul, then these demons are blown about like dark clouds from one part of the heart to another, transforming themselves into sinful passions or distractions, in order to eclipse the remembrance of God and draw the mind away from discourse with grace.

—Theophan the Recluse, *The Fruits of Prayer*

The demons have no means of taking possession of a man's spirit or body, no power forcibly to enter his soul, unless they first deprive him of all holy thoughts, and make him empty and devoid of spiritual contemplation.

—John Cassian, *The Art of Prayer*

These devils keep us in terror, because we lay ourselves open to being terrorized. We become attached to honors, possessions, and pleasures. Then they join forces with us, since by loving and desiring what we should loathe we become our own enemies. Then they will do us great harm. . . . But if we loathe everything for God's sake, embrace the Cross and try to serve Him truly, the devil will fly from such realities as from the plague.

—Teresa of Ávila, *Life*

But the demon is never fatigued or weakened in his effort at tempting souls. The Almighty, however, is not wanting in his providence; for He limits and restrains the power of the demons, so that they cannot pass the measure set for them, nor exert all their indefatigable powers for the persecution of souls.

—Mary of Agreda, *The Mystical City of God*

When questioned about the future, the demons give ambiguous or equivocal answers about things of which they are ignorant, and if things turn out wrong, they put the blame on interpreters or soothsayers.

—Robert Bellarmine, *The Mind's Ascent to God by the Ladder of Created Things*

As to the demons, they are false and deceitful mediators, who, though their uncleanness of spirit frequently reveals their misery and malignity, yet, by virtue of the levity of their aerial bodies and the nature of the places they inhabit, do contrive to turn us aside and hinder our spiritual progress; they do not help us towards God, but rather prevent us from reaching Him.

—Augustine, *The City of God*

The demons, then, have knowledge without charity, and are thereby so inflated or proud, that they crave those divine honors and religious services which they know to be due to the true God, and still, as far as they can, exact these from all over whom they have influence.

—Augustine, *The City of God*

The evil spirits, cunning thieves that they are, can take use by surprise and rob us of all we possess. They are watching day and night for the right moment. They roam incessantly seeking to devour us and to snatch from us in one brief moment of sin all the grace and merit we have taken years to acquire. Their malice and their experience, their cunning and their numbers ought to make us ever fearful of such a misfortune happening to us.

—Louis de Montfort, *Treatise on True Devotion to the Blessed Virgin*

For neither the devils nor their satellites and servants can hurt us, without the permission of Almighty God. If God is our defender, how easily will He dispel all perils!

—Francis Xavier, *letter*

The devils cannot do anything against us without God's permission. But with God's permission they are powerful. All wickedness, all the passions are inspired by them. But listen: God allows them to suggest sin to a person, but they cannot force him to do it. We ourselves are responsible for accepting or rejecting their seductive suggestions.

—John Damascene, *The Orthodox Faith*

There are three principal weapons that the devil likes to carry in order to wound our souls. They are gluttony, arrogance and ambition.

—Ambrose, *On the Gospel of St. Luke*

Demons are exorcised in the Spirit of God.

—Basil the Great, *On the Holy Spirit*

Desires

Desire means the soul is sick, while continence means the soul is healthy.

—Basil the Great, *letter*

For he who knows not how to govern his desires, like a man run away with by wild horses, is overthrown, bruised, torn and injured.

—Ambrose, *Concerning Virgins, to Marcellina, His Sister*

The bodily eye sees, but let the eye of the heart be closed; let modesty of mind remain.

—Ambrose, *Concerning Repentance*

You see, then, that our mind is the cause of our guilt. And so the flesh is innocent, but is often the minister of sin. Let not, then, desire of beauty overcome you. Many nets and many snares are spread by the devil.

—Ambrose, *Concerning Repentance*

Man possesses by his free choice what he desires, whether it is good or base.

—Gregory of Nyssa, *Commentary on the Inscriptions of the Psalms*

The soul lives by avoiding what it dies by desiring. Keep yourselves clean from the monstrous savagery of pride, from sluggish delights of sensuality, and from the false name of knowledge, so that the wild beasts may be tamed, the cattle mastered, and the serpents rendered harmless.

—Augustine, *Confessions*

Everyone knows that we must avoid evil desires, for by their indulgence we become evil likewise; but I would urge you not to desire those things which are dangerous to the soul, such as balls and similar perilous amusements, honors, etc., offices, visions and raptures. In all such things there is a great risk of vanity and delusion.

—Francis de Sales, *The Devout Life*

However small and insignificant your desires may be, do not allow them to disquiet you, for if you do, they will be followed by greater and more important desires, which will find your heart more disposed to anxiety and disorder.

—Francis de Sales, *The Devout Life*

Therefore, if you earnestly desire to be delivered from some evil, or to attain to some good, above all things calm and tranquillize your mind, and compose your judgment and will; then quietly and gently pursue your aim, adopting suitable means with some method.

—Francis de Sales, *The Devout Life*

You should notice that all pleasures, joys, and affections are ever caused in the soul by the will and desire for things which appear to you good, fitting, and delectable, since the soul considers these to be pleasing and precious; and in this way the desires of the will are drawn to them, and fears to lose them; and thus, through its affections for things and rejoicing in them, the soul becomes perturbed and unquiet.

—John of the Cross, *letter to a religious penitent, 1589*

Whoever seeks anything, he does not seek God.

—Henry Suso, *sermon*

The flesh fights most stubbornly against the spirit, and carnal desires usually subdue even the strongest souls, but the love of God easily conquers the love of the flesh, and the fear of God easily casts down the fear of the world.

—Robert Bellarmine, *The Mind's Ascent to God by the Ladder of Created Things*

All human thoughts and desires, even when present and really existing, are very profound so that neither angels nor demons nor men can penetrate to investigate them.

—Robert Bellarmine, *The Mind's Ascent to God by the Ladder of Created Things*

Desire nothing for yourself, either good or bad. For yourself, want only what God wants.

—Josemaría Escrivá, *The Forge*

Detachment

It is detachment above all detachment to be detached in one's detachment.

—Henry Suso, *Little Book of Eternal Wisdom*

For inner detachment it is important always to have nature under rein.

—Henry Suso, *The Life of the Servant*

A beginner, before he is permanently established in God, can quite easily lose the way. To prevent this I can find nothing better than that, as far as possible, a person completely give up all things that take him outside himself, and that he make his way into himself and remain within himself.

—Henry Suso, *letter*

A spiritual person should be so detached that if someone were to strike him on one cheek, he would offer the other.

—Henry Suso, *sermon*

Your detachment must be bottomless. How bottomless? If a stone were to fall into a bottomless pool, it would have to sink forever because it would never reach bottom. So should a person sink and fall endlessly into the unfathomable God and have his ground in him.

—Henry Suso, *sermon*

What is the spiritual practice of a completely detached person? Losing self.

—Henry Suso, *The Life of the Servant*

I cannot understand how humility exists, or can exist, without love, or love without humility, and it is impossible for these two virtues to exist save where there is great detachment from all created things.

—Teresa of Ávila, *The Way of Perfection*

In order to hear God, people should stand firm and be detached in their sense life and affections.

—John of the Cross, *The Dark Night of the Soul*

Detachment. How hard it is! Oh, to be fastened by nothing but three nails and to have no more feeling in my flesh than the Cross!

—Josemaría Escrivá, *The Way*

One clear sign of detachment is genuinely not to consider anything as one's own.

—Josemaría Escrivá, *The Forge*

Your happiness will grow in the measure in which you detach your heart from all earthly things so as to consecrate it entirely to God.

—Claude de la Colombière, *letter*

Do all you can to love everyone. If you are not yet able to, at the very least don't hate anyone. Yet you won't even manage this if you have not reached detachment from the things of the world.

—Maximus the Confessor, *Centuries on Charity*

Your life consists in drawing nearer to God: to do this you must endeavor to detach yourself from visible things and remember that in a short time they will all be taken from you.

—John of Ávila, *letter to a friend, 1565*

Determination

Compromise is a word found only in the vocabulary of those who have no will to fight—the lazy, the cunning, the cowardly—for they consider themselves defeated before they start.

—Josemaría Escrivá, *The Way*

With God there are no *impossibles*. They are overcome always.

—Josemaría Escrivá, *The Forge*

Devil

The devil performs his craftiness through the work of people.

—Hildegard of Bingen, *Scivias*

For the devil shows foul and stinking ways to people. And the devil pierces people with blemishes—as a snake stings people with poison—and cruelly strikes them down.

—Hildegard of Bingen, *Scivias*

I resist the struggle of the devil which lifts itself up against me.

—Hildegard of Bingen, *Scivias*

He [the devil] is not, however, called "prince" because he has any authority over or is master of the world—away with such blasphemy! He has not even authority over pigs!—but because he enslaves those who have nailed themselves to the world through their lust for the wealth and goods which are in it and thus has them under his power. He is called prince of darkness because, having himself fallen from the light at the beginning by his revolt, he will be the eternal heir of darkness.

—Symeon the New Theologian, *Ethical Discourses*

If someone should slap you on the right cheek and you do not turn him the other, but instead strike him in return, you have become at once a soldier and subordinate of Satan the adversary, and you have struck not just your brother, but, in him, also the One Who said not to strike but to turn the other cheek.

—Symeon the New Theologian, *Ethical Discourses*

I believe the devil is very successful in preventing those who practice prayer from advancing further by giving them false notions of humility.

—Teresa of Ávila, *Life*

The deceiver knows that any soul who resolutely persists in prayer is lost to him, and that, thanks to the goodness of God, every time he brings it down he only helps it to leap up again even higher in His service. This is a matter of some concern to Satan.

—Teresa of Ávila, *Life*

The devil can play plenty of tricks all the same; and so there is nothing more certain than that we must always be fearful and proceed with caution.

—Teresa of Ávila, *Life*

In every respect we must be careful and alert, for the devil never slumbers. And the nearer we are to perfection, the more careful we must be, since his temptations are then much more cunning because there are no others that he dare send us; and if, as I say, we are not cautious, the harm is done before we realize it.

—Teresa of Ávila, *The Way of Perfection*

For the devil does not allow a single bad habit to disappear] and the very weakness of our mortal nature destroys the virtues in us.

—Teresa of Ávila, *The Way of Perfection*

It was of great service to me to learn that—with the Lord's permission—the devil can do so much harm to a body and soul, even though they do not belong to him. What will he do to them, then, I thought, when they are truly in his possession! This gave me a new desire to deliver myself from such dangerous company.

—Teresa of Ávila, *Life*

The Devil invites men to the water of death, that is, to which he has, and, blinding them with the pleasures and conditions of the world, he catches them with the hook of pleasure, under the pretense of good, because in no other way could he catch them, for they would not allow themselves to be caught if they saw that no good or pleasure to themselves were to be obtained thereby.

—Catherine of Siena, *Dialogue*

The Devil often places himself upon the tongues of creatures, causing them to chatter nonsensically, with the purpose of preventing the prayer of the soul.

—Catherine of Siena, *Dialogue*

To the just man the appearance and vision of the Devil causes no harm or fear, for fear and harm can only be caused to him by sin; but those who have passed their lives lasciviously and in many sins, receive both harm and fear from the appearance of the devils, not indeed the harm of despair if they do not wish it, but the suffering of condemnation, of the refreshing of the worm of conscience, and of fear and terror at their horrible aspect.

—Catherine of Siena, *Dialogue*

For I realize that though the devil lost beatitude he did not lose his intelligence, and with that intelligence—or better, cleverness—I know, as I said, that he could deceive me. But then I turn to the tree of the most holy cross of Christ crucified; there I lean; there I want to nail myself fast. I have no doubt that if I am nailed fast with him in love and in deep humility, the devils will have no power over me. And this is not because of my own power but because of the power of Christ crucified.

—Catherine of Siena, *letter to a religious, c. 1374*

Unless we either preserve our baptismal grace, or, by true penance, renounce the Devil again, and return to the service of God, and persevere in it until the end of our life, we cannot possibly live well, nor be delivered from a miserable death.

—Robert Bellarmine, *The Art of Dying Well*

Oh, how different are the ways of God from the ways of men! The King of Heaven and earth rejoices in simplicity and sobriety, and is chiefly solicitous to fill, enrich, and exhilarate the soul. But men prefer listening to their concupiscence and their enemy the Devil before God.

—Robert Bellarmine, *The Art of Dying Well*

The devil is able and successful to the extent that others believe what he says and consider him a good spirit.

—John of the Cross, *The Ascent of Mount Carmel*

The devil . . . can through suggestion ingrain many intellectual ideas so deeply in the soul that they will seem to be true; and if the soul is not humble and distrustful he will doubtless bring it to believe a thousand lies.

—John of the Cross, *The Ascent of Mount Carmel*

The devil finds it pleasing to suggest to souls and impress on them apprehensions and feelings.

—John of the Cross, *The Dark Night of the Soul*

How terribly ugly Satan is! The poor damned souls that have to keep him company! Just the sight of him is more disgusting than all the torments of hell.

—Faustina Kowalska, *Divine Mercy in My Soul*

Today I have fought a battle with the spirits of darkness over one soul. How terribly Satan hates God's mercy! I see how he opposes his whole work.

—Faustina Kowalska, *Divine Mercy in My Soul*

For the devil drags a monk headlong to death by way of no other sin than that of submission to private judgment and the neglect of the advice of our elders.

—John Cassian, *Conferences*

The Devil is the origin of evil, the source of wickedness, the foe of the world, and ever the hater of successful men. He sets his snares, plans falls, digs ditches, arranges wrecks, stimulates bodies, pricks souls, suggests thoughts, stirs up enmities, makes virtues seem odious and vices attractive, sows errors, nourishes grudges, disturbs the peace, breaks up affection, tears unity apart, has a great relish of evil and none of good, profanes the things of God and disorders those of men.

—Peter Chrysologus, *sermon*

Satan does not sleep and—with God's permission—he will often suggest to you all kinds of "wise" counsels. He will point out to you other so-called "obligations," other "joys"; but whoever loves the Immaculate sincerely and with all his heart will easily recognize the enemy and repel him.

—Maximilian M. Kolbe, *letter to newly invested brothers in Grodno, 1927*

There is a nature in which evil does not or even cannot exist; but there cannot be a nature in which there is no good. Hence not even the nature of the devil himself is evil, in so far as it is nature, but it was made evil by being perverted. Thus he did not abide in the truth, but could not escape the judgment of the Truth; he did not abide in the tranquility of order, but did not therefore escape the power of the Ordainer. The good imparted by God to his nature did not screen him from the justice of God by which order was preserved in his punishment; neither did God punish the good which He had created, but the evil which the devil had committed.

—Augustine, *The City of God*

The evil spirit often disguises himself as an angel of light, and now and then tricks us by his illusions. All of us must be ever alert for these tricks and should pay particular attention to learning how to recognize and overcome them. Experience has shown that the most effective and surest remedy in such cases is to discuss them as soon as possible with those appointed by God for this.

—Vincent de Paul, *Common Rules or Constitutions of the Congregation of the Mission*

Let us beware of the malice and craftiness of Satan, who does not want anyone to turn his mind and heart to God.

—Francis of Assisi, *early Rule*

Yet thou are not the sole author of the evil, but there is also another most wicked prompter, the devil. He indeed suggests, but does not get the mastery by force over those who do not consent.

—Cyril of Jerusalem, *Catecheses*

The devil also transfigures himself into an angel of light; not that he may reascend to where he was, for having made his heart hard as an anvil, he has henceforth a will that cannot repent; but in order that he may envelop those who are living an Angelic life in a midst of blindness, and a pestilent condition of unbelief.

—Cyril of Jerusalem, *Catecheses*

Therefore, most beloved brethren, the mind stands ready and armed against all the deceitful plots or the open threats of the devil, always as prepared to repulse, as the enemy is always prepared to attack.

—Cyprian of Carthage, *Jealousy and Envy*

The most fearful enemy that God has set up against the devil is Mary, his holy Mother. From the time of the earthly paradise, although she existed then only in his mind, he gave her such a hatred for his accursed enemy, such ingenuity in exposing the wickedness of the ancient serpent and such power to defeat, overthrow and crush this proud rebel, that Satan fears her not only more than angels and men but in a certain sense more than God himself.

—Louis de Montfort, *Treatise on True Devotion to the Blessed Virgin*

For Satan, knowing that he has little time—even less now than ever—to destroy souls, intensifies his efforts and his onslaughts every day. He will not hesitate to stir up savage persecutions and set treacherous snares for Mary's faithful servants and children whom he finds more difficult to overcome than others.

—Louis de Montfort, *Treatise on True Devotion to the Blessed Virgin*

Where Mary is present, the evil one is absent.

—Louis de Montfort, *Treatise on True Devotion to the Blessed Virgin*

If we do not entrust ourselves to God, we sell ourselves to the devil.

—Paulinus of Nola, *letter*

Begone, Satan; begone, proud and envious one, never again will you hinder the conversion and salvation of souls.

—Anthony Mary Claret, *autobiography*

Devotion

Devotion is in itself a single virtue, but it prepares and moves us forward to all the other virtues, and gives a general impulse to them all.

—Peter of Alcántara, *Treatise on Prayer & Meditation*

Devotion, as Saint Thomas says, is nothing else than a certain promptitude and facility in well-doing, which banishes from our soul all difficulty and heaviness and makes us prompt and ready to undertake all that is good. It is a spiritual nourishment, a refreshment, a dew from heaven, a breath wafted to us from the Holy Spirit, a supernatural *affection*. It so regulates, strengthens and transforms the heart of man as to give him a new taste and keenness for spiritual things, and a new distaste and horror for sensual things.

—Peter of Alcántara, *Treatise on Prayer & Meditation*

Devotion is the crown of sweetness, the queen of virtues, the perfection of charity.

—Francis de Sales, *The Devout Life*

Although it is lawful to amuse yourself, to dance, dress, hear good plays, and join in society, yet to be attached to such things, is contrary to devotion and extremely hurtful and dangerous. The evil lies not in *doing* the thing, but in *caring* for it.

—Francis de Sales, *The Devout Life*

Indeed, our external pursuits are rather helped than hindered by spiritual retreat and short devotions of the soul.

—Francis de Sales, *The Devout Life*

People shine in the highest God, and God shines in people since the Word of God was made flesh wondrously. Therefore, God in heaven is worthy of the praise and glory of every creature.

—Hildegard of Bingen, *Scivias*

We should not worry, therefore, as I have said before, if we are not conscious of our devotion. We should instead thank the Lord for allowing us to wish to please Him, even though our works are poor.

—Teresa of Ávila, *Life*

Jesus, our Savior, true God and true man must be the ultimate end of all our other devotions; otherwise they would be false and misleading. He is the Alpha and the Omega, the beginning and the end of everything. . . . He alone is everything to us and he alone can satisfy our desires.

—Louis de Montfort, *Treatise on True Devotion to the Blessed Virgin*

Have only a few private devotions, but be constant in them.

—Josemaría Escrivá, *The Way*

Let us subject our necks only to His yoke, which is sweet, and to His burden, which is light, so that in freedom we may be borne over every yoke of the Enemy's power to the realms of heaven.

—Paulinus of Nola, *letter*

May I love and contemplate you alone and may my lamp ever burn and shine before you.

—Columban, *sermon*

Inspire us with a love for you as great as the affection and attachment which is due to you as our God. May affection for you pervade our hearts. May attachment to you take possession of us all. May love of you fill all our senses. May we know no other love except you who are eternal, a love so great that the many waters of these heavens and land and sea will fail to quench it.

—Columban, *sermon*

For devotion it suffices us simply to know that we shall have a God; a God who is One, a living, an ever-living God; always like unto Himself; who has no Father, none mightier than Himself, no successor to thrust Him out from His kingdom: who in name is manifold, in power infinite, in substance uniform.

—Cyril of Jerusalem, *Catecheses*

Discernment

Discernment is—and is recognized to be—a solid understanding of the will of God in all times, in all places, in all things; and it is found only among those who are pure in heart, in body and in speech.

—John Climacus, *The Ladder of Divine Ascent*

You need great discrimination in order to distinguish between good and evil. So do not readily or lightly put your trust in appearances, but weigh things well, and after testing everything carefully cleave to what is good and reject what is evil. . . . You must test and discriminate before you give credence to anything.

—Gregory of Sinai, *The Philokalia*

Every rational being, for whom the Savior came, ought to examine his way of life and know himself and discern between evil and good, so that he may be freed through his coming.

—Anthony, *letter*

I want you to know, my children, that I do not cease to pray to God for you, day and night, that he may open the eyes of your hearts that you may see all the secret evils which they pour upon us every day in this present time. I ask God to give you a heart of knowledge and a spirit of discernment, that you may be able to lift your hearts before the Father as a pure sacrifice in all sanctity, without blemish.

—Anthony, *letter*

Thus there exists a reasonable measure between being too small and being too large, which always calls us back from any excess on either side, providing in every case what is constant with need and opposing the unreasonable demands of superfluous desire. And this measure of true discernment, weighing all our actions in the scales of justice, does not allow us to err from what is just or to make a mistake, if we follow it closely as our guide.

—Columban, *Rule*

Just as error overtakes those who have no path, so for those who live without discernment excess is near at hand, always contrary to the virtues, which lie between extremes. Its onset is dangerous when beside the straight path of discernment our enemies place the stumbling blocks of wickedness and the temptations of various kinds of error. Therefore we must pray to God continually to illumine with the light of true discernment this way that is surrounded on all sides by the deep darkness of the world so that his true worshipers may be able to come to him through this darkness without error.

—Columban, *Rule*

Hence it is very clear that no virtue can come to full term or can endure without the grace of discernment. . . . With discernment it is possible to reach the utmost heights with the minimum of exhaustion. Without it there are many who despite the intensity of their struggle have been quite unable to arrive at the summit of perfection. For discernment is the mother, the guardian, and the guide of all virtues.

—John Cassian, *Conferences*

True discernment is attained when one is really humble.

—John Cassian, *Conferences*

For he who neglects to look forward by consideration to what he is about to do advances his steps with his eyes closed; proceeds on and accomplishes his journey, but goes not in advance of himself by looking forward; and therefore the sooner falls, because he gives no heed through the eyelid of counsel to where he should set the foot of action.

—Gregory the Great, *The Book of Pastoral Rule*

The Creator of all teaches us that we ought to be mindful of our own nature, and to discern the vileness of our body; for no one can see divine things except one who through knowledge of his vileness cannot be puffed up.

—Ambrose, *Concerning Widowhood*

You must not trust, then, wholly to your bodily eyes; that which is not seen is more really seen, for the object of sight is temporal, but that other eternal, which is not apprehended by the eye, but is discerned with the mind and spirit.

—Ambrose, *On the Mysteries*

The power and activity of overseeing things is characteristic of God. Therefore, the person who has in himself what he desires becomes an overseer as well as a discerner of the nature of things.

—Gregory of Nyssa, *Commentary on the Inscriptions of the Psalms*

Discipline

Discipline is a teacher of religion and of true piety; she does not threaten in order to inflict pain, or chastise in order to work injury.

—Valerian, *homily*

Those who submit to the Lord with simple heart will run the good race. If they keep their minds on leash they will not draw the wickedness of demons onto themselves.

—John Climacus, *The Ladder of Divine Ascent*

If we cannot restrain our tongue, or control our bodies and employ them in good works, can we complain that God does not call us to higher things?

—John of Ávila, *letter to a disciple, 1563*

Fastings, vigils, scriptural meditation, nakedness, and total deprivation do not constitute perfection but are the means to perfection. They are not themselves the end point of a discipline, but an end is attained through them.

—John Cassian, *Conferences*

Three things keep a wandering mind in place—vigils, meditation, and prayer. Constant attention to them and a firm concentration upon them will give stability to the soul.

—John Cassian, *Conferences*

You must attack your rebellious body, curb your sharpened tongue, recollect your distracted mind, so that your heart is not like a public house, a common wine cellar, a tavern, where anyone can come in and where everyone can do as he pleases. Drive them out, drive out this low company or you can certainly never receive our gentle Lord. Remember that he has bidden you to be his bride. And so see to it that you don't become a barmaid!

—Henry Suso, *letter*

You say that you can't do more? Could it be that . . . you can't do less?

—Josemaría Escrivá, *The Way*

Discipline of the body, if it is combined with peace of mind, purifies it from all material tendencies.

Discipline of the soul makes it humble and purifies it from the impressions that push it in a material direction.

—Isaac of Nineveh, *The Philokalia*

Discretion

Discretion is necessary in everything.

—Teresa of Ávila, *Life*

For great harm comes of bad company, since we are inclined by nature to follow the worse rather than the better.

—Teresa of Ávila, *Life*

Get used to saying No.

—Josemaría Escrivá, *The Way*

Don't waste your time and energy—which belong to God—throwing stones at the dogs that bark at you on your way. Ignore them.

—Josemaría Escrivá, *The Way*

Remain silent, and you will never regret it: speak, and you often will.

—Josemaría Escrivá, *The Way*

Never give your opinion if you are not asked for it, even if you think your view is best.

—Josemaría Escrivá, *The Way*

There must be some that wear out their bodies with abstinence: but because they have no discretion, they be a great way from God.

—Abbot Antony, *saying*

If we dwell upon the harms that have been wrought on us by man, then we amputate from our mind the power of dwelling upon God.

—Abbot Macarius, *saying*

To make a good choice on any matter whatever, we must first meditate with a pure and upright intention on the end of our creation, which is the glory of God and our salvation. Therefore our choice ought never to fall on anything that does not lead us to this end; for it is evident that the means ought always to be subordinate to the end, and not the end to the means.

—Ignatius of Loyola, *Spiritual Exercises*

When the time of discretion is come, the soul can, by her free will, make choice either of good or evil, according as it pleases her will; and so great is this liberty that man has, and so strong has this liberty been made by virtue of the glorious blood, that no demon or creature can constrain him to one smallest fault without his free consent.

—Catherine of Siena, *Dialogue*

It is up to you, while you are leading this life, to have God angry and an enemy or a friend who is pleased with you.

—Robert Bellarmine, *The Mind's Ascent to God by the Ladder of Created Things*

Doubt

To doubt is the greatest insult to the Divinity.

—Padre Pio, *Counsels*

Drunkenness

He who drinks wine out of necessity does no evil; but he who takes it to such an excess that he becomes intoxicated offends God mortally, loses his judgment, drowns his reason in the wine he drinks, and if he happens to die in this state, is damned.

—Francis de Sales, *Oeuvres*

Duty

Don't shirk your duty. Carry it out conscientiously, even though others neglect theirs.

—Josemaría Escrivá, *The Way*

Put your heart aside. Duty comes first, but, when fulfilling your duty, put your heart into it: be gentle.

—Josemaría Escrivá, *The Way*

E

Eating

One must not be a slave to wine or crave for meat, or generally delight in any food or drink, for the athlete ought to observe temperance in all things.

—Basil the Great, *letter to Gregory of Nazianzus*

I would have it so that every day one should deny oneself a little in eating, so as not to be satisfied.

—Abbot Pastor, *saying*

The Fathers did eat only bread and salt and were made strong in the work of God, while they straightened themselves: wherefore let us confine ourselves to this same bread and salt. For it behooves them that serve God to be straightened in themselves, for the Lord himself said, "Straight is the gate and narrow is the way that leadeth unto life."

—Abbot John, *saying*

Fastidiousness in eating often takes necessity as its pretext, or fear of one's health. Most often it is sensuality or a failure to mortify ourselves. All those who wish to imitate the Blessed Virgin's way of life must be content with ordinary meats, simply prepared, bread without choice, etc. If we were only a little advanced in virtue, we would know the profit there is in living poorly and putting aside all the fastidiousness for which we must one day render a severe account.

—Marguerite Bourgeoys, *Autographic Writings*

We must, above all, in our repasts, be on our guard against avidity, precipitation, or that effusion of the soul which is bestowed in a manner on the food. It is requisite that we should always rule our appetite and practice temperance both in the quantity of nourishment and the manner of taking it.

—Ignatius of Loyola, *Spiritual Exercises*

To extirpate any bad habit of excess in eating or drinking, it would be well to determine before the repast, and before the want of it is yet felt, the quantity that on reflection we judge it well to take. The portion thus determined we ought to content ourselves with, even when nature asks for more, and Satan backs the demand. To conquer both, we might even retrench something more.

—Ignatius of Loyola, *Spiritual Exercises*

As Christ's spouse avoid wine as you would avoid poison. Wine is the first weapon that devils use in attacking the young. The restlessness of greed, the windiness of pride, the delights of ostentation are nothing to this.

—Jerome, *letter to Eustochium, 384*

The Greeks have a pretty proverb which perhaps in our language loses some of its force: "A fat paunch never breeds fine thoughts."

—Jerome, *letter to Nepotian*

I do not condemn food "which God created to be enjoyed with thanksgiving," but I assert that for young men and girls some food is an incentive to sensuality. Neither Etna's fire, nor Vulcan's isle, nor Vesuvius and Olympus, seethe with such burning heat as does the youthful marrow when it is flushed with wine and inflamed by feasting.

—Jerome, *letter to Furia, 394*

A frugal diet which leaves you always hungry is to be preferred to a three days' fast, and it is much better to go short every day than occasionally to satisfy your appetite to the full. That rain is best which falls slowly to earth: a sudden and excessive shower which comes tumbling down washes away the soil.

—Jerome, *letter to Furia, 394*

What shall I say about the belly, the queen of the passions? If you can deaden or half-deaden it, do not relent. It has mastered me, beloved, and I worship it as a slave and vassal, the abettor of the demons and dwelling-place of the passions.

—Gregory of Sinai, *The Philokalia*

For when the stomach is heavy the intellect is clouded, and you cannot pray resolutely and with purity.

—Gregory of Sinai, *The Philokalia*

For if abstinence [of food and drink] goes too far, then it will be a vice and not a virtue, for virtue sustains and contains many goods.

—Columban, *Rule*

Through God's favor, we are admonished to be abstemious in diet and sober in drink. I have no doubt that this is to prevent hearts now uplifted with heavenly strength from being emasculated by worldly allurements or souls from being less watchful in prayer and petition by being weighed down with lavish feasting.

—Cyprian of Carthage, *letter to presbyters and deacons*

Over-eating is the forerunner of impurity.

—Josemaría Escrivá, *The Way*

Education and learning

Read often and learn all you can. Let sleep steal upon you with a book in your hand, and let the sacred page catch your drooping head.

—Jerome, *letter to Eustochium, 384*

No art is learned without a master. Even dumb animals and herds of wild beasts follow leaders of their own.

—Jerome, *letter to Rusticus, 411*

Among all the benefits that learning bestows on men, there is none more excellent than this, that by study we are taught to seek in that very study not praise, but utility. Such has been the teaching of the most learned men, especially of philosophers, who are the guides of human life.

—Thomas More, *letter to his children's tutor, c. 1518*

The educator should be convinced that his efforts are important, even though he cannot always measure the results of his efforts, even though sometimes he can never be aware of them at all. He must never forget that, above all, the primary and most essential Educator is not the human being but God himself.

—Edith Stein, *Essays on Woman*

Where there is a sound family life and where the parents, especially the mother, really fulfill their vocation, the school's task will easily be one of restraint; it will not have much more to do than to reinforce the child's upbringing at home. But this is not the typical situation today. The destruction of the family life has placed a greater responsibility on the school.

—Edith Stein, *Essays on Woman*

See also: SPIRITUAL STUDY

Ego

Egoism is the source of the passions.

From egoism spring gluttony, avarice, conceit. From gluttony springs lust, from avarice greed, from conceit springs pride.

All the other vices, without exception, are merely consequences of this one thing: anger, melancholy, rancor, sloth, envy, slander and so on.

At the beginning of all the passions there is egoism, just as at the end there is pride.

—Maximus the Confessor, *Centuries on Charity*

Emotions

Love is the source of all emotions.

—Thomas Aquinas, *Summa of Christian Teaching*

For the soul perceives its own being in the stirring of the emotions. Through the emotions, it comes to know what it is and how it is; it also grasps through them the relationship of another being to itself, and then, consequently, the significant of the inherent value of exterior things, of unfamiliar people and impersonal things.

—Edith Stein, *Essays on Woman*

It is only the person who is deeply involved with life whose emotions are stirred.

—Edith Stein, *Essays on Woman*

End times

Further, the Lord has announced to us that at the dissolution of the universe, signs will appear in the sun, in the moon and in the stars. The sun shall be turned into blood and the moon shall not give her light, signs of the consummation of all things.

—Basil the Great, *homily on the Hexaemeron*

At the end of the time appointed by God for the world to last, and after many signs and terrible wonders which shall fill all men with fear and terror, a deluge of fire will come and consume the whole earth, sparing nothing of all that we behold.

—Francis de Sales, *The Devout Life*

When the Lord comes to give judgment the universe will utter a mournful groan; the tribes of men will beat their breasts; kings once most mighty will shiver with naked flanks; Jupiter with all his offspring will then be shown amid real fires; Plato with his disciples will be revealed as but a fool; Aristotle's arguments will not help him. Then you the poor rustic will exult, and say with a smile, "Behold my crucified God, behold the judge."

—Jerome, *letter to Helidorus, 374*

In the hour of God's punishment as the earth is trampled under foot—the time of the final judgment, the despair that all things on earth are vile will come to those who are disloyal to God.

—Hildegard of Bingen, *Scivias*

For when the judgment is finished, this heaven and earth shall cease to be, and there will be a new heaven and a new earth. For this world shall pass away by transmutation, not by absolute destruction.

—Augustine, *The City of God*

Envy

Plagued by envy, how do you fancy yourselves as holy at all, you who are not recognized as either a believer or a Christian for the sake of your love of God and of neighbor? It is obvious to everyone who listens to the divine Scripture that this is the case, and that he who suffers from envy has the devil within himself and cannot be said to be of Christ because he has no love for his neighbor.

—Symeon the New Theologian, *Ethical Discourses*

People will employ a hundred and one devices to conceal their envy from others. If someone speaks well of another in our presence, we keep silence: we are upset and annoyed. If we must say something, we do so in the coldest and most unenthusiastic fashion. No, my dear brethren, there is not a particle of charity in the envious heart.

—John Baptiste Marie Vianney, *sermon*

I do not believe there is a more ugly and dangerous sin than envy because it is hidden and often covered by the attractive mantle of virtue or of friendship.

—John Baptiste Marie Vianney, *sermon*

Envy is a public plague which spares no one.

—John Baptiste Marie Vianney, *sermon*

Therefore, whoever envies his brother the god which the Lord says or does in him commits a sin of blasphemy, because he envies the Most High Who says and does every good.

—Francis of Assisi, *saying*

The envious are to be told that, when they fail to keep themselves from spite, they are being sunk into the old wickedness of the wily foe.

—Gregory the Great, *The Book of Pastoral Rule*

Don't envy your betters, or grieve those who surpass you, or censure those who fall behind, but agree with those who urge you on.

—Columban, *letter, c. 610*

Nothing is so divisive as envy, which is a deadly evil, in a certain sense more deadly than greed.

A greedy person is happy when he gets something. An envious one is happy, not when he himself gets something, but when someone else does not. He sees his own personal profit, not in the good that comes his way, but in the evil that happens to someone else.

—John Climacus, *homily on the First Letter to the Corinthians*

Eternity

Eternity principally characterizes God who is utterly unchangeable. Indeed, because he is his own varying existence, God and eternity are the same thing.

—Thomas Aquinas, *Summa Theologica*

There is but *one eternity;* if the soul be once lost, it is lost for ever.

—Alphonsus Liguori, *sermon*

Before you had a being, God loved you. Before your father or mother was born, God loved you: yes, even before the creation of the world, he loved you. And how long before creation has God loved you? Perhaps for a thousands years, or for a thousand ages. It is needless to count years or ages; God loved you from eternity.

—Alphonsus Liguori, *sermon*

Just as eternity had no origin before the beginning of the world, it will have no end after the end of the world; the world's beginning and end will be enclosed, so to speak, in a unique cycle of understanding.

—Hildegard of Bingen, *Book of Divine Works*

Eternity lives in the Father because no one existed before Him and because eternity has no beginning, just as the works of God have no beginning.

—Hildegard of Bingen, *letter to Bishop Eberhard II of Bamberg*

Eternity! that voice to be everywhere understood. ETERNITY! to love and serve Him only who is to be loved and eternally served and praised in heaven.

—Elizabeth Seton, *Collected Writings*

Eternity—oh, how near it seems to me now! . . . Oh, how long will be the duration of the beautiful day in which there is no night. Oh, that we may spend it in praising, blessing and adoring forever.

—Elizabeth Seton, *Collected Writings*

Indeed You are unity itself not divisible by any mind. Life and wisdom and the other [attributes], then, are not parts of You, but all are one and each of them is wholly what You are and what all the others are. Since, then, neither You nor Your eternity which You are have parts, no part of You or of Your eternity is anywhere or at any time, but You exist as a whole everywhere and Your eternity exists as a whole always.

—Anselm, *Proslogion*

Satan once loved me ardently in the death [of sin]: let him behold me reigning with Thee throughout the ages.

—Hilary of Poitiers, *hymn*

Have you seen the dead leaves fall in the sad autumn twilight? Thus souls fall each day into eternity. One day, the fallen leaf will be you.

—Josemaría Escrivá, *The Way*

Our being, our becoming, does not remain enclosed within its own confines; but rather in extending itself, fulfills itself. However, *all* of our being and becoming and acting in time is ordered from eternity, has a meaning for eternity, and only becomes clear to us and insofar as we put it in the light of eternity.

—Edith Stein, *Essays on Woman*

He will say to us at the end of our days: be it done as you desire; and because of what you have done, come, enjoy eternity.

—Francis de Sales, *Oeuvres*

Eucharist

The heart which is preparing to receive the Holy Eucharist should be like a crystal vase, filled with the purest and most limpid water. We should not allow the slightest impure atom to make its appearance.

—Elizabeth Seton, *Collected Writings*

Eternal Wisdom, on the one hand, wished to prove his love for man by dying in his place in order to save him, but on the other hand, he could not bear the thought of leaving him. So he devised a marvelous way of dying and living at the same time, and of abiding with man until the end of time. So, in order to fully satisfy his love, he instituted the sacrament of Holy Eucharist and went to the extent of changing and overturning nature itself.

—Louis de Montfort, *The Love of Eternal Wisdom*

It is most important that the Holy Eucharist becomes life's focal point: that the Eucharistic Savior is the center of existence; that every day is received from His hand and laid back therein; that the day's happenings are deliberated with Him. In this way, God is given the best opportunity to be heard in the heart, to form the soul, and to make its faculties clear-sighted and alert for the supernatural.

—Edith Stein, *Essays on Woman*

The Eucharist is a fire which inflames us, that, like lions breathing fire, we may retire from the altar being made terrible to the Devil.

—John Chrysostom, *homily*

Evil

There is nothing evil by nature, but it is by use that evil things become such. So I say, says he, that man was made with a free will, not as if there were already evil in existence, which he had the power of choosing if he wished, but on account of his capacity of obeying or disobeying God.

For this was the meaning of the gift of Free Will. And man after his creation receives a commandment from God; and from this at once rises evil, for he does not obey the divine command; and this alone is evil, namely, disobedience, which had a beginning.

—Methodius, *Concerning Free Will*

Now one says in Holy Writ, that "man has learned evil." I say, then, that disobedience to God is taught. For this alone is evil which is produced in opposition to the purpose of God, for man would not learn evil by itself. He, then, who teaches evil is the Serpent.

—Methodius, *Concerning Free Will*

Evil is not a living animated essence; it is the condition of the soul opposed to virtue, developed in the careless on account of their falling away from good.

—Basil the Great, *homily on the Hexaemeron*

Do not then go beyond yourself to seek for evil, and imagine that there is an original nature of wickedness. Each of us, let us acknowledge it, is the first author of his own vice.

—Basil the Great, *homily on the Hexaemeron*

Things that do not please us seem to be evil and harmful, however good and fitting they may be.

—John of the Cross, *letter*

For to be in evil means a lack of true existence, since evil does not exist by itself but is a deficiency of the beautiful.

—Gregory of Nyssa, *Commentary on the Inscriptions of the Psalms*

Once every trace of evil has been abolished, everyone will be conformed to Christ and will share one radiant form which had clothed our nature from the very beginning.

—Gregory of Nyssa, *Commentary on the Inscriptions of the Psalms*

Man has an innate temper. He is sorely afflicted by evil when there is no occasion for it.

—Gregory of Nyssa, *Commentary on the Inscriptions of the Psalms*

Alienation from God, Who is Life, is an evil; the cure, then, of this infirmity is, again to be made friends with God, and so to be in life once more.

—Gregory of Nyssa, *On Infants' Early Death*

Although he is not the Creator or Abettor of evils, nevertheless he rules over these evils with the utmost prudence. Why, then, should my most gentle and at the same time most mighty Lord not allow evil to exist, since evil cannot overthrow his eternal plan in the slightest way? What, moreover, could make his own power appear more manifest, his wisdom more awesome, his mercy more tender than that he can omnipotently bring good out of evil, wisely keep in order what has been set in order, and mercifully confer happiness on the miserable?

—Aelred of Rievaulx, *Mirror of Charity*

The root of all evils is self-centeredness just as, on the other hand, the root of all virtues is charity. As long as this poisonous root remains in the depths of the soul, even though some of the twigs on the surface may be pruned back, others will inevitably continue to sprout from the re-invigorated base until the very root from which these pernicious shoots spring up has been utterly torn out and nothing more remains.

—Aelred of Rievaulx, *Mirror of Charity*

The evil should always be anxious as regards their wretched works, since even each of their thoughts lies open to the view of the strict Judge.

—Bede the Venerable, *homily on the Gospels*

But there is another reason why the wicked are left at large: so that they may not be deprived of the advantages of conversion from their evil ways, which certainly could not happen if they had been rendered incapable of doing evil.

—John Chrysostom, *On Providence*

He hates evil, who hates his own sins, and blesses and loves every one of his brethren.

—Abbot Poemon, *saying*

It is true that we all have inclinations to evil: some are prone to anger, other to sadness, others to envy, others to vanity and vainglory, others to avarice; and if we live according to such or similar inclinations we are lost.

—Francis de Sales, *Oeuvres*

It is a perilous thing to live in the world and in conversation with the wicked. An evil man will love sensual pleasure so much and consider it so precious that he will not quit the delight that he takes in it for all the wealth and honors in the world.

—Francis de Sales, *Oeuvres*

Yes, my dear brethren, in everything that we see, in everything that we hear, in all we say and do, we are conscious of the fact that we are drawn towards evil.

—John Baptiste Marie Vianney, *sermon*

For man, unassisted by God's grace, is even worse than the devil, because the devil is a spirit without a body, while man, without the grace of God, is a devil incarnate. Man has a free will, which, according to the ordination of God, is nowhere bound, so that he can do all the evil that he wills; to the devil, this is impossible, since he can act only by the divine permission; and when man surrenders to him his evil will, the devil employs it, as the instrument of his temptation.

—Catherine of Genoa, *Life and Doctrine*

God, despite his omnipotence and supreme goodness, allows evils he could prevent to exist in the world, if removing them would cause greater good to be lost or greater evil to ensue.

—Thomas Aquinas, *Summa Theologica*

Nothing can be essentially or completely evil, for if all good was eliminated in something there would be no subject left to be evil.

—Thomas Aquinas, *Summa Theologica*

If God did not permit bad, many goods would disappear: fire cannot exist without consuming air nor lions survive without killing asses; nor could we praise the righting of wrongs or the endurance of suffering if wickedness did not exist.

—Thomas Aquinas, *Summa Theologica*

It is always the same with those who do evil: they labor long only to yield death as their everlasting punishment.

—Patrick, *letter to the Soldiers of Coroticus*

Evil is a deliberate kind of knowledge. Or, rather, it is a deformity of the devil. There is no truth in it. And it imagines it can avoid being detected by many.

—John Climacus, *The Ladder of Divine Ascent*

When confronted by evils, we should choose the least.

—John Climacus, *The Ladder of Divine Ascent*

If men were to lay all their evils together, to be afterwards divided by equal portions amongst them, most men would rather take what they brought than stand to division; yet such is the partial judgment of self-love, that every man judgeth his self-misery too great, fearing he shall find some circumstance to increase it and make it tolerable: thus by thought he aggravates evil.

—Robert Southwell, *letter to a friend, 1591*

The Name of Jesus is a standard in battle, that is to say, in the fight against evil.

—Bernadine of Siena, *sermon*

Those who cause evil suffer more than others, because they have done evil to them. But much worse, woe woe betide those who hinder good and with their example are the cause of everybody else's evil.

—Maria Maddalena de' Pazzi, *The Dialogues*

A good person is soft and flexible to each good thing and separates evil from himself or herself.

—Hildegard of Bingen, *Scivias*

An evil thought sheds its danger when it is brought out into the open, and even before the verdict of discernment is proffered the most foul serpent which, so to speak, has been dragged out of its dark subterranean lair into the light by the fact of open avowal retreats, disgraced and denounced. Its dangerous promptings hold sway in us as long as these are concealed in the heart.

—John Cassian, *Conferences*

Good never leads to evil.

—Teresa of Ávila, *The Way of Perfection*

Ever since man deserted the true light, he delights only in darkness in accord with the popular saying: "To a man accustomed to evil, evil seems sweet."

—Bridget of Sweden, *Book of Questions*

But whenever thou forgettest God, forthwith thou beginnest to devise wickedness and to commit iniquity.

—Cyril of Jerusalem, *Catecheses*

If thou be not willing, the eye sees not amiss, the ear hears nothing which it ought not, the hand is not stretched out for wicked greed, the foot walketh not toward injustice, thou hast not strange loves, commitest no fornication, covetest not thy neighbor's wife. Drive out wicked thoughts from thine heart, be as God made thee, and thou wilt rather give thanks to thy Creator.

—Cyril of Jerusalem, *Catecheses*

For if a Christian has withdrawn from the fury and contention of the flesh as from the storms of the sea, and has now begun to be tranquil and gentle in the harbor of Christ, he ought not to admit into his heart either anger or discord, for it is not right for him to render evil for evil or to hate.

—Cyprian of Carthage, *The Good of Patience*

Those who take notice of what is evil in their neighbors, and yet refrain their tongue in silence, withdraw, as it were, the aid of medicine from observed sores, and became the causers of death, in that they would not cure the venom which they could have cured. The tongue, therefore, should be discreetly curbed, not tied up fast.

—Gregory the Great, *The Book of Pastoral Rule*

Excommunication

Since those who are excommunicated are cut off from the Church, they forfeit their share of all the good that is done, and this is a far greater loss than that of all material things.

—Thomas Aquinas, *letter on articles of faith*

F

Failure

You haven't failed; you have gained experience. On you go!

—Josemaría Escrivá, *The Way*

Things done in the service of God never fail through lack of money: they fail through lack of spirit.

—Josemaría Escrivá, *The Forge*

Faith

Faith darkens and empties the intellect of all its natural understanding and thereby prepares it for union with the divine wisdom.

—John of the Cross, *The Dark Night of the Soul*

When the soul is clothed in faith the devil is ignorant of how to hinder her, neither is he successful in his efforts, for faith gives her strong protection—more than do all the other virtues—against the devil, who is the mightiest and most astute enemy.

—John of the Cross, *The Dark Night of the Soul*

It is incontestably necessary for us first of all to lay the foundation of faith securely in the depths of our souls, then through the manifold forms of virtue to erect inward piety as a kind of fortress wall, and then, the soul having been walled all around and virtue, as it were, planted within it as on a solid foundation, then indeed one must raise the roof of this edifice, the roof of which is the divine knowledge of God, and so complete the whole house of the Spirit.

—Symeon the New Theologian, *Ethical Discourses*

May faith be the torch which illuminates, animates and sustains you, so that all your actions and sufferings may be for God alone Who should be served in privation as well as in consolation.

—Margaret Mary Alacoque, *Life and Writings of St. Margaret Mary*

[Faith is] to live ever in loving kindness and in humbleness, and to do good to one's neighbor.

—Abbot Pimenion, *saying*

The power of faith is enormous. It is so great that it not only saves the believer: thanks to one person's faith others are saved also.

—Cyril of Jerusalem, *Catecheses*

Faith can be said to be nothing else than an adhesion of the understanding and will to divine truths.

—Francis de Sales, *Oeuvres*

Now there is nothing stronger than truth, in which consists the valor of faith. Men indeed have this strength. They have power and mastery over all animals. Yet because we do not always realize that this is in us, we often fear like weaklings and cowards, stupidly taking flight before the beasts. The strength of faith, on the contrary, consists partly in knowing its power.

—Francis de Sales, *Oeuvres*

If you are armed with the armor of faith, nothing can harm you.

—Francis de Sales, *Oeuvres*

Faith is first and foremost a fidelity to truth, indeed to Truth himself; but since Truth himself is the ultimate goal of our activities faith also directs our behavior.

—Thomas Aquinas, *Summa Theologica*

Faith is the mental disposition through which eternal life starts up in us, causing our mind to assent to what it does not see.

—Thomas Aquinas, *Summa Theologica*

Only the man who has faith and is inspired by charity can rise above the miseries, the meannesses, and the malice of this world; instead, the man who lets himself be overcome by the spirit of illicit gain, of overweening hatred, and of impurity, is doomed to suffer, first here below, because he can never be entirely satisfied, and later in the other world.

—Pope John XXIII, *Daily Papal Messages*

You can't help feeling the fascination of a soul that knows what it wants, and lives by faith.

—Pope John XXIII, *Daily Papal Messages*

Faith is the beginning, and love is the end; and the union of the two together is God. All that makes for a soul's perfection follows in their train, for nobody who professes faith will commit sin, and nobody who possesses love can feel hatred.

—Ignatius of Antioch, *Epistle to the Ephesians*

A man who asserts that he has true faith and yet continues to sin is like a man without eyes. And the man who has no faith but who does good is like someone who draws water and then pours it into a barrel with holes.

—John Climacus, *The Ladder of Divine Ascent*

Faith gives wings to prayer, and without it no one can fly upward to heaven.

—John Climacus, *The Ladder of Divine Ascent*

No man has faith who does not believe that he has received his being from God; neither has he faith, who thinks that any other than the Almighty can give him strength to become good, for holiness is a higher gift than mere existence.

—John of Ávila, *letter to a disciple, 1563*

Souls that have faith, leave to the fools of this world the care of realizing a fortune on this Earth; seek you to make a fortune for the next life, which shall be eternal. The present life must end, and end very soon.

—Alphonsus Liguori, *sermon*

Faith, like active prayer, is a grace. For prayer, when activated by love through the power of the Spirit, renders true faith manifest—the faith that reveals the life of Jesus.

—Gregory of Sinai, *The Philokalia*

For wherever fear of God takes root, the wisdom of the human mind can be found. And God will help put faith in such a mind which God finds so satisfying.

—Hildegard of Bingen, *Scivias*

Faith reaches holiness with good works.

—Hildegard of Bingen, *Scivias*

Indeed, is it not clear that the soul of the faithful person, the most worthy of all creatures because of the grace of God, is greater than heaven itself? For the heavens with the rest of creation cannot contain their Creator. Only the faithful soul is His dwelling place and throne, and this only through charity which the wicked do not have.

—Clare of Assisi, *letter to Agnes of Prague*

Faith is powerful to do all things, for nothing is impossible to the believer; faith makes all things attainable and possible.

—Mary of Agreda, *The Mystical City of God*

Faith enlivens the other virtues and serves as a nourishment of the just man and a support in his labors.

—Mary of Agreda, *The Mystical City of God*

Many people have faith, but a faith which is habitual rather than active, like a sword buried in its scabbard.

—Robert Bellarmine, *The Mind's Ascent to God by the Ladder of Created Things*

And the righteous shall live by faith.

—Paul, *Romans 1:17*

Life eternal is the supreme good, death eternal the supreme evil, and that to obtain the one and escape the other we must live rightly. And this it is written, "The just lives by faith," for we do not as yet see our good, and must therefore live by faith; neither have we in ourselves power to live rightly, but can do so only if He who has given us faith to believe in His help does help us when we believe and pray.

—Augustine, *The City of God*

The families which do not live by faith seek their peace in the earthly advantages of this life; while the families which live by faith look for those eternal blessings which are promised, and use as pilgrims such advantages of time and of earth as do not fascinate and divert them from God, but rather aid them to endure with greater ease, and to keep down the number of those burdens of the corruptible body which weigh upon the soul.

—Augustine, *The City of God*

According to St. Thomas, the act of faith is twofold, interior and exterior. The interior act of that of believing; but to confess with the mouth those things which are of faith is an exterior act of faith.

—Vincent Ferrer, *sermon*

Unity of faith exists when we are all one, when we are all similarly recognize that we're bound together.

—John Chrysostom, *homily*

None of the philosophers before the coming of Christ could by bending all effort to the task know as much about God and things necessary for eternal life as after the coming of Christ a little old woman knows through her faith.

—Thomas Aquinas, *Commentary on Apostles' Creed*

Nor does He require precious gifts, but the good odor of faith, which the altars of your heart send forth and the disposition of a religious mind exhales.

—Ambrose, *Concerning Widowhood*

He who has kept good faith has deserved that good faith should be kept with him; he who has made good profit, because he has not sought his own benefit, has gained a claim to a heavenly reward.

—Ambrose, *Concerning Widowhood*

Simple faith is both the cause and the effect of Wisdom in our soul. The more faith we have, the more we shall possess Wisdom. The more we possess it, the stronger our faith. Without seeing, without feeling, without tasting and without faltering.

—Louis de Montfort, *The Love of Eternal Wisdom*

For that the grace is there is a matter of faith, on account of Him Who has promised to give it being Divine; while the testimony as to His Divinity comes through the Miracles.

—Gregory of Nyssa, *The Great Catechism*

If you have not faith, do not fear beasts so much as your faithlessness, which renders you susceptible of all corruption.

—Basil the Great, *homily on the Hexaemeron*

For, when enlightened by faith, the soul hath visions of God, and as far as is possible beholds God, and ranges round the bounds of the universe, and before the end of this world already beholds the Judgment, and the payment of the promised rewards.

—Cyril of Jerusalem, *Catecheses*

Be simple in faith but well trained in manners; demanding in your own affairs but unconcerned in those of others.

—Columban, *letter, c. 610*

There are some who pass through life as through a tunnel, without ever understanding the splendor, the security and the warmth of the sun of faith.

—Josemaría Escrivá, *The Way*

We cannot give way in matters of faith. But don't forget that in order to speak the truth there is no need to ill-treat anyone.

—Josemaría Escrivá, *The Forge*

Whoever lives in the strong faith that nothing happens without the knowledge and will of God is not easily disconcerted by astonishing occurrences or upset by the hardest of blows. He will stay quiet and face the facts clearly; he will discover the right guidelines for his practical behavior in the overall situation.

—Edith Stein, *Essays on Woman*

To be sure, life built on faith should be the fruit of religious formation. Faith, however, is not a matter of imagination or pious emotion; but, on the contrary, it is an intellectual recognition (if not a rational permeation) and a voluntary acceptance by the will; a complete development of faith is one of the most profound acts of the individual, one in which all his powers become acute.

—Edith Stein, *Essays on Woman*

It is an error to think that faith is so entirely a gift of God that it is not in our power to increase and strengthen it.

—Claude de la Colombière, *spiritual reflections*

For what is faith but a carriage to carry us to the fatherland?

—Aelred of Rievaulx, *Mirror of Charity*

If you observe the heavens, says Scripture, their order will be a guide for you towards faith. They do in fact reveal the Artist who made them. If you then observe the beauty of the earth, it will help you to increase your faith.

—Basil the Great, *On Psalm 32*

By faith we believe that the world must come to an end by the final judgment.

—Bonaventure, *The Soul's Journey Into God*

Family

Happiness is to be found only in the home and in the family circle where God is loved and honored, and everyone loves and helps and cares for the other.

—Théophane Vénard, *letter to his brothers, 1851*

Society is suffering acutely because of the lack of Christian mothers. Since society is based on the family, its very shape and fate is largely in the hands of women. If they were given a thorough Christian education and well-grounded in Christian principles, the whole of society would rise generated in newness of life.

—Placid Riccardi, *letter to his brother, 1906*

May God pour down every blessing on you, your family, your children. He who emptied himself with such generosity so as to enrich men and comfort them in every need will not do less for one who loves and serves him from the depths of his being. Wait patiently for his consolation.

—Placid Riccardi, *letter to his brother, 1906*

A household cannot be a democracy, ruled by everyone, but the authority must necessarily rest in one person.

—John Chrysostom, *homily*

As with a general whose troops are so well organized on the front that the enemy cannot find a place to penetrate for an attack, so it is with husband and wife: when the concerns of everyone in the house are the same, harmony reigns in the family, but if not, the entire household is easily broken up and destroyed.

—John Chrysostom, *homily*

The family burden which the husband bears in addition to his professional duties would seem all too heavy if his helpmate did not stand by his side; she is called in accordance with her nature to carry more than half of this load.

—Edith Stein, *Essays on Woman*

Any social condition is an unhealthy one which compels married women to seek gainful employment and make it impossible for them to manage their home. And we should accept as normal that the married woman is restricted to domestic life at a time when her household duties exact her total energies.

—Edith Stein, *Essays on Woman*

But if it sometimes happens that married people should be oppressed with the number of their children, whom, through poverty, they cannot easily support, there is a remedy pleasing to God. And this is for the couple, by mutual consent, to separate from the marriage-bed and spend their days in prayer and fasting.

—Robert Bellarmine, *The Art of Dying Well*

Fasting

But let your fasts be moderate, since if they are carried to excess they weaken the stomach, and by making more food necessary to make up for it lead to indigestion, which is the parent of lust. A frugal, temperate diet is good for both body and soul.

—Jerome, *letter to Rusticus, 411*

Enfeebling the body by nightwatches and fasting is only acceptable to God if it can claim some virtue; if it is done with due discretion and curbs our passions without overburdening our nature.

—Arsenius, *saying*

Fasting ends lust, roots out bad thoughts, frees one from evil dreams. Fasting makes for purity of prayer, an enlightened soul, a watchful mind, a deliverance from blindness. Fasting is the door of compunction, humble sighing, joyful contrition, and end to chatter, an occasion for silence, a custodian of obedience, a lightening of sleep, health of the body, an agent of dispassion, a remission of sins, the gate, indeed, the delight of Paradise.

—John Climacus, *The Ladder of Divine Ascent*

Fasting is a virtue only when it is accompanied by conditions which render it pleasing to God. Thus it happens that it profits some and not others, because it is not undertaken by all in the same manner.

—Francis de Sales, *Oeuvres*

We must fast with our whole heart, that is to say, willingly, whole-heartedly, universally and entirely.

—Francis de Sales, *Oeuvres*

If you fast without humility, it is worth nothing and cannot be pleasing to the Lord.

—Francis de Sales, *Oeuvres*

Fasting is the support of our soul: it gives us wings to ascend on high, and to enjoy the highest contemplation.

—John Chrysostom, *homily on Genesis*

No one fasts for human praise, but for the pardon of his sins.

—Augustine, *sermon*

The chief end of fasting is mortification of the flesh, so that the spirit may be strengthened more. For this purpose, we must use only spare and unsavory diet.

—Robert Bellarmine, *The Art of Dying Well*

What we gain from fasting does not compensate for what we lose through anger.

—John Cassian, *Conferences*

For we fast by abstaining from wine and flesh, not because we abhor them as abominations, but because we look for our reward; that having scorned things sensible, we may enjoy a spiritual and intellectual feast; and that having now sown in tears we may reap in joy in the world to come.

—Cyril of Jerusalem, *Catecheses*

A strict fast is a penance most pleasing to God.

—Josemaría Escrivá, *The Way*

Fate

So if God, who created the whole world, also guides it, where will chance, fate, and fortune govern a single created thing?

—Paulinus of Nola, *letter*

Fear

I do not now fear God, but I love him, for love casteth fear out of doors.

—Abbot Anthony, *saying*

The mind, therefore, that is bound by the bondage of fear knows not the grace of liberty. For good should be loved for itself, not pursued because of the compulsion of penalties.

—Gregory the Great, *The Book of Pastoral Rule*

There is, as I have said, nothing to fear so long as we walk truthfully in His Majesty's presence with a clean conscience.

—Teresa of Ávila, *Life*

I do not fear death half as much as I do my weak and detestable person.

—Elizabeth Seton, *Collected Writings*

Our fear increases if we fly from it, while our courage grows stronger if we resist.

—Peter of Alcántara, *Treatise on Prayer & Meditation*

Fear is the first temptation which the enemy presents to those who have resolved to serve God, for soon as they are shown what perfection requires of them they think, "Alas, I shall never be able to do it." . . . Do not trouble yourself and do not frame these idle fears that you are not able to accomplish that to which you have bound yourself, since you are armed and encompassed with the truth of God and with his word.

—Francis de Sales, *Oeuvres*

The slothful and cowardly fear everything and find everything difficult and trying because they amuse themselves in thinking, with the foolish and slothful imagination which they have created for themselves, more about future difficulties than what they have to do at present.

—Francis de Sales, *Oeuvres*

Neither fear nor love of self can turn the soul to God; they may sometimes change the aspect or influence the actions of a man, but they will never change his heart.

—Bernard of Clairvaux, *letter to Guy the Carthusian Prior*

We should always hold fast to the fear of God. It is the root of all spiritual knowledge and right action. When the fear of God rules in the soul everything goes well both within and without. Try to kindle this sense of fear in your heart every morning before you do anything else. Then it will go on working by itself as a kind of pendulum.

—Theophan the Recluse, *The Fruits of Prayer*

Fear arising from guilt is evil.

—Peter Chrysologus, *sermon*

Someone who keeps away from the blandishments of sin because he is afraid will return to the object of his choice as soon as the obstacle of fear is removed. Hence he will not acquire any firm stand in what is good. He will have no rest from temptation since he will not be possessed by the sturdy and continuous peace of chastity.

—John Cassian, *Conferences*

I long to see you free of all slavish fear, as I reflect how fear cuts off the vigor of holy resolution and wholesome desire. So I have asked and will continue to ask the good gentle Jesus to free you from all slavish fear, leaving you only holy fear.

—Catherine of Siena, *letter to Pope Gregory XI, at Avignon, 1376*

Flattery

No one needs the words of flatterers except him who knows himself to be unworthy of praise. He who is worthy gets praised in more modest fashion through the devotion of his friends. But, he who is under a feeling of unworthiness thinks that his acts are being scrutinized if he goes away without praise.

—Valerian, *homily*

The Lord is so jealous of the souls especially beloved by Him, that He will immediately turn away from them if they recompense themselves by their flatteries; since by this levity they become unworthy of his favors.

—Mary of Agreda, *The Mystical City of God*

It is not possible to unite in a soul the adulations of the world and the caresses of the Most High. For these latter are sincere, holy, pure, and lasting: they humiliate, cleanse, pacify and illumine the heart; while on the other hand the flatteries of creatures are vain, fleeting, deceitful, impure and false, issuing from the mouths of those who are all liars (Psalms 115:11); and whatever is deceitful is a work of the enemy.

—Mary of Agreda, *The Mystical City of God*

There are those who take enjoyment in flattery, patting each other on the back and conniving with each other. While take care not to offend one another, they incur each other's ruin, because they do not enjoy themselves in the liberty of justice or in the Lord.

—Aelred of Rievaulx, *Mirror of Charity*

Avoid flattery. Flattery confirms sinners in their evil desires by giving them praise.

Avoid flatterers. Flatterers' tongues rivet souls to their fate.

—Augustine, *On Psalm 140*

Forgiveness

And in this mortal life mercy and forgiveness are the path which always leads us to grace.

—Julian of Norwich, *Showings*

If you wish the happiness of having your sins forgiven, you must have nothing belonging to anyone else which you should and could pay back.

—John Baptiste Marie Vianney, *sermon*

One must not bear a grudge against a man who has sinned and repents, but forgive him heartily.

—Basil the Great, *letter to Gregory of Nazianzus*

What does ignorance of God beget us? Despair! A man who ponders all the evil he has done becomes anxious about himself. If he does not know how good and forgiving the Lord is, how willing to forgive and welcome him back, he falls into despair and becomes impenitent. He does not realize that Omnipotent Goodness could manage all his affairs, not wanting anyone to perish but that the sinner could be converted and live.

—Bernard of Clairvaux, *On the Canticle of Canticles*

If we pray to the Lord to forgive us, we ourselves must be forgiving; we are all under the eyes of our Lord and God, and every one of us must stand before the judgment-seat of Christ, where each of us will have to give an account of himself.

—Polycarp of Smyrna, *epistle to the Philippians*

How can he who will not obey the command of God to pardon his neighbor, expect to obtain from God the forgiveness of his own sins?

—Alphonsus Liguori, *sermon*

I have looked so closely into my heart that I cannot find there any single good action. I know my sins and they are more than the sand upon the shore. Water like the sea is little compared to the extent of my sins. But I trust in your God that he will forgive me the whole extent of my sinfulness and look upon me again.

—Pelagia the Penitent, *Vita Sanctae Pelagiae, Metricis*

God immediately forgives everything to those who ask forgiveness in a spirit of humility and contrition and who ceaselessly invoke his holy name.

—Gregory of Sinai, *The Philokalia*

Even if your wife sins against you more times than you can count, you must forgive and pardon everything.

—John Chrysostom, *sermon*

He who knows how to forgive prepares for himself many graces from God. As often as I look upon the cross, so often will I forgive with all my heart.

—Faustina Kowalska, *Divine Mercy in My Soul*

If you wish God to forgive you your offenses against him, forgive your enemies what they have done to injure you. At the very instant when you forgive your enemy, God will forgive you.

—Vincent Ferrer, *sermon*

For when the Lord forgave all sins, He made an exception of none.

—Ambrose, *Concerning Repentance*

God is able whensoever He wills to forgive us our sins, even those which we think cannot be forgiven.

—Ambrose, *Concerning Repentance*

Fornication

see ADULTERY; LUST; PASSIONS

Friendship

Friendship, therefore, is that virtue by which spirits are bound by ties of love and sweetness and out of many are made one.

—Aelred of Rievaulx, *Spiritual Friendship*

For we are compelled by the law of charity to receive in the embrace of love not only our friends but also our enemies. But only those do we call friends to whom we can fearlessly entrust our heart and all its secrets; those, too, who, in turn, are bound to us by the same law of faith and security.

—Aelred of Rievaulx, *Spiritual Friendship*

In friendship are joined honor and charm, truth and joy, sweetness and good-will, affection and action. And all these take their beginning from Christ, advance through Christ, and are perfected in Christ.

—Aelred of Rievaulx, *Spiritual Friendship*

Friendship, therefore, heightens the joys of prosperity and mitigates the sorrows of adversity by dividing and sharing them. Hence, the best medicine in life is a friend.

—Aelred of Rievaulx, *Spiritual Friendship*

If somebody asks me, "What is best in this life?" I shall answer, "Friends!"

—Gregory of Nazianzus, *letter to Palladios*

Just as human law aims primarily at friendship between men, so God's law aims primarily at friendship of man for God. But love is based on likeness, and to love God, who is most good, man must become good himself.

—Thomas Aquinas, *Summa Theologica*

All love is not friendship; for we may love without being loved, and then love but not friendship exists, for friendship is mutual love, and unless it is mutual, it is not friendship.

—Francis de Sales, *The Devout Life*

I would bid you love everyone with the love of charity, but have no friendship save with those who can interchange virtuous love with you, since the more your friendship stands on the foundation of virtue, the more perfect it will be.

—Francis de Sales, *The Devout Life*

If we have a friend who has never done anything hard for us, we still know how sincere his friendship is. But if he endures difficulties and sufferings for our sake, then we have a proof that his friendship is real, indeed. . . . True friendship rejoices when it has to suffer for a beloved friend.

—Maximilian M. Kolbe, *article on discipline, 1934*

The bond of friendship between eternal Wisdom and man is so close as to be beyond our understanding. Wisdom is for man and man is for Wisdom.

—Louis de Montfort, *The Love of Eternal Wisdom*

Have no enemies. Have only friends: friends on the right—if they have done or have wished to do you good; and on the left—if they have harmed or tried to harm you.

—Josemaría Escrivá, *The Way*

In a Christian, in a child of God, friendship and charity are one and the same thing. They are a divine light which spreads warmth.

—Josemaría Escrivá, *The Forge*

Dangers in Friendship

Friendship arising from the mere gratification of the senses is utterly gross and unworthy of that name, as is that arising from vain and superficial merits which also depend upon the senses only. Always dispose of a part of your means by giving freely alms to the poor, for you impoverish yourself by that which you give, and the more it is the more you are impoverished. Undoubtedly God will restore it to you in this world as well as in the next, for nothing brings such prosperity as almsgiving.

—Francis de Sales, *The Devout Life*

You must be aware that you be not deceived in your friendships under any pretext whatever, for Satan often deludes those who love.

—Francis de Sales, *The Devout Life*

True and living friendship cannot exist amid sin. . . . Sin destroys that friendship where it effects an entrance: if the sin is but accidental, it will be put to flight by a friendly correction; but if it be rooted and permanent, then friendship will perish, for it can exist only where virtue is.

—Francis de Sales, *The Devout Life*

Our friend becomes an enemy if he would cause us to sin.

—Francis de Sales, *The Devout Life*

The Devil employs vicious friends as decoys to draw so many souls into the snare of sin.

—Alphonsus Liguori, *sermon*

One scandalous companion is enough to corrupt all who treat him as a friend.

—Alphonsus Liguori, *sermon*

The world is filled with disloyalty, deception and inconstancy. When no more advantage is to be gained, friendship is over.

—Henry Suso, *Little Book of Eternal Wisdom*

For, when we are unwarily joined in friendship with the wicked, we are bound in their sins.

—Gregory the Great, *The Book of Pastoral Rule*

G

Gambling

If I let you go, and if I dismiss this assembly, some will run to the dice, where they will find bad language, sad quarrels and the pangs of avarice. There stands the devil, inflaming the fury of the players with the dotted bones, transporting the same sums of money from one side of the table to the other, now exalting one with victory and throwing the other to despair, now swelling the first with boasting and covering his rival with confusion.

—Basil the Great, *homily on the Hexaemeron*

Generosity

For what use is it when you give as much of your wealth as someone might give a spoonful of water from the ocean, and you don't imitate the widow's generosity of spirit?

—John Chrysostom, *homily*

But you are afraid and you fear lest, if you begin to act very generously, your patrimony come to an end because of your generous action and you perchance be reduced to penury; be undisturbed on this score, be secure. That cannot be ended, whence expenditure is made in the service of Christ, whence the heavenly work is celebrated. I do not promise you on my own authority but I vouch for it on the faith of holy Scriptures and on the authority of the divine promise.

—Cyprian of Carthage, *Works and Almsgiving*

Why do you pile up the burden of your patrimony, that the richer you have been in the sight of the world, the poorer you may become in the sight of God? Divide your returns with your God; share your gains with Christ; make Christ a partner in your earthly possessions that He also may make you co-heir of His heavenly kingdom.

—Cyprian of Carthage, *Works and Almsgiving*

We are taught how fitting it is to be merciful and liberal towards the poor, and that this liberality should not be checked by the consideration of our poverty, since liberality is determined not by the amount of our possessions, but by the disposition of giving. . . . For the piece of money out of a small stock is richer than treasures out of abundance, because it is not the amount that is given but the amount that remains which is considered.

—Ambrose, *Concerning Widowhood*

Whatever you give to the poor you do without a doubt put out at interest. This interest will yield you its returns later on when the labors of every man will be evaluated and multiplied honor conferred.

—Valerian, *homily*

Gentleness

Jesus is also gentle in his words. When he dwelt on earth he won everyone over by his gentle speech. Never was he heard to raise his voice or argue heatedly.

—Louis de Montfort, *The Love of Eternal Wisdom*

We should remember that he [Christ] himself said that by gentleness we inherit the earth. If we act on this we will win people over so that they will turn to the Lord. That will not happen if we treat people harshly or sharply.

—Vincent de Paul, *Common Rules or Constitutions of the Congregation of the Mission*

If the highest end of virtue is that which aims at the advancement of most, gentleness is the most lovely of all, which does not hurt even those whom it condemns, and usually renders those whom it condemns worthy of absolution. Moreover, it is the only virtue which has led to the increase of the Church which the Lord sought at the price of His own Blood, imitating the loving kindness of heaven, and aiming at the redemption of all, seeks this end with a gentleness which the ears of men can endure, in presence of which their hearts to not sink, nor their spirits quail.

—Ambrose, *Concerning Repentence*

Gloating

He who rejoices at the fall of another rejoices at the victory of the devil.

—Ambrose, *Concerning Repentance*

Glory

It seems to me that we have nothing to fear when we look to God only and seek His glory alone; since He takes into account the good will alone of a heart that loves Him.

—Margaret Mary Alacoque, *Life and Writings of St. Margaret Mary*

To have the right idea of glory and to love it, you should consider all the riches of the world and its delights as mud and vanity and weariness, as they truly are, and do not esteem anything, however signal and precious, except being in God's grace. All that is best here below is ugly and bitter when compared to those eternal goods for which we were created. And however brief the ugliness and bitterness, it will last forever in the soul that esteems it.

—John of the Cross, *letter*

Pleasure and glory strip us of divine glory; temperance and patience weave back the divine garment.

—Theoleptos of Philadelphia, *letter*

No matter what the multitude of men may do, they have abundant help in heaven.

Nevertheless, they ask God in prayer to grant their erroneous fantasies such as power, honor, wealth, or that miserable, petty glory which excites our human nature.

—Gregory of Nyssa, *Commentary on the Inscriptions of the Psalms*

Thus, while it is one thing not to seek out that glory which is of men, it is another to depend on God's glory and seek it without fail.

—Symeon the New Theologian, *Ethical Discourses*

No plans we make for God are ever accomplished without trouble. The more the devil tries to upset them, the more glory for God can we hope for.

—Claude de la Colombière, *letter*

God in himself has no need to receive glory from you. But he wants you to become worthy to receive glory from him.

—Basil the Great, *Commentary on Psalm 28*

In a word, all the glory of the labors we have undergone in this world, in order to acquire a large income, a high character for valor, for learning and for genius, shall end in our being thrown into a pit to become the food for worms.

—Alphonsus Liguori, *sermon*

There is no glory in having a gift without knowing it. But to know only that you have it, without knowing that it is not of yourself that you have it, means self-glorying, but no true glory in God.

—Bernard of Clairvaux, *On Loving God*

To him who possess virtues it is a great virtue to despise glory; for contempt of it is seen by God, but is not manifest to human judgment.

—Augustine, *The City of God*

Gluttony

If you become surfeited with food, or still more with drink, the peace of God will cease to act in you. If you are angry, you will lose this peace for a long while.

—Bishop Ignatius of Antioch, in *The Art of Prayer*

A stuffed belly produces fornication, while a mortified stomach leads to purity. The man who pets a lion may tame it but the man who coddles the body makes it ravenous.

—John Climacus, *The Ladder of Divine Ascent*

Keep mistress gluttony under control and every abode will then give you dispassion, but let her take hold of you and every place outside the grave will be a menace to you.

—John Climacus, *The Ladder of Divine Ascent*

Gluttony is the hypocrisy of the stomach which complains of being empty when it is well fed, and bellows that it is hungry when it is full almost to bursting.

—John Climacus, *The Ladder of Divine Ascent*

Master gluttony before it masters you!

—John Climacus, *The Ladder of Divine Ascent*

In eating, one should not display the gluttony of a mad guzzler, but observe always restraint, moderation, and self-discipline regarding pleasures, without letting the mind idle away from the thought of God.

—Basil the Great, *letter to Gregory of Nazianzus*

The bread from heaven satisfies our every taste and hunger, making the pleasures of gluttony appear insipid.

—Anthony of Padua, *Sermones*

When the belly is distended with gluttony, the virtues of the soul are destroyed through lechery.

—Gregory the Great, *The Book of Pastoral Rule*

Gluttony is an ugly vice. Don't you feel a bit amused and even disgusted, when you see a group of dignified gentlemen, seated solemnly around a table, stuffing fatty substances into their stomachs, with an air of ritual, as if that were an end in itself?

—Josemaría Escrivá, *The Way*

God

Adoration and Praise of God

Most noble balm of divinity! Like an ocean of love, you empty yourself in eternal light and in eternal budding of life. You transform as you diffuse yourself until the end of time.

—Gertrude the Great, *The Herald of Divine Love*

O Lord, may I place all my happiness in remaining with thee. One thing alone I desire, and I ask it from thy love—to dwell always close to thee, in body or at least in heart; to behold thy eucharistic beauty and glory; to feed ever on thy love; to pass my days and nights, as far as thou dost wish, in blessing, in loving and contemplating thee!

—Gertrude the Great, *Love, Peace and Joy*

O Lord, tell me what satisfaction would be most acceptable to thy heart, and I will try to accomplish it, were it even to exhaust all my strength.

—Gertrude the Great, *Love, Peace and Joy*

Oh, how I long to be consumed with so burning a love that my heart could liquefy itself and be lost entirely in thee!

—Gertrude the Great, *Love, Peace and Joy*

No creature suffices to praise you worthily. You alone are sufficient to yourself who are never deficient in yourself. Your face, mellifluous above honey and the honeycomb, fattens the souls of saints.

—Gertrude the Great, *Spiritual Exercises*

You are God, you are Father, you are Spirit, and you are also love. Never, never will I tire of calling you with this name of love.

—Maria Maddalena de' Pazzi, *The Forty Days*

In the life to come our minds will see the true God himself, and our outer worship will need no symbols but will consist in praise of God from heart and mind. At present however God's truth can only express itself to us in symbols we can sense.

—Thomas Aquinas, *Summa Theologica*

Thou hast shown me a spark of thy pure and simple love, and it has kindled in my heart a flame that devours me. Nowhere on earth can I find repose, nor can I feel or see aught beside me. I am lost and beside myself; I am led captive and wounded nigh unto death, and wait only on thy providence, which will satisfy every one of my desires, which is in the order of salvation.

—Catherine of Genoa, *Life and Doctrine*

O my Lord, what a true friend You are, and how powerful! You can do everything when you will, and you never cease to will if we love You! Let all things praise you, Lord of the world. O that a voice might go forth over the earth, proclaiming how faithful You are to Your friends! All things fail, but You, Lord of them all, never fail.

—Teresa of Ávila, *Life*

O my Lord, how abundantly you display Your power! There is no need to seek reasons for Your will, for You transcend all natural reason and make all things possible. Thus you show us that we need do no more than truly love You, and truly forsake everything for You, and that You, my Lord, will then make everything easy.

—Teresa of Ávila, *Life*

O King of glory and Lord of all kings, Your kingdom is not hedged about by trifles, for it is infinite. We have no need of third parties through whom to approach You.

—Teresa of Ávila, *Life*

Lord, you are my God and my Lord, and never have I seen You. You have created me and re-created me and You have given me all the good things I possess, and still I do not know You. In fine, I was made in order to see You, and I have not yet accomplished what I was made for.

—Anselm, *Proslogion*

You exist so truly, Lord my God, that You cannot even be thought not to exist.

—Anselm, *Proslogion*

Since, then, nothing is greater than You, no place or time confines You but You exist everywhere and always. And because this can be said of You alone, You alone are unlimited and eternal.

—Anselm, *Proslogion*

You are life and light and wisdom and blessedness and eternity and many suchlike good things; and yet You are nothing save the one and supreme good, You who are completely sufficient unto Yourself, needing nothing, but rather He whom all things need in order that they may have being and well-being.

—Anselm, *Proslogion*

I snuggle to the heart of God like a baby to its mother's breast.

—Faustina Kowalska, *Divine Mercy in My Soul*

I feel in my soul an unfathomable abyss which only God can fill. I lose myself in Him as a drop does in the ocean.

—Faustina Kowalska, *Divine Mercy in My Soul*

O gentle Lord, since loving imitation of your meek way of life and your suffering from love is so very pleasing to you, I shall spend all my efforts from now on to imitate you joyfully rather than to lament with weeping, though I should do both according to your words.

—Henry Suso, *Little Book of Eternal Wisdom*

Denial of God

For he is dead who wholly casts God out of his heart. He, then, who does not wholly cast Him out, but under pressure of torments has denied Him for a time, is half dead.

—Ambrose, *Concerning Repentence*

Goodness of God

For God is good—or rather, of all goodness He is the Fountainhead, and it is impossible for one who is good to be mean or grudging about anything.

—Athanasius, *On the Incarnation*

And so since a being is good insofar as it is perfect, God's being is his perfect goodness; for in God to exist, to live, to be wise, to be happy, and anything else is obviously belonging to perfection and goodness, are one and the same in God, as if everything adding up to his goodness were God's very being.

—Thomas Aquinas, *Summa Theologica*

Now, the cause of all things being united to God, namely, his goodness, which all things reflect, is exceedingly great and deeply seated in God, since he himself is his own goodness. Wherefore in God not only is there true love, but also most perfect and most abiding love.

—Thomas Aquinas, *Summa Theologica*

God wills himself to exist, and also other things with himself as their goal, for it befits God's goodness to offer other things a share in it. Nothing but his own goodness causes God to will other things, and he wills many such things in the one simple, single act of willing his own goodness.

—Thomas Aquinas, *Summa Theologica*

Now, since a thing is lovable to the extent that is good, and since the goodness of God is infinite, he is infinitely lovable. However, no creature is capable of loving God infinitely, because an infinite act is impossible to a finite power. Consequently, only God, whose power to love matches his goodness, can love himself perfectly according to the first degree of perfection.

—Thomas Aquinas, *On the Perfection of the Spiritual Life*

Since God is forever Goodness itself, he is always just and merciful. It is the property of goodness to communicate itself, for of itself it is communicative, and to this end it uses mercy and justice: mercy to do good, and justice to punish and uproot whatever prevents us from experiencing the effects of this goodness of our God, this God whose mercy is his justice and whose justice is his mercy.

—Francis de Sales, *Oeuvres*

For I know that my God is not merely bounteous Bestower of my life, the generous Provider for all my needs, the pitiful consoler of all my sorrows, the wise Guide of my course: but that he is far more than that. He saves me with an abundant deliverance: he is my eternal Preserver, the portion of my inheritance, my glory.

—Bernard of Clairvaux, *On Loving God*

God watches over the affairs of those who truly love him without their worrying about them.

—John of the Cross, *letter*

God in fact is perfectly good. He is the One toward whom all things tend. His nature is unchangeable, supreme dignity superabundant love, an inexhaustible treasure.

—Basil the Great, *Commentary on Psalm I*

HAND OF GOD

God's hand is God's power; and He, working invisibly, effects visible results.

—Augustine, *The City of God*

How amazing and pitiful is it that the soul be so utterly weak and impure that the hand of God, though light and gentle, should feel so heavy and contrary. For the hand of God does not press down or weigh on the soul, but only touches it; and this mercifully, for God's aim is to grant it favors and not chastise it.

—John of the Cross, *The Dark Night of the Soul*

HUMANITY AND GOD

Let us know that although we are strangers to the Lord while in the body, we are present to the eyes of God.

—Columban, *sermon*

God never costs too dear, however much we pay for him.

—John of Ávila, *letter to a widow, 1568*

One hour is not a long time, one hour to speak to the good God. We have so many things to ask of him, we could stay with him forever.

—Brother André, *Brother André According to Witnesses*

Most people judge God's power by their own limited understanding.

—Thérèse of Lisieux, *The Story of a Soul*

How true it is that God alone knows the secrets of our hearts! We ourselves are so shortsighted.

—Thérèse of Lisieux, *The Story of a Soul*

The first rules we must observe are the commandments of God. All other rules are merely things dependent upon them and they can produce nothing if they are not rooted in them.

—Marguerite Bourgeoys, *Autographic Writings*

Open your heart so that the word of God may enter it, take root in it, and bear fruit there for eternal life.

—John Baptiste Marie Vianney, *sermon*

O Lord! I desire to make this compact with thee: I will give this sinful being of mine into thy hands, for thou alone canst hide it in thy mercy, and so dispose of me that nothing of myself can any more be seen. Occupy me wholly with thy love, which will enlighten me in every other love and keep me wholly lost in thee, holding me so engrossed by thee that I shall find neither time nor place for self.

—Catherine of Genoa, *Life and Doctrine*

The Master is never so far away that the disciple needs to raise his voice in order to be heard: He is always right at his side.

—Teresa of Ávila, *The Way of Perfection*

The person guarding himself from lowly, earthly things draws near to a great [divine] nature transcending every human thought; he imitates God by good deeds and associates himself with God's own nature.

—Gregory of Nyssa, *Commentary on the Inscriptions of the Psalms*

Never make a decision without stopping to consider the matter in the presence of God.

—Josemaría Escrivá, *The Way*

All my greatness is but small to you, all my strength is weak to you, all my wisdom is foolish to you. I shall run toward the scents of your ointments, O Lord.

—Aelred of Rielvaux, *Mirror of Charity*

Oh! happy is he who wishes for nothing but God; for God will satisfy all the desires of his heart.

—Alphonsus Liguori, *sermon*

Nature and Power of God

Great is the Lord and there is no measure or end to his greatness. He is great not only because his omnipotence is his height, his unfathomable wisdom is his depth, his mercy which reaches everywhere is his breadth, his justice which is like a rod of iron is his length, but also because each of these attributes is great with the magnitude of infinite breadth, length, height and depth.

—Robert Bellarmine, *The Mind's Ascent to God by the Ladder of Created Things*

God is the truest fountain of being since he receives being from no other being and all receive from him. God receives being from no being because existence stems from God's essence, and his very essence is his existence so that it cannot be or be thought that God has not always existed or does not always exist.

—Robert Bellarmine, *The Mind's Ascent to God by the Ladder of Created Things*

God never goes outside himself because he is all good in himself. Before the world came to exist he was as rich and happy as he was later because nothing was made by God which was not always in God to a higher degree.

—Robert Bellarmine, *The Mind's Ascent to God by the Ladder of Created Things*

Since God cannot be encompassed by any image, form or particular knowledge, in order to be united with him the soul should not be limited by any particular form or knowledge.

—John of the Cross, *The Ascent of Mount Carmel*

No creature, none of its actions and abilities, can reach or encompass God's nature.

—John of the Cross, *The Ascent of Mount Carmel*

For he who created all things from nothing is greater than all that can be seen whole, and greater than all that is, and thus when he is seen, he is invisible, since he alone knows who he is and how great he is.

—Columban, *sermon*

The One Triune God is an ocean that cannot be crossed or explored. High is the heaven, broad the earth, deep the sea and long the ages; but higher and broader and deeper and longer is his knowledge. For he has been adorned by nature, he who created it from nothing.

—Columban, *sermon*

The holy fathers explain that what is unknowable in God is his essence, while what may be known is that which pertains to his essence, namely, goodness, wisdom, power, divinity and majesty.

—Gregory Palamas, *Topics of Natural and Theological Science and on the Moral and Ascetic Life: One Hundred and Fifty Texts*

Nothing is hidden from the Lord; even our most secret thoughts are ever present to him.

—Ignatius of Antioch, *Epistle to the Ephesians*

God is in all things by his presence, his power and his substance . . . by his power, because all things are within his power, and by his presence, because all things are opened to his sight, and by his substance he is present in all things.

—Thomas Aquinas, *Summa Theologica*

God's perfect actuality in existing, free from all matter and potentiality, makes him completely knowable and completely knowing. So he knows himself as well as he can be known, he perfectly comprehends himself.

—Thomas Aquinas, *Summa Theologica*

It is clear that no creature has anything generically in common with God, so that God cannot be known in his essence through any created species at all, not only through a sensible species but not even through an intelligible one. Hence, for God himself to be known in his essence God himself must become the form of the intellect knowing him and unite with it not so as to constitute one nature but as the intelligible species is to the knower.

—Thomas Aquinas, *Compendium of Theology*

What, then, is my God? What, I ask, unless the Lord God? Who is the Lord but the Lord? Or who is God but our God?

Most high, most good, most mighty, most almighty; most merciful and most just; most hidden and most present; most beautiful and most strong; stable and incomprehensible; unchangeable, yet changing in all things; never new, and never old, yet renewing all things; leading proud men into senility, although they know it not; ever active, and ever at rest; gathering in, yet needing nothing; supporting, fulfilling, and protecting things; creating, nourishing, and perfecting them; searching them out, although nothing is lacking in you.

—Augustine, *Confessions*

For absolutely nothing defiles our God: none from the will, none from necessity, none from any unforeseen chance. He is God, and what he wills for himself is good, and he himself is that same good, whereas to be corrupted is not good. Nor are you forced to do anything against your will, because your will is not greater than your power. But it would be greater if you were greater than yourself. God's will and power are God himself.

—Augustine, *Confessions*

What is God? Who is like to him in greatness? Nations before him are as a drop of water; the universe as a grain of sand; the whole human race as nothing.

—Ignatius of Loyola, *Spiritual Exercises*

God is the foundation of our natural reason; and God is the teaching of Holy Church, and God is the Holy Spirt, and they are all different gifts, and he wants us to have great regard for them, and to accord ourselves to them. For they work continually in us, altogether, and those are great things; and of this greatness he wants us to have knowledge here, as it were in an ABC.

—Julian of Norwich, *Showings*

The properties [of God] are these: life, love and light. In life is wonderful familiarity, in love is gentle courtesy, and in light is endless nature.

—Julian of Norwich, *Showings*

For God is the unity that knows nothing similar to it. If this were not so, then God could scarcely be called "the One."

—Hildegard of Bingen, *Book of Divine Works*

God is divided by no divisions, either in the beginning or at the end. God is to be understood just as God is by all of God's thinking creatures.

—Hildegard of Bingen, *Scivias*

In its foreknowledge and in its workings the Godhead is like a wheel, a whole. In no way is it to be divided because the Godhead has neither beginning nor end. No one can grasp it, for it is timeless. And just as a wheel encloses within itself what lies hidden within it, so also does the Holy Godhead enclose everything within itself without limitation, and it exceeds everything. For no one could disperse its might or overpower it or complete it.

—Hildegard of Bingen, *Book of Divine Works*

He is beautiful without a blemish, great without quantity, good without need of qualification, eternal without the duration of time, strong without any weakness, living without touch of decay, true without deceit, present in all places, filling them without occupying them, existing in all things without occupying any space. There is no contradiction in his kindness, nor any defect in his wisdom.

—Mary of Agreda, *The Mystical City of God*

The Father dwells in inaccessible light, and God is spirit, and no one has ever seen God. Therefore He cannot be seen except in the Spirit because it is the Spirit that gives life; the flesh has nothing to offer.

—Francis of Assisi, *admonition*

We must believe the Deity to be not only almighty, but just, and good, and wise, and everything else that suggests excellence.

—Gregory of Nyssa, *The Great Catechism*

That Deity should be born in our nature, ought not reasonably to present any strangeness to the minds of those who do not take too narrow a view of things. For who, when he takes a survey of the universe is so simple as not to believe that there is Deity in everything, penetrating it, embracing it, and seated in it? For all things depend on Him who is nor can there be anything which has not its being in Him Who is.

—Gregory of Nyssa, *The Great Catechism*

That the omnipotence of the Divine nature should have had the strength to descend to the humiliation of humanity, furnishes a clearer proof of that omnipotence than even the greatness and supernatural character of the miracles.

—Gregory of Nyssa, *The Great Catechism*

It is difficult to conceive God but to define Him in words is an impossibility.

—Gregory of Nazianzus, *theological oration*

The Divine Nature cannot be apprehended by human reason, and that we cannot even represent to ourselves all its greatness.

—Gregory of Nazianzus, *theological oration*

Compared with their Author, the sun and moon are but a fly and an ant. The whole universe cannot give us a right idea of the greatness of God; and it is only by signs, weak and slight in themselves, often by the help of the smallest insects and of the least plants, that we raise ourselves to Him.

—Basil the Great, *homily on the Hexaemeron*

Yet the beholding of heaven and earth does not make us know God better than the attentive study of our being does; I am, says the Prophet, fearfully and wonderfully made; that is to say, in observing myself I have known Thy infinite wisdom.

—Basil the Great, *homily on the Hexaemeron*

O my God, Thy people know Thee not! Oh, if they only knew Thee, Thou wouldst be loved still more. If they knew Thy Wisdom, Thy omnipotence, Thy goodness, Thy beauty, and all Thy divine attributes, all Thy people would be as the seraphim, afire with divine love.

—Anthony Mary Claret, *autobiography*

He is encompassed like treasure by the earthen vessel of our tabernacle, the Same Who is in every respect both incomprehensible and uncircumscribed. Without form or shape He takes form in us who are small, He Who fills all things uncircumscribably and transcends both grandeur and plentitude.

—Symeon the New Theologian, *Ethical Discourses*

Union with God

There is no way to union with God without annihilating the memory as to all forms. This union cannot be wrought without a complete separation of the memory from all forms that are not God.

—John of the Cross, *The Ascent of Mount Carmel*

To understand the nature of this union, one should first know that God sustains every soul and dwells in it substantially, even though it may be that of the greatest sinner in the world. This union between God and creatures always exists. By it he conserves their being so that if the union should end they would immediately be annihilated and cease to exist.

—John of the Cross, *The Ascent of Mount Carmel*

A soul makes room for God by wiping away all the smudges and smears of creatures, by uniting its will perfectly to God's; for to love is to labor to divest and deprive oneself for God of all that is not God. When this is done the soul will be illumined by and transformed in God.

—John of the Cross, *The Ascent of Mount Carmel*

For if in any way the will can comprehend God and be united with him, it is through love and not through any gratification of the appetite.

—John of the Cross, *letter*

Wherefore, in order to become united with Him, a man must empty and strip himself of every inordinate affection of desire and pleasure for all that can be distinctly enjoyed, whether it be high or low, temporal or spiritual, to the end that the soul may be purged and clean from all inordinate desires, joys, and pleasures whatsoever and may thus be wholly occupied, with all its affections, in loving God.

—John of the Cross, *letter to a religious penitent, 1589*

In order for the soul to succeed in reaching God and to become united with him, it must have the mouth of its will opened to God alone, and freed from any morsel of desire, to the end that God may satisfy and fill it with his love and sweetness.

—John of the Cross, *letter to a religious penitent, 1589*

When a man's senses are perfectly united to God, then what God has said is somehow mysteriously clarified. But where there is no union of this kind, then it is extremely difficult to speak of God.

—John Climacus, *The Ladder of Divine Ascent*

The interior of my soul is like a large and magnificent world in which God and I live. Except for God, no one is allowed there. At the beginning of this life with God, I was dazzled and overcome with awe. His radiance blinded me, and I thought He was not in my heart; and yet those were the moments when God was working in my soul. Love was becoming purer and stronger, and the Lord brought my will into the closest union with His own holy Will. No one will understand what I experience in that splendid palace of my soul where I abide constantly with my Beloved. No exterior thing hinders my union with God.

—Faustina Kowalska, *Divine Mercy in My Soul*

A soul that is united with God must be prepared for great and hard-fought battles.

—Faustina Kowalska, *Divine Mercy in My Soul*

This union of my soul with God is my wealth in poverty and joy in deepest afflictions.

—Elizabeth Seton, *Collected Writings*

A true philosopher is one who perceives in created things their spiritual Cause, or who knows created things through knowing their Cause, having attained a union with God that transcends the intellect and a direct, unmediated faith. He does not simply learn about divine things, but actually experiences them.

—Gregory of Sinai, *The Philokalia*

No unity with God is possible except by an exceedingly great love.

—Dimitri of Rostov, *The Inner Closet of the Heart*

Let him who wishes to contemplate the invisible things of God in the unity of his essence fix his attention first on being itself, and let him see that being itself is so certain in itself that it cannot be thought not to be.

—Bonaventure, *The Soul's Journey Into God*

I have no longer either soul or heart; but my soul and heart are those of my Beloved.

—Catherine of Genoa, *Life and Doctrine*

The principle means of union with God must be found in the reception of the sacraments and in prayer.

—Francis de Sales, *letter to a married woman, 1604*

The closer I am to the embrace of God, the sweeter is the kiss of God. The more lovingly we both embrace, the more difficult it is for me to depart. The more God gives me, the more I can give and still have more. The more quickly I leave the Lord, the sooner I must return. The more the fire burns, the more my own light increases. The more I am consumed by love, the brighter I shall shine! The greater my praise of God, greater my desire is to love the Lord.

—Mechtilde of Magdeburg, *The Flowing Light of the Godhead*

For if you can make your life as close to the passionless calm of the divine nature as possible, then your soul will be restored to the image of God. And if you can achieve this similarity to God, you will also have attained the image of the divine life which lasts for ever in its eternal happiness.

—Basil the Great, *On Ascetic Discourse*

What God is like in his own nature and in his own being no one on earth has ever discovered nor will ever be able to discover. We shall only discover this when what is similar to God, namely, our soul, is united to the Supreme Being—only when the image attains to the prototype to which it is straining.

For the time being, all we can possibly grasp is a mere feeble reflection, a faint ray of the great Light.

—Gregory of Nazianzus, *oration*

Voice of God

When . . . we hear with the inner ear some part of the speech of God, we approximate to the angels. But in this work I need not labor to give an account of the ways in which God speaks. For either the unchangeable Truth speaks directly to the mind of the rational creature in some indescribable way, or speaks through the changeable creature, either presenting spiritual images to our spirit, or bodily voices to our bodily sense.

—Augustine, *The City of God*

God speaks to us through preachers and through readings, by all his creatures and by his precepts. He wishes to be heard especially by those he has received into his service. They do not please him when they are preoccupied with frivolous thoughts, with their own inclinations or their good friends, particularly on the mornings of Communion days and during the half hour for preparation in the evening. This recollection is very necessary after recreation and I do not see that it is preserved.

—Marguerite Bourgeoys, *Autographic Writings*

It is true that the voice of God, having once fully penetrated the heart, becomes strong as the tempest and loud as the thunder; but before reaching the heart it is weak as a light breath which scarcely agitates the air. It shrinks from noise, and is silent amid agitation.

—Ignatius of Loyola, *Spiritual Exercises*

Word of God

Always give good heed to the Word of God, whether you hear or read it in private, or hearken to it when publicly preached: listen with attention and reverence; seek to profit by it, and do not let the precious words fall unheeded; receive them into your heart as a costly balsam; imitate the Blessed Virgin who "kept all the sayings concerning her son 'in her heart.' " And remember that according as we hearken to and receive God's words, we will hearken and receive our supplications.

—Francis de Sales, *The Devout Life*

When we think of God's word we do not deem the Word to be something unsubstantial, or the result of instruction, nor an utterance of the voice, not what after being uttered passes away, nor what is subject to essentially self-subsisting, with a faculty of will ever-working, all-powerful.

—Gregory of Nyssa, *The Great Catechism*

The Word of God is a substantial and personified being, Himself both God and the Word; Who has embraced in Himself all creative power, or rather Who is that very power with an impulse to all good; Who works out effectually whatever He will by having a power concurrent with His will; Whose will and work is the life of all things that exist; by Whom, too, man was brought into being and adorned with the highest excellences after the fashion of Deity.

—Gregory of Nyssa, *The Great Catechism*

For God's love and love of God, see LOVE.

For God's will, see WILL.

See also: FORGIVENESS; JUDGMENT; JUSTICE; MERCY; PROVIDENCE.

Godliness

For the method of godliness consists of these two things, pious doctrines, and virtuous practice: and neither are the doctrines acceptable to God apart from good works, nor does God accept the works which are not perfected with pious doctrines.

—Cyril of Jerusalem, *Catecheses*

Goodness

Everything—whether it has knowledge or not—tends to good. . . . Therefore, since all natural things have been directed by a certain natural inclination toward their ends by the first mover, God, whatever is willed or intended by God is that to which everything is naturally inclined. But inasmuch as God's will can have no other end than himself, and he is essentially goodness, everything must be naturally inclined to good.

—Thomas Aquinas, *On Truth*

For needful it was that neither His light should be unseen, nor His glory without witness, nor His goodness unenjoyed, nor that any other quality observed in the Divine nature should in any case lie idle, with none to share it or enjoy it. If, therefore, man comes to his birth upon these conditions, namely to be a partaker of the good things in God, necessarily he is framed of such a kind as to be adapted to the participation of such good.

—Gregory of Nyssa, *The Great Catechism*

That the life of man is at present subject to abnormal conditions is no proof that man was not created in the midst of good. For since man is the work of God, Who through His goodness brought this creature into being, no one could reasonably suspect that he, of whose constitution goodness is the cause, was created by his Maker in the midst of evil.

—Gregory of Nyssa, *The Great Catechism*

He who is good by nature does nothing except good.

—Gregory of Nyssa, *Commentary on the Inscriptions of the Psalms*

For he who is good to both good and wicked is better than he who is good only to the good. And he who is good to the wicked by both punishing and sparing them is better than he who is good to the wicked only by punishing them.

—Anselm, *Proslogion*

If one does not know what is better, one must reflect, consider and seek advice, because one must not act with an uncertain conscience. When uncertain, say to yourself: "Whatever I do will be good. I have the intention of doing good." The Lord God accepts what we consider good, and the Lord God also accepts and considers it as good. One should not worry if, after some time, one sees that these things are not good. God looks at the intention with which we begin, and will reward us accordingly. This is a principle we ought to follow.

—Faustina Kowalska, *Divine Mercy in My Soul*

Gossip

We must not mimic outsiders, nor talk about families and criticize them, their households, their reputations, etc.

—Marguerite Bourgeoys, *Autographic Writings*

When you hear ill of anyone, refute the accusation if you can in justice do so; if not, apologize for the accused on account of his intentions . . . and thus gently check the conversation, and if you can, mention something else favorable to the accused.

—Francis de Sales, *The Devout Life*

The tongue of the scandalmonger is like the worm which gnaws at the good fruit—that is, the best actions that people do—and tries to turn them all to bad account. The tongue of the scandalmonger is a grub which taints the most beautiful of the flowers and upon them leaves behind it the disgusting trace of its own slime.

—John Baptiste Marie Vianney, *sermon*

There is yet another form of wrongdoing which is all the more deplorable in that it is more common, and that is licentious talk. There is nothing more abominable, my dear breathren, nothing more horrible than such talk. . . . It outrages God, it scandalizes our neighbor.

—John Baptiste Marie Vianney, *sermon*

Very often it requires only one immodest or unseemly word to start a thousand evil thoughts, a thousand shameful desires, perhaps even to cause a fall into an infinite number of sins and to bring innocent souls evil of which they had been happily ignorant.

—John Baptiste Marie Vianney, *sermon*

One should not speak idle talk, for it is neither useful to those who listen, nor necessary or permissible with regard to God.

—Basil the Great, *letter to Gregory of Nazianzus*

Let us clothe ourselves in a mutual tolerance of one another's views, cultivating humility and self-restraint, avoiding all gossip and backbiting, and earning our justification by deeds and not words.

—Clement of Rome, *first epistle to the Corinthians*

In your conversations, be careful not to give pain to any companion, either present or absent, by turning him into ridicule. You may say: *I do it through jest;* but, such jests are contrary to charity.

—Alphonsus Liguori, *sermon*

Joy in hearing useless things gives direct rise to distraction of the imagination, gossiping, envy, uncertain judgments, and wandering thoughts, from which flow many other pernicious kinds of harm.

—John of the Cross, *The Ascent of Mount Carmel*

There is life, but there is also death in the tongue. Sometimes we kill with the tongue: we commit real murders.

—Faustina Kowalska, *Divine Mercy in My Soul*

No one should speak deprecatingly about other countries or provinces, as this usually causes no small trouble.

—Vincent de Paul, *Common Rules or Constitutions of the Congregation of the Mission*

Those who are spoken badly of in a frivolous and idle way will have a bigger reward, but those who speak badly of them will have a sentence and a punishment that's more grievous.

—John Chrysostom, *homily*

Excuse thyself from talking many idle words: neither backbite, nor lend a willing ear to backbiters; but rather be prompt to prayer.

—Cyril of Jerusalem, *Catecheses*

Gossip is a disease that infects and poisons the apostolate. It goes against charity, means a waste of energy, takes away peace and destroys one's union with God.

—Josemaría Escrivá, *The Way*

See also: SLANDER

Grace

Only the power of grace can uproot and form fallen nature anew; it happens from within, never from without.

—Edith Stein, *Essays on Woman*

Only by the means of grace can nature be liberated from its dross, restored to its purity, and made free to receive divine life. And this divine life itself is the inner driving power from which acts of love come forth.

—Edith Stein, *Essays on Woman*

There is nothing better in the world than to be in the grace of God.

—Josemaría Escrivá, *The Way*

With God's grace, you have to tackle and carry out the impossible, because anybody can do what is possible.

—Josemaría Escrivá, *The Forge*

God always gives sufficient grace to whoever is willing to receive it. This is an established truth and all theologians are in agreement with it.

—Francis de Sales, *Oeuvres*

It is very difficult to say what initiates the fall of sinners. It is nevertheless very certain, as theologians say, that it is not grace that fails them, but rather it is they who fail grace.

—Francis de Sales, *Oeuvres*

A soul in a state of grace attracts the looks and ravishes the heart of God.

—Ignatius of Loyola, *Spiritual Exercises*

When you are in a state of grace, you are free.

—Ignatius of Loyola, *Spiritual Exercises*

Grace increases in proportion as man makes use of it. Hence it is evident that God gives man from day to day all that he needs, no more and no less, and to each according to his condition and capacity.

—Catherine of Genoa, *Life and Doctrine*

A soul in the state of grace need fear nothing from devils, for they are so cowardly that they flee from the gaze of a child.

—Thérèse of Lisieux, *The Story of a Soul*

Oh, how contrary to human nature are the divine teachings! Without the help of grace, it would be impossible not only to follow them but to even understand them.

—Thérèse of Lisieux, *The Story of a Soul*

Great graces are often attached to what seems trifling.

—Margaret Mary Alacoque, *Life and Writings of St. Margaret Mary*

Grace does five things: first it heals our soul, so that secondly we will do good, thirdly actually do the good we will, fourthly persevere in doing good, and finally come to glory.

—Thomas Aquinas, *Summa Theologica*

Man cannot rise from sin without the help of grace.

—Thomas Aquinas, *Summa Theologica*

Grace makes the soul like to God.

—Thomas Aquinas, *Summa Theologica*

Our parents begot us by blood and the will of the flesh (John 1:13), but priests make us children of God; blessed regeneration, true freedom, and adoption according to grace.

—John Chrysostom, *letter to Basil the Great, 386*

A drop of grace filled all things with knowledge; through it miracles were wrought and sins forgiven.

—John Chrysostom, *On Psalm 44*

Jesus is in the Church as the first fountain of grace; the Blessed Virgin is there as the channel through which graces are given to the faithful. The Saints are the streams which contain each one its portion of this same grace. All graces are in the fountain as in their prime source.

—John Eudes, *The Holy Name of Mary*

In order to obtain God's graces by prayer, it is necessary, first, to take away sin; for God does not hear obstinate sinners. For example: if a person entertains hatred toward another, and wishes to take revenge, God does not hear his prayer.

—Alphonsus Liguori, *sermon*

You have united the depth of my evil to the precious gold of your love so that the jewels of your grace might be encased in me.

—Gertrude the Great, *The Herald of Divine Love*

Let us meekly recognize our weakness, knowing that we cannot stand for the twinkling of an eye except with the protection of grace, and let us reverently cling to and trust only in God.

—Julian of Norwich, *Showings*

Grace was sent out to save nature and destroy sin and bring it back again to the blessed place from which it came, which is God, with more nobility and honor by the powerful operation of grace.

—Julian of Norwich, *Showings*

Grace builds up everything, because grace is always present in believers. Those who commit themselves irrevocably to grace, will pass under its guidance, and it shapes and forms them in a way known only to itself.

—Theophan the Recluse, *letter*

He who bears grace in his heart, surrenders himself wholly to the action of grace, and it is grace that acts in him. For him this truth is more evident, not only than any mathematical truth, but even than any experience in his exterior life, because he has already ceased to live outside himself and is wholly concentrated within. He has now only one care, always to be faithful to the grace present within him.

—Theophan the Recluse, *The Fruits of Prayer*

If you fail to receive grace it is because of your lack of faith and your negligence; if you find it again it is because of your faith and your diligence.

—Gregory of Sinai, *The Philokalia*

People who have received grace are as if impregnated and with child by the Holy Spirit; but they may abort the divine seed through sinning, or divorce themselves from God through intercourse with the enemy lurking within them.

—Gregory of Sinai, *The Philokalia*

As a corpse which can have no feeling or movement of itself, but only when it is moved and lifted by others, so those, who are drowned in the stream of disordinate love of the world, are dead to grace.

—Catherine of Siena, *Dialogue*

Be attentive to the voice of Grace.

—Elizabeth Seton, *Collected Writings*

The Lord God grants His graces in two ways: by inspiration and by enlightenment.

If we ask God for a grace, He will give it to us; but let us be willing to accept it. And in order to accept it, self-denial is needed.

—Faustina Kowalska, *Divine Mercy in My Soul*

Invoke the intercession of the angels and saints to obtain grace from the Lord.

—Mary of Agreda, *The Mystical City of God*

And what is grace? The Son of God, whom the Father sent into the world, not so that He might judge the world, but that the world might be saved by Him (John 3:17).

—Elisabeth of Schönau, *Third Book of Visions*

Cleanse thy vessel, that thou mayest receive grace more abundantly.

—Cyril of Jerusalem, *Catecheses*

For it is of the Lord to vouch for a continuance of heavenly sacraments, and to promise that the grace of spiritual joy shall not fail, to grant the defenses of life, the seals of faith, the gifts of virtues.

—Ambrose, *Concerning Widowhood*

It is not of the waters but of grace that a man is cleansed.

—Ambrose, *On the Mysteries*

He Who Himself was the light of the world granted to His disciples to be the light of the world through grace.

—Ambrose, *Concerning Repentence*

Nor it is not a single but a twofold grace that every one who believes should also suffer for the Lord Jesus. He, then, who believes receives his grace, but he receives a second, if his faith be crowned by suffering.

—Ambrose, *Concerning Repentence*

The desire for divine Wisdom must indeed be a great grace from God because it is the reward for the faithful observance of his commandments.

—Louis de Montfort, *The Love of Eternal Wisdom*

When Mary has taken root in a soul she produces in it wonders of grace which only she can produce; for she alone is the fruitful virgin who never had and never will have her equal in purity and fruitfulness.

—Louis de Montfort, *Treatise on True Devotion to the Blessed Virgin*

Now everything from God reveals grace to us and brings it by different means to the eyes of those who contemplate the divine wonders on high. Grace is not manifested by one means only, but it variously deals with the circumstances into which we have fallen due to our inclination toward evil.

—Gregory of Nyssa, *Commentary on the Inscriptions of the Psalms*

The person failing to comprehend [God's] grace is blind. After receiving a pearl, he throws it away as a common pebble, thereby freely depriving himself of its possession by his ignorance of the beautiful.

—Gregory of Nyssa, *Commentary on the Inscriptions of the Psalms*

Nothing whatever is more profitable for the soul which has chosen to study God's law day and night than searching the divine scriptures. The meaning of the Holy Spirit's grace is hidden in them. It fills a man's spiritual perception with every pleasure, lifts it entirely from earthly things and the lowliness of what is visible, and makes it both angelic in form and a sharer in the angels' very life.

—Symeon the New Theologian, *Ethical Discourses*

Gratitude

If a soul is naturally loving and grateful, the memory of a favor received makes it turn to God more than all the tortures of hell that it can picture to itself. At least, that was certainly the case with me, wicked though I am.

—Teresa of Ávila, *Life*

I thank my parents, companions and friends for all the charity they have shown me in putting up with all my defects, and I thank them for all the favors and all the assistance which in their goodness they have given me. . . . I ask them to continue to give me the charity of their prayers, and when I am separated from them, I firmly hope that I will see them again one day in Paradise.

—Joseph Cafasso, *prayer on preparation for death*

Greed

We are tempted to commit sins of greed on the mountain of success in our state in life, in the glory that comes from our successes. Note that greed is not restricted to money, but also includes a desire for honors and places of distinction. The more a greedy person possesses, the more does he strive to ascend. And so it happens that when a greedy, ambitious person falls, his fall is disastrous.

—Anthony of Padua, *Sermones*

God, who cannot lie, promises that he will return to the almsgiver treasure in heaven and a hundredfold besides and life everlasting, but the greedy man is fearful and cannot be brought to believe and prefers to hide his treasure where rust corrodes and thieves break in and steal rather than lay up his treasure in heaven where a thief cannot creep up nor rust corrode.

—Robert Bellarmine, *The Mind's Ascent to God by the Ladder of Created Things*

Experience indeed teaches that possessions heaped up by greedy rich men go to their prodigal heirs, who quickly run through what their greedy parents gathered. Meanwhile, the sin of avarice remains and will remain forever, and the worm of conscience will not die nor will the fire of hell be extinguished.

—Robert Bellarmine, *The Mind's Ascent to God by the Ladder of Created Things*

But we call the greedy poor, who are always craving and always wanting. For they may possess ever so great an amount of money; but whatever be the abundance of that, they are not able but to want.

—Augustine, *The City of God*

There are two kinds of avarice. One is temporal, and it is that by which we are avid to acquire wealth, honors and the goods of this life. There are many such avaricious people in the world. . . . There is another kind of avarice which clings to what it has and is unwilling to part with it for anything. This is highly dangerous and steals in everywhere, even into religion and spiritual things.

—Francis de Sales, *Oeuvres*

No matter how many such things one has, he is always lusting after what he has not; never at peace, he sighs for new possessions. Discontented, he spends himself in fruitless toil; and finds only weariness in the evanescent and unreal pleasures of the world. In his greediness, he counts all that he has clutched as nothing in comparison with what is beyond his grasp, and loses all pleasure in his actual possessions by longing after what he has not, yet covets. No man can ever hope to own all things.

—Bernard of Clairvaux, *On Loving God*

The pretext of almsgiving is the start of avarice, and the finish is detestation of the poor. The collector is stirred by charity, but, when the money is in, the grip tightens.

—John Climacus, *The Ladder of Divine Ascent*

Guard against all avarice. Indeed, it acts in such a way that your works will be deceitful and you will defraud your neighbors and cheat and perjure the name of the Lord and gather unjust wealth, which plunges its owners into ruin.

—Elisabeth of Schönau, *The Book of the Ways of God*

Whoever craves money loses the faith, whoever collects money squanders the grace.

—Maximus of Turin, *sermon*

The person who is avaricious always takes advantage of someone else; he feasts himself on others' downfall.

—Maximus of Turin, *sermon*

Grief

To grieve to excess over the failings for which we must render an account is neither safe nor necessary. It is more likely to be damaging or even destructive. Still worse is it then and perfectly useless to wear oneself out grieving over others' misdeeds. Above all it is playing into the hands of the devil, and harmful to the soul.

—John Chrysostom, *letter to Olympias, 404*

It is a loving act to show sadness when our dear ones are torn from us, but it is a holy act to be joyful through hope and trust in the promises of God. . . . Thankful joy is more acceptable to God than long and querulous grief.

—Paulinus of Nola, *letter*

Tears bestowed on the dead are especially vain—they do nothing for the one whom God has taken, and they oppress the one left behind. . . . Granted our love may weep for a time, but our faith must ever rejoice. We should long for those who have been sent before us, but we should not lose hope of gaining them back.

—Paulinus of Nola, *letter*

H

Happiness

Above all, I beg of you to always be gay, joyful and happy, for this is the true mark of the spirit of God, who wishes that we should serve him in peace and contentment; do not be uneasy or anxious, but do all things with liberty of mind and in the presence of God.

—Margaret Mary Alacoque, *Life and Writings of St. Margaret Mary*

The word "beatitude," or "happiness," indicates clearly what it is, for it signifies a place of consolation where all joys and blessings are found and experienced.

—Francis de Sales, *Oeuvres*

Neither wealth, nor honors, nor vanity can make a man happy during his life on earth, but only attachment to the service of God, when we are fortunate enough to realize that and to carry it out properly.

—John Baptiste Marie Vianney, *sermon*

Only the service of God will console us and make us happy in the midst of all the miseries of life.

—John Baptiste Marie Vianney, *sermon*

Do you want to be happy, my friends? Fix your eyes on heaven; it is there that your hearts will find that which will satisfy them completely.

—John Baptiste Marie Vianney, *sermon*

To think ourselves imperfect, and others perfect—that is happiness. That creatures should recognize that we are without virtue takes nothing from us, makes us no poorer; it is they who by this lose interior joy; for there is nothing sweeter than to think well of our neighbor.

—Thérèse of Lisieux, *Counsels and Reminisces*

Experience taught me that the only way to get happiness in this world is to hide oneself away and remain in ignorance of all created things.

—Thérèse of Lisieux, *The Story of a Soul*

Real happiness will come, not in gratifying our desires or in gaining transient pleasures, but in accomplishing God's will for us: even as we pray every day: "Thy will be done in earth as it is in heaven."

—Bernard of Clairvaux, *On Loving God*

Happy the soul which reclines upon the breast of Christ and takes its rest within the arms of the Word. How grateful we should be for that grace.

—Bernard of Clairvaux, *On the Canticle of Canticles*

There is a joy that is not granted to the wicked, but only to those who worship you for your own sake, and for whom you yourself are joy. This is the happy life, to rejoice over you, to you, and because of you: this it is, and there is no other.

—Augustine, *Confessions*

Joy in the truth is the happy life. This is joy in you who are the truth, O God, "my light," "the salvation of my countenance, my God." This happy life all men desire; this life which alone is happy all men desire; all men desire joy in the truth.

—Augustine, *Confessions*

Earthly happiness, like smoke, gradually fades away until it is no more seen. The years we pass here are but as a brief dream, from which we wake to find that it has all been an illusion.

—John of Ávila, *letter to a widow, 1568*

Since happiness is nothing other than the enjoyment of the highest good and since the highest good is above, no one can be made happy unless he rises above himself, not by an ascent of the body, but of the heart. But we cannot rise above ourselves unless a higher power lifts us up.

—Bonaventure, *The Soul's Journey Into God*

But happiness I had only in terms of the best and ultimate end. Therefore human desire seeks nothing except the highest good or what leads to or has some likeness to it.

—Bonaventure, *The Soul's Journey Into God*

My goal is God . . . and my happiness is in accomplishing His will, and nothing in the world can disturb this happiness for me: no power, no force of any kind.

—Faustina Kowalska, *Divine Mercy in My Soul*

It is well known that one of the greatest obstacles, which hinders a man from attaining his supreme happiness and good, is the evil inclination of the heart and the difficulty and disinclination experienced in doing what is right. Were it not for this, it would be a very easy thing to run in the path of virtue and to attain the end for which he was created.

—Peter of Alcantara, *Treatise on Prayer & Meditation*

This is the ground and foundation of our happiness—a becoming less and an annihilation of oneself. Whoever wants to become something he is not, must of necessity become less of that which he is.

—Henry Suso, *sermon*

The heavenly kingdom will have the most, or rather all, of the good things that can be desired. Everybody who lives in that kingdom will be happy—happiness is the sum total from adding all good things together.

—Robert Bellarmine, *The Mind's Ascent to God by the Ladder of Created Things*

Oh, what happiness has a missionary who makes it his chief endeavor to render himself pleasing to God, who strives to rid himself of all impediments and to acquire what he lacks! This labor makes us pleasing to God.

—Vincent de Paul, *Conferences*

Perfect action itself is happiness. The highest object, however, is God. But the most perfect permanent disposition is charity . . . and therefore it is written that God is the end of the righteous will as is charity and good delight, and happiness; yet so that God is the ultimate end with happiness completing charity, and delight as a subordinate end joined to the ultimate end.

—Thomas Aquinas, *Commentary on Sentences*

For happiness is a word for the ultimate end of man and his highest good. And the end and the good are the will's objective.

—Thomas Aquinas, *Debated Questions*

Now, the end of our desire is God. So the act by which we are primarily united to him is originally and essentially our happiness. But through the act of the intellect we are primarily united to him, and so the vision of God, which is an intellectual act, is essentially and originally our happiness.

—Thomas Aquinas, *Debated Questions*

Man's beatitude or happiness consists in this: to see God through God's essence, although a man may be quite remote from God in the perfection of his happiness; for God possesses this happiness through his own nature, but man has it by a participation in the divine light.

—Thomas Aquinas, *Summa Theologica*

Happiness is another name for God.

—Thomas Aquinas, *Summa Theologica*

Natural wealth, like food and drink, clothing and transport, housing and the like, doesn't suffice to make us happy. Such things are only means of supporting human life: man is wealth's goal rather than wealth man's.

—Thomas Aquinas, *Summa Theologica*

Nothing is more consoling than to know divine Wisdom. Happy are those who listen to him; happier still are those who desire him and seek him; but happiest of all are those who keep his laws. Their hearts will be filled with that infinite consolation which is the joy and happiness of the eternal Father and the glory of the angels.

—Louis de Montfort, *The Love of Eternal Wisdom*

Just actions are truly the first steps towards a happy life.

—Basil the Great, *homily on the Hexaemeron*

The goal of a life in accord with virtue is happiness.

—Gregory of Nyssa, *Commentary on the Inscriptions of the Psalms*

If we feel we are beloved sons of our Heavenly Father, as indeed we are, how can we fail to be happy all the time?

—Josemaría Escrivá, *The Forge*

Others may look for happiness from their riches or their talents; they may rely upon the innocence of their lives, the rigor of their penance, the number of their good works, or the fervor of their prayers; but for me, O Lord, my confidence shall be my confidence itself.

—Claude de la Colombière, *sermon*

Where there is no love, there is no delight. Finally, the greater the love for the highest good, the greater the delight and the greater the happiness.

—Aelred of Rievaulx, *Mirror of Charity*

The blind perversity of us miserable humans is lamentable. Although we desire happiness ardently, not only do we not do those things by which we may obtain our desire, but rather, with contrary disaffection, we take steps to add to our misery. In my opinion, we would never do this if a false image of happiness were not deceiving us or a semblance of real misery frightening us off from happiness.

—Aelred of Rievaulx, *Mirror of Charity*

Harmony

A pure and simple realization: beings of opposite natures can unite in a concord of harmony.

—Athanasius, *Against the Pagans*

But in the universe there is no disorder, only order; no disharmony, only concord. So we need to reflect: there has always been the Lord to unite so many different elements and to make of them a complete harmony.

—Athanasius, *Against the Pagans*

To realize the true meaning of Brotherhood it should be written not on the walls, but in the heart. There is a beautiful give and take in the different relationships of life where all are united in one great love in him who sacrificed his life for us, our Lord and Savior Jesus Christ. If only everyone could feel this, how perfect would be the harmony on earth.

—Théophane Vénard, *letter to his brothers, 1851*

Harmony is the excellence of our actions, and in heaven our actions will not disturb harmony but will perfect it in such a way that our actions will not be detrimental to each other, but each will aid the other to continue and persevere for the glory of the pure love of God, which will render them capable of subsisting together.

—Francis de Sales, *Oeuvres*

Haste

The hasty, while they forestall the time of good deeds, pervert their merit, and often fall into what is evil, while failing together to discern what is good. Such persons look not at all to see what things they are doing when they do them, but for the most part, when they are done, become aware that they ought not to have done them.

—Gregory the Great, *The Book of Pastoral Rule*

Hate

Whoever hates his brother is in darkness.

—Thomas Aquinas, *Summa Theologica*

For no one ever undermines those whom they love, and belittling others is the firstborn son of hatred.

—Columban, *sermon*

To pay back hatred with love is the summit of perfect love.

—Valerian, *homily*

Hatreds die when an injury is not pondered; anger has no power if the voice of one person is lacking in a quarrel. Consequently, a double victory awaits patience: a man has overcome the impulses of his own temper and restrained the conduct of another.

—Valerian, *homily*

For as long as we live in hatred for our neighbors we are hating our own selves, because hatred deprives us of divine charity. How stupidly blind not to see that with the sword of hatred for our neighbors we are killing ourselves!

—Catherine of Siena, *letter to Charles V, king of France, 1376*

We must love our enemies and do good to those who hate us.

—Francis of Assisi, *saying*

Sinners continually hate and persecute the elect, openly and secretly. The elect are a burden to them. They despise them, criticize them, ridicule them, insult them, rob them, deceive them, impoverish them, hunt them down and trample them into the dust; while they themselves are making fortunes, enjoying themselves, getting good positions for themselves, enriching themselves, rising to power and living in comfort.

—Louis de Montfort, *Treatise on True Devotion to the Blessed Virgin*

Has so-and-so slandered you? Don't give in to hatred. If you hate the slanderer, you are hating a person and therefore breaking the commandment to love. The evil done with words you are now doing by your deeds. On the other hand, if you keep the commandments, you are helping the other as much as you can to become free from this sin.

—Maximus the Confessor, *Centuries on Charity*

Healing

The Lord did not come to make a display. He came to heal and to teach suffering men. For one who wanted to make a display the thing would have been just to appear and dazzle the beholders. But for Him who came to heal and to teach the way was not merely to dwell here, but to put Himself at the disposal of those who needed Him, and to be manifested according as they could bear it, not vitiating the value of the Divine appearing by exceeding their capacity to receive it.

—Athanasius, *On the Incarnation*

And be not afraid that there will be any delay in healing. He who is healed by Christ has no hindrances. You must use the remedy which you have received; and as soon as He has given the command, the blind man sees, the paralytic walks, the dumb speaks, the deaf hears, she that has a fever ministers, the lunatic is delivered. And do you, then, who ever after an unseemly fashion languish for desire of anything, entreat the Lord . . . and fear no delay.

—Ambrose, *Concerning Widowhood*

Health

Two things here on earth are essential: health and a friend. They are the two things most to be prayed for. Woe to the person who despises them.

Health and friendship are natural gifts. God has made human beings for living—hence health—and for not living alone—hence the search for friendship.

—Augustine, *Sermon Denis*

When our purpose is to serve our Lord better, it may be good to ask health of him as the one who can give it to us. Yet it must be done only on this condition, that it be his will.

—Francis de Sales, *Oeuvres*

Heart

He [God] is so close, in fact, that he even hears the desires of our hearts.

—Vincent Ferrer, *sermon*

The heart is a small vessel, but all things are contained in it; God is there, the angels are there, and there also is life and the Kingdom, the heavenly cities and the treasures of grace.

—Dimitri of Rostov, *The Inner Closet of the Heart*

Into every duty a God-fearing heart must be put, a heart constantly permeated by the thought of God; and this will be the door through which the soul will enter into an active life.

—Theophan the Recluse, *letter*

To be sober means not to let the heart cling to anything except God. Cleaving to other things makes the soul drunk, and it begins to do quite unaccountable things. To be vigilant means to watch carefully, lest something evil springs up in the heart.

—Theophan the Recluse, *The Fruits of Prayer*

As the son of grace touches the heart, the seed of prayer is sown there, and there straightway follows the turning of mind and heart towards God. Thoughts of God then follow in due course.

—Theophan the Recluse, *Fruits of Prayer*

When we strive with diligent sobriety to keep watch over our rational faculties, to control and correct them, how else can we succeed in this task except by controlling our mind, which is dispersed abroad through the senses, and bringing it back to the world within, into the heart itself, which is the storehouse of all our thoughts?

—Gregory Palamas, *The Art of Prayer*

The most important work that a spiritual wrestler can do, is to enter within the heart, there to fight Satan; to hate and repel the thoughts that he inspires and to wage war upon him.

—Marcarius of Egypt, *homily*

The heart rules over the whole human organism, and when grace takes possession of the pastures of the heart, it reigns over all a man's thoughts and members. For the intellect and all the thoughts of the soul are located there.

—Gregory Palamas, *In Defense of Those Who Devoutly Practice a Life of Stillness*

The heart is the first organ in the human body to be formed. The heart symbolizes humility, for it is in the heart that this virtue has its principal seat: "Learn from me," says the Lord, "for I am gentle and humble of heart."

—Anthony of Padua, *Sermones*

The deeper the roots of humility are embedded in the heart, the higher rises the edifice of good deeds.

—Anthony of Padua, *Sermones*

Do you suppose that, because we cannot hear Him, He is silent? He speaks clearly to the heart when we beg Him from our hearts to do so.

—Teresa of Ávila, *The Way of Perfection*

The only hard heart is one which is not aghast at itself because it feels nothing. What is a hard heart? It is one which is not torn by regret nor softened by devotion nor moved by prayers. It does not yield to threats and is hardened by scourging. It is ungrateful for benefits and heedless of advice.

—Robert Bellarmine, *The Mind's Ascent to God by the Ladder of Created Things*

Lift up the eyes of your heart to the sacred light, watch closely and see the glory and majesty of the Lord.

—Elisabeth of Schönau, *First Book of Visions*

Stand in the path of the vision you have chosen. Cleanse the eyes of your heart so that you may raise them in contemplation of the light in which life dwells, which is your redemption.

—Elisabeth of Schönau, *The Book of the Ways of God*

No heart ever achieved true pleasure or complete joy or constant peace of heart through a creature.

—Henry Suso, *Little Book of Eternal Wisdom*

Allegorically, the altar is the heart of every devout Christian, on which is offered to God the sacrifice of which David speaks: "The sacrifice to God is a contrite and humble heart." (Psalms 50:19) A contrite heart implies the turning away from sin, and in this way a sacrifice is offered to God on the altar of the heart.

—Vincent Ferrer, *sermon*

Blessed is the servant who safeguards the secrets of the Lord in his heart.

—Francis of Assisi, *saying*

Cleanness of heart is nothing less than the love and grace of God. The pure of heart are called blessed by our Savior (Matthew 5:8), and to call them blessed is equivalent to saying that they are taken with love, for blessedness is derived from nothing else but love.

—John of the Cross, *The Dark Night of the Soul*

For the heart has such power that it subjects all things to itself; this it does by desiring to be subject to nothing and losing all care so as to burn more in love.

—John of the Cross, *letter*

To possess God in all, you should possess nothing at all. For how can the heart that belongs to one belong completely to the other?

—John of the Cross, *letter*

Heaven

At present we have a human body but in the future we will have a celestial one, because there are human bodies and celestial bodies. There is a human splendor and a celestial splendor. The splendor that can be attained on earth is temporary and limited while that of heaven lasts forever, which will be shown when the corruptible becomes incorruptible and the mortal immortal.

—Basil the Great, *Consolation in Adversity*

We shall be excluded from the kingdom if our faults and sins remain with us. And we shall be excluded from the kingdom if we think that our omnipotent Lord is powerless. The only person who could think that God is powerless is someone who believed they could not be improved by him.

—Basil the Great, *Consolation in Adversity*

We claim that we desire the kingdom of heaven, and yet we neglect those things that ensure we could gain entry there. And although we make no efforts to fulfil the Lord's commands, we still imagine our foolishness that we will receive the same honors as those who have fought against sin right up to their death.

—Basil the Great, *The Greater Rules*

Our rest will be in Heaven. O Heaven, Heaven, whoever thinks on you will not suffer from weariness!

—Joseph Cafasso, *second panegyric on St. Joseph Cafasso by St. John Bosco*

I am every day more convinced that happiness in Heaven is for those who know how to be happy on earth.

—Josemaría Escrivá, *The Forge*

Enter eagerly into the treasure-house that lies within you, and so you will see the treasure-house of heaven: for the two are the same, and there is but one single entry into them both. The ladder that leads to the Kingdom is hidden within you, and is found in your own soul. Dive into yourself and in your soul you will discover the rungs by which to ascend.

—Isaac of Ninevah, *The Art of Prayer*

Do not imagine then, my dear souls, that our spirit will be dulled or drowsy by the abundance and joys of eternal happiness. Quite the contrary! It will be very alert and agile in its various activities.

—Francis de Sales, *Oeuvres*

There our good angels will give us greater joy than we can imagine when we recognize them and they speak to us so lovingly of the care they had for our salvation during our mortal life, reminding us of the holy inspirations they gave us, as a sacred milk which they drew from the breast of Divine Goodness, to attract us to seek the incomparable sweetness we now enjoy.

—Francis de Sales, *Oeuvres*

Not only will there be conversation between the Divine Persons, but also between God and us. And what will this divine conversation be? Oh, what will it be indeed! It will be such as no man may speak. It will be an intimate conversation so secret that no one will understand it except God and the soul with whom it is made. God will say to each of the blessed a word so special that there will be no other like it. But what will this word be? Oh, it will be the most loving word that one can ever imagine. Think of all the words which can be spoken to melt a heart, and the most affectionate names that can be heard, and then say that these words are meaningless in comparison with the word which God will give to each soul in heaven above.

—Francis de Sales, *Oeuvres*

In heaven we shall live and not be able to die, for we shall enjoy eternal glory, life that was purchased for us by our Savior's death. We shall possess it securely, without fear of losing it. Our Lord came as Savior to save us all from dying. For his death acquired for us that life in which we shall never die, the life of glory.

—Francis de Sales, *Oeuvres*

Life is passing, Eternity draws nigh; soon shall we live the very life of God. After having drunk deep at the fount of bitterness, our thirst will be quenched at the very source of all sweetness.

—Thérèse of Lisieux, *Counsels and Reminisces*

In heaven the good God will do all I wish, because I have never done my own will on earth.

—Thérèse of Lisieux, *Counsels and Reminisces*

For it is meet that those who are not satisfied by the present should be sustained by the thought of the future, and that the contemplation of eternal happiness should solace those who scorn to drink from the river of transitory joys.

—Bernard of Clairvaux, *On Loving God*

Where is the heaven that we do not see, before which all this which we see is earth? For this corporeal whole, since it is not everywhere whole, has in such wise received form and beauty in its least parts, all of which the very lowest is our earth, but to that heaven of heaven even our earth's heaven is but earth. Not unreasonably are both these great bodies but earth before the indescribable heaven which is the Lord's and not the sons' of men.

—Augustine, *Confessions*

I interpret the heaven of heaven as the intellectual heaven, where it belongs to intellect to know all at once, not in part, not in a dark manner, not through a glass, but as a whole, in plain sight, face to face, not this thing now and that thing then, but, as has been said, it knows all at once, without any passage of time.

—Augustine, *Confessions*

In heaven you have all you desire.

—Alphonsus Liguori, *sermon*

In Heaven, the soul is certain that she loves God, and that he loves her; she sees that the Lord embraces her with infinite love, and that this love shall not be dissolved for all eternity.

—Alphonsus Liguori, *sermon*

In beholding the beauty of God, the soul shall be so inflamed and so inebriated with divine love, that she shall remain happily lost in God; for she shall entirely forget herself, and for all eternity shall think only of loving and praising the immense good which she shall possess forever, without the fear of having it in her power ever to lose it.

—Alphonsus Liguori, *sermon*

There is no middle place: you must be forever happy in Heaven, or overwhelmed with despair in Hell.

—Alphonsus Liguori, *sermon*

Today I was in heaven, in spirit, and I saw its inconceivable beauties and the happiness that awaits us after death. I saw how all creatures give ceaseless praise and glory to God. I saw how great is happiness in God, which spreads to all creatures, making them happy; and then all the glory and praise which springs from this happiness returns to its source; and they enter into the depths of God, contemplating the inner life of God, the Father, the Son, and the Holy Spirit, whom they will never comprehend or fathom.

—Faustina Kowalska, *Divine Mercy in My Soul*

Looking up into the heavens we see there a veritable multitude of stars thrown across the empty spaces, whence a whole infinity of things might come down on us. How shall we not stand astonished and abashed at seeing the immensity of heaven, and, what greater still, that of the Sovereign Lord who made it?

—Peter of Alcantara, *Treatise on Prayer & Meditation*

And what can one say of all the other blessings of heaven? There, will be health, and no sickness; liberty, and no servitude; beauty, and no unsightliness; immortality, and no decay; abundance, and no want; repose, and no cares; security, and no dread; knowledge, and no error; satiety, and no feelings of revulsion; joy, and no sorrow; honor, and no contention.

—Peter of Alcantara, *Treatise on Prayer & Meditation*

But, my soul, if your faith is strong and vigilant, you cannot deny that after this life, which flits away like a shadow, if you remain firm in faith, hope, and love, you will see God clearly and truly as he is in himself and you will possess him and enjoy him far better and more intimately than you now enjoy created things.

—Robert Bellarmine, *The Mind's Ascent to God by the Ladder of Created Things*

The angel of the Lord came to me and snatched my spirit from my body, and suddenly I came with him and he led me into the height before the door that is in the sight of the Lord. I looked in and I saw many thousands of crowned saints standing by and ministering to God, and I saw the four animals around the throne. Indeed, angels and archangels, cherubim and seraphim stood before the throne of God, and throwing themselves down they worshiped Him and in a clear voice they said, "Holy, holy, holy Lord, all powerful God, who was and who is and who is to come."

—Elisabeth of Schönau, *First Book of Visions*

The souls of the elect are daily and constantly transferred by the hands of the holy angels from the places of purgation to a place of rest where they are fitted into the supernal city. Each is assigned its place there according to the order of the blessed spirits that has been appointed by God, and each soul has a brightness according to the quality of its merits. This is that structure, and the master of this whole operation is the archangel Michael.

—Elisabeth of Schönau, *Third Book of Visions*

Hell

The damned are in the infernal abyss . . . where they endure unutterable torments in every sense and in every member; because, as every sense and member has participated in their sin, so must they participate in its punishment. The eyes, as the reward of their false and evil gazing, will endure the horrible sight of devils and of hell; the ears, which delighted in unholy conversation, will never hear aught save weeping, lamentations, and despair, and so with the other senses.

—Francis de Sales, *The Devout Life*

The damned will be enveloped in flames as in a garment. The fire will penetrate all the members of his body—and what a fire!

—Ignatius of Loyola, *Spiritual Exercises*

As the purified spirit finds no repose but in God, for whom it was created, so the soul in sin can rest nowhere but in hell, which by reason of its sins, has become its end.

—Catherine of Genoa, *Life and Doctrine*

The greatest pain in Hell is the loss of God, that sovereign good, who is the source of all the joys in Paradise.

—Alphonsus Liguori, *sermon*

Live in fear of the day of judgment and have a great horror of hell.

—Benedict, *Rule*

He, therefore, is a fool indeed, who despises so great a good, and chooses rather to receive in this life, the earnest money of Hell, walking by the lower road with great toil, and without any refreshment or advantage.

—Catherine of Siena, *Dialogue*

Close your ears to the whisperings of hell and bravely oppose its onslaughts.

—Clare of Assisi, *letter to Ermentrude of Bruges*

Everyone who has the world's honors and its joy is driven by various cares and is involved in bitter things that lead to hell.

—Bridget of Sweden, *Book of Questions*

Tell me, are you still asking why hell exists? Ask that question no longer, but ask why there's only one hell.

—John Chrysostom, *homily*

It is of faith that Heaven exists for the good and Hell for the wicked. Faith teaches that the pains of Hell are eternal, and it also warns us that one single mortal sin suffices to condemn a soul forever because of the infinite malice by which it offends an infinite God.

—Anthony Mary Claret, *autobiography*

Although the sinner does not believe in Hell, he shall nevertheless go there if he has the misfortune to die in mortal sin—even though he neither believes in Hell or even thinks about it.

—Anthony Mary Claret, *autobiography*

If I love, there will be no hell for me.

—Josemaría Escrivá, *The Forge*

When the Devil tempts you, remember Hell;—the thought of Hell will preserve you from that land of misery. I say, remember Hell, and have recourse to Jesus Christ and to most holy Mary, and they will deliver you from sin, which is the gate of Hell.

—Alphonsus Liguori, *sermon*

God threatens Hell, not to send us there, but to deliver us from that place of torments.

—Alphonsus Liguori, *sermon*

Some foolish worldlings say: *If I go to Hell I shall not be alone there.* Miserable fools! do you not see that the greater number of your companions, the more insufferable shall be your torments?

—Alphonsus Liguori, *sermon*

In Hell there is continual weeping; but what is the object of the bitterest tears of the unhappy damned? It is the thought of having lost God through their own fault.

—Alphonsus Liguori, *sermon*

If Hell were not eternal, it would not be so frightful a chastisement.

—Alphonsus Liguori, *sermon*

Holiness

Those who imagine they can attain to holiness by any wisdom or strength of their own will find themselves after many labors, and struggles, and weary efforts, only the farther from possessing it, and this in proportion to their certainty that they themselves have gained it.

—John of Ávila, *letter to a disciple, 1563*

Do not forget that holiness consists not in extraordinary actions, but in performing your duties towards God, yourself and others well.

—Maximilian M. Kolbe, *text for the Assumption, 1940*

To be holy isn't easy, but it isn't difficult either. To be holy is to be a good Christian, to resemble Christ. The more closely a person resembles Christ, the more Christian he is, the more he belongs to Christ, the holier he is.

—Josemaría Escrivá, *The Forge*

Holy Spirit

The infusion of the Holy Spirit does not lie within our power. It comes as Spirit Himself wishes. And when it comes, this infusion will so greatly animate the powers of our spirit that the song of God breaks out of itself. Freedom of choice lies only between leaving this song to be sung in the heart alone, or expressing it aloud for all to hear.

—Theophan the Recluse, *letter*

Charity, or love, is in reality the Holy Spirit, the Spirit of truth. As charity covers a multitude of sins, so too does the grace of God, which makes one do penance.

—Anthony of Padua, *Sermones*

As soon as the water of the Holy Spirit begins to enter into the human heart, fleshly love immediately begins to grow cold.

—Robert Bellarmine, *The Mind's Ascent to God by the Ladder of Created Things*

Every just person who is filled with the Holy Spirit, just as Paul was, is the heaven of the Holy Spirit. Indeed, all just people may be compared to one heaven because there is one heart and one soul in them and one spirit rules them.

—Elisabeth of Schönau, *Third Book of Visions*

From all eternity the Father begets the Son, and the Holy Spirit proceeds from them both.

—Maximilian M. Kolbe, *notes, 1937*

The first disposition proper and necessary for the reception of the grace of the Holy Ghost is corporal abstinence from inordinate food, drink, sleep, speech, laughter, luxury, intimacy with men or women, and over-indulgence in the society of others. Such abstinence is proper and necessary for the reception of the Holy Ghost.

—Vincent Ferrer, *sermon*

If you abstain from worldly affairs, bodily pleasures and the like, then the fire of the Holy Ghost will burn in you.

—Vincent Ferrer, *sermon*

If, therefore, today you wish to receive the Holy Ghost, be at peace with one another, following the example of the apostles, for otherwise you cannot receive him.

—Vincent Ferrer, *sermon*

For though remission of sins is given equally to all, the communion of the Holy Ghost is bestowed in proportion to each man's faith. If thou hast labored little, thou receivest little; but if thou hast wrought much, the reward is great. Thou art running for thyself, see to thine own interest.

—Cyril of Jerusalem, *Catecheses*

He then is in no wise full of the Holy Spirit, who either in the calm of meekness forsakes the fervor of zeal, or again in the ardor of zeal loses the virtue of meekness.

—Gregory the Great, *The Book of Pastoral Rule*

The Holy Spirit tells us that Wisdom is for ever seeking throughout the world for souls worthy of him (Wisdom 6:17), and he fills these holy souls with his presence making them "friends of God and prophets" (Wisdom 7:27) . . . When Wisdom enters a soul, he brings all kinds of good things with him and bestows vast riches upon that soul.

—Louis de Montfort, *The Love of Eternal Wisdom*

Through the Holy Spirit the saints become eyewitnesses of the world to come.

—Symeon the New Theologian, *Ethical Discourses*

Holiness is attained with the help of the Holy Spirit, who comes to dwell in our souls, through grace given us by the sacraments and as a result of a constant ascetical struggle.

—Josemaría Escrivá, *The Forge*

One of the greatest gifts the Holy Spirit can bestow on us is to give us peace in time of struggle, calm in the midst of trouble, so that in time of desolation we are armed with so virile a courage that nature, the devil, and even God himself, who seems to be against us, cannot withstand.

—Claude de la Colombière, *retreat notes*

The gift of the Holy Spirit makes us capable of practicing prayer continually. When the Holy Spirit has established his temple in a person, that person cannot but pray without ceasing. Whether waking or sleeping, prayer does not fade from his soul.

—Isaac of Nineveh, *The Philokalia*

A person who trusts that he can find rest in the delights and abundance of earthly things is deceiving himself. By the frequent disorders of the world, and at last by its end, such a one is proven convincingly to have laid the foundation of his tranquility on the sand. But all those who have been breathed upon by the Holy Spirit, and have taken upon themselves by the very pleasant yoke of the Lord's love, and following his example, learned to be gentle and humble of heart, enjoy even in the present some image of the future tranquility.

—Bede the Venerable, *homily on the Gospels*

The [Holy] Spirit is in heaven, but he fills the world with his ubiquitous presence which cannot be constrained. He is wholly present in each, and yet wholly with God.

—Basil the Great, *On Faith*

When we hear of a spirit, then it is impossible to conceive of a circumscribed nature, subject to change and variation, just like a creature. But we approach the all-highest with our minds and are compelled to conceive of an intelligent essence of unlimited power and infinite magnitude, unmeasured by times or epochs, generous in the bestowing of good things, one turned to by all things needing sanctification, desired by all things living in virtue, and they are watered by his inspiration and helped on towards their natural and proper end.

—Basil the Great, *On the Holy Spirit*

The Spirit is not united to the soul by spacial proximity (for how could that which has no body be approached by a body?), but rather by the departure of the passions which came upon the soul on account of its friendship with the body and which have alienated it from its fellowship with God.

—Basil the Great, *On the Holy Spirit*

Through him hearts are raised up, the weak are led by the hand, and those who are making progress are perfected.

—Basil the Great, *On the Holy Spirit*

Honor

Where there is no honor, there is contempt; where there is contempt, insult is frequent; where there is insult, there is indignation; where there is indignation, there is no rest; where there is no rest, the mind is often diverted from its purpose.

—Jerome, *letter to Helidorus, 374*

I believe that honor and money nearly always go together, and that he who desires honor never hates money, while he who hates money cares little for honor.

—Teresa of Ávila, *The Way of Perfection*

And we must honor all theologians and those who minister the most holy divine words and respect them as those who minister to us spirit and life.

—Francis of Assisi, *The Testament*

Hope

Hope is the power behind love. . . . When hope fails, so does love.

—John Climacus, *The Ladder of Divine Ascent*

He wishes us to have recourse to Himself before all others, and to place our only hope in Him, that He may also center in Him all our love.

—Alphonsus Liguori, *sermon*

Hope too shuts out the onset of all sins. "Those who hope in Him do not commit sin." (Psalms 33:23)

—John Cassian, *Conferences*

Hope is sure of pardon and is without fear of being punished. Hope knows of the good works done. Hope is able to be on the lookout for the promised reward.

—John Cassian, *Conferences*

Thus hope, by means of the reasoning powers, maintains the middle road between despair and presumption, not permitting man to presume on his own powers for the attainment of eternal glory or to set aside meritorious activity on his own part, nor allowing fear or despondency to hinder Him from exerting himself toward it on account of the Lord's assurances of final success. In this security, guaranteed by divine faith in all that pertains to these things and applied in prudent and sound reasoning, man hopes without fear of being deceived and yet also without presumption.

—Mary of Agreda, *The Mystical City of God*

Hope has this characteristic: It covers all the senses of a person's head so they do not become absorbed in any worldly thing, nor is there any way some arrow from the world might wound them. Hope allows the soul only a visor that it may look toward heavenly things, and no more.

—John of the Cross, *The Dark Night of the Soul*

When the mind's capacity for speculation becomes inactive, our faculty for hope is also put to rest.

—Gregory of Nyssa, *Commentary on the Inscriptions of the Psalms*

I may even lose thy grace by sin, but I will never lose my hope. I will keep it even to the last moment of my life, and all the demons in hell shall try in vain to tear it from me. In peace I will sleep and I will rest.

—Claude de la Colombière, *sermon*

What is hope but food for the journey to support us in the miseries of this life?

—Aelred of Rievaulx, *Mirror of Charity*

Hospitality

It is also good for us to attend to the precept of hospitality, to be ready to give to strangers, for we, too, are strangers in the world.

—Ambrose, *Concerning Widowhood*

This is the law of hospitality—that the person who is welcomed makes the one who welcomes him like himself. This is what John the Evangelist indicated most clearly with respect to those who welcomed the Son of God when he said: "But however many welcomed Him, to them He gave the power to become sons of God." (John 1:12)

—Maximus of Turin, *sermon*

Humanity

Body, soul, and God are the man who is created according to the image of God and made worthy of becoming God.

—Symeon the New Theologian, *Ethical Discourses*

God created humanity as man and woman, and He created both according to His own image. Only the purely developed masculine *and* feminine nature can yield the highest attainable likeness to God. Only in this fashion can there be brought about the strongest interpenetration of all earthly and divine life.

—Edith Stein, *Essays on Woman*

It is a great honor that God bestowed on men and women the image of his eternity and likeness to his own character.

—Columban, *sermon*

If the Ocean is good and worthy of praise before God, how much more beautiful is the assembly of a Church like this, where the voices of men, of children, and of women, arise in our prayers to God mingling and resounding like the waves which beat upon the shore.

—Basil the Great, *homily on the Hexaemeron*

And if you turn to him you will understand our origin and destiny because his is the glory for ever and ever.

—Basil the Great, *On Paradise*

In man is found a certain likeness to God which is taken from God as from the exemplar.

—Thomas Aquinas, *Summa Theologica*

Bearing the image of God in ourselves, all of us are consequently the image of each other. Together we constitute the image of one portrait, that of God.

—Francis de Sales, *Oeuvres*

Our Lord, in coming into the world, has so raised our nature higher than all the angels, the cherubim, and all that is not God, and has made us so like himself, that we can say with certainty that we resemble God perfectly. In becoming man, he has taken our likeness and given us his.

—Francis de Sales, *Oeuvres*

To what extent did the greatness of God lower itself for each one of us, and to what extent does he wish to exalt us? To unite us so perfectly with himself as to make us one same thing with him.

—Francis de Sales, *Oeuvres*

He dwelt among us in his flesh to show us that he wished to make use of his humanity as a tool or instrument to accomplish the works which belong to his divinity.

—Francis de Sales, *Oeuvres*

God brought you out of nothing, and made you what you are out of his sole goodness, without requiring any assistance on your part.

—Francis de Sales, *The Devout Life*

God did not create you because he had any need of you, for you are wholly useless to him, but only that he might exercise towards you his goodness, bestowing on you his grace and glory.

—Francis de Sales, *The Devout Life*

Man was created for a certain end. This end is to praise, to reverence, and to serve the Lord his God, and by this means to arrive at eternal salvation.

—Ignatius of Loyola, *Spiritual Exercises*

I come from God; hence I belong to God. God is my creator; hence he is my Lord and my Master. To deny this consequence would be to deny my reason.

—Ignatius of Loyola, *Spiritual Exercises*

God can dispose of me according to his pleasure; he can take from me fortune, health, honor, life; my duty is to receive everything from his hand with submission and without complaint.

—Ignatius of Loyola, *Spiritual Exercises*

I am not made for a mortal man; I am not made for myself; I am not made for an angel. An intelligent and immortal being, I am too great for a creature, however noble, to be my end. My end is that of the angel; is that of Jesus Christ; is that of God himself. God does not exist, could not exist, except to know himself and to love himself; and I only exist, or could exist, to know and to love God.

The dominion of God is immortal, like myself; it begins with time, and continues through eternity; death, which deprives men of all their rights, is unable to do anything against the rights of God.

—Ignatius of Loyola, *Spiritual Exercises*

Man was created to praise and adore the Lord his God, and in serving him to save himself. This is his end.

—Ignatius of Loyola, *Spiritual Exercises*

God created me, and in creating me, made me the noblest creature of the visible world. All my being bears the stamp of his divine perfections.

—Ignatius of Loyola, *Spiritual Exercises*

For you have made us for yourself, and our heart is restless until it rests in you.

—Augustine, *Confessions*

For before I was, you were, and I was nothing to which you could grant being. Yet, behold! I am, because of your goodness, which preceded all that you made me to be, and all out of which you made me.

—Augustine, *Confessions*

Man's nature is such that truth tastes bitter and pleasant vices are esteemed.

—Jerome, *letter, 385*

For while we were created in God's image and likeness, by reason of our own perversity we hide ourselves behind changing masks, and as on the stage one and the same actor now figures as a brawny Hercules, and now relaxes into the softness of a Venus or the quivering tone of a Cybele, so we who, if we were not of the world, would be hated by the world, have a counterfeit mask for every sin to which we are inclined.

—Jerome, *letter, 385*

I am certain in my heart that "all that I am" I have received from God.

—Patrick, *letter to the soldiers of Coroticus*

Man is created more perfectly in God's image than the angels, both because he possesses in himself a sustaining and quickening power and because he has the capacity for sovereignty.

—Gregory Palamas, *Topics of Natural and Theological Science and on the Moral and Ascetic Life: One Hundred and Fifty Texts*

Anyone who really wants to build a ladder to God should start by considering himself. Each of us is a creature and an image too of God, and nothing is closer to us than ourselves. . . . He who examines his whole self and considers what lies hidden within will find the whole world in shortened form, from which he will ascend without difficulty to the maker of all things.

—Robert Bellarmine, *The Mind's Ascent to God by the Ladder of Created Things*

The end for which man was created is none other than God himself.

—Robert Bellarmine, *The Mind's Ascent to God by the Ladder of Created Things*

Consider, O human being, in what great excellence the Lord God has placed you, for He created and formed you to the image of His beloved Son according to the body and to His likeness according to the Spirit.

—Francis of Assisi, *saying*

We might say that eternal Wisdom made copies, that is, shining likenesses of his own intelligence, memory, and will, and infused them into the soul of man so that he might become the living image of the Godhead. In man's heart he enkindled the fire of the pure love of God. He gave him a radiant body and virtually enshrined within him a compendium of all the various perfections of angels, animals, and other created things.

—Louis de Montfort, *The Love of Eternal Wisdom*

And God formed humanity according to the divine image and likeness. God already had it in mind that this very form should enclose the holy Godhead. For the same reason God delineated all of creation in the human species, just as the whole world emerged from the divine Word.

—Hildegard of Bingen, *Book of Divine Works*

God is the living light in every respect. From God all lights shine. Therefore, we remain a light that gives off light through God.

—Hildegard of Bingen, *Book of Divine Works*

And after all the other creatures were created, God created humanity so that we human beings would find waiting for us all the things we might need. And God illuminated humanity with the living breath of the spirit.

—Hildegard of Bingen, *Book of Divine Works*

Humanity holds the misery of damnation in those who were disgraced through the worst deception of the devil, and it holds the happiness of redemption in those who were chosen through their desire for salvation.

—Hildegard of Bingen, *Scivias*

Humanity stands, as it were, at a crossroad. If human beings seek in the light for salvation from God, they will receive it. But if they choose evil, they will follow the Devil to the place of punishment.

—Hildegard of Bingen, *Book of Divine Works*

Moreover, nothing in creation had erred from the path of God's purpose for it, save only man. Sun, moon, heaven, stars, water, air, none of these had swerved from their order, but, knowing the Word as their Maker and their King, remained as they were made. Men alone having rejected what is good, have invented nothings instead of the truth, and have ascribed the honor due to God and the knowledge concerning Him to demons and men in the form of stones.

—Athanasius, *On the Incarnation*

Humility

The Holy Spirit confers true humility. However intelligent, sensible, and clever a man may be, if he does not possess the Holy Spirit within him, he cannot know himself properly; for without God's help he cannot see the inner state of his soul.

—Metropolitan Innocent of Moscow, *The Art of Prayer*

The holy fathers teach that there are two kinds of humility: to regard oneself as lower than everyone else, and to ascribe all one's achievement to God. The first is the beginning, the second the consummation.

—Gregory of Sinai, *The Philokalia*

Those who say or do anything without humility are like people who build in winter or without bricks and mortar. Very few acquire humility and know it through experience; and those who try to talk about it are like people measuring a bottomless pit.

—Gregory of Sinai, *The Philokalia*

Be humble towards God and gentle with your neighbor. Judge and accuse no one but yourself, and ever excuse others. Speak of God always to praise and glorify him, speak of your neighbor only with respect—do not speak of yourself at all, either well or ill.

—Margaret Mary Alacoque, *Life and Writings of St. Margaret Mary*

It is no great matter that thy mind should be with God: but if thou didst see thyself less than any of his creatures, that were something.

—Abbot Sisois, *saying*

It is a remarkable thing: God so loves humility that he sometimes tests us, not to make us do evil but to teach us by our own experience what we really are, permitting us to say or do some foolish thing, giving us reason to humble ourselves.

—Francis de Sales, *Oeuvres*

We must indeed keep ourselves humble because of our imperfections, but this humility must be the foundation of a great generosity, for one without the other degenerates into imperfection. Humility without generosity is only a deception and a cowardice of heart which makes us think that we are good for nothing and that others should never think of using us in anything great. On the other hand, generosity without humility is only presumption.

—Francis de Sales, *Oeuvres*

For if you have not humility, you have not charity, and if you are without charity you are without humility. It is almost impossible to have charity without being humble and to be humble without having charity. These two virtues have such an affinity with one another that the one can never be without the other.

—Francis de Sales, *Oeuvres*

Now humility and patience have such an affinity with one another that one can hardly exist without the other. He who desires to be humble must be patient enough to endure the contempt, the censure, the reprehensions that the humble suffer.

—Francis de Sales, *Oeuvres*

O God! with how much humility and spiritual abasement ought we to live on this earth! But also what great reason to anchor our hope and confidence completely in Our Lord!

—Francis de Sales, *Oeuvres*

The kestrel has a peculiar property of frightening away birds of prey with its looks and cries, for which reason the dove seeks it beyond all other birds, and lives fearlessly in its neighborhood; and so humility repulses Satan and preserves us in the gifts and graces of the Holy Spirit. For this reason all the saints, and especially the King of Saints and His Mother, ever honored and cherished this virtue above all others.

—Francis de Sales, *The Devout Life*

Assuredly nothing can so humble us before the compassion of God as the abundance of his mercies; nothing so humble us before his justice as the abundance of our misdeeds.

—Francis de Sales, *The Devout Life*

True humility does not affect to be humble, and makes few lowly speeches, for she not only desires to hide other virtues, but above all, to hide herself.

—Francis de Sales, *The Devout Life*

A really humble man would rather let another say that he is contemptible and worth nothing, than say so himself.

—Francis de Sales, *The Devout Life*

If you ask me what are the most profitable humiliations, I reply that undoubtedly those will do us most good and serve God best which are accidental or attendant upon our position in life, because these we do not seek for ourselves, but receive them as God sends them, and his choice is always better than ours.

—Francis de Sales, *The Devout Life*

Humility perfects us towards God, mildness or gentleness toward our neighbor.

—Francis de Sales, *The Devout Life*

And one must always keep in mind that which the fathers taught, that neither widowhood nor virginity have any merit in heaven, except that which is assigned to them by humility.

—Francis de Sales, *The Devout Life*

It appears to me that humility is the truth. I know not whether I am humble, but I know that I see the truth in all things.

—Thérèse of Lisieux, *Counsels and Reminisces*

It is a great joy to me, not only when others find me imperfect, but above all when I feel that I so am: compliments, on the contrary, cause me nothing but displeasure.

—Thérèse of Lisieux, *Counsels and Reminisces*

The reason Christ especially recommended humility to us is because it most effectively removes the main obstacle to our spiritual welfare, the preoccupation with earthly greatness that holds us back from striving for spiritual and heavenly things.

—Thomas Aquinas, *Summa Theologica*

Humility frees and disposes us to receive God's blessing: charity and the other virtues that will move us directly to God and are therefore more to be prized than humility.

—Thomas Aquinas, *Summa Theologica*

Humility and purity are the wings which carry us to God and make us almost divine. Remember: that a bad man who is ashamed of the wrong things he is doing, is nearer to God than a good man who blushes at doing the right thing.

—Padre Pio, *Spiritual Maxims*

A man truly humble within himself will never find his tongue betraying him. What is not in the treasury cannot be brought out through the door.

—John Climacus, *The Ladder of Divine Ascent*

Humility is a spiritual teaching of Christ led spiritually like a bride into the inner chamber of the soul of those deemed worthy of it, and it somehow eludes all description.

—John Climacus, *The Ladder of Divine Ascent*

The wonderful Fathers proclaimed physical labor to be the way to and the foundation of humility. To this I would add obedience and honesty of heart, since these are by nature opposed to self-aggrandizement.

—John Climacus, *The Ladder of Divine Ascent*

The Son of God came down from heaven and taught us by his life and words the way to heaven, and that way is humility, as he said: "He that humbleth himself shall not be exalted" (Luke 18:14). Therefore, if you wish God to give you a new heart, you must first of all amend your deeds, and then lament your faults and accuse yourself of your sins.

—John of Ávila, *letter to a disciple, 1563*

Fever may hinder your prayers, but it cannot prevent you from being humble.

—Sebastian Valfrè, *letter to an invalid, 1690*

O most humble Virgin, make us share in thy humility; make us detest all pride and vanity, and love humiliation in all places, at all times, and in all things, according to the divine precept: *"Humilia te in omnibus*—humility in all things," not indeed that we may be afterwards exalted and glorified, but that God may be glorified and exalted in us; for he who exalts himself abases God, and he who abases himself, exalts God.

—John Eudes, *The Holy Name of Mary*

The cry of the humble man penetrates the Heavens, and he will not depart till God hears his prayer.

—Alphonsus Liguori, *sermon*

Whenever the devil wishes to capture something, that object should protect and arm itself with humility because Lucifer certainly fled from humility, even as the serpent hides itself in a cave when humility is present.

—Hildegard of Bingen, *Scivias*

Throughout our lives it is well for us to recognize the worthlessness of our nature if only in order to keep our humility.

—Teresa of Ávila, *Life*

Reflect that true humility consists to a great extent in being ready for what the Lord desires to do with you and happy that He should do it, and in always considering yourselves unworthy to be called His servants.

—Teresa of Ávila, *The Way of Perfection*

Avoid being bashful with God, as some people are, in the belief that they are being humble. It would not be humility on your part if the King were to do you a favor and you refused to accept it; but you would be showing humility by taking it, and being pleased with it, yet realizing how far you are from deserving it.

—Teresa of Ávila, *The Way of Perfection*

The first step of humility is unhesitating obedience, which comes naturally to those who cherish Christ above all.

—Benedict, *Rule*

Oh my Jesus! . . . Let me mount to Thee on the steps of humility, on which Thou camest down to me.

—Elizabeth Seton, *Collected Writings*

All heavenly visions, revelations and feelings—or whatever else one may desire to think on—are not worth as much as the least act of humility. Humility has the effect of charity: It neither esteems nor seeks its own, it thinks no evil save of self, it thinks no good of self but of others.

—John of the Cross, *The Ascent of Mount Carmel*

Humility, humility, and ever humility, as we can do nothing of ourselves; all is purely and simply God's grace.

—Faustina Kowalska, *Divine Mercy in My Soul*

Nothing is difficult for the humble.

—Faustina Kowalska, *Divine Mercy in My Soul*

Satan defeats only the proud and the cowardly, because the humble are strong.

Nothing will confuse or frighten a humble soul.

—Faustina Kowalska, *Divine Mercy in My Soul*

However much a soul may be enriched and favored by God, she should never cease to turn her eyes inward upon herself, to consider her own unworthiness, to fold her wings and to humble herself before such great majesty.

—Peter of Alcántara, *Treatise on Prayer & Meditation*

Humility is more noble than other virtues because it humbly bears things that are less noble and less esteemed. . . . Just as the heart cannot suffer pain or infirmity, so true humility cannot suffer, that is, be sorrowful at injury it receives, nor be saddened at another's good fortune. And this is as it should be, because if humility is false, the whole edifice of the other virtues collapses.

—Anthony of Padua, *Sermones*

If you wish to achieve true knowledge of Scripture you must hurry to achieve unshakeable humility of heart. This is what will lead you not to the knowledge which puffs a man up but to the lore which illuminates through the achievement of love. It is impossible for the unclean of heart to acquire the gift of spiritual knowledge.

—John Cassian, *Conferences*

True patience and humility can only be acquired and kept when the innermost heart is humble.

—John Cassian, *Conferences*

Then love humility, my soul, if you want to be truly exalted. Imitate the spotless Lamb, imitate the Virgin Mother, imitate the cherubim and seraphim. All of them are the more humble the higher they are.

—Robert Bellarmine, *The Mind's Ascent to God by the Ladder of Created Things*

The higher you are, the lower you should be; indeed, humility is the great virtue by which one arrives at a crown.

—Elisabeth of Schönau, *letter to the sisters in Dirstein*

May your holy humility teach me prudently to shun all snares of the enemy.

—Gertrude the Great, *Spiritual Exercises*

For the greater we are, the more we should humble ourselves and recognize our own nothingness. If we know ourselves, we humble ourselves, not holding our head high or becoming bloated with pride. Rather we bow our head in acknowledgment of the goodness God has showered on us.

—Catherine of Siena, *letter to Cardinal Pietro Corsini of Florence, at Avignon, 1376*

We should also remember that humility is the route to heaven. A loving acceptance of it when we are humiliated usually rises up, guiding us, as it were, step by step from one virtue to the next until we reach heaven.

—Vincent de Paul, *Common Rules or Constitutions of the Congregation of the Mission*

The more one is humbled, the more one is exalted. Just as, in the case of water, the more a person pushes it down, the more the water rises in height; and the greater the distance from which one shoots, the more it hits the mark, so is it the case with humility.

—John Chrysostom, *homily*

Let the humble be told, then, that when they abase themselves, they ascend to the likeness of God; let the haughty be told that, when they exalt themselves, they fall into the imitation of the apostate angel.

—Gregory the Great, *The Book of Pastoral Rule*

What is more sublime than humility, which, while it depresses itself to the lowest, conjoins itself to its Maker who remains above the highest?

—Gregory the Great, *The Book of Pastoral Rule*

What else is so dear to God and welcome as a contrite and humble heart, and pride laid low in a spirit of humility? It is such a condition of soul that God Himself comes to dwell and make His rest, and that every machination of the devil remains ineffective. All the corrupting passions of sin vanish completely.

—Symeon the New Theologian, *Ethical Discourses*

Without humility it is not possible to become the recipient of the gifts of the Spirit.

—Symeon the New Theologian, *Ethical Discourses*

You are humble not when you humble yourself, but when you are humbled by others and you bear it for Christ.

—Josemaría Escrivá, *The Way*

Humility is born of knowing God and knowing oneself.

—Josemaría Escrivá, *The Forge*

A humble man sees only his own faults. It is a sign of little virtue to notice the imperfections of others.

—Claude de la Colombière, *spiritual notes*

For the one who loses humility will not be able to preserve chastity of the flesh.

—Aelred of Rielvaux, *sermon*

Hypocrisy

Hypocrisy is the mother of lying and frequently its cause. Some would argue that hypocrisy is nothing other than a meditation on falsehood, that it is the inventor of falsehood laced with lies.

—John Climacus, *The Ladder of Divine Ascent*

Hypocrisy is born of self-conceit, and self-conceit is contrary to being poor in spirit.

—Gregory Palamas, *To the Most Reverend Nun Xenia*

I

Ideas

It is obvious that all who assert that everything happens by chance cannot admit the existence of ideas. . . . Likewise all who assert that everything comes from God by necessity of nature and not by a will-decision cannot admit ideas, because those acting through the force of natural necessity do not themselves choose the end.

—Thomas Aquinas, *On Truth*

Idleness

Idleness is the enemy of the soul.

—Benedict, *Rule*

A powerful remedy against temptations of the flesh, and all sins of impurity, is to *flee idleness*; for no one is more exposed to such temptations than he who has nothing to do, who spends his time in gazing at people out of the window, or in chatting with his friends.

—Robert Bellarmine, *The Art of Dying Well*

Idleness is a great help to temptation.

—Francis de Sales, *Oeuvres*

And since a lazy life is the enemy of virtues, especially of chastity, each of us is to avoid being idle and should always make good use of his time.

—Vincent de Paul, *Common Rules or Constitutions of the Congregation of the Mission*

For the slothful one is as it were awake in that he feels aright, though he grows torpid by doing nothing: but slothfulness is said to cast into a deep sleep, because by degrees even the wakefulness of right feeling is lost, when zeal for well-doing is discontinued.

—Gregory the Great, *The Book of Pastoral Rule*

Idleness is something inconceivable in a man who has the soul of an apostle.

—Josemaría Escrivá, *The Way*

If you were in fact compelled to sin, if you were the victim of violence, then you would be forgiven for it. On the other hand, if you sin through idleness, do not expect forgiveness.

—John Chrysostom, *On the Letter to the Ephesians*

Work is not shameful; idleness is.

—John Chrysostom, *Priscilla and Aquila*

The cradle of all temptations and all useless and unhealthy thoughts is idleness. Idleness contains all sin.

The idle are never servants of God. Those who do not do what they must with fidelity and fervor, those who do not do it with the intention of serving God, are idle when they come to act.

And it is ridiculous to look for idle works to escape idleness. An idle work is one that has no usefulness or is done with no intention of becoming useful: useful in the first place to one's own conscience, enriching the heart's treasure.

—Bernard of Clairvaux, *letter to the brethren*

Ignorance

Ignorance produces a wretched soul, and a mind full of nothing does itself terrible damage!

—Basil the Great, *Consolation in Adversity*

Illness

After talking with the sick we should pray for them, so that they accept their share of sufferings for the forgiveness of their sins. We can also pray to the Lord that the doors of heaven will be opened for them when they die.

—Brother André, *Brother André According to Witnesses*

We can show how much we care not by judging others, and by visiting the sick who need comfort so as to understand that God is visiting them. . . . It would also do a lot of good to those in good health. They have a lot to learn from the sick.

—Brother André, *Brother André According to Witnesses*

Sickness is a good thing, for it helps us to reconsider our past life and make up through repentance and suffering.

—Brother André, *Brother André According to Witnesses*

Illness can occur sometimes to cleanse us from our sins and sometimes to humble our thinking. When our ever-gracious Master and Lord discovers people getting lazy in their religious lives, he may humble their bodies by illness, as if by a lighter form of asceticism. Illness too can sometimes purify the soul from evil thoughts and passions.

—John Climacus, *The Ladder of Divine Ascent*

You may well be content to serve our Lord in illness, for when he calls people to suffer instead of working for him, he is calling them to a higher state. During our earthly exile, it is most fitting that we should carry the cross with Christ, who loved it so dearly that he chose to die on it. We can do this better in sickness than in health, for illness is repugnant to flesh and blood and can never cause vainglory.

—John of Ávila, *letter to a layman, 1560*

Accept your illness then willingly, and be grateful to our Lord who sent it. If you bear this cross and burden well, he will send you interior and more painful trials, which he keeps for his dearest friends, to conform them to himself. For though Christ's visible cross was great, it was not to be compared to that which, unknown to men, he bore in his soul.

—John of Ávila, *letter to a layman, 1560*

Everything, whether you are well or sick, reduces itself to conforming yourself to God's sweet will; and one who can make good use of sickness will not be less perfect than one who makes good use of health and prosperity.

—Sebastian Valfrè, *letter to an invalid, 1690*

Every illness and every trial is permitted by God as the means whereby we can best ensure our salvation and as the material most fitted for our sanctification.

—Sebastian Valfrè, *letter to an invalid, 1690*

To exercise a special charity towards the sick, is also very pleasing to God. . . . Be careful to relieve them by alms, or by little presents, and to serve them as well as you can, at least by endeavoring to console them by your words, and by exhortations to practice resignation to the will of God, and to offer to him all their sufferings.

—Alphonsus Liguori, *sermon*

In sickness itself, or amidst casual happenings, so long as the soul is a loving one it is always possible to pray by offering up the distraction itself and remembering Him for whom we are suffering it.

—Teresa of Ávila, *Life*

The virtues of the infirm are meekness, humility, patience, resignation and gratitude for help received.

—Elizabeth Seton, *Collected Writings*

I thank God for this illness and these physical discomforts, because I have the time to converse with the Lord Jesus.

—Faustina Kowalska, *Divine Mercy in My Soul*

Obedience is one of the virtues most needed in the sick. They should be completely obedient to doctors and chaplains, as well as to the nurse and anyone else involved in their care.

—Vincent de Paul, *Common Rules or Constitutions of the Congregation of the Mission*

For the sick, unless the physician be called to them by the prayers of others, cannot pray for themselves. The flesh is weak, the soul is sick and hindered by the chains of sins, and cannot direct its feeble steps to the throne of the physician. The angels must be entreated for us, who have been to us as guards; the martyrs must be entreated, whose patronage we seem to claim for ourselves by the pledge as it were of their bodily remains.

—Ambrose, *Concerning Widowhood*

Do not fear, because the Lord is great, that perhaps He will not condescend to come to one who is sick, for He often comes to us from heaven; and is wont to visit not only the rich but also the poor and the servants of the poor.

—Ambrose, *Concerning Widowhood*

There is greater grace in the infirmity of the body than in its soundness.

—Ambrose, *Concerning Repentance*

O my God, how good thou art. Thou does use the very sicknesses of man's body to heal the soul.

—Anthony Mary Claret, *autobiography*

By the sickness he sends you, God asks of you great contempt for all things, great indifference about life and death, perfect abandonment to his divine will, a sovereign and infinite respect for this adorable will which you must prefer to everything else and in which you must find your pleasure, and also a great love of the cross, especially all that humiliates body and mind.

—Claude de la Colombière, *letter*

Not infrequently, illness is an opportunity to correct one's faults.

—Basil the Great, *The Greater Rules*

If your body is racked with every sort of pain, do not become depressed, allowing your spirit to be broken, and do not feel driven to cry out against God; but instead you should call to mind the example of Job who surpassed all others by his patience.

—Basil the Great, *Consolation in Adversity*

It is not enough to be ill because such is God's will, but we must be ill as he wills, when he wills, and how long it pleases him, entrusting our health to whatever he ordains for us, without asking for anything. We must let him act and, without trying to foresee what is requisite for our cure, we must abandon to our superiors and leave the care of ourselves to them. We are not to concern ourselves with anything but bearing our illness as long as God pleases.

—Francis de Sales, *Oeuvres*

We must make good use of it [illness] and not have too much special treatment if can we do without it. It is a time of blessing when we have prepared well for it, but it can be a great danger because of the devil, who not having been able to destroy us during our life, will do his best to destroy us at the time of our death.

—Marguerite Bourgeoys, *Autographic Writings*

Illumination

If, in meditating on divine things, our most merciful God should favor you, as is His wont, with some heavenly illumination, do not let it escape from your mind, but note it down in some little book to assist your memory. Believe me, that a great part of the real spiritual profit of God's servants consists in such observation, and in carefully recalling to mind pieces of knowledge of this sort given to them in mental prayer and meditation. . . . I advise you, therefore, strongly to make a little journal, and to note down carefully in it the secret illuminations with which God has enlightened your mind in your daily meditations.

—Francis Xavier, *letter*

The brighter the light, the more the owl is blinded; and the more one looks at the brilliant sun, the more the sun darkens the faculty of sight, deprives and overwhelms it in its weakness.

Hence when the divine light of contemplation strikes the soul not yet entirely illumined, it causes spiritual darkness, for it not only surpasses the act of natural understanding but it also deprives the soul of this act and darkens it.

—John of the Cross, *The Dark Night of the Soul*

While it is one thing to be satisfied with cheap clothing and not to desire splendid robes, it is something else again to be clothed with God's own light.

—Symeon the New Theologian, *Ethical Discourses*

Illumine me with the true light, O compassionate One, so that I may see the glory which You had with Your Father before the world was made. Abide even in me, as You have said, so that I, too, may become worthy of abiding in You, and may then consciously enter into You and consciously possess You within myself.

—Symeon the New Theologian, *Ethical Discourses*

For your teaching, Lord, does not fill the ear with fine-sounding words but is breathed into the mind by your gentle Spirit.

—Aelred of Rielvaux, *sermon*

Illusion

For the mind itself lies to itself about itself, and feigns with respect to good work to love what it does not love, and with respect to the world's glory not to love what it does love.

—Gregory the Great, *The Book of Pastoral Rule*

Imagination

Control the imagination strictly: it is the only route by which Satan can slip thoughts into the mind to deceive it.

—Hesychius of Sinai, *The Philokalia*

Immortality

Our life is mortal, indeed, having been deprived of immortality. But the person knowing that he is in the midst of two lives, crosses over from mortality to immortality. By eliminating the former, the bad one, he gives victory to the latter.

—Gregory of Nyssa, *Commentary on the Song of Songs*

For His return from death becomes to our mortal race the commencement of our return to the immortal life.

—Gregory of Nyssa, *The Great Catechism*

For He Who lives forever did not sink down into the conditions of a bodily birth from any need to live, but to call us back from death to life.

—Gregory of Nyssa, *The Great Catechism*

We will undoubtedly come to eternal life; but if we are content with human prudence, with satisfying our self-love, and our particular loves which please our sensuality, we will take a great many false steps which lead to perdition.

—Marguerite Bourgeoys, *Autographic Writings*

Before death, while we are still in mortal flesh, we eat the labors of our hands, we swallow with an effort the food so gained; but after death, we shall begin eagerly to drink in the spiritual life and finally, reunited to our bodies, and rejoicing in fullness of delight, we shall be refreshed with immortality.

—Bernard of Clairvaux, *On Loving God*

We are all created from one invisible essence, having a beginning but no end; thus, they who know themselves know that the essence of unity is immortal.

—Anthony, *letter*

For no one who is sick with his own sins, and far from being whole, can minister the remedies of the healing of immortality.

—Ambrose, *Concerning Widowhood*

If we wish to have the roots of immortality deeply embedded in our heart we must have in our mind knowledge of eternal Wisdom. To know Jesus Christ incarnate Wisdom, is to know all we need.

—Louis de Montfort, *The Love of Eternal Wisdom*

For over the boundless space which separates things mortal and divine He has established His mediation like a bridge to connect the two, so that by this path the earthly may be joined with the heavenly, once the celestial incorruption has permeated our corrupt nature, once immortality, in the words of Scripture, has swallowed up our mortality, and our life, victorious in Christ and from Christ, has conquered and absorbed death.

—Paulinus of Nola, *letter*

Impatience

For the very virtue of charity, which is the mother and guardian of all virtues, is lost through the vice of impatience.

—Gregory the Great, *The Book of Pastoral Rule*

Imperfection

The saints point out that there is no one without imperfections.

—Vincent de Paul, *Conferences to the Daughters of Charity*

We should have a strong and constant resolution never to be so cowardly as to commit any imperfection voluntarily.

—Francis de Sales, *Oeuvres*

Thus in every rational creature there is found perfection and imperfection, signs of the two principles from which it has come forth into existence. Since everything that issues from God is good and lovable, it follows that everything in the creature that is good and lovable issues from God as its first source; likewise, any imperfection found there comes from the nothingness from which it has been drawn. These two faces are found not only in rational creatures but in everything created by God.

—Francis de Sales, *Oeuvres*

Even the rose is not so perfect as to be without some imperfection. Though it is very beautiful in the morning, in full bloom, with a delightful and pleasing fragrance, yet in the evening it is so faded and wilted that its condition can be used to symbolize the voluptuousness and delights of the worldly life.

—Francis de Sales, *Oeuvres*

All creatures have something of perfection and of imperfection.

—Francis de Sales, *Oeuvres*

Every man has some imperfection, no matter how holy he may be—and some perfection, no matter how wicked.

—Francis de Sales, *Oeuvres*

God permits even his servants to be tempted, as well as to try their fidelity, as to purify them from their imperfections.

—Alphonsus Liguori, *sermon*

People are terribly blind and want to do great feats, undertake something as though they wanted to take God by storm, doing everything themselves according to their own will and self-confident in their own nature. No, not by fighting but by abandoning, by dying, by decreasing and abandoning! As long as there is a drop of blood in you that is unmortified and unconquered, you are imperfect.

—Henry Suso, *sermon*

Ingratitude

Thou knowest, O my God, the cause of my most bitter grief, of my deepest confusion—my infidelity, my irreverence, my ingratitude in the use of thy benefits. Yes, if thou, so great, hadst given to me, so undeserving, a mere thread of tow, it would have been my duty to show thee more reverence and more love than I have done after so many graces.

—Gertrude the Great, *Love, Peace and Joy*

Ingratitude is an enemy of the soul—the emptying out of merits, the routing of virtue, the ruin of God's benefits.

Ingratitude is a burning wind, drying up the font of piety, the dew of mercy, the flowing waters of grace.

—Bernard of Clairvaux, *On the Canticle of Canticles*

Iniquity

see EVIL

Intuition

God knows all things perfectly at the same moment by a single, simple intuition.

—Robert Bellarmine, *The Mind's Ascent to God by the Ladder of Created Things*

Lift up your eyes now, my soul, and see what a gulf separates your knowledge from the wisdom of your creator. By many acts, running here and there you hardly know one thing perfectly, but your Creator by one act intuits all things and himself most clearly and distinctly.

—Robert Bellarmine, *The Mind's Ascent to God by the Ladder of Created Things*

J

Jealousy

The manifold and fruitful destruction of jealousy is widely spread. It is the root of all evils, the source of all disasters, the nursery of sins, the substance of transgressions. From it hatred rises; animosity precedes from it. Jealousy inflames avarice, when one cannot be content with its own on seeing another richer. Jealousy incites ambition when one sees another more exalted in honors. When jealousy blinds our senses and reduces the secrets of the mind to its sway, fear of God is scorned, the teaching of Christ is neglected, the day of judgment is not provided for.

—Cyprian of Carthage, *Jealousy and Envy*

Jealousy has no terminus; it is a continually abiding evil and a sin without end, and as he who is envied proceeds with greater success, to this extent does the envious one burn to a greater heat with the fires of envy.

—Cyprian of Carthage, *Jealousy and Envy*

It is a vain imagination that love is exalted by jealousy. It may testify that love is great, but not that it is good, pure and perfect; since the perfection of love presupposes confidence in the virtue of what we love, whereas jealousy presupposes lack of confidence.

—Francis de Sales, *The Devout Life*

Joy

Since He is joy, He does not accept entry into a house of sorrow and grief, just like the busy bee will not go into a house full of smoke. If, however, you have prepared yourself with joy and without anxiety, He will be found once more inside you. Therefore allow the Master to take His rest untroubled upon the couch of your soul.

—Symeon the New Theologian, *Ethical Discourses*

Joy is a Christian possession which we will have as long as we keep fighting, for it is a consequence of peace.

—Josemaría Escrivá, *The Forge*

Try to fulfill each day's task steadily and cheerfully. Be merry, really merry. The life of a true Christian should be a perpetual jubilee, a prelude to the festivals of eternity.

—Théophane Vénard, *letter to his brother Eusebius, 1851*

Judgment

God's Judgment

Death is in itself very fearful, but much more terrible in regard to the judgment that it summoneth us unto. Your soul will then experience the most terrible fears, if you do not recover yourself into the fold and family of God's church.

—Robert Southwell, *letter to his father, 1589*

In what hour we do cover up our brother's sins, God shall cover ours: and in what hour we do betray our brother's shames, in like manner God shall betray our own.

—Abbot Pastor, *saying*

God alone will judge.

—Patrick, *letter to the soldiers of Coroticus*

I would remind you that we shall have to give an account at the judgment of our indiscretion as well as of our self-indulgence.

—Catherine dei Ricci, *letter to a layman, 1561*

Sinners know that the moment they consent to mortal sin, God condemns them to Hell.

—Alphonsus Liguori, *sermon*

It is the common opinion of theologians, that, at the very moment and in the very place in which a soul departs from the body, the divine tribunal is erected, the accusation is read, and the sentence is passed by Jesus Christ, the Judge. At this terrible tribunal each of us shall be presented, to give an account of all our thoughts, of all our words, and of all our actions.

—Alphonsus Liguori, *sermon*

In the balance of the Lord, a holy life and good works make the scale descend; but nobility, wealth, and science, have no weight. Hence, if found innocent, the peasant, the poor, and the ignorant, shall be rewarded. But the man of rank, of wealth, or of learning, if found guilty, shall be condemned.

—Alphonsus Liguori, *sermon*

For now the axe is laid to the root of the trees. Every tree, therefore, that doth not yield good fruit, shall be cut down and cast into the fire.

—John the Baptist, *Matthew 3:10*

When God comes to judge you, you will not be able to say that you did not know what you should have done.

—John Baptiste Marie Vianney, *sermon*

All your needs will be taken account of at the last day.

—Mechtilde of Magdeburg, *The Flowing Light of the Godhead*

Indeed, God's judgment does not exceed the measure of human sins in fixing the punishment due for such sins. Instead, sins are judged correctly because our Protector and Guide holds equitably the scale of judgment.

—Hildegard of Bingen, *Book of Divine Works*

People are not able to flee in any way from the most equal scale of God's judgment.

They are not able to hold back what they merit—either the glory and joy of life or the punishment and grief of death—for God sees all most keenly.

—Hildegard of Bingen, *Scivias*

A very clear proof of the fact that a soul has not yet cut loose from the corruption of sin is when it feels no sympathizing pity for the wrongdoing of others but holds instead to the strict censoriousness of a judge. For how can someone attain a perfection of heart if he does not possess what the apostle described as the Law's consummation when he said, "Carry one another's burdens and in this way you will fulfill the law of Christ." (Galatians 6:2) . . . And therefore it is most certain that he yields to the very sins which he condemns in someone else with unmerciful and inhuman severity. "The stern king will tumble into evil." (Proverbs 13:17) "He who shuts his ears to the cry of the poor will himself call out, and there will be none to listen to him." (Proverbs 21:13)

—John Cassian, *Conferences*

The person who turns to good is set free, even if his life is marred by a multitude of mistakes and the sum of his evil deeds seems like a thousand years. It is nothing as far as turning to God is concerned, for his eye always considers the present, not the past.

—Gregory of Nyssa, *Commentary on the Inscriptions of the Psalms*

Human Judgment

When judging other people, why do you put into your criticism the bitterness of your own failures?

—Josemaría Escrivá, *The Way*

Let us be slow to judge. Each one sees things from his own point of view, as his mind, with all its limitations, tells him, and through eyes that are often dimmed and clouded with passion.

—Josemaría Escrivá, *The Way*

If your heart is gentle, your judgment will be gentle; if it is charitable, your judgment will be so too.

—Francis de Sales, *The Devout Life*

To pass judgment on another is to usurp shamelessly a prerogative of God, and to condemn is to ruin one's soul.

—John Climacus, *The Ladder of Divine Ascent*

He who judges without certain grounds, that another has committed a mortal sin, is guilty of a grievous fault.

—Alphonsus Liguori, *sermon*

Often we judge things to be bad while in the sight of God they are not so.

—John Baptiste Marie Vianney, *sermon*

For it seems to me that the habit of judging keeps the soul far from Thee, so I do not wish to fall into this snare.

—Catherine of Siena, *Dialogue*

How liable we are to err in our judgments regarding others except we thoroughly know the motives of their actions.

—Elizabeth Seton, *Collected Writings*

But those who have received the power to judge others should receive judgment with mercy as they themselves desire to receive mercy from the Lord.

—Francis of Assisi, *letter to the faithful*

Justice

God is not unjust. He will not slam the door against the man who humbly knocks.

—John Climacus, *The Ladder of Divine Ascent*

Executioners do not do something extraordinary; they are servants of justice, and the sword by which criminals are put to death is not against the Law.

—Gregory of Nazianzus, *letter*

The course of justice is also part of this world order and requires punishment of sinners.

—Thomas Aquinas, *Summa Theologica*

It does not cost more to side with justice, but then one must have a conscience and reason calmly as to the object of life: in a word, serve and love God.

—Théophane Vénard, *letter to his brothers, 1851*

God deserves honor and our neighbor [deserves] our care, charity and love. But this justice is not done properly. Oh, how many of us are in fact full of injustice; and we are so foolish to believe that we do justice to our neighbors and to ourselves! We are unjust toward ourselves because so often our pride takes us away from ourselves!

—Maria Maddalena de' Pazzi, *The Dialogues*

God the Father is changeless in justice and spares the unjust only because they pray to the divine Son for forgiveness. For God looks at the divine Word made flesh and is reminded that it is through the Word that all creatures were made.

—Hildegard of Bingen, *letter to Abbot Helenger*

God cast out all those who prize evil rather than justice.

—Hildegard of Bingen, *Scivias*

His justice is so great and penetrating that it reaches deep into the heart of things, and all things stand before Him in naked truth, and nothing can withstand Him.

—Faustina Kowalska, *Divine Mercy in My Soul*

Once charity begins, justice begins; as charity increases, justice increases; when charity is perfect, justice is perfect.

—Robert Bellarmine, *The Mind's Ascent to God by the Ladder of Created Things*

Where there is no true justice there can be no right. For that which is done by right is justly done, and what is unjustly done cannot be done by right.

—Augustine, *The City of God*

Justice is that virtue which gives everyone his due.

—Augustine, *The City of God*

The grace of the Holy Spirit does not permit delay. When God is asking his creatures for anything, he asks gently leaving them entirely free. But the longer we delay in responding to his gentle request the less we hear his voice, and the longer his voice goes undeeded the more his justice is asserted.

—Louis de Montfort, *letter*

What crimes are committed in the name of justice!

If you were a dealer in fire-arms and someone offered to buy a gun from you, so that he might use the weapon to kill your mother, would you sell it to him?—Yet, wasn't he ready to pay you a just price for it?

University professor, journalist, politician, diplomat: reflect.

—Josemaría Escrivá, *The Way*

K

Kindness

I will be kind to everybody, particularly to those whom I find troublesome.

—Anthony Mary Claret, *autobiography*

Knowledge

Love without knowledge is only darkness to the wise soul.

—Mechtilde of Magdeburg, *The Flowing Light of the Godhead*

I don't think it is possible to have virtue or the fullness of grace without dwelling within the cell of our heart and soul, where we will gain the treasure that is life for us; I mean the holy abyss that is holy knowledge of ourselves and of God.

—Catherine of Siena, *letter to Abbess Nicolosa, c. 1374*

If, then, you wish to build in your heart the sacred tabernacle of spiritual knowledge, clear all the stain of sin away from you and wipe out all the concerns of this present world. For it is impossible that a soul which is in the slightest way taken up with worldly cares should win the gift of knowledge or bear the fruit of spiritual awareness or should concentrate on spiritual readings.

—John Cassian, *Conferences*

The fact is that it is impossible for an unclean soul to acquire spiritual knowledge, no matter how hard it labors at the reading of the Scriptures. No one pours some rare ointment or the best honey or a precious liquid into a foul and filthy container. A jar once shot through by evil smells will more easily contaminate the most fragrant myrrh than receive from it some sweetness or capacity to please.

—John Cassian, *Conferences*

To attain spiritual knowledge there is no other route except the following, which has been so aptly described by one of the prophets: "Sow integrity for yourselves, reap a harvest of the hope of life, light up within you the light of knowledge." (Hosea 10:12) First, then, we must sow integrity for ourselves, that is, we must propagate real perfection in us with the works of justice. Second, we must reap the hope of life. In other words, the fruits of spiritual virtue must be gathered by way of the expulsion of the sins of the flesh and in this way it will be possible for us to turn on the light of knowledge within us.

—John Cassian, *Conferences*

God makes things exist by his knowing them and, therefore, the existence of things depends on God's knowledge. The soul can somehow guess about future events. God sees all future events no less clearly than past and present events.

—Robert Bellarmine, *The Mind's Ascent to God by the Ladder of Created Things*

Made like unto God, you too by a single intuition, one which remains forever, may see at once God in himself and yourself and all created things in God.

—Robert Bellarmine, *The Mind's Ascent to God by the Ladder of Created Things*

Brothers, if the full knowledge of the true wisdom and the knowledge of God were going to be given to us through letters and formal study, what need would there be then for faith, or for divine Baptism or even communication in the mysteries?

—Symeon the New Theologian, *Ethical Discourses*

If you have received from God the gift of knowledge, however limited, beware of neglecting charity and temperance. They are virtues which radically purify the soul from passions and so open the way of knowledge continually.

—Maximus the Confessor, *Centuries on Charity*

The way of spiritual knowledge passes through inner freedom and humility. Without them we shall never see the Lord.

—Maximus the Confessor, *Centuries on Charity*

One can come to a certain knowledge of God, a knowledge superior to that of others. If we call that perfect knowledge, however, it is not perfect in an absolute sense, but only when compared with the knowledge of other people.

—Gregory of Nazianzus, *oration*

L

Laughter

Laughter is a sign of friendliness so long as it is not coarse. . . . You ought not to laugh always simply because you have the capacity, any more than a horse is always neighing because it is capable of neighing.

We ought to control our laughter, to learn to laugh in moderation, being very careful not to let go of ourselves.

—Clement of Alexandria, *The Teacher*

Leadership

You will never be a leader if you see others only as stepping stones to get ahead. You will be a leader if you are ambitious for the salvation of all mankind.

—Josemaría Escrivá, *The Way*

Leisure

Too little play is not as bad as too much; like salt, one needs only a little to give savor to life.

—Thomas Aquinas, *Summa Theologica*

Light

God is light and the vision of Him as is light. Thus, in the vision of the light there is knowledge first of all that God is, just as in the case of a man there is first hearing about him, then sight of him, and with the sight of him the knowledge that the man about whom one has heard does in fact exist.

—Symeon the New Theologian, *Ethical Discourses*

Just as the darkness does not go away unless the light is present, so the disease of the soul is not banished unless He Who takes away our infirmities comes and unites Himself with us. He is called health when he comes because He chases away every disease and infirmity of the soul and gives us back our health; and he is called light, Who is transcends all light, because He illumines us; and life, Who is beyond all life, because he vivifies us.

—Symeon the New Theologian, *Ethical Discourses*

The Lord uses us as torches, to make that light shine out. Much depends on us; if we respond many people will remain in darkness no longer, but will walk instead along paths that lead to eternal life.

—Josemaría Escrivá, *The Forge*

For mortals this life is a race: we run it on earth that we may receive our crown elsewhere.

—Jerome, *letter, 384*

Living

Sow, sow God's word! Make good on the talents entrusted to you! God has given you, and your neighbors as well, not merely one talent but ten. These are the ten commandments, the very life of our soul. So be enterprising in your use of them.

—Catherine of Siena, *letter to a frater in Pisa, c. 1374*

The soul who loves virtuously, places the root of her tree in the valley of true humility; but those who live miserably are planted on the mountain of pride, whence it follows that since the root of the tree is badly planted, the tree can bear no fruits of life but only of death.

—Catherine of Siena, *Dialogue*

Every part of the journey is of importance to the whole.

—Teresa of Ávila, *The Way of Perfection*

Living well is not only doing good things but doing them well, choosing them in a right way and not simply acting on impulse or emotion. Right choosing involves having a right goal and suitably acting to achieve that goal.

—Thomas Aquinas, *Summa Theologica*

What gives a man dignity is not his wealth or good fortune or noble birth but a worthy and virtuous life and the dignity of his labor.

—Pope John XXIII, *letter to cousin Agnese, May 4, 1946*

Let the world indulge its madness. Let it wear itself out, for it cannot endure and passes like a shadow. It is growing old and, I think, is in its last decrepit stage. But we, buried deep in the wounds of Christ, why should we be dismayed?

—Peter Canisius, *letter to Jesuits in Cologne, 1552*

Our life is like the print of a cloud in the air, like a mist dissolved in the sun, like a passing shadow, like a flower that soon fadeth, like a dry leaf carried with every wind, like a vapor that soon vanishes out of sight.

—Robert Southwell, *letter to Catholics in prison, 1584*

It is from experience that we reap what is profitable, and it is experience that refutes the fruitless arguments of contentious braggarts.

—Gregory Palamas, *In Defense of Those Who Devoutly Practice a Life of Stillness*

Your way of acting should be different from the world's way; the love of Christ must come before all else. You are not to act in anger or nurse a grudge. Rid your heart of all deceit. Never give a hollow greeting of peace or turn away when someone needs your love. Bind yourself to no oath lest it prove false, but speak the truth with heart and tongue.

—Benedict, *Rule*

The debt we pay for this beautiful creation and the many enjoyments of this life are to be borne in some degree by us all. Human life and sorrow are inseparable.

—Elizabeth Seton, *Collected Writings*

When all is over, when the silver cord is loosed, and the spirit returned to Him who gave it, then He who has witnessed its struggles will give it rest. In the meantime exertions and sacrifices must be made.

—Elizabeth Seton, *Collected Writings*

If, then, we wish to learn the art of living well and dying well, let us not follow the crowd, which only believes and values what is seen; we must follow Christ and His Apostles, who, by word and deed, have taught us that present things are to be despised, and "the hope and coming of the glory of the great God and our Savior Jesus Christ" is alone to be desired and expected.

—Robert Bellarmine, *The Art of Dying Well*

The objective of our life is the kingdom of God, but we should carefully ask what we should aim for. If we do not look very carefully into this we will wear ourselves out in useless strivings. For those who travel without a marked road there is the toil of the journey—and no arrival at a destination.

—John Cassian, *Conferences*

There is no arrival unless there is a definite plan to go.

—John Cassian, *Conferences*

What is our life but a torch which is forever consuming itself? The more resplendently it burns, the more rapidly it will fail.

—Peter of Alcantara, *Treatise on Prayer & Meditation*

What, indeed, is this world if not a wheel going round? Look at everything that is of the world and you will not find anything that is not subject to mutability, and mutability, by its turning, rolls down its subjects from one state to another. Now, indeed, through certain advances one is lifted up to better things, but then through various failings one sinks down to worse. In this state of changeableness, the good and the evil walk on the wheel, but in different ways.

—Elisabeth of Schönau, *Third Book of Visions*

The spirit of the world is restless, and wishes to do everything. Let us leave it to itself. Let us have no desire to choose our own paths, but walk in those which God may be pleased to prescribe for us.

—Vincent de Paul, *letter to a Polish missionary, 1659*

For where there's transgression accusations [follow], but, where there's righteous living, [there follow] praises and crowns.

—John Chrysostom, *homily*

Above all, you who've recently put on Christ and received the descent of the Spirit, take care every day that the brightness of your clothing receive no blemish or wrinkle (Ephesians 5:27) on any part; neither through inappropriate comments nor through listening to frivolity, nor through wicked thoughts, nor through your eyes darting carelessly and at random over whatever they chance upon.

—John Chrysostom, *baptismal instruction*

Your guardianship of the faith ought therefore to be good, that integrity of life and silence may endure unblemished.

—Ambrose, *On the Mysteries*

Life is movement, tending to an end.

—Maximilian M. Kolbe, *article, 1933*

The world must change if souls pass from this life to a new life.

—Basil the Great, *homily on the Hexaemeron*

Be submissive to good, unbending to evil, gentle in generosity, untiring in love, just in all things.

—Columban, *letter, c. 610*

Your life should be a psalm not resounding with earthly utterances—thoughts are these utterances—but you should be a pure, audible sound coming from heaven above.

—Gregory of Nyssa, *Commentary on the Inscriptions of the Psalms*

Thus everyone who conducts himself soberly and justly with a healthy attitude in this life, and who bears with the courage and patience the pains and sorrows of those trials and tribulations which come upon him, whether from visible or invisible enemies, wisely redeems his time and makes good use of the evil days of the present life.

—Symeon the New Theologian, *Ethical Discourses*

Your life, your work, should never be negative, nor *anti* anything. It is—it must be—positive, optimistic, youthful, cheerful, and peaceful.

—Josemaría Escrivá, *The Forge*

Without God's help it is impossible to live a clean life.

—Josemaría Escrivá, *The Forge*

Whoever has been called to eternal life ought to resemble the Incorruptible. For this reason, let our whole life be springtime; let the truth within us never grow old.

—Clement of Alexandria, *The Teacher*

Live a holy life and you will be praising God with your whole life.

—Augustine, *On Psalm 148*

Lord's Prayer

see PRAYER

Love

ATTRIBUTES AND NATURE OF LOVE

The most necessary virtue of all is love.

—Anthony Mary Claret, *autobiography*

Why do we not burn with the divine fire which he has come to enkindle on earth! We ought to be consumed therein. To love and be consumed by this sacred fire will be my constant endeavor.

—Margaret Mary Alacoque, *Life and Writings of St. Margaret Mary*

In order to make good use of time we must love ardently and constantly; we must surrender ourselves entirely to love, leaving it to act for us. Be satisfied to adhere to it in everything, but always with profound humility.

—Margaret Mary Alacoque, *Life and Writings of St. Margaret Mary*

For love is repaid with love alone.

—Francis de Sales, *Oeuvres*

Love is the chief among the passions of the soul. It is the king of all the heart's impulses; it draws all things to itself, and makes us like to what we love.

—Francis de Sales, *The Devout Life*

We must make no compromise with a love that is contrary to the love of God.

—Francis de Sales, *The Devout Life*

But true love is the love of a lover. It is rarely found, for nothing touches it, neither good nor evil. The lover gives his life gladly for the beloved. He does not know his own interests or even his own needs. Sickness and health are alike to him; prosperity and adversity, life and death; consolation and desolation are alike to him.

—Marguerite Bourgeoys, *Autographic Writings*

Love is an affection of the soul, not a contract: it cannot rise from a mere agreement, nor is it so to be gained. It is spontaneous in its origin and impulse; and true love is its own satisfaction.

—Bernard of Clairvaux, *On Loving God*

Learn from Christ to love tenderly, lest we be seduced by the glory of the world or the delights of the flesh; prudently, lest we be deceived by the spirit of lies and deceit; bravely, lest being overcome by adversity we flee from the love of the Lord. Let the courage of God who is Christ strengthen you.

—Bernard of Clairvaux, *On the Canticle of Canticles*

I love because I love, I love that I may love. Love is a great thing so long as it continually returns to its fountainhead, flows back to its source, always drawing from there the water which constantly replenished it.

—Bernard of Clairvaux, *sermon*

True love does not demand a reward, but it deserves one.

—Bernard of Clairvaux, *On Loving God*

Love is the eternal law whereby the universe was created and is ruled. Since all things are ordered in measure and number and weight, and nothing is left outside the realm of law, that universal law cannot itself be without a law, which is itself. So love though it did not create itself, does surely govern itself by its own decree.

—Bernard of Clairvaux, *On Loving God*

Whether man will or no, he cannot help making an act of love.

—Catherine of Siena, *Dialogue*

Love is had only by loving. If you want love, you must begin by loving—I mean you must want to love. Once you want it, you must open the eye of your understanding to see where and how love is to be found. And you will find it within your very self.

—Catherine of Siena, *letter to a nobleman's wife*

Love is so powerful that it makes one heart and one will of lover and beloved. Whatever the one loves, so does the other; if it were otherwise, it would not be perfect love.

—Catherine of Siena, *letter to Cardinal Iacopo Orsini, 1374*

Love exhales a continual perfume, by which man suffers himself to be allured, and so powerful is this fragrance that however great may be the torments through which he passes to salvation, there is no martyrdom he would not suffer gladly to attain it.

—Catherine of Genoa, *Life and Doctrine*

Love makes men just, simple, pure, rich, wise, and contented, and with its sweetness lessens every grief.

—Catherine of Genoa, *Life and Doctrine*

O love, thy bonds are so sweet and so strong that they bind angels and saints together, and so firm and so close that they are never broken; men who are bound by this chain are so united that they have but one will and one aim, and all things among them are in common, both temporal and spiritual. In this union there is no difference between rich and poor, between nation and nation; all contradiction is excluded, for by this love crooked things are made straight and difficulties reconciled.

—Catherine of Genoa, *Life and Doctrine*

I know that without love all we do is worthless.

—Thérèse of Lisieux, *The Story of a Soul*

Love alone attracts me. I no longer wish for either suffering or death and yet both are precious to me.

—Thérèse of Lisieux, *The Story of a Soul*

Of course one may stumble and be guilty of small faults, but love, able to draw good from everything, will very quickly destroy all that displeases Jesus and will fill one's heart with deep and humble peace.

—Thérèse of Lisieux, *The Story of a Soul*

I no longer want anything except to love until I die of love. I am free and fear nothing.

—Thérèse of Lisieux, *The Story of a Soul*

In order for love to be fully satisfied it must descend to nothingness and transform that nothingness to living fire. I know, Lord, that "love is repaid by love alone." And so I have sought and I have found the way to ease my heart—by giving you love for love.

—Thérèse of Lisieux, *The Story of a Soul*

Love finds nothing hard: no task is difficult if you wish to do it.

—Jerome, *letter, 384*

Love binds us fast to God. Love casts a veil over sins innumerable. There are no limits to love's endurance, no end to its patience. Love is without servility, as it is without arrogance. Love knows no divisions, promotes no discord; all the works of love are done in perfect fellowship.

—Clement of Rome, *first epistle to the Corinthians*

Love grants prophecy, miracles. It is an abyss of illumination, a fountain of fire, bubbling up to inflame the thirsty soul. It is the condition of angels, and the progress of eternity.

—John Climacus, *The Ladder of Divine Ascent*

But true love is not in word only but also in action and truth.

—Columban, *sermon*

Love endures everything, love is stronger than death, love fears nothing.

—Faustina Kowalska, *Divine Mercy in My Soul*

Pure love is capable of great deeds, and it is not broken by difficulty or adversity. As it remains strong in the midst of difficulties, so too it perseveres in the toilsome and drab life of each day. It knows that only one thing is needed to please God: to do even the smallest things out of great love—love and always love.

—Faustina Kowalska, *Divine Mercy in My Soul*

Great love can change small things into great ones, and it is only love which lends value to our actions.

—Faustina Kowalska, *Divine Mercy in My Soul*

Love is a mystery that transforms everything it touches into things beautiful and pleasing to God. The love of God makes a soul free.

—Faustina Kowalska, *Divine Mercy in My Soul*

Love is not only higher than fear and hope, but higher than all the charisms, however great and however marvelous these may be in human reckoning.

—John Cassian, *Conferences*

If you have the will to love, you have already given a proof that you love.

—Maximilian M. Kolbe, *letter to friars in Japan, 1933*

A single act of love makes the soul return to life. Let us often make use of this means.

—Maximilian M. Kolbe, *letter to Polish friars, 1940*

Everything that is done out of Love acquires greatness and beauty.

—Josemaría Escrivá, *The Way*

Do everything for Love. Thus there will be no little things: everything will be big. Perseverance in little things for love is heroism.

—Josemaría Escrivá, *The Way*

Love is sacrifice; and sacrifice for Love's sake is a joy.

—Josemaría Escrivá, *The Forge*

Love in the darkness and uncertainty in which God wishes you to be: What does it matter where the love comes from, provided it be followed by good results?

—Claude de la Colombière, *letter*

Love cannot be compelled. You do not love because you are forced to love: you love spontaneously, of your own free will.

—John Chrysostom, *On the Letter to the Ephesians*

In the very nature of every human being has been sown the seed of the ability to love. You and I ought to welcome this seed, cultivate it carefully, nourish it attentively and foster its growth by going to the school of God's commandments with the help of his grace.

—Basil the Great, *The Greater Rules*

True love requires one to will another's good as one's own.

—Thomas Aquinas, *Summa of Christian Teaching*

Love is orderly and just, when the greater good is preferred to the lesser good. Need we be reminded that among all good things that affect man, the good of the soul is paramount, and after that comes the good of the body, with the lowest place being occupied by the good that consists in external things?

—Thomas Aquinas, *On the Perfection of Religious Life*

God's love

Love is our Lord's meaning. . . . Before God made us he loved us, which love was never abated and never will be. And in this love he has done all his works, and in this love he has made all things profitable to us, and in this love our life is everlasting. In our creation we had beginning, but the love in which he created us was in him from without beginning. In this love we have our beginning, and all this shall we see in God without end.

—Julian of Norwich, *Showings*

The love which Our Lord had during his passion puts into full light God's love for us.

—Brother André, *Brother André According to Witnesses*

But God loves us so much that although he sees us so blind and deaf to our own advantage, yet he does not for that reason cease to knock continually at our hearts by his holy inspirations, that he may so enter and make therein tabernacles for himself into which creatures can never enter more.

—Catherine of Genoa, *Life and Doctrine*

The intimate, amorous relation which God sustains with the heart of man is a secret between him and the heart.

—Catherine of Genoa, *Life and Doctrine*

Divine love brings with it every good and banishes every evil.

—Catherine of Genoa, *Life and Doctrine*

God's love shows itself just as well in the simplest soul which puts up no resistance to his grace as it does in the loftiest soul.

—Thérèse of Lisieux, *The Story of a Soul*

There is a city of God, and its Founder has inspired us with a love which makes us covet its citizenship.

—Augustine, *The City of God*

Neither death, nor life, nor angels, nor principalities, nor powers . . . nor any other creature, shall be able to separate us from the love of God.

—Paul, *Romans 8:38, 39*

God loves, he desires nothing else than to be loved; for he loves only that he may be loved.

—Bernard of Clairvaux, *sermon*

For love fulfills every wish of God.

—Hildegard of Bingen, *Book of Divine Works*

Who would suppose that you, O infinite, eternal God, have loved me for centuries and even before the centuries began? Indeed, you have loved me simultaneously with your existence as God; consequently you have loved me always and will always love me. Even though I did not yet exist, you already loved me, O good God. You called me from nothingness to existence.

—Maximilian M. Kolbe, *meditation, 1929*

The essence of the love of God will always consist not in feeling good, not in remembering or thinking or understanding or imagining, but exclusively in fulfilling God's will at every moment of our lives and in submitting ourselves completely to this will.

—Maximilian M. Kolbe, *letter to a brother, 1935*

The only real love is God's Love!

—Josemaría Escrivá, *The Way*

Love of God

If you love the world, you withdraw from God. If you withdraw from the love of the world and begin to love God, you then approach God. So we approach God when we grow in love of God. God approaches us when God deigns to have mercy on us.

—Aelred of Rielvaux, *sermon*

Hence we must attempt in return to repay the acts of his divine kindness by loving God the Father with our whole heart, our whole soul [and] our whole strength.

—Bede the Venerable, *homily on the Gospels*

It is not necessary to acquire riches, nor to obtain dignities, nor to gain a great name. The only thing necessary is to love God.

—Alphonsus Liguori, *sermon*

God has not created us, nor does he preserve our lives, that we may labor to acquire riches or Earthly honors, or that we may indulge in amusements: but that we may love and serve him in this world, in order to love and enjoy him for eternity in the next.

—Alphonsus Liguori, *sermon*

If indeed we loved the good God as we should, it would be a lot easier for us to put into practice the Christian virtues of patience and charity . . . for we can't love God without loving our neighbor. We would serve him better in our daily work. We would find it less tiring to say our morning and night prayers for those who are so busy that they cannot find the time even to go to mass.

—Brother André, *Brother André According to Witnesses*

It is not necessary to spend 15 or 20 years in colleges and universities to love the Lord.

—Brother André, *Brother André According to Witnesses*

Therefore in the love of God no measurement is proposed beyond which it is not fitting to proceed; but no matter how much anyone loves, he will always love further, and for this reason it is said that there is no prefixed measure beyond which it is not fitting to progress.

—Thomas Aquinas, *Commentary on Sentences*

Since all that one does is directed to the ultimate end through one's intention and all one's acts are disposed in accordance with the ultimate end, it will come to pass that when he is in a state of eternal beatitude, the rational creature will be loving God with his whole heart as long as his intention directs every thought and every love and every desire and every action to God.

—Thomas Aquinas, *On the Perfection of the Spiritual Life*

God is to be loved as our ultimate goal, to which everything is to be referred. Rightly then a certain totality is commanded in our love of God. In heaven we will love God with all our heart actually intent on him at all times; on the way there the whole of our heart is to be disposed to God, in such a way that it will not receive into itself anything opposed to God's love.

—Thomas Aquinas, *Summa Theologica*

God is the most lovable of all things, and meditation on his nature is the strongest incentive there is to love and devotion; but because our minds are not strong in themselves, we need to be led to knowledge, and so to love of God by way of the world we sense, and above all by thinking of Christ the man, so that *by seeing God with our eyes we can be lifted up to love what we cannot see.*

—Thomas Aquinas, *Summa Theologica*

You know, God, that I have never wanted anything but to love you alone. I long for no other glory. Your love has gone before me from my childhood, it has grown with me, and now it is an abyss whose depths I cannot plumb. Love attracts love and mine soars up to you, eager to fill the abyss of your love, but it is not even a drop of dew lost in the ocean. To love you as you love me, I must borrow your love—only then can I have peace.

—Thérèse of Lisieux, *The Story of a Soul*

O divine love, where shall I find words to speak of thee? I am conquered and subdued by thee; I am dying of love and I do not feel love; I am annihilated in love and I do not know love; I feel love acting within me, and its action I do not understand; I feel my heart burning with love, and yet I do not see the flame of love.

—Catherine of Genoa, *Life and Doctrine*

Love is a divine flame: and as material fire ever burns and consumes, according to its nature, so in man the love of God is by its nature ever working toward its end, and for its part never ceases to benefit and serve him whom it holds so dear; he who does not know its power has but himself to blame, since God never tires of doing good to man while he is in this life, and has always the most tender love for him.

—Catherine of Genoa, *Life and Doctrine*

You want me to tell you why God is to be loved and how much. I answer, the reason for loving God is God himself; and the measure of love due to him is immeasurable love. . . . We are to love God for himself, because of a twofold reason: nothing is more reasonable, nothing is more profitable.

—Bernard of Clairvaux, *On Loving God*

Therefore even the infidel who knows not Christ but does at least know himself, is bound to love God for God's own sake. He is unpardonable if he does not love the Lord his God with all his heart, and with all his soul, and with all his mind; for his own innate justice and common sense cry out from within that he is bound wholly to love God, from whom he has received all things.

—Bernard of Clairvaux, *On Loving God*

Because love is natural, it is only right to love the Author of nature first of all.

—Bernard of Clairvaux, *On Loving God*

But if we are to love our neighbors as we ought, we must have regard to God also: for it is only in God that we can pay the debt of love aright. Now a man cannot love his neighbor in God, except he love God himself; wherefore we must love God first, in order to love our neighbors in him.

—Bernard of Clairvaux, *On Loving God*

Whosoever loves God aright loves all God's creatures.

—Bernard of Clairvaux, *On Loving God*

God is so perfect and so amiable that he ought to be loved above all things, and that nothing ought to be loved except for him. Faith and reason proclaim this truth.

—Ignatius of Loyola, *Spiritual Exercises*

To love God is the true object of our heart.

—Ignatius of Loyola, *Spiritual Exercises*

Divine love suffices to prevent us from willfully doing anything which could displease the Beloved of our souls. Indeed, I cannot understand how a heart that belongs to God and truly wishes to love him, can deliberately offend him.

—Margaret Mary Alacoque, *Life and Writings of St. Margaret Mary*

When the heart has no love of itself, it will be forever aroused to love you alone!

—Mechtilde of Magdeburg, *The Flowing Light of the Godhead*

There is no other path but through the burning love of the Crucified, a love which so transformed Paul into Christ when he was carried up to the third heaven (2 Corinthians 12:2) that he could say: With Christ I am nailed to the cross. I live, now not I, but Christ lives in me (Galatians 2:20).

—Bonaventure, *The Soul's Journey Into God*

I find so much contentment in the love of God, that I am obliged to consider how any one can raise his eyes to the light of heaven and be insensible to it.

—Elizabeth Seton, *Collected Writings*

Now when the fear of God is perfect, love is also perfect, which means that the transformation of the soul in God through love is accomplished.

—John of the Cross, *The Ascent of Mount Carmel*

For where there is true love of God, love of self and of one's own things finds no entry.

—John of the Cross, *The Dark Night of the Soul*

God must be loved with the whole understanding, without deceit, with the whole will, without reserve or division, with the whole mind, without forgetfulness, without diminution, without negligence or remissness.

—Mary of Agreda, *The Mystical City of God*

The motive of charity in loving God is none else than God Himself; for He must be loved for his own sake, being the highest Good and most perfect goodness and holiness.

—Mary of Agreda, *The Mystical City of God*

And in order that thou mayest be diligent, cultivate love; for love is a fire, which does not have its effect until the material is prepared; therefore let thy heart always be disposed and prepared. Whenever the Most High bids thee or communicates to thee anything for the welfare of souls, or especially for their eternal salvation, devote thyself to it entirely; for they are bought at the inestimable price of the blood of the Lamb and of divine love.

—Mary of Agreda, *The Mystical City of God*

Love God not for your own sake, for your own profit, but love him for his sake, because he is the highest Good and is worthy of being loved. Then your love will be perfect and not mercenary.

—Catherine of Siena, *letter to a nobleman's wife*

Lord, you alone know that no one can love something he cannot at all know. Therefore, since I shall now love you alone, let me get to know you better so that I can learn to love you completely.

—Henry Suso, *Little Book of Eternal Wisdom*

To me, a city that doesn't have citizens who love God is worth less than any village, and less honorable than any cave.

—John Chrysostom, *homily*

May the perfect love of God reign in our hearts!

—Louis de Montfort, *letter*

Whatever I shall have to do or suffer in this miserable life, I intend that it be proof of love for my God, so that living, I shall live only to love, and dying, I may die in order to love still more.

—Joseph Cafasso, *prayer on preparation for death*

Unless someone loves God first of all with all his soul and proves his love for Him by denying both himself and the world, he is unworthy mystically of God's manifestation in the revelation of the Holy Spirit, nor does he possess Him as head, but is instead a dead body in spiritual works, is deprived of Christ, the life of all.

—Symeon the New Theologian, *Ethical Discourses*

You have more love of God than you think.

—Claude de la Colombière, *spiritual reflections*

Whoever loves God loves his neighbor.

—Basil the Great, *The Greater Rules*

We will certainly deserve great punishment if, having known that we are so dearly loved by our good Savior, we nevertheless are so ungrateful as to not love him with all our heart and power, nor follow with all our strength and all our care the examples he has given us in his life, passion and death.

—Francis de Sales, *Oeuvres*

He died of love for us, we should also die of love for him; or, if we cannot die of love, at least we should live for him alone.

—Francis de Sales, *Oeuvres*

You will always find his eyes fixed upon you with unchangeable love.

—Francis de Sales, *The Devout Life*

LOVE OF OTHERS

Love one another as Jesus Christ has loved us, not because of any merit that may be found in us, but only because he created us in his image and likeness.

—Francis de Sales, *Oeuvres*

Let us love, then, to the whole extent of our hearts, in order to please our heavenly Father, but let us love reasonably; that is, let our love be guided by reason, which desires that we love the soul of the neighbor more than his body. But let us love his body also, and then, in proper order, all that pertains to the neighbor, each thing according to its merits, for the proper exercise of this love.

—Francis de Sales, *Oeuvres*

If we love a vicious person, our friendship too will be evil; for since it cannot be founded on true virtue, it must rest in some false good or mere sensual attraction.

—Francis de Sales, *The Devout Life*

I find that there are several kinds of love in human society: there is the love of strangers, of travelers, of the poor, of associates, of angels, of parents and of lovers. All these loves can be good or indifferent. It is only the love of the lover which penetrates the heart of God. Only to this love is nothing refused.

—Marguerite Bourgeoys, *Autographic Writings*

God is not satisfied if we preserve the love we owe our neighbor; we must preserve our neighbor in the love he ought to have for us. We must give the cloak to him who wishes to have the tunic rather than take him to court.

—Marguerite Bourgeoys, *Autographic Writings*

The effect of true love is the reciprocal communication of all good things between the persons who love each other; whence it follows that charity cannot exist without sacrifice.

—Ignatius of Loyola, *Spiritual Exercises*

To love our neighbor's welfare as much as our own: that is true and sincere charity out of a pure heart, and a good conscience, and of faith unfeigned. . . . Whosoever loves his own prosperity only is proved thereby not to love good for its own sake, since he loves it on his own account.

—Bernard of Clairvaux, *On Loving God*

As you esteem yourself so must you consider your neighbor. If you love yourself because you love God, you will have the same love for your neighbor. As for your enemies, esteem them not for what they are but for what they may one day become.

—Bernard of Clairvaux, *On the Canticle of Canticles*

For that is a true and sincere charity to be attributed entirely to a pure heart and unfeigned faith which leads us to love our neighbor's good as well as our own. The man who loves his own good in preference to his neighbor's good, or who loves only for his own good, proves that his love is not disinterested.

—Bernard of Clairvaux, *letter to Guy the Carthusian Prior*

Loving only friends to the exclusion of enemies goes unrewarded by God.

—Thomas Aquinas, *Summa Theologica*

Do not search about for the words to show people you love them. Instead, ask God to show them your love without your having to talk about it. Otherwise you will never have time enough both for loving gestures and for compunction.

—John Climacus, *The Ladder of Divine Ascent*

I tell you that if Truth Himself had not declared that there is no greater love than to lay down one's life for one's friends, I should conceive it a thing equally noble to do what the Apostle tells the Corinthians: "I die daily, I affirm it, by the very pride that I take in you, brethren, in Jesus Christ our Lord."

—John de Brébeuf, *letter to Jesuits in France, 1636*

Therefore we ought to love one another warmly, for he who loves his neighbor loves God, and he who loves God loves his own soul.

—Anthony, *letter*

The love of husband and wife is the force that welds society together. Men will take up arms and even sacrifice their lives for the sake of this love.

—John Chrysostom, *homily*

When you are looking for a bridegroom or a bride, ask this first of all, whether your intended is loved by God and enjoys good will from above. If these blessings are present, everything else follows. If they are absent, even if the goods of this life are present in great abundance, they are of no benefit.

—John Chrysostom, *sermon*

For that person truly loves his enemy who is not hurt by an injury done to him, but, because of love of God, is stung by the sin of his soul. Let him show his love by his deeds.

—Francis of Assisi, *saying*

We need to love our neighbor, not just because he is pleasant or helpful or rich or influential or even because he shows us gratitude. These motives are too self-serving, unworthy of our Lady's Knights. Genuine love rises above creatures and soars up to God. In him, by him and through him it loves all men, both good and wicked, friends and enemies.

—Maximilian M. Kolbe, *article on spiritual combat, 1924*

For when you love someone because he is a source of advantage or of pleasure, you are really loving not the friend but yourself, because you are seeking from him a good that serves your purpose or serves your pleasure. To love your neighbor in that manner is to love him as you love wine or a horse. Such things we do not love as ourselves, as though wishing them well; rather we are turning whatever good is in them to our own advantage. Thus the commandment to love our neighbor as ourselves requires that our charity toward him be genuine.

—Thomas Aquinas, *On the Perfection of Religious Life*

It is possible, accordingly, to judge how perfect is one's love for one's neighbor by considering what a man gives up for the love of his neighbor.

—Thomas Aquinas, *On the Perfection of Religious Life*

Since slavery is so opposed to true life that is akin to death, if anyone permits himself to be enslaved for the love of his neighbor, this love would be on the same level as one who exposes himself to the danger of death for the love of his neighbor.

—Thomas Aquinas, *On the Perfection of Religious Life*

Labor with all your might to gain for yourselves the love of the people. You will be far better able to help them if they love you than if they fear you.

—Francis Xavier, *letter to Jesuit missionaries*

Have a great love for those who contradict and fail to love you, for in this way love is begotten in a heart that has no love. God so acts with us, for he loves us that we might love by means of the very love he bears toward us.

—John of the Cross, *letter*

If you do not think, therefore, about the fault of your fellow-man, if you suffer the pain he causes you and have forbearance, behold! You have love! For it is love which incites you to good works and patience.

—Theoleptos of Philadelphia, *letter*

Yet readiness to do good to someone who hates us is a characteristic of perfect love alone.

—Maximus the Confessor, *Centuries on Charity*

An enemy is by definition one who obstructs, ensnares and injures others. He is therefore a sinner. We ought to love his soul by correcting him and doing everything possible to bring him to conversion. We ought to love his body too by coming to his aid with the necessities of life.

—Basil the Great, *The Lesser Rules*

Show love towards hatred and tolerance toward persecution.

—Basil the Great, *letter*

Perfect love is that by which we are ordered to love the Lord with our whole heart, our whole soul and our whole strength, and our neighbor as ourselves. Neither of these [two kinds of] love is capable of being perfect without the other, because God cannot be loved apart from our neighbor, nor our neighbor apart from God.

—Bede the Venerable, *homily on the Gospels*

Loyalty

A truly loyal friend sees nothing in his friend but his heart.

—Aelred of Rielvaux, *Spiritual Friendship*

Lust

If thou hast not these imaginings, thou art without hope: for if thou hast not the imagination thereof, thou hast the deed itself. For he who fights not in his mind against sin, nor gainsays it, sins in the flesh. And he who sins in the flesh, hath of no trouble from the imagination thereof.

—Abbot Cyrus of Alexandria, *saying*

By lust the Devil triumphs over the entire man, over his body and over his soul; over his memory, filling it with that remembrance of unchaste delights, in order to make him take complacency in them; over his intellect, to make him desire occasions of committing sin; over the will, by making it love its impurities as his last end, and as if there were no God.

—Alphonsus Liguori, *sermon*

When we live according to our soul's desire, we deny ourselves out of love of God, and become strangers to the lusts of the flesh. This is what the saints and the just have done.

—Hildegard of Bingen, *Book of Divine Works*

In the realm of evil thoughts none induces to sin as much as do thoughts that concern the pleasure of the flesh.

—Thomas Aquinas, *On the Perfection of the Spiritual Life*

The single are to be admonished not to think that they can have intercourse with disengaged women without incurring the judgment of condemnation.

—Gregory the Great, *The Book of Pastoral Rule*

Lust is fed by feastings, nourished by delicacies, kindled by wine, and inflamed by drunkenness. Still more dangerous than these are the incentives of words, which intoxicate the mind as it were with a kind of wine of the vine of Sodore. Let us be on our guard against abundance of this wine, for when the flesh is intoxicated the mind totters, the heart wavers, the heart is carried to and fro.

—Ambrose, *Concerning Repentance*

A body immersed in delights is a body that breeds lust of every kind.

—John Chrysostom, *homily on the Epistle to the Hebrews*

Filthy talk makes us feel comfortable with filthy action. But the one who knows how to control the tongue is prepared to resist the attacks of lust.

—Clement of Alexandria, *The Teacher*

As long as we are held down by this frail body; as long as we keep our treasure in earthen vessels, and the flesh lusteth against the spirit, the spirit against the flesh: so long can there be no sure victory.

—Jerome, *letter, 384*

M

Malice

Worms thrive in a rotten tree; malice thrives in the deceptively meek and silent. He who has expelled malice has found forgiveness, but he who hugs it is deprived of mercy.

—John Climacus, *The Ladder of Divine Ascent*

The mother of all wickedness is pleasure and malice. If these are in a man, he will not see the Lord; and to abstain from the first without giving up the second will not be of much use.

—John Climacus, *The Ladder of Divine Ascent*

The passions of the mind, love, hate, anger, envy, and the others which are included under the term "malice"—so blind the mind that they prevent it from discerning truth, but they work like tinted lenses which make white seem red or lenses designed to make small things appear large or large things small or things far away appear close or things close appear distant.

—Robert Bellarmine, *The Mind's Ascent to God by the Ladder of Created Things*

How can God justly punish with eternal torments, a sin that lasts but a moment? I answer, that the grievousness of a crime is measured not by its duration, but by the enormity of its malice.

—Alphonsus Liguori, *sermon*

Men find it a grave evil and an unbearable fire to see in happiness those whom they once held in contempt. The rich man's malice does not leave him, even though he already endures its punishment.

—Peter Chrysologus, *sermon*

Just as gold is purged in the fire, even so, through the malice of the wicked, souls are purged and educated and drawn back from things that must not be done.

—Bridget of Sweden, *Book of Questions*

If a sin is of infinite malice, the preventing of a sin is the preventing of an infinite injustice to God, our good Father.

—Anthony Mary Claret, *autobiography*

Man

Man is the source and end of woman.

—Thomas Aquinas, *Summa Theologica*

Marriage

Husbands and wives should live peacefully in their union of marriage; they should be mutually edifying to each other, pray for one another, bear patiently with one another's faults, encourage virtue in one another by good example, and follow the holy and sacred rules of their state, remembering that they are the children of the saints and that, consequently, they ought not to behave like pagans, who have not the happiness of knowing the one true God.

—John Baptiste Marie Vianney, *sermon*

The marriage bond is to be avoided at all costs by those tending to perfection, because this bond entangles a person in worldly cares.

—Thomas Aquinas, *On the Perfection of the Spiritual Life*

Husband and wife should bear with each other, *supportantes invicem in caritate*, as St. Paul enjoins. Everyone has faults. If they are patiently endured, peace will reign happily, but if each little peccadillo is going to arouse friction and put the other out of temper, it will be impossible to live in harmony.

—Robert Bellarmine, *letter to his niece, 1614*

The wife must love her husband as if there were no other man in the world, in much the same way as the husband should love her as if no other woman existed.

—Robert Bellarmine, *letter to his niece, 1614*

A wife ought to love her husband, and be loved by him in return; but she should love him with fear and reverence, so that her love should not prevent her fear; otherwise, she might become a tyrant.

—Robert Bellarmine, *The Art of Dying Well*

Husband and wife are equally responsible for the honor of their marriage bed.

—John Chrysostom, *homily*

There is no relationship between human beings so close as that of husband and wife, if they are as united as they ought to be.

—John Chrysostom, *homily*

But one's partner for life, the mother of one's children, the source of one's every joy, should never be fettered with fear and threats, but with love and patience. What kind of marriage can there be when the wife is afraid of her husband? What sort of satisfaction could a husband himself have, if he lives with his wife as if she were a slave, and not with a woman by her own free will?

—John Chrysostom, *homily*

Your wife is God's creation. If you reproach her, you are not condemning her but Him who made her.

—John Chrysostom, *homily*

A wife should respect her husband even when he shows her no love, and a husband should love his wife even when she shows him no respect. Then they will both be found to lack nothing, since each has fulfilled the commandment given to him.

—John Chrysostom, *homily*

A wife should never nag her husband: "You lazy coward, you have no ambition! Look at our relatives and neighbors; they have plenty of money. Their wives have far more than I do." Let no wife say any such thing; she is her husband's body, and it is not for her to dictate to her head, but to submit and obey.

—John Chrysostom, *homily*

Where chastity and holiness are at stake, the husband has no greater privilege than the wife. He is punished equally with her if he breaks the laws of marriage, and with good reason.

—John Chrysostom, *sermon*

Marriage is not an evil thing. It is adultery that is evil, it is fornication that is evil. Marriage is a remedy to eliminate fornication.

—John Chrysostom, *sermon*

If you take a bad wife, you must endure the annoyance.

—John Chrysostom, *sermon*

When there is an infection in our bodies, we do not cut off the limb, but try to expel the disease. We must do the same with a wife. If there is some wickedness in her, do not reject your wife, but expel the evil.

—John Chrysostom, *sermon*

In particular, you must not seek money when you are about to take a bride. You must consider that marriage is not a business venture but a fellowship for life.

—John Chrysostom, *sermon*

When God divided these two He assigned the management of the household to the woman, but to the men He assigned all the affairs of the city, all the business of the marketplace, courts, council-chambers, armies, and all the rest.

—John Chrysostom, *sermon*

Let each of you love his wife as himself, and let the wife see that she respects her husband.

—Paul, *Ephesians 5:33*

Let there be one home, one table, a shared wealth, one bed, and one soul for you, and make room for the fear of the Lord in your midst. Fear of the Lord is the ornament of the marriage bed; the marriage bed that is devoid of it will be judged cursed and unclean by the Lord.

—Elisabeth of Schönau, *The Book of the Ways of God*

With patience and compassion let the man support the frailties of the woman and the woman support the frailties of the man. Do not disdain each other; instead, vie in showing the greater honor to each other. Bitter and contentious words should never arise between you; rather, reprove each other's excesses in the spirit of gentleness and good severity.

—Elisabeth of Schönau, *The Book of the Ways of God*

As long as the wedding cake lasts the man will be infatuated. But afterwards he will come to himself and say: "That foolish woman wishes to be the master." And then squabbling will begin at home.

—Vincent Ferrer, *sermon*

The good wife ought to honor her husband and look upon him as her lord.

—Vincent Ferrer, *sermon*

Husbands and wives are to be admonished, that those things wherein they sometimes displease one another they bear with mutual patience, and by mutual exhortations remedy. For it is written, "Bear ye one another's burdens, and so ye shall fulfil the laws of Christ" (Galatians 6:2).

—Gregory the Great, *The Book of Pastoral Rule*

The marriage bond is not then to be shunned as though it were sinful, but rather declined as being a galling burden. For the law binds the wife to bear children in labor and sorrow, and is in subjection to her husband, for that he is lord over her.

—Ambrose, *Concerning Widowhood*

Marriage is the key to the control of the desires; it is the seal of unshakeable friendship; it is drink from a hidden spring; strangers cannot taste it; it bubbles up yet cannot be drawn from the outside.

Those who are united in the flesh form one soul and purify their religion by their reciprocal love.

—Gregory of Nazianzus, *First Poem*

Let married people remain on their cross of obedience, which is in marriage. It is the best and most practical cross of them and one of the most demanding, in that there is almost continual activity—and occasions for suffering are more frequent in this state than in any other. Do not desire, therefore, to descend from this cross under any pretext whatever. Since God has placed you there, remain there always.

—Francis de Sales, *Oeuvres*

It was God who brought Eve to Adam and gave her to him as his wife, and it is God, my friends, who with his invisible hand bound the knot which unites you and gave you to one another; therefore give good heed that you cherish a love which is holy, sacred and divine.

—Francis de Sales, *The Devout Life*

If two pieces of wood are carefully glued together, their union will be so close that it is easier to break them in some fresh place than where they were joined; and God so unites man and wife, that it is easier to sever soul and body than those two.

—Francis de Sales, *The Devout Life*

There is no union so precious and so fruitful between husband and wife as that of holy devotion, in which they should mutually lead and sustain each other.

—Francis de Sales, *The Devout Life*

For since the bringing of children into the world is the principal end of marriage, to do anything in order to prevent the accomplishment of this end is always mortal sin.

—Francis de Sales, *The Devout Life*

It is no great thing to love a husband while he lives, but to love him so much after his death to refuse all other, is a degree of love only appertaining to true widows.

—Francis de Sales, *The Devout Life*

Martyrdom

The martyrs get a birth at the time of their death. They get a new beginning through their end, and a new life through their execution. They who were thought to be extinguished on earth shine brilliantly in heaven.

—Peter Chrysologus, *sermon*

Precious is this death which has purchased deathlessness at the price of one's own blood, which has received a crown from God for the supreme act of valor.

—Cyprian of Carthage, *letter to martyrs*

Whatever honors the religious may pay in the places of the martyrs, they are but honors rendered to their memory, not sacred rites or sacrifices offered to dead men as to gods.

—Augustine, *The City of God*

Just as the waters that bubble forth from the springs aren't contained within their own hollows but well over and flow beyond, so too the grace of the Spirit that accompanies these bones and dwells with the saints both extends towards others who follow it with faith and flows from mind into body, and from body into clothing, and from clothing into shoes, and from shoes into a person's shadow.

—John Chrysostom, *homily after the remains of martyrs*

I mean that to honor a martyr is to imitate a martyr.

—John Chrysostom, *homily on martyrs*

They [martyrs] can entreat for our sins, who, if they had any sins, washed them in their own blood; for they are the martyrs of God, our leaders, the beholders of our life and of our actions. Let us not be ashamed to take them as intercessors for our weakness, for they themselves knew the weaknesses of the body, even when they overcame.

—Ambrose, *Concerning Widowhood*

Whoever honors the martyrs, then, honors Christ as well, and whoever rejects His holy ones rejects God, too.

—Maximus of Turin, *sermon*

Although all the saints are everywhere and are useful to everyone, nonetheless those who have put up with suffering for our sake intercede especially for us. For when a martyr suffers he suffers not for himself alone but also for his co-citizens; he suffers for himself for the reward, for his co-citizens an example; he suffers for himself peace, for his co-citizens salvation.

—Maximus of Turin, *sermon*

Martyrdom means bearing witness to God. Every soul that seeks in pureness of heart to know God and obeys the commandments of God is a martyr, bearing witness by life or by words.

—Clement of Alexandria, *Miscellaneous Studies*

Mary

Love, serve, and honor Mary with all your heart, and you will gain and possess entirely the heart of the Heavenly Father. He will love you and bless you abundantly, and she will repeat, after her Divine Son: "For the Father Himself loveth you, because you have loved me."

—John Eudes, *The Holy Name of Mary*

If we wish to recover lost grace, let us seek Mary, by whom this grace has been found. She never lost the divine grace; she always possessed it.

—Alphonsus Liguori, *sermon*

The happiness of those gone to Mary!—to be face to face with her.

—Elizabeth Seton, *Collected Writings*

How happy this earth to possess Mary so long. A secret blessing to the rising church. The perfect praise arising from earth to the blessed Trinity so long as she remained. How darkened in the sight of angels when she was removed from it.

—Elizabeth Seton, *Collected Writings*

Oh, Mary, glorious happy mother, even through the ignomities of her Soul. Her full conformity to His will!

—Elizabeth Seton, *Collected Writings*

As Mother of God and mother of all God's children, she is exalted above all creatures on the throne of glory; maternity itself is glorified through her. As Virgin, she manifests an incomparable beauty pleasing to God, along with the fruitfulness of virginal purity. As Queen, she evidences the conquering power of a serving love and of purity intact. Every woman who wants to fulfill her destiny must look to Mary as the ideal.

—Edith Stein, *Essays on Woman*

Mary stands at the crucial point in human history and especially at the crucial point in of the history of woman; in her, motherhood was transfigured and physical maternity surmounted.

—Edith Stein, *Essays on Woman*

The imitation of Mary includes the imitation of Christ because Mary is the first Christian to follow Christ, and she is the first and most perfect model of Christ. Indeed, that is why the imitation of Mary is not only relevant to women but to all Christians. But she has a special significance for women, one in accord with their nature, for she leads them to the feminine form of the Christian image.

—Edith Stein, *Essays on Woman*

The title of Mary as our mother is not merely symbolic. Mary is our mother in the most real and lofty sense, a sense which surpasses that of earthly maternity. She begot our life of grace for us because she offered up her entire being, body and soul, as the Mother of God.

—Edith Stein, *Essays on Woman*

The Blessed Mary is like a full moon, perfect in every way. A half-moon, with its spots and "horns," is imperfect. The glorious Virgin Mary, however, was spotless in her birth, having been sanctified in her mother's womb and protected by the angels. She never waned, never showed the "horns" of pride, but always shone full and perfect. This is the light that is said to have dispelled the darkness.

—Anthony of Padua, *Sermones*

The Virgin Mary was also like a shimmering rainbow in the conception of the Son of God. A rainbow is formed when the sun enters a cloud. It is made up of four colors: the color of soot, a watery blue, a golden yellow, and a fiery red. At the Annunciation, the sun of justice, the Son of God, entered the cloud, the glorious Virgin Mary. For this reason, the Virgin became like a shimmering rainbow. This rainbow is a sign of the covenant of peace and reconciliation between God and sinners.

The sooty color in the rainbow symbolizes the poverty of the Blessed Mary. The watery color is her humility, the golden yellow is the symbol of her charity, and the fiery red, whose flame cannot be cut or harmed by a sword, symbolizes her incorruptible virginity.

—Anthony of Padua, *Sermones*

Hence from her first instant in the womb of her mother, She was wiser, more prudent, more enlightened, and more capable of comprehending God and all his works, than all the creatures have been or ever will be in eternity, excepting of course her most holy Son.

—Mary of Agreda, *The Mystical City of God*

The beauty, grace and elegance of our Queen were incomparable; for all the natural graces and gifts, which were hers in a most perfect degree, were reenforced by the splendor of supernatural or divine grace, and effected a marvelous union of grace and beauty in all her being and activity, enthralling all in love and admiration of Her.

—Mary of Agreda, *The Mystical City of God*

The Immaculate stands at the extreme limit between God and creation. She is a faithful image of God's perfection and sanctity. Our soul's degree of perfection depends on the union of our will with that of God. The greater the perfection, the closer the union. Because the most Blessed Virgin surpasses in perfection all the angels and saints, her will is united with and made one in the closest manner with the will of God. She lives and acts solely in God and through God. Hence, by accomplishing the will of the Immaculate we accomplish by that very fact the will of God.

—Maximilian M. Kolbe, *article, 1938*

Oh, what a companionship yours is. Truly, truly, being familiar with you is by far better than life. Your scent is like the innermost balsam of divine peace and favor. You are the superabundant and exceedingly rich storehouse of divine consolation. If only, O charity, queen, you led me into your pantry that I might pleasantly taste your better wines, which lie hidden there. Lo, all your vessels are brimful with God and overflowing with the Holy Spirit.

—Gertrude the Great, *Spiritual Exercises*

As into a very precious vessel, more and more graces have been poured into her soul and she has never failed to make good use of them. Therefore, with every good reason, she should be honored by all creatures and served in a particular way by Christians since she is the only pure creature who has ever found favor in the eyes of God. This makes her the astonishment of the heavenly court and the admiration of all humanity.

—Louise de Marillac, *Spiritual Writings*

In Maria are seen at the riches of heaven congregated and collected into one.

—Lawrence of Brindisi, *sermon*

Blessed and revered may you be, my Lady, O Virgin Mary, most holy Mother of God. You are, in truth, his best creation; and no one has ever loved him so intimately as you, O glorious Lady.

—Bridget of Sweden, *prayer*

Let your true devotion to your loving Mother Mary be manifest everywhere and to everyone, so that you may spread everywhere the fragrance of Jesus and, carrying your cross steadfastly after our good Master, gain the crown and kingdom which is waiting for you.

—Louis de Montfort, *letter*

The Fathers of the Church tell us that Mary is an immense ocean of all the perfections of God, the great storehouse of all his possessions, the inexhaustible treasury of the Lord, as well as the treasurer and dispenser of all his gifts. Because God gave her his Son, it is his will that we should receive all gifts through her, and that no heavenly gift should come down upon earth without passing through her as a channel. Of her fulness we have all received, and any grace or hope of salvation we may possess is a gift which comes to us from God through Mary.

—Louis de Montfort, *The Love of Eternal Wisdom*

Only through Mary, then, can we possess divine Wisdom.

—Louis de Montfort, *The Love of Eternal Wisdom*

I declare with the saints: Mary is the earthly paradise of Jesus Christ the new Adam, where he became man by the power of the Holy Spirit, in order to accomplish in her wonder beyond our understanding. She is the vast and divine world of God where unutterable marvels and beauties are to be found. She is the magnificence of the Almighty where he hid his only Son, as in his own bosom, and with him everything that is most excellent and precious.

—Louis de Montfort, *Treatise on True Devotion to the Blessed Virgin*

We must do everything through Mary, that is, we must obey her always and be led in all things by her spirit, which is the Holy Spirit of God.

—Louis de Montfort, *Treatise on True Devotion to the Blessed Virgin*

O my Mother Mary, my hope, the consolation of my soul and the object of my love, do thou remember the many graces I have asked from thee, all of which thou hast so graciously given me. Can it be that I now find this perennial fountain of graces exhausted? No, it has never been heard, nor shall it ever be heard, that anyone devoted to thee has been rejected.

—Anthony Mary Claret, *autobiography*

O Mary, dear Mother Mary, how beautiful it would be to die with thee and to be assisted by thee; I hope and I ask as the greatest of your favors that you come to assist me at the last moments of my life. Oh then when I shall see thee I shall throw myself into thy arms!

—Joseph Cafasso, *second panegyric on St. Joseph Cafasso by St. John Bosco*

Love our Lady. And she will obtain for you abundant grace to conquer in your daily struggle.

—Josemaría Escrivá, *The Way*

But if we praise her with our voice let us not insult her by our behavior. Let us not pretend to praise her but do so in very truth. . . . Truly to praise the humility of Saint Mary is to do everything in our power to cultivate humility. Truly to praise her chastity is to detest and scorn all impurity and all wantonness. Truly to praise her charity is to direct all our thoughts and energies to the perfect love of God and neighbor.

—Aelred of Rielvaux, *sermon*

How many kinds of virtues shine forth in one Virgin! The secret of modesty, the banner of faith, the service of devotion, the Virgin within the house, the companion for the ministry, the mother of the temple.

—Ambrose, *Concerning Virgins, to Marcellina, His Sister*

Meditation

Through the study of books one seeks God; by meditation one finds him.

—Padre Pio, *Spiritual Maxims*

Whoever does not meditate is like someone who never looks in the mirror before going out, doesn't bother to see if he's tidy, and may go out dirty without knowing it.

—Padre Pio, *Spiritual Maxims*

When there is no time for both, meditation is to be preferred to vocal prayer, because it is more fruitful.

—Padre Pio, *Counsels*

If you habitually meditate upon him [God], your whole soul will be filled with him, you will learn his expression, and learn to frame your actions after his example.

—Francis de Sales, *The Devout Life*

Meditation fills our will, the affective part of the soul, with good impulses, such as the love of God and of our neighbor, the desire of heaven and its glories, zeal for the salvation of souls, imitation of the life of our Savior, compassion, veneration, holy joy, fear of God's displeasure, of judgment and hell, hatred of sin, confidence in the mercy and goodness of God, repentance for our past sins. And we should seek to enlarge and confirm our souls as much as possible in these affections.

—Francis de Sales, *The Devout Life*

Meditation consists in calling to mind some dogmatic or moral truth, and reflecting on or discussing this truth according to each one's capacity, so as to move the will and produce in us amendment.

—Ignatius of Loyola, *Spiritual Exercises*

In times of dryness and desolation, we must be patient, and wait with resignation the return of consolation, putting our trust in the goodness of God. We must animate ourselves by the thought that God is always with us, that he only allows this trial for our greater good, and that we have not necessarily lost his grace because we have lost the taste and feelings of it.

—Ignatius of Loyola, *Spiritual Exercises*

You will not be alone if you are with him.

—Ignatius of Loyola, *Spiritual Exercises*

One should aspire at keeping the mind in quietude. The eye that wanders continually around, now sideways, now up and down, is unable to distinctly see what lies under it; it ought rather to apply itself firmly to the viable object if it aims at a clear vision. Likewise, the spirit of man, if it is dragged about by the world's thousand cares, has no way to attain a clear vision of the truth.

—Basil the Great, *letter to Gregory of Nazianzus*

We become a temple of God when our continuous meditation on him is not constantly interrupted by ordinary worries, and the spirit is not disturbed by unexpected emotions.

—Basil the Great, *letter to Gregory of Nyssa*

Meditation gives birth to perseverance, and perseverance ends in perception, and what is accomplished with perception cannot easily be rooted out.

—John Climacus, *The Ladder of Divine Ascent*

But the Name of Jesus is more than a light, it is also food. Do you not feel increase of strength as often as you remember it? What other name can so enrich a man who meditates?

—Bernard of Clairvaux, sermon on the *Song of Songs*

It is by means of prayer that God dispenses all his favors, but particularly the great gift of divine love. To make us ask this love, meditation is a great help. Without meditation we shall ask little or nothing from God. We must, then, always, every day, and several times in the day, ask God to give us the grace to love him with our whole heart.

—Alphonsus Liguori, *sermon*

Never let the thought of Him leave your mind but meditate constantly on the mysteries of the Cross and the anguish of His mother as she stood beneath the Cross.

—Clare of Assisi, *letter to Ermentrude of Bruges*

When spiritual persons cannot meditate, they should learn to remain in God's presence with a loving attention and a tranquil intellect, even though they seem to themselves to be idle. For little by little and very soon the divine calm and peace with a wondrous, sublime knowledge of God, enveloped in divine love, will be infused into their souls.

—John of the Cross, *The Ascent of Mount Carmel*

His presence is known when we meditate on the fact that the sands of the sea are numbered by Him, that He keeps a count of the waves.

—John Cassian, *Conferences*

The work of meditation is to consider, with attentive study, the things of God, now busy on one, now on another, in order to move our hearts to some appropriate sentiments and affections of the will—striking the flint to secure a spark.

—Peter of Alcántara, *Treatise on Prayer & Meditation*

Let the truth be in your hearts, as it will be if you practice meditation, and you will see clearly what love we are bound to have for our neighbors.

—Teresa of Ávila, *The Way of Perfection*

Where there is rest and meditation, there is neither anxiety nor restlessness.

—Francis of Assisi, *saying*

No one presumes to teach an art till he has first, with intent meditation, learnt it.

—Gregory the Great, *The Book of Pastoral Rule*

When you meditate on all these things, I earnestly advise you to write down, as a help to your memory, those heavenly lights which our merciful God so often gives to the soul which draws near to Him, and with which He will also enlighten yours when you strive to know His will in meditation, for they are more deeply impressed on the mind by the very act and occupation of writing them down. And should it happen, as it usually does, that in course of time these things are either less vividly remembered or entirely forgotten, they will come with fresh life to the mind by reading them over.

—Francis Xavier, *letter*

You have to meditate often on the same themes, keeping on until you *rediscover* an old discovery.

—Josemaría Escrivá, *The Forge*

Meekness

Meekness works alongside obedience, guides a religious community, checks frenzy, curbs anger. It is a minister of joy, an imitation of Christ, the possession of angels, a shackle for demons, a shield against bitterness. The Lord finds rest in the hearts of the meek, while a turbulent spirit is the home of the devil.

—John Climacus, *The Ladder of Divine Ascent*

Blessed is he who, slandered and despised every day for the Lord's sake, still restrains himself. He will be in the chorus of martyrs and will talk familiarly with angels.

—John Climacus, *The Ladder of Divine Ascent*

God wishes us to be meek even towards ourselves. When a person commits a fault, God certainly wishes him to humble himself, to be sorry for his sin, and to purpose never fall into it again; but he does not wish him to be indignant with himself, and give way to trouble and agitation of mind; for, while the soul is agitated, a man is incapable of doing good.

—Alphonsus Liguori, *sermon*

Just as the surest cure for lying is to unsay a falsehood as soon as we are conscious of having told it, so the best cure for anger is to make immediate reparation in meekness; for, as the proverb says, fresh wounds are always the easiest to heal.

—Francis de Sales, *The Devout Life*

Mercy

For the all-merciful God never abandons one of his creatures while it remains in this life, but often visits it with some inspiration, by which man finds himself aided when he listens to it, although, if he resists it, he often becomes worse, by reason of his ungrateful neglect of preventing grace.

—Catherine of Genoa, *Life and Doctrine*

O Jesus, do not hide from me, for I cannot live without You. Listen to the cry of my soul. Your mercy has not been exhausted, Lord, so have pity on my misery. Your mercy surpasses the understanding of all Angels and people put together; and so, although it seems to me that you do not hear me, I put my trust in the ocean of your mercy, and I know that my hope will not be deceived.

—Faustina Kowalska, *Divine Mercy in My Soul*

God will not deny his mercy to anyone. Heaven and earth may change, but God's mercy will never be exhausted.

—Faustina Kowalska, *Divine Mercy in My Soul*

So it behooves us, if we would have Christ for a frequent guest, to fill our hearts with faithful meditations on the mercy he showed us in dying for us, and on his mighty power in rising again from the dead.

—Bernard of Clairvaux, *On Loving God*

In Christ there are two proofs of the gentleness of his nature. He patiently awaits the return of the sinner and he gently receives the penitent. This twofold mercy abounds in the heart of the Lord Jesus—his long-suffering in waiting for the sinner and his readiness in granting pardon.

—Bernard of Clairvaux, *On the Canticle of Canticles*

Mercy does not oppose justice, but fills it out. God's justice is based on his mercy, for nothing is due to any creature except because of something it already is or will be because of God's goodness. Mercy starts all God's works and grows in all that follows, God always giving beyond the measure of a creature's due.

—Thomas Aquinas, *Summa Theologica*

Let us entreat his mercy and goodness, casting ourselves upon his compassion and wasting no more energy in quarrels and a rivalry which only ends in death.

—Clement of Rome, *first epistle to the Corinthians*

How can God pardon the dying sinner, when he sees that all his acts of sorrow, and all his promises, proceed not from the heart, but from a dread of death and of approaching damnation?

—Alphonsus Liguori, *sermon*

The mercy of God is different from the acts of his mercy: the former is infinite, the latter are finite. God is merciful, but he is also just.

—Alphonsus Liguori, *sermon*

He will show you mercy, if you wish to change your life; but if you intend to continue to offend him, he tells you that he will take vengeance on your sins by casting you into Hell.

—Alphonsus Liguori, *sermon*

And as he makes the sun rise over the just and the wicked, he always sends his light over everyone and shows his mercy to everyone, but they don't want to receive it.

—Maria Maddalena de' Pazzi, *The Dialogues*

O most sweet God of my life and the only love of my soul, your overabundance of mercy has led me through the many obstacles I have placed in the way of your love.

—Gertrude the Great, *The Herald of Divine Love*

Because the Deity is goodness itself, true mercy and an abyss of loving bounty—or, rather, he is that which embraces and contains this abyss, since he transcends every name that is named . . . and everything we can conceive—we can receive mercy only by union with him.

—Gregory Palamas, *Three Texts on Prayer and Purity of Heart*

O sweet Mercy, how kindly you are mixed in every cup.

—Elizabeth Seton, *Collected Writings*

The Judge will show mercy in proportion as we show it.

—Elizabeth Seton, *Collected Writings*

Practice acts of mercy. In our own sufferings they give us confidence before God; they contribute much to the value of our prayers, which can no longer be called mere arid petitions, and they secure for them a reception full of mercy, seeing they proceed themselves from a merciful heart.

—Peter of Alcántara, *Treatise on Prayer & Meditation*

His mercy is so great that He has forbidden none to strive to come and drink of this fountain of life. Blessed be He for ever!

—Teresa of Ávila, *The Way of Perfection*

Let then mortals, who have sinned against God, undeceive themselves: without penance there shall be no grace, without reform no pardon, without pardon no glory. But just as these are not conceded to those that are unworthy, so they are also never denied to those that are worthy; nor is ever the mercy of God withheld from any one who seeks to obtain it.

—Mary of Agreda, *The Mystical City of God*

God is such an inexhaustible wellspring of boundless mercy and natural goodness that never was there a devoted mother who as willingly stretched out her hand to her own child that she had carried under her heart, seeing it in a raging fire, as God does to the penitent, even if it were possible that he had the sins of all men himself and committed them a thousand times every day.

—Henry Suso, *sermon*

If you should suffer some disadvantage in helping a needy neighbor, reflect how much you will differ from your Lord, who gave his life and blood to help you. Thus it will come about that without any hope of earthly reward and without any motive of vainglory, but only out of pure love for God and your neighbor, you will make progress in the virtue of mercy.

—Robert Bellarmine, *The Mind's Ascent to God by the Ladder of Created Things*

Rich is the mercy of Our God, and abundantly does He bestow grace upon grace on those who love Him.

—Elisabeth of Schönau, *Second Book of Visions*

The remedies for propitiating God have been given in the words of God himself; divine instructions have taught that God is satisfied by just works, that sins are cleansed by the merits of mercy.

—Cyprian of Carthage, *Works and Almsgiving*

It is obvious that mercy destroys stains more effectively than well water because well water only cleanses the skin of the body, while the bounty of mercy purifies the interior regions of the soul.

—Maximus of Turin, *sermon*

He who is loved receives not harshness but mercy.

—Ambrose, *Concerning Repentance*

I commend to Thy mercy also all those unhappy sinners who are hanging over the brink of hell.

—Joseph Cafasso, *prayer*

You must never treat anyone unmercifully. If you think someone is not worthy of your mercy, you should realize that you don't deserve mercy either.

—Josemaría Escrivá, *The Forge*

He from whom a poor man never goes away sad sends ahead integral fruits of mercy to the Lord.

—Valerian, *homily*

Miracles

If we characterize miracles—or marvels—as things that need a marvelous cause like the power of God, then the creation and all other things only God can do are miracles.

—Thomas Aquinas, *Summa Theologica*

In studying nature we have not to inquire how God the Creator may, as He freely wills, use His creatures to work miracles and thereby show forth His power; we have rather to inquire what Nature with its immanent causes can naturally bring to pass.

—Albertus Magnus, *De Coelo et Mundo*

A person struck by the greatness of miracles shakes in mind and body, and when the person has been stunned by this shaking, the person then thinks about his or her own weakness.

—Hildegard of Bingen, *Scivias*

God does not work miracles and grant favors by means of some statues so these statues may be held in higher esteem than others, but so he may awaken the dormant devotion and affection of the faithful through his wonderful works.

—John of the Cross, *The Ascent of Mount Carmel*

The working of signs and miracles is not always necessary nor useful to everyone nor granted to everyone. Humility, therefore, is the teacher of all virtues. It is the surest foundation for a heavenly building. It is the personal and splendid gift of the Savior. It achieves all the miracles which Christ worked and does so without risk of vanity.

—John Cassian, *Conferences*

Let us allow her [Mary] to do in us and through us whatever she desires, and she will surely accomplish miracles of grace, and we ourselves will become holy, great saints, very great saints, because we shall succeed in becoming like her, and by means of us she will win over the entire world and every individual soul.

—Maximilian M. Kolbe, *letter to Polish seminarians, 1934*

May all your miraculous works, whatever is grasped within the circumference of heaven, earth, and the abyss, be jubilant to you and forever give you that praise which, going out from you, flows back into you, its source.

—Gertrude the Great, *Spiritual Exercises*

Yes, this is still the age of miracles: we too would work them if we had faith!

—Josemaría Escrivá, *The Way*

The working of miracles and gifts of healing are performed through the Holy Spirit.

—Basil the Great, *On the Holy Spirit*

We cannot but believe that all miracles, whether wrought by angels or by other means, so long as they are so done as to commend the worship and religion of the one God in whom alone is blessedness, are wrought by those who love us in a true and godly sort, or through their means, God Himself working in them.

—Augustine, *The City of God*

For we cannot listen to those who maintain that the invisible God works no visible miracles; for even they believe that he made the world, which surely they will not deny to be visible.

—Augustine, *The City of God*

For man himself is a greater miracle than any miracle done through his instrumentality.

—Augustine, *The City of God*

The ultimate reason for believing miracles is the omnipotence of the Creator.

—Augustine, *The City of God*

Those things which are regarded as impossible will be accomplished according to the word, and by the power of that God who predicted and effected that the incredulous nations should believe incredible wonders.

—Augustine, *The City of God*

Miracles were necessary before the world believed, in order that it might believe.

—Augustine, *The City of God*

Christ, the man, among all the works of God is, just as the sun among the stars, the most august of God's miracles.

—Lawrence of Brindisi, *sermon*

A miracle, we say, is a supernatural and divine work, exceeding the nature of man, which none except a divine hand is able to have worked: for, "Nothing is impossible for God, the Word of all."

—Lawrence of Brindisi, *sermon*

Not all can merit the miracles of divine power, but they who are aided by the pursuits of religious devotion, and that they lose the fruits of divine working who are devoid of reverence for heaven.

—Ambrose, *Concerning Widowhood*

Miserliness

A miser loves no one except for his own profit.

—Catherine of Siena, *Dialogue*

Waves never leave the sea. Anger and gloom never leave the miserly.

—John Climacus, *The Ladder of Divine Ascent*

Moderation

We should endeavor to follow the rule of moderation, avoiding the excesses of both luxury and physical abuse, so our bodies are not ruined by either obesity or starvation in following the commandments. For both extremes can do equal harm, and so we must avoid letting our body get out of control by a life of ease, and abusing it so that it is made weak and unresponsive. For in both these states the soul is deprived of the time to look with freedom upon high things, since it is distracted and obsessed by the sensation of pain, being dragged down to the level of the ill-used body.

—Basil the Great, *On Ascetic Discourse*

Modesty

Modesty, as we all know is that virtue which teaches us how to do all things in the right way. It sets before our eyes how Jesus did things, and it tells us to do the same.

—Anthony Mary Claret, *autobiography*

Be ever sober, ever chaste, ever modest.

—Columban, *letter, c. 610*

Money and wealth

Do you have wealth? It is a good thing. But only if your use of it is good. You will not be able to make good use of it if you are evil: wealth is an evil for the evil, a good for the good. Not that it is a good in the sense that is makes you good, but it is converted into good when it is in the hands of the good.

—Augustine, *sermon*

Make a present of the money you have to spare without asking for interest: it will benefit you and others.

It will benefit you insofar as you have made your money safe. It will benefit the others insofar as they are able to use it.

—Basil the Great, *On Psalm 14*

Anyone who submits to paying interest becomes a slave for the rest of his life.

—Basil the Great, *On Psalm 14*

Thrift is a good companion for those who are on the road to heaven.

—Clement of Alexandria, *The Teacher*

In short, you should know that it is not riches but men's use of them which is blameworthy or acceptable to God. To realize this, read how the holy fathers Abraham and Job became dear to God by use of their wealth. Indeed, in that Gospel in which the rich man in hell who despised Lazarus is unnamed, we note that the rich Joseph of Arimathea is cited by name.

—Paulinus of Nola, *letter*

Let us not seek wealth, nor high social position (these are external things), but true nobility of soul.

—John Chrysostom, *homily*

Let no one marry a woman for her money; such wealth is base and disgraceful.

—John Chrysostom, *homily*

Money is everything now, and so everything has become corrupted and ruined, because we are possessed by this passion for money.

—John Chrysostom, *homily*

Wealth is a hindrance, because it leaves us unprepared for the hardships of life.

—John Chrysostom, *homily*

Wealth is regarded as a good thing by most people. But that is not entirely true: it depends how you use it. If wealth were a good thing in itself and on its own account, then everyone who possesses it ought to be good. Yet not all rich people are virtuous, only those who manage their money in a responsible way. Therefore wealth is not a good thing in itself, it is only an instrument for doing good.

—John Chrysostom, *Commentary on Isaiah*

If everyone honors you as a friend, but they admit that you are of no worth, but that they're compelled to honor you because of your wealth, how could they dishonor you [more] in another way? The result is that wealth causes us dishonor, being more worth honor than those themselves who possess it, and a sign of weakness rather than power.

—John Chrysostom, *homily*

Haven't I said to you constantly that wealth is a runaway slave?

—John Chrysostom, *homily on Eutropius*

What can be bought with this money that we desire? Can it be anything of value? Anything that is permanent? If not, what do we want it for? All that it provides is a dismal ease which costs us very dear. What it obtains for us is hell; what it buys is fire everlasting and torments without end.

—Teresa of Ávila, *Life*

All men would be friendly, one to another, if the world were to lose interest in honor and money. I really believe that this would be a remedy for everything.

—Teresa of Ávila, *Life*

Worrying about getting money from other people seems to me like thinking about what other people enjoy. However much you worry, you will not make them change their minds nor will they become desirous of giving you alms. Leave these anxieties to Him Who can move everyone, Who is the Lord of all money and of all who possess money.

—Teresa of Ávila, *The Way of Perfection*

The businessman who keeps stored away in a sack the money with which he could carry on gainful trading is recognized as being quite a fool.

—Valerian, *homily*

It is a great happiness for a Christian to be actually rich but poor in spirit, for thus he can use wealth and its advantages in this world and yet have the merit of poverty as regards the next.

—Francis de Sales, *The Devout Life*

Moon

Now it is not without a secret reason of the Divine Maker of the universe, that the moon appears from time to time under different forms. It presents a striking example of our nature. Nothing is stable in man; here from nothingness he raises himself to perfection; there after having hastened to put forth his strength to attain his full greatness he suddenly is subject to gradual deterioration, and is destroyed by diminution. Thus, the sight of the moon, making us think of the rapid vicissitudes of human things, ought to teach us not to pride ourselves on the good things of this life, and not to glory in our power, not to be carried away by uncertain riches, to despise our flesh which is subject to change, and to take care of the soul, for its good is unmoved. If you cannot behold without sadness the moon losing its splendor by gradual and imperceptible decrease, how much more distress should you be at the sight of a soul, who, after having possessed virtue, loses its beauty by neglect, and does not remain constant to its affections, but is agitated and constantly changes because its purposes are unstable. What Scripture says is very true, "As for a fool he changeth as the moon." (Sirach 27:11)

—Basil the Great, *homily on the Hexaemeron*

You are changed like the moon so that you who shortly before were shining with a devout faith are afterwards eclipsed by the weakness of unfaith. You are changed like the moon when your mind is emptied of wisdom as the lunar sphere is deprived of light; and just a small covering of clouds passes over it, but you the vilest darkness of the mind invades. O, fool, you were changed like the moon! For it quickly returns to its fulness, but not even over a long time are you converted to wisdom; it speedily gathers up the light it had lost, but not even slowly do you get back the faith that you denied.

—Maximus of Turin, *sermon*

Mortification

All the time that we deprive ourselves of anything which gives us pleasure to do, we are practicing a fast which is very pleasing to God because fasting does not consist solely of privations in eating and drinking, but of denying ourselves that which please our taste most.

—John Baptiste Marie Vianney, *sermon*

It is also true that we should practice mortification in many things to make reparation for our sins. There is no doubt that the person who lives without mortifying himself is someone who will never succeed in saving his soul.

—John Baptiste Marie Vianney, *sermon*

When someone rings for us, or knocks at our door, we must mortify ourselves so as not even to do one stitch more before answering. I have practiced that; and it is, I assure you, a source of peace.

—Thérèse of Lisieux, *Counsels and Reminisces*

Our body is like an ass which we must beat, but not too much, because otherwise it will fall down and it won't carry us anymore.

—Padre Pio, *Spiritual Maxims*

We must completely crush our evil passions and desires by mortifying our senses; our hearts also must be athirst if, by God's grace, they are to be filled with love. Then his goodness will be able to look with favor upon the sacrifice of self you offer up frequently to his divine Majesty, and upon the services you render to the poor.

—Louise de Marillac, *letter to religious sisters, 1655*

I send you this hair shirt to use when you find it difficult to recollect yourself at times of prayer, or when you are anxious to do something for the Lord. It is good for awakening love, but you are on no account to put it on after you are dressed, or to sleep in it. It can be worn on any part of the body, and put on in any way so long as it feels uncomfortable. Even a mere nothing like this makes one so happy when it is done for God out of a love for him.

—Teresa of Ávila, *letter to her brother Toledo, 1577*

God hides the prize of eternal glory in our mortifications and in the victory over ourselves, which we always strive for with great gentleness.

—Jane Frances de Chantal, *letter to a superior, 1627*

Mortification . . . which is intolerable to the proud and hard-hearted, becomes the comfort of those who take pleasure only in what is humble and gentle.

—Columban, *Rule*

There are three different ways of mortification: not to argue back in the mind, not to speak with an unbridle tongue, not to go wherever we wish.

—Columban, *Rule*

The road and ascent to God, then, necessarily demands a habitual effort to renounce and mortify the appetites; the sooner this mortification is achieved, the sooner the soul reaches the top. But until the appetites are eliminated, one will not arrive no matter how much virtue is practiced.

—John of the Cross, *The Ascent of Mount Carmel*

Anyone who does not conquer the appetites is wicked.

—John of the Cross, *The Ascent of Mount Carmel*

As the tilling of soil is necessary for its fruitfulness—untilled soil produces only weeds—mortification of the appetites is necessary for one's spiritual fruitfulness. I venture to say that without this mortification all that is done for the sake of advancement in perfection and in knowledge of God and of oneself is no more profitable than seed sown on uncultivated ground.

—John of the Cross, *The Ascent of Mount Carmel*

The Spirit of the Lord, however, wants the flesh to be mortified and looked down upon, considered of little worth and rejected. It strives for humility and patience, the pure, simple and true peace of the spirit. Above all, it desires the divine fear, the divine wisdom and the divine love of the Father, Son and Holy Spirit.

—Francis of Assisi, *early Rule*

Wisdom is not satisfied with half-hearted mortification or mortification of a few days, but requires one that is total, continuous, courageous and prudent if he is to give himself to us.

—Louis de Montfort, *The Love of Eternal Wisdom*

If we would possess Wisdom, we must mortify the body, not only by enduring patiently our bodily ailments, the inconveniences of the weather and the difficulties arising from other people's actions, but also by deliberately undertaking some penances and mortifications, such as fasts, vigils and other austerities practiced by holy penitents. It requires courage to do that because the body naturally idolizes itself, and the world considers all bodily penance as pointless and rejects them. The world does and says everything possible to deter people from practicing the austerities of the saints.

—Louis de Montfort, *The Love of Eternal Wisdom*

Constrain yourself in every way and always train yourself for discomfort by reducing comfort little by little, that you may both weaken the strength of the flesh and fortify the soul. For the vanquishing of the flesh secures the victory of the soul and the reasonable distress of the body can bring forth an outpouring of joy for the spirit.

—Theoleptos of Philadelphia, *letter*

If the grain of wheat does not die, it remains unfruitful. Don't you want to be a grain of wheat, to die through mortification, and to yield a rich harvest? May Jesus bless your wheat field!

—Josemaría Escrivá, *The Way*

Make sure you practice this very interesting mortification: that of not making your conversation revolve around yourself.

—Josemaría Escrivá, *The Forge*

To preserve holy purity and live a clean life you have to love and practice daily mortification.

—Josemaría Escrivá, *The Forge*

We should accept mortification with those same sentiments that Jesus Christ had in his Holy Passion.

—Josemaría Escrivá, *The Forge*

Music

The songs of birds and the sound of music should remind us of the eternal and ever new canticle of Heaven.

—Anthony Mary Claret, *autobiography*

The first true archetype is music, for harmony and concord harmonize all things with respect to each other through an order, arrangement and system. The Maker of the universe works skillfully through his ineffable word of wisdom by those things which were always rooted in wisdom. If the entire world order is a kind of musical harmony whose artisan and creator is God as the Apostle says (Hebrews 11:10), the man is a microcosm, an imitator of him who made the world.

—Gregory of Nyssa, *Commentary on the Inscriptions of the Psalms*

Remove from your lives shameful, immodest, and Satanic music, and don't associate with people who enjoy such profligate entertainment.

—John Chrysostom, *homily*

Mystical marriage

In this tranquillity the understanding sees itself raised upon a new and strange way, above all natural understanding, to the Divine light, much as one who, after a long sleep, opens his eyes to the light which he was not expecting.

—John of the Cross, *The Spiritual Canticle*

I ask Jesus to draw me into the flames of his love and to unite me so closely to him that he lives and acts in me. I feel that the more the fire of love encompasses my heart, the more I shall say: "Draw me," and the more will those souls who are near to mine "run swiftly in the sweet odor of the Beloved." Yes, they will run and we shall run together, for souls on fire cannot stay still.

—Thérèse of Lisieux, *The Story of a Soul*

As marriage takes place between man and woman for the begetting of several more so, between the flesh and the spirit a certain union, like that of marriage, takes place, for the bringing forth of children; that is, virtuous acts and meritorious works. The flesh without spirit is worth nothing, for it is the spirit which moves the flesh to acts of virtue and meritorious exercises, which are called children.

—Vincent Ferrer, *sermon*

To be the bride of Christ means to belong to the Lord: it means to put the love of Christ before all things, not merely by theoretical conviction but in the tug of the heart and in practical life. To become so one must be detached from all creatures, free of a fixation on oneself and on others; and that is the deepest, most spiritual meaning of purity.

—Edith Stein, *Essays on Woman*

Nature

Nature does nothing in vain.

—Thomas Aquinas, *On the Power of God*

Whatever happens by chance happens only rarely, but experience shows that harmony and utility are present in nature always, or almost so. This cannot be the effect of mere chance; it must exist because some end is intended.

—Thomas Aquinas, *On Truth*

God is the cause of the universe, a cause which does not depend on any other cause. This is the teaching of our eyes when we look at the ordering of nature.

—Gregory of Nazianzus, *oration*

Nothing gives us as much joy as the sky which is like a pure transparent veil, like a meadow with a thousand flowers—the stars, like a crown for their heads.

—John Chrysostom, *On Providence*

I shall never forget the impression the sea made on me. I could not take my eyes from it. The majestic roaring of its waves filled me with a sense of power and majesty of God.

—Thérèse of Lisieux, *The Story of a Soul*

Since the stars keep their proper distances and never tire in turning in their orbit, they seem to behave like a joyous chorus of noble virgins who are ever dancing skillfully through the sky.

—Robert Bellarmine, *The Mind's Ascent to God by the Ladder of Created Things*

Obedience

Simply obey. God does not ask anything else of you.

—Francis de Sales, *Oeuvres*

Be willing to languish in obedience to his will, and prepare to die when he calls you, that you may be with him and praise him forever.

—Francis de Sales, *The Devout Life*

Happy are those who are obedient, for God will not suffer them to go astray.

—Francis de Sales, *The Devout Life*

Where there is no obedience there is no virtue, where there is no virtue there is no good, where there is no good there is no love, where there is no love, there is no God, and where there is no God there is no Paradise.

—Padre Pio, *Spiritual Maxims*

Under the old law anyone who refused obedience to the priests was put outside the camp and stoned by the people, or else he was beheaded and expiated his contempt with his blood. Today the disobedient are smitten with the spiritual sword, or they are expelled from the Church and torn in pieces by the ravening jaws of demons.

—Jerome, *letter, 374*

Obedience is the burial place of the will and the resurrection of lowliness.

—John Climacus, *The Ladder of Divine Ascent*

Obedience is more pleasing to God than all the sacrifices of penitential works, or of alms-deeds, which we can offer to him.

—Alphonsus Liguori, *sermon*

Those who keep the commandments out of obedience return to God more quickly.

—Gregory of Sinai, *The Philokalia*

We must, then, prepare our hearts and bodies for the battle of holy obedience to

God's instructions. What is not possible to us by nature, let us ask the Holy One to supply by the help of grace.

—Benedict, *Rule*

Thus nothing must be rejected by Christ's true disciples in their obedience, however hard and difficult it may be, but it must be grasped with enthusiasm and with joy, since if obedience is not of this kind, then it shall not be acceptable to the Lord, who says: "And he who does not take up his cross and follow me is not worthy of me." (Matthew 10:38)

—Columban, *Rule*

What destroys obedience? Look at the first man and thou wilt see the cause which destroyed the obedience imposed on him by Me, the Eternal Father. It was pride, which was produced by self-love, and desire to please his companion. This was the cause that deprived him of the perfection of obedience, giving him instead disobedience, depriving him of the life of grace, and slaying his innocence, wherefore he fell into impurity and great misery, and not only he, but the whole human race, as I said to thee.

—Catherine of Siena, *Dialogue*

The whole of your faith is founded upon obedience, for by it you prove your fidelity.

—Catherine of Siena, *Dialogue*

A soul is obedient in proportion to her humility, and humble in proportion to her obedience.

—Catherine of Siena, *Dialogue*

As obedience is the most pleasing homage to the Sovereign Master, I am certainly not going astray while I act only through obedience.

—Elizabeth Seton, *Collected Writings*

A disobedient soul will win no victory, even if the Lord Jesus himself, in person, were to hear its confession.

—Faustina Kowalska, *Divine Mercy in My Soul*

The vow of obedience is the principle one in religion; for it implies a total renunciation and denial of one's will.

—Mary of Agreda, *The Mystical City of God*

Whoever struggles against what he must do under obedience makes life difficult for himself, because doing little unwillingly is worse than doing much willingly.

—Henry Suso, *letter*

Proud people are never obedient because their pride makes them unwilling to bend or submit to anyone.

—Catherine of Siena, *letter to nuns, 1376*

By holy obedience we do away with self-love, which spoils everything; by obedience the smallest of our actions become meritorious. It protects us from illusions of the devil, enables us to overcome our enemies, and brings us surely, as though while sleeping, into the harbor of salvation.

—Louis de Montfort, *The Love of Eternal Wisdom*

Since the Author of Salvation himself redeemed us through His obedience, how much more ought we His servants to offer the service of our humility and obedience.

—Ambrose, *On the Mysteries*

If obedience does not give you peace, it is because you are proud.

—Josemaría Escrivá, *The Way*

Someone who "does not learn how to obey" will never learn to command.

—Josemaría Escrivá, *The Forge*

God requests human obedience so that his love and his pity may have an opportunity of doing good to those who serve him diligently. The less God has need of anything, the more human beings need to be united with him. Consequently, a human being's true glory is to persevere in the service of God.

—Irenaeus, *Against Heresies*

For just as the various activities required in our daily life have their own objects and their respective ways of being done, so also there is one rule and canon prescribed for all our works, which is to fulfil God's commandments according to his will. Hence it is impossible for our work to be done properly unless it is carried out in obedience to the will of him who has prescribed it.

—Basil the Great, *The Greater Rules*

Order

"Orderly" is when everything pertaining to an issue, both interiorly and exteriorly, is not left out of consideration, including the consequences. "Disorderly" is when one of these things has been neglected.

—Henry Suso, *Little Book of Truth*

The peace of all things is the tranquility of order.

—Augustine, *The City of God*

Without a plan of life you will never have order.

—Josemaría Escrivá, *The Way*

P

Pain

No one born passes this life without pain, bodily or mental.

—Catherine of Siena, *Dialogue*

For how would the one who doesn't know pain ever be healed unless they learnt this very lesson first?

—John Chrysostom, *homily on "My Father's Working Still"*

Parents and parenthood

A mother at her confinement should preserve modesty as far as possible in her state and never lose sight of the fact that she is in the presence of God and in the company of her guardian angel.

—John Baptiste Marie Vianney, *sermon*

If a mother's love could be a fortune to you, you would be rich indeed! Alas, it is poor coin in this world; but be assured it will bear interest in heaven, where it solicits, I may truly say day and night, every blessing on you.

—Elizabeth Seton, *letter to her son, William*

Because our parents have educated us, we should obey them.

—Thomas Aquinas, *sermon*

If you do not admit the blessing of the natural life for which you are indebted to your parents, then you are unworthy of what is greater—the life of grace—and all the more unworthy of the life of glory, the greatest of all blessings.

—Thomas Aquinas, *sermon*

Now, because we are indebted to our parents from our birth, we should honor them above every superior from whom we receive only temporal things. . . . Moreover, because in our childhood we receive food from our parents, in their old age we should support them.

—Thomas Aquinas, *sermon*

The first virtue of godliness in Christians is to honor their parents, to requite the troubles of those who begot them, and with all their might to confer on them what tends to their comfort (for if we should repay them ever so much, yet we shall never be able to return their gift of life, that they may also enjoy the comfort provided by us, and may confirm in us in those blessings which Jacob the supplanter shrewdly seized.

—Cyril of Jerusalem, *Catecheses*

To be a mother is to nourish and protect true humanity and bring it to development.

—Edith Stein, *Essays on Woman*

The commandment to love our parents belongs to both natural law and to divine positive law, and I have always called it a "most sweet precept."

Do not neglect your obligation to love your parents more each day, to mortify yourself for them, to pray for them, and to be grateful to them for all the good you owe them.

—Josemaría Escrivá, *The Forge*

Passions

Those who do not know how to walk in the way of the Spirit are likely to fail to keep a watchful eye on the passions that rage within them, and let themselves be entirely taken up with the body. They then reach one or two opposite states. Either they become gluttonous, profligate, miserable, choleric, full of rancor, and this quenches their spirit, or they overdo the mortification and lose their clarity of thought.

—Maximus the Confessor, *Centuries on Charity*

Those brought down by wine often wash with water, but those brought down by passion wash with their tears.

—John Climacus, *The Ladder of Divine Ascent*

Whatever power thou hast, strive that the life which is within thee may be according to God, and may conquer the passions of the outer man.

—Abbot Arsenius, *saying*

When the winds are strong and violent, the pilot lowers the sails and casts anchor. So, when we find ourselves assailed by any bad passion, we should always lower the sails; that is, we should avoid all the occasions which may increase the passion, and should cast anchor by uniting ourselves to God, and by begging of him to give us strength not to offend him.

—Alphonsus Liguori, *sermon*

For when any passion takes possession of the heart, it obscures the truth, and makes the soul incapable of distinguishing between good and evil.

—Alphonsus Liguori, *sermon*

All bad passions spring from self-love. This is, as Jesus Christ teaches all who follow him, the principal enemy which we have to contend with; and this enemy we must conquer by self-denial.

—Alphonsus Liguori, *sermon*

When we coddle the flesh in order to foster its desires, then the passion becomes evil and self-indulgence gives rise to the carnal passions and renders the soul diseased.

—Gregory Palamas, *To the Most Reverend Nun Xenia*

At least men are merciful from time to time, but the passions—they won't be satisfied until they have destroyed you!

—John Chrysostom, *homily*

Sex is not evil, but it is a hindrance to someone who desires to devote all her strength to a life of prayer.

—John Chrysostom, *homily*

With your flesh conquered, then your spirit will reign in you. As a result, you will know God in your soul, and you may knowingly keep God's commandments and fulfill them without laziness. In this manner, all the strength of your body and soul will be subjected to God.

—Hildegard of Bingen, *Scivias*

But, when a man, a creature put together from earthly stuff, overcomes his earthly stigma, vanquishes the urges of his blood and overwhelms the passions of his flesh, he mounts above the sky and flies to the very abode of God. Thus he becomes greater than the heavens. He excels the angels, not by his nature, but by his merits.

—Peter Chrysologus, *sermon*

It is when the soul serves God that it exercises a right control over the body; and in the soul itself the reason must be subject to God if it is to govern as it ought the passions and other vices.

—Augustine, *The City of God*

For when the appetites and concupiscences are quenched, the soul dwells in spiritual peace and tranquility. Where neither the appetites or concupiscence reign, there is no disturbance but only God's peace and consolation.

—John of the Cross, *The Dark Night of the Soul*

If then you are also fleshly because of unbelief and wickedness, because of neglect and transgression of the commandments, I say that you have fattened your heart and have stopped up its ears, and that the eye of your soul has been veiled by the passions. How in that case would you be able to recognize a spiritual and holy man?

—Symeon the New Theologian, *Ethical Discourses*

How is that heart of yours getting along? Don't worry: the saints—who were perfectly ordinary, normal beings like you and me—also felt those "natural" inclinations. And if they had not felt them, their "supernatural" reaction of keeping their heart—soul and body—for God, instead of giving it to creatures, would have had little merit.

—Josemaría Escrivá, *The Way*

Those who copulate can generate nothing save by the creative energy of God.

—Augustine, *The City of God*

We cannot belong to ourselves; we must belong to God or to our passions. We have only the one choice of the one yoke or the other. Which appears the most honorable?

—Ignatius of Loyola, *Spiritual Exercises*

We must know that the constant invocation of the Name of God is a medicine which cures not only all the passions but also their effects.

—Barsanouphios and John, in *The Art of Prayer*

Patience

Look upon yourself as a tree planted beside the water, which bears its fruit in due season; the more it is shaken by the wind, the deeper it strikes its roots into the ground.

—Margaret Mary Alacoque, *Life and Writings of St. Margaret Mary*

There is no other remedy for your ills but patience and submission to the will of God.

—Margaret Mary Alacoque, *Life and Writings of St. Margaret Mary*

Better is the patient than the arrogant (Ecclesiastes 7:9); because, in truth, one that is patient chooses to suffer any evils whatever rather than that his hidden good should come to be known through the vice of ostentation.

—Gregory the Great, *The Book of Pastoral Rule*

For victory over cities is a less thing, because that which is subdued is without; but a far greater thing is that which is conquered by patience, since the mind itself is by itself overcome, and subjects itself to itself, when patience compels it to bridle itself within.

—Gregory the Great, *The Book of Pastoral Rule*

Patience is the sponge of the sorrows that come upon [us] against [our] will, for it receives and accepts as well the misfortunes that strike from the outside and makes humble the spirit of the soul.

—Theoleptos of Philadelphia, *letter*

Our Lord so loved patience that he wished to become its mirror and pattern. He endured scourging and ill treatment with invincible patience; he supported so many blasphemies, so many calumnies, without saying a word.

—Francis de Sales, *Oeuvres*

He who desires to be patient must be humble, because one cannot long support the labors and adversities of life without the humility which makes us gentle and patient.

—Francis de Sales, *Oeuvres*

A truly patient man neither complains himself nor wishes others to complain for him; he speaks honestly, simply, and truly of his trial without complaining, bemoaning or exaggeration; and if he is pitied he receives pity with patience likewise, unless it is bestowed on some evil which does not exist.

—Francis de Sales, *The Devout Life*

The great happiness of man is thus to possess his soul; and the more perfect our patience, the more perfectly do we possess our souls.

—Francis de Sales, *The Devout Life*

We must be patient not only under sickness, but further, we must bear the particular complaints which God sends us; take the place where he wills us to be among those with whom he surrounds us, and under the privations he appoints for us, and so on with all other trials.

—Francis de Sales, *The Devout Life*

One should be patient, whatever one has to suffer.

—Basil the Great, *letter to Gregory of Nazianzus*

Keep well dug into your minds the words of Our Lord: In patience you will possess your soul.

—Padre Pio, *Spiritual Maxims*

Patience is the guardian of all the other virtues, and, if it fails, we may lose in one moment the labor of many days.

—John of Ávila, *letter to a disciple, 1563*

Patience cannot be proved in any other way than by suffering, and patience is united with love.

—Catherine of Siena, *Dialogue*

Remembering the comparison of my unworthiness with Thy goodness, let my soul wait with patience, and glorify Thee for Thy patience with me.

—Elizabeth Seton, *Collected Writings*

Very wisely, then, do the saints tell us that the true touchstone for a man is not the relish he may experience in prayer, but his patience in tribulation, self-abnegation and the doing of the will of God, to which, of course, spiritual consolations may themselves undoubtedly contribute.

—Peter of Alcántara, *Treatise on Prayer & Meditation*

A servant of God cannot know how much patience and humility he has within himself as long as he is content. When the time comes, however, when those who should make him content do the opposite, he has as much patience and humility as he has at that time and no more.

—Francis of Assisi, *saying*

If, however, we who have renounced the devil and the world suffer trials and the attacks of the devil and the world more frequently and more violently, how much more ought we to maintain patience, with which, as our helper and companion, we may endure all afflictions.

—Cyprian of Carthage, *The Good of Patience*

Patient waiting is necessary that we may fulfill what we have begun to be, and through God's help, that we may obtain what we hope for and believe.

—Cyprian of Carthage, *The Good of Patience*

Patience, however, beloved brethren, not only preserves what is good, but also repels what is evil. Devoted to the Holy Spirit and cleaving to heavenly and divine things, it struggles with the bulwark of its virtues against the acts of the flesh and the body whereby the soul is stormed and captured.

—Cyprian of Carthage, *The Good of Patience*

Let patience be strong and stable in the heart, and then the sanctified body and temple of God will not be corrupted by adultery, innocence dedicated to justice will not be infected by the contagion of deceit, and the hand that has held the Eucharist will not be sullied by the bloodstained sword.

—Cyprian of Carthage, *The Good of Patience*

For as patience is a good of Christ, so, on the contrary, impatience is an evil of the devil; and as man in whom Christ lives and abides is found to be a patient man, so he is always impatient whose mind is possessed by the wickedness of the devil.

—Cyprian of Carthage, *The Good of Patience*

It is patience that both commends us to God and saves us for God.

—Cyprian of Carthage, *The Good of Patience*

Peace

Learn this lesson well, once and for all: God is the only Master of our hearts; he alone can give solid peace, and our whole confidence must rest in him only.

—Claude de la Colombière, *letter*

Keep your heart in peace and let nothing trouble you, not even your faults. You must humble yourself and amend them peacefully, without being discouraged or cast down, for God's dwelling is in peace.

—Margaret Mary Alacoque, *Life and Writings of St. Margaret Mary*

The spirit of God does all things in peace. Let us have recourse to God with love and confidence, and he will receive us into the arms of his mercy.

—Margaret Mary Alacoque, *Life and Writings of St. Margaret Mary*

Unless a man shall say in his heart, "I alone and God are in this world," he shall not find quiet.

—Abbot Allois, *saying*

True peace is born of doing the will of God, and bearing with patience the sufferings of this life, and does not come from following one's own whim or selfish desire, for this always brings, not peace and serenity, but disorder and discontent.

—Pope John XXIII, *Daily Papal Messages*

Live completely at peace because there will be light.

—Padre Pio, *letter, 1915*

Let us turn our eyes to the Father and Creator of the universe, and when we consider how precious and peerless are his gifts of peace, let us embrace them eagerly for ourselves. Let us contemplate him with understanding, noting with the eyes of the spirit the patient forbearance that is everywhere willed by him, and the total absence of any friction that marks the ordering of his whole creation.

—Clement of Rome, *first epistle to the Corinthians*

O burning furnace, we enjoy the true vision of peace only in you. You judge and purify the gold of the elect and lead the soul to eagerly search for you in your eternal truth, our highest good.

—Gertrude the Great, *The Herald of Divine Love*

Peace is associated with humility.

—Hildegard of Bingen, *Book of Divine Works*

Human passions and weaknesses are never extinct, but they cannot triumph in a heart possessed by Peace. She is lovely; make acquaintance with her. She will not be angry that you neglected her so long.

—Elizabeth Seton, *Collected Writings*

The true peacemakers are those who preserve peace of mind and body for love of our Lord Jesus Christ, despite what they suffer in this world.

—Francis of Assisi, *saying*

A priest who is not at peace with himself will not be able to inspire peace in another soul.

—Faustina Kowalska, *Divine Mercy in My Soul*

Peace is nourished from the rich fruitfulness of charity. It is the nursling daughter of faith, the supporting column of justice. Peace is a suitable pledge of future hope. Peace, which unites those present, invites the absent. This peace reconciles earthly things with the heavenly and human matters with those divine.

—Peter Chrysologus, *sermon*

When we set our heart on other people it is not set on anything stable, for a human being is alive today and tomorrow is dead. So if we wish to have peace we must rest our heart and soul with faith and love in Christ crucified.

—Catherine of Siena, *letter to a senator's wife, c. 1374–75*

For peace is a good so great, that even in this earthly and mortal life there is no word we hear with such pleasure, nothing we desire with such zest, or find to be more thoroughly gratifying.

—Augustine, *The City of God*

Whoever gives even moderate attention to human affairs and to our common nature, will recognize that if there is no man who does not wish to be joyful, neither is there any one who does not wish to have peace. For even they who make war desire nothing but victory—desire, that is to say, to attain to peace with glory. For what else is victory than the conquest of those who resist us? And when this is done there is peace.

—Augustine, *The City of God*

He, then, who prefers what is right to what is wrong, and what is well-ordered to what is perverted, sees that the peace of unjust men is not worthy to be called peace in comparison with the peace of the just.

—Augustine, *The City of God*

He will surround you with His shield of peace. . . . Everywhere will He guard and bless your entrances and departures, so that in every place you may find the Son of peace and your peace may come on all who receive you.

—Paulinus of Nola, *letter*

Whoever has peace in his heart "prepares a place" for the Lord and calls upon Him with courage and love. And He Who is called upon and longed for appears instantly and fills the soul with endless joy.

—Theoleptos of Philadelphia, *letter*

There is no peace except in perfect forgetfulness of self; we must resolve to forget even our spiritual interests, so that we may seek nothing but God's glory.

—Claude de la Colombière, *retreat notes*

I see that you have at last found the secret of true peace: not to examine your present state and to abandon the past and future entirely to God's mercy; to have a great idea of his goodness, which is infinitely greater than you can express, and to believe, in spite of anything that tries to persuade you to the contrary, that you are loved by him in spite of all your miseries.

—Claude de la Colombière, *letter*

Do not let your peace depend upon what is outside you; you will see that Our Lord will supply for everything when you are satisfied with him alone, and you will find more in him than all creatures together.

—Claude de la Colombière, *letter*

So you want peace of heart? Then do not seek health, nor wealth, nor fame, nor power, nor luxury. Seek wisdom in God's sight, stick to the virtues, and nothing will be able to make you sad.

—John Chrysostom, *To the People of Antioch*

Penance and penitence

Penance should be but the means to increase virtue according to the needs of the individual, and according to what the soul sees she can do in the measure of her own possibility.

—Catherine of Siena, *Dialogue*

Penance is the purifier of the soul.

—Elizabeth Seton, *Collected Writings*

A gloomy and constrained penance is so unworthy of the Beloved and so unedifying to His dear ones.

—Elizabeth Seton, *Collected Writings*

We can do penance at every moment of our life, provided we do it with love.

—Maximilian M. Kolbe, *notes, 1940*

According to the holy Doctors, for every mortal sin a man is obliged by God to seven years of penance in this world, or the equivalent in purgatory; the reason being that every mortal sin is an offense against the seven Gifts of the Holy Ghost.

But the quality of penance is not fixed, so Christ willed to remain seven years in Egypt, that is in a narrow place, to show that it is becoming to remain for seven years in the narrow place of penitence, and after that a man is free from the imposed penalty.

—Vincent Ferrer, *sermon*

But he who has heaped up sin must also increase his penitence. For greater sins are washed away by greater weeping.

—Ambrose, *Concerning Repentance*

Let us then keep the feast on good food, doing penance yet joyful in our redemption, for no food is sweeter than kindness and gentleness.

—Ambrose, *Concerning Repentance*

Let then, nothing call you away from penitence, for this you have in common with the saints, and would that such sorrowing for sin as that of the saints were copied by you.

—Ambrose, *Concerning Repentance*

Good, then, is penitence, and if there were no place for it, every one would defer the grace of cleansing by baptism to old age. And a sufficient reason is that it is better, to have a robe to mend, than one to put on; but as that which has been repaired once is restored, so that which is frequently mended is destroyed.

—Ambrose, *Concerning Repentance*

Doing penance for one's sins is a first step toward obtaining forgiveness and winning eternal salvation. . . . No individual Christian can grow in perfection, nor can Christianity itself gain in vigor, except it be on this basis of penance.

—Pope John XXIII, *Paenitentiam Agere*

Perfection

The best occupation for perfect souls is to make one's life a praise of God.

—Gregory of Nyssa, *Commentary on the Inscriptions of the Psalms*

As perfection consists in trying to please God in everything and to please him only, we must not hesitate when we get an opportunity of pleasing him and of being praised by him however much we displease men and lose their esteem.

—Claude de la Colombière, *spiritual notes*

God should be desired above all else; that is the way to progress in love. In attaining to God there will be perfect blessedness because there will be perfect love of the perfect good.

—Aelred of Rievaulx, *Mirror of Charity*

Among the stage leading to perfection, friendship is the highest.

—Aelred of Rielvaux, *Spiritual Friendship*

The perfect person does not only try to avoid evil. Nor does he do good for fear of punishment, still less in order to qualify for the hope of a promised reward.

The perfect person does good through love.

—Clement of Alexandria, *Miscellaneous Studies*

Anyone who works day and night to succor the destitute is nearing perfection.

—Basil the Great, *The Greater Rules*

Human beings must undergo a rigorous training if they are to overcome their great lack of virtues and reach the state of perfection.

—Basil the Great, *On Paradise*

Whatever good thing is done is made perfect only by love.

—Bede the Venerable, *homily on the Gospels*

What a great pity that the desire for perfection is not itself sufficient for having it, but that it must be acquired by the sweat of our brow and hard work!

—Francis de Sales, *Oeuvres*

God has not placed perfection in the multiplicity of acts we perform to please him, but only in the way we perform them, which is simply to do the little we do according to our vocation, in love, by love, and for love.

—Francis de Sales, *Oeuvres*

All Christian perfection consists in this point: to ask God for nothing and to refuse nothing.

—Francis de Sales, *Oeuvres*

His will is that we be perfect, uniting ourselves to him, and imitating him to the utmost of our capacity.

—Francis de Sales, *The Devout Life*

The way of perfection is the way of divine wisdom. Perfection in terms of the Gospel does not ask for dispensation. . . . Divine wisdom would have us work at mortifying our senses, our eyes, our moods, our passions. It would have us suffer contempt and even love it, endure poverty and inconvenience and all that displeases nature especially in drinking, in eating, in clothing, in sleeping and in speaking. We must withdraw from all conversations and familiarities even though they are permitted by human prudence.

—Marguerite Bourgeoys, *Autographic Writings*

Our Lord is not content to have those who wish to follow the way of perfection keep the commandments. He wills that they leave everything and themselves as well; that they lose their lives in this world to find them again in the next; that interiorly as well as exteriorly they embrace poverty in everything, contempt, humiliations, suffering and all the rest.

—Marguerite Bourgeoys, *Autographic Writings*

Much later, when I understood what perfection was, I realized that to become a saint one must suffer a great deal, always seek what is best, and forget oneself. I understood that there were many kinds of sanctity and that each soul was free to respond to the approaches of Our Lord and to do little or much for him—in other words, to make a choice among the sacrifices he demands.

—Thérèse of Lisieux, *The Story of a Soul*

At the start of my spiritual life, when I was thirteen or fourteen, I used to wonder what more I could ever learn about spiritual perfection. I thought it impossible to understand it better. But I soon came to know that the farther one travels along the road, the farther away the goal seems to get.

—Thérèse of Lisieux, *The Story of a Soul*

The outer man is composed of many members, but the inner man comes to perfection through his mind—by attention to himself, by fear of the Lord, and by the grace of God.

—Dimitri of Rostov, *The Inner Closet of the Heart*

The achievement of passionlessness and sanctity—in other words, of Christian perfection—is impossible without acquiring inner prayer. All the Fathers are agreed on this.

—Theophan the Recluse, *letter*

For if a beginner tries hard, with God's help, to gain the summit of perfection, I think he will never reach heaven alone, but will take many others with him. God will prize him as a good captain and give him his company; and the devil will put such perils and difficulties in his way that he will need not merely a little courage but a great deal, also much help from God, if he is not to turn back.

—Teresa of Ávila, *Life*

Perfect souls are in no way repelled by trials, but rather desire them and pray for them and love them. They are like soldiers: the more wars there are, the better they are pleased, because they hope to emerge from them with the greater riches. If there are no wars, they serve for their pay, but they know they will not get very far on that.

—Teresa of Ávila, *The Way of Perfection*

When perfection is not in the soul, everything which the soul does for itself and for others is imperfect.

—Catherine of Siena, *Dialogue*

Every perfection and every virtue proceeds from charity, and charity is nourished by humility, which results from the knowledge and holy hatred of the self, that is, sensuality.

—Catherine of Siena, *Dialogue*

Perfection does not consist in experiencing consolation. It consists in surrendering one's will to God's will, whether this be burdensome or easy.

—Henry Suso, *letter*

Essential to perfection is the perfect observance of the command to love. And since whatever flows from perfect love—blessing men who curse you, for example—is a consequence of perfection, we are commanded to be ready to do such things when necessary, and a superabounding charity will do them even without necessity.

—Thomas Aquinas, *Summa Theologica*

There is a primary perfection of human nature in the state of glory when man will have all that is possible for human nature to have; but there is a secondary perfection in created nature, when, for example, a man has all that he ought to have according to that time.

—Thomas Aquinas, *Commentary on Sentences*

Man's perfection consists in loving God and neighbor. . . . But we should "love, not in word or speech, but in action in truth" (John 3:18). To love in this way a man must do two things: avoid evil and do good.

—Thomas Aquinas, *sermon*

A thing is said to be perfect absolutely when it has acquired all those attributes that its nature implies.

—Thomas Aquinas, *On the Perfection of the Spiritual Life*

The perfection of the spiritual life, therefore, consists first and principally in loving God.

—Thomas Aquinas, *On the Perfection of the Spiritual Life*

Abraham possessed such a degree of perfection that neither great possessions nor the use of marriage shook his mind from perfect love of God. But if anyone lacking this strength of mind attempted to arrive at perfection saddled both with riches and with marriage, he would be guilty both of a presumptuous error and of making light of Our Lord's counsels.

—Thomas Aquinas, *On the Perfection of the Spiritual Life*

It is therefore of the utmost importance that, in seeking the perfection that can be attained only by the union with Jesus, we rid ourselves of all the evil that is in us. Otherwise our infinitely pure Lord, who has an infinite hatred for the slightest stain on our souls, will refuse to unite us to himself and will drive us from his presence.

—Louis de Montfort, *Treatise on True Devotion to the Blessed Virgin*

Since true devotion comes from the heart and looks only to the truth and substance represented by spiritual objects, and since everything else is imperfect attachment and possessiveness, any appetite for these things must be uprooted if some degree of perfection is to be reached.

—John of the Cross, *The Dark Night of the Soul*

Persecution

Let no persecution lessen thy love, which many waters cannot quench, nor many rivers drown.

—Ambrose, *On the Mysteries*

I believe that anyone who wishes to be devout and live piously in Jesus will suffer persecution and will have a daily cross to carry. But he will never manage to carry a heavy cross, or carry it joyfully and perseveringly, without a trusting devotion to our Lady, who is the very sweetness of the cross.

—Louis de Montfort, *Treatise on True Devotion to the Blessed Virgin*

I pray, my brother, that we may be found worthy to be cursed, censured, and ground down, and even to be executed in the name of Jesus Christ, as long as Christ Himself is not killed in us.

—Paulinus of Nola, *letter*

For I have deliberately lightened myself of baggage and of oppressive clothing that I may swim unencumbered through this rough sea of the present life which bars our way to God with baying sins like hounds between. At Christ's command and with His help I have cast off all garments of the flesh and anxiety of the morrow. I do not boast of having done this.

—Paulinus of Nola, *letter to Augustine*

The world has always tried to hinder and persecute me. But our Lord has had care of me and has frustrated all its evil plans.

—Anthony Mary Claret, *autobiography*

Perseverance

The crown will be given neither to beginners, nor to the advanced, but to the victorious, to those who persevere to the end.

—Margaret Mary, *Life and Writings of St. Margaret Mary*

If we are calm and persevering, we shall find not only ourselves, but our souls, and with that, God himself.

—Padre Pio, *Spiritual Maxims*

In the spiritual life one must always go on pushing ahead and never go backwards; if not, the same thing happens as to a boat which when it loses headway gets blown backwards with the wind.

—Padre Pio, *Spiritual Maxims*

Spin a little every day; thread by thread weave your design until it is finished and you will infallibly succeed. But be careful not to hurry, because you will tangle the thread with knots and confuse the spindle. Therefore advance always, and even if you progress at a slow pace, you will still travel far.

—Padre Pio, *letter, 1917*

I pray my God that he will grant me perseverance and allow me to prove a faithful witness right up to the time of my passing over, for my God's sake.

—Patrick, *letter to the soldiers of Coroticus*

An active soul is a provocation to demons, yet the greater our conflicts the greater our rewards. There will be no crown for the man who has never been under attack, and the man who perseveres in spite of any failures will be glorified as a champion by the angels.

—John Climacus, *The Ladder of Divine Ascent*

The more he gives, the more he desires to give. He loves to see the trust which makes us persist in knocking unceasingly.

—Placid Riccardi, *letter to his brother, 1906*

If, then, we wish to persevere and to be saved—for no one can be saved without perseverance—we must pray continually. Our perseverance depends, not on one grace, but on a thousand helps which we hope to obtain from God during our whole lives, that we may be preserved in his grace.

—Alphonsus Liguori, *sermon*

Perseverance: a gratuitous grace, yet forfeited so often!

—Elizabeth Seton, *Collected Writings*

The appetites sap the strength needed for perseverance in the practice of virtue.

—John of the Cross, *The Ascent of Mount Carmel*

The spirit points in a certain direction. There is an unwavering purpose in the mind. If this is not held on to with all eagerness and dedication there can be no coming to the longed-for fruits of the goal.

—John Cassian, *Conferences*

Keep your options open when there's no problem, but dig in when you must choose.

—Columban, *letter, c. 610*

Though weary, don't give up.

—Columban, *letter, c. 610*

Don't tell Jesus that you want consolation in prayer. If he gives it to you, thank him. Tell him always that you want perseverance.

—Josemaría Escrivá, *The Way*

To begin is easy; to persevere is sanctity.

—Josemaría Escrivá, *The Way*

Discouragement is an enemy of your perseverance. If you don't fight against discouragement you will become pessimistic first, and lukewarm afterwards. Be an optimist.

—Josemaría Escrivá, *The Way*

Don't lose heart. Carry on! Carry on with that holy stubbornness which in spiritual terms is called *perseverance*.

—Josemaría Escrivá, *The Forge*

Pessimism

Reject your pessimism and don't allow those around you to be pessimistic. God should be served with cheerfulness and abandonment.

—Josemaría Escrivá, *The Forge*

Piety

Those who are pious, with a piety devoid of affectation, carry out their professional duty perfectly, since they know that their work is a prayer raised to God.

—Josemaría Escrivá, *The Forge*

Pilgrimage

O ye who fear the Lord, praise Him in the places where ye are. Change of place does not effect any drawing nearer unto God, but wherever thou mayest be God will come to thee, if the chambers of thy soul be found of such a sort that He can dwell in thee and walk in thee. But if thou keepest thine inner man full of wicked thoughts, even if thou wast on Golgotha, even if thou wast on the Mount of Olives, even if thou stoodest on the memorial rock of the Resurrection, thou wilt be as far away from receiving Christ into thyself, as one who has not even begun to confess Him.

—Gregory of Nyssa, *On Pilgrimages*

Since we are travelers and pilgrims in the world, let us ever ponder on the end of the road, that is of our life, for the end of our roadway is our home.

—Columban, *sermon*

Whoever makes a pilgrimage, therefore, does well to make it alone, even if this must be done at an unusual time. I would never advise going along with a large crowd, because one ordinarily returns more distracted than before. Many who go on pilgrimage do so more for the sake of recreation than devotion.

—John of the Cross, *The Ascent of Mount Carmel*

Pleasure

But no one can live entirely without sensual and physical pleasure.

—Thomas Aquinas, *Summa Theologica*

One should not judge pleasure according to the senses. One should judge pleasure according to the truth.

—Henry Suso, *The Life of the Servant*

The person who's drunk can't even enjoy pleasure. For pleasure is an outcome of moderation; [the outcome] of immoderation [is] insensibility. How can a person perceive the pleasure of the beverage, when they can't tell if they're sitting or lying? How could they enjoy festivity, when they can't see the sun itself because of the thick cloud of alcohol? For such is the extent of the darkness they encounter that the sun's rays are insufficient to dissolve that gloom.

—John Chrysostom, *homily on martyrs*

The wisdom of the flesh is the love of pleasure. This is the wisdom shown by the worldly-wise who seek only the satisfaction of the senses. They want to have a good time. They shun everything that might prove unpleasant or mortifying for the body, such as fasting, and other austerities. Usually they think only of eating, drinking, playing, laughing, enjoying life and having a good time.

—Louis de Montfort, *The Love of Eternal Wisdom*

A soul given up to pleasure naturally feels aversion toward the bitterness of self-denial.

—John of the Cross, *The Dark Night of the Soul*

When something distasteful or unpleasant comes your way, remember Christ crucified and be silent.

—John of the Cross, *letter*

I call pleasure love of one's body. The soul's happiness has no part in anything unreasonable and is not slavishly devoted to pleasure.

—Gregory of Nyssa, *Commentary on the Inscriptions of the Psalms*

Possessions

I doubt that it is possible to desire to possess honestly that which another possesses, for by this desire we must involve the other's loss.

—Francis de Sales, *The Devout Life*

Therefore do not let your desires for that which you have not assume a definite shape, and do not fix your heart on that which you have; do not be overpowered by such losses as you may meet with, and then you may venture to think that although you are rich in fact, you are not in spirit, but that being poor in spirit, you are blessed, for the kingdom of heaven is yours.

—Francis de Sales, *The Devout Life*

Our possessions are not our own; God has given them to us that we may cultivate them, and it is his will that we should render them useful and fruitful. By our care thereof we render to him an acceptable service.

—Francis de Sales, *The Devout Life*

All the goods of this world cannot content the heart of man, which has been created to love God, and can find no peace out of God.

—Alphonsus Liguori, *sermon*

Truly, my children, I talk to you *as to wise men*, so that you understand what I will tell you: "Unless each one of you hates all earthly possessions, and renounces them and all their workings by all his heart and stretches out the hand of his heart to heaven and to the Father of all, he cannot be saved."

—Anthony, *letter*

If the bridegroom shows his wife that he takes no pleasure in worldly excess, and will not stand for it, their marriage will remain free from the evil influences that are so popular these days.

—John Chrysostom, *homily*

Temporal goods are given to us by the liberality of God, and He will demand an account of them, for they were committed to us for disposal as well as possession.

—Robert Bellarmine, *The Art of Dying Well*

Your God is gentle and mild. He does not command that while you are a pilgrim on earth you must utterly forgo creaturely consolations; indeed, he created all things to serve you. But he did command that you use them with moderation, sobriety, and temperance, that you share them cheerfully with the needy, that your possessions not be your master but you theirs, and that you use them to attain God.

—Robert Bellarmine, *The Mind's Ascent to God by the Ladder of Created Things*

Be willing to do without material things rather than lose the spiritual, especially in this dear holy work that God has put into your hands.

—Catherine of Siena, *letter to Louis, duke of Anjou, 1376*

Let the lovers of this world keep their possessions, though they be as great as they desire; for me, my God alone is sufficient!

—Joseph Cafasso, *saying*

Poverty

Even as stout garments trodden underfoot and turned over in the washing are made clean and white, so is a strong soul made steadfast by voluntary poverty.

—Abbot Syncletica, *saying*

The treasure house of the monk is voluntary poverty. Wherefore, my brother, lay up thy treasure in heaven: for there abide the ages of quiet without end.

—Abbot Hyperichius, *saying*

Do not be ashamed of being poor, or of seeking charitable alms; receive what is given you in humility and bear refusals with meekness.

—Francis de Sales, *The Devout Life*

Always dispose of a part of your means by giving freely alms to the poor, for you impoverish yourself by that which you give, and the more it is the more you are impoverished. Undoubtedly God will restore it to you in this world as well as in the next, for nothing brings such prosperity as almsgiving.

—Francis de Sales, *The Devout Life*

Oh, the holiness and richness of making one's self poor by almsgiving!

—Francis de Sales, *The Devout Life*

Love poverty and the poor; for by this love you will become truly poor yourself, since we become like to that which we love, as says holy scripture.

—Francis de Sales, *The Devout Life*

If you are really poor, then above all be poor in spirit, and make a virtue of necessity by using that precious stone poverty to the best advantage. We do not see its glory in this world, and yet it is of the greatest beauty and value.

—Francis de Sales, *The Devout Life*

Poverty is a tool or training for perfection, since by renouncing wealth we also remove certain obstacles to charity: concerns, love of wealth, vainglory and pride.

—Thomas Aquinas, *Summa Theologica*

The foundation for perfect love is voluntary poverty, whereby one lives without any private property: *if you want to be perfect, go and sell what you have and give it to the poor, and come, follow me.* Involuntary poverty holds spiritual dangers, and men fall into many sins trying to escape it. . . . It is difficult to preserve charity in the midst of riches: *a rich man finds it hard to enter the kingdom of heaven.*

—Thomas Aquinas, *Summa Theologica*

What matters is that I should never be ashamed of my poverty, indeed I should be proud of it, just as the lords of this world are proud of their noble lineage, their title of nobility, their liveries. I am of the same family as Christ—what more can I want? Do I need anything? Providence will abundantly provide, as always hitherto.

—Pope John XXIII, *Journal of a Soul*

Rich men should provide for the poor and the poor should thank God for giving them somebody to supply their wants.

—Clement of Rome, *first epistle to the Corinthians*

A man who has embraced poverty offers up prayer that is pure, while a man who loves possessions prays to material images.

—John Climacus, *The Ladder of Divine Ascent*

Poverty is rightly called gold, since it makes its possessor resplendent and wealthy. Where true poverty is found, there is sufficiency; where there is abundance, there is want.

—Anthony of Padua, *Sermones*

Indeed, what poverty can be greater and more holy than that of the man who recognizing that he has no defense and no strength begs each day for the largess of another and who understands that his life and being are at every moment sustained by divine help?

—John Cassian, *Conferences*

Poverty is good and contains within itself all the good things in the world. It is a great domain—I mean that he who cares nothing for the good things of the world has dominion over them all.

—Teresa of Ávila, *The Way of Perfection*

If, on one hand, possessions throttle the spirit and tyrannically oppress it in its weakness, if they suppress the soul's most noble privilege of following eternal goods and God himself: it is certain, on the other hand, that voluntary poverty restores to man the nobility of his condition and, liberating him from vile servitude and reinstating him his noble freedom and mastery of all things.

—Mary of Agreda, *The Mystical City of God*

For I assure thee, my dearest, there is no more acceptable gift to the Most High than voluntary poverty. There are very few in the world in our days who use well the temporal riches and offer them to their God and Lord with the generosity and love of these holy Kings.

—Mary of Agreda, *The Mystical City of God*

The virtue of poverty can be infringed even by the undisciplined craving for personal belongings.

—Vincent de Paul, *Common Rules or Constitutions of the Congregation of the Mission*

Consolation is to be offered to those who are tried in the furnace of poverty; and fear is to be induced in those whom the consolation of temporal glory lifts up; that both those may learn that they possess riches which they see not, and these become aware that they can by no means keep the riches that they see.

—Gregory the Great, *The Book of Pastoral Rule*

It is a murderous crime to despise the poor on our own judgment, for no act of God has set them apart from us.

—Paulinus of Nola, *letter*

But the faithful man, most strange paradox, in poverty is rich: for knowing that we need only to have food and raiment, and being therewith content, he has trodden riches under foot.

—Cyril of Jerusalem, *Catcheses*

Lack of resources lessens pride and leaves the way open to the holy virtue of humility. It disposes the heart to receive new graces, and makes it climb the steep path to perfection with remarkable facility. Those fluids which are lighter are the ones which rise to the top, while the thick, heavy fluids cleave to the bottom.

—Anthony Mary Claret, *autobiography*

Experience has taught me that if the poor are treated well and given decent ways of gaining a livelihood, they are on the whole virtuous; but on the other hand, if they are neglected, their goodness degenerates into evil.

—Anthony Mary Claret, *autobiography*

Rather than in not having, true poverty consists in being detached, in voluntarily renouncing one's dominions over things.

That is why there are poor who are really rich. And vice-versa.

—Josemaría Escrivá, *The Way*

Poverty is like a galloping horse. It catches up with you quickly, it begins to chase you again and you find yourself in trouble as before, only further in debt than at first. A loan in fact does not do away with poverty: it only postpones it. Because that is so, put up with the hardships of poverty today and don't put them off till tomorrow.

—Basil the Great, *On Psalm 14*

When the poor are helped there ought to be these two conditions: generosity and joy.

—John Chrysostom, *On the Letter to the Romans*

Power

Power will rest with you just so long as your principles remain sound. The real key-bearer of the kingdom of Heaven it is he who opens up true knowledge to the worthy and shuts to the unworthy.

—Columban, *letter to Pope Boniface IV, 613*

Prayer

Answers to prayer

When requests are made to God and are not immediately answered, the reason may be one of the following: either that the petition is premature, or because it has been made unworthily or vaingloriously, or because, if granted, it would lead to conceit, or because negligence and carelessness would result.

—John Climacus, *The Ladder of Divine Ascent*

It also sometimes happens that we seek things entirely related to salvation with our eager petitions and devoted actions, and yet we do not immediately obtain what we ask. The result of our petition is postponed to some future time, as when we daily ask the Father on bended knees, saying, "Your kingdom come," (Matthew 6:10), and nevertheless we are not going to receive the kingdom as soon as our prayer is finished, but at the proper time.

—Bede the Venerable, *homily on the Gospels*

He will give either what we ask, or what he knows to be more profitable to us.

—Bernard of Clairvaux, *sermon*

If you are not successful in your prayer, do not expect success in anything. It is the root of all.

—Theophan the Recluse, *letter*

If, as we pray, no hesitation cuts across us and no uneasiness undermines our confidence in what we ask for, if we feel in the flush of prayer that we have been granted what we sought, then I have no doubt that our prayers have effectively reached through to God. Our conviction that God is looking at us and that He has the power to grant what we ask of Him earns us the right to be heard and to be given what we seek.

—John Cassian, *Conferences*

How to pray

We must pray without ceasing, in every occurrence and employment of our lives—that prayer which is rather a habit of lifting up the heart to God as in a constant communication with Him.

—Elizabeth Seton, *Collected Writings*

When you are praying, don't rack your brains to find words. On many occasions the simple, monotonous stammering of children has satisfied their Father who is in heaven.

—John Climacus, *The Ladder of Divine Ascent*

For He [God] says: pray wholeheartedly, though it seems to you that this has no savor for you; still it is profitable enough, though you may not feel that. Pray wholeheartedly, though you may feel nothing, though you may see nothing, yes, though you think that you could not, for in dryness and in barrenness, in sickness and in weakness, then is your prayer most pleasing to me, though you think it almost tasteless to you. And so is all your living prayer in my sight.

—Julian of Norwich, *Showings*

There is no need of much speaking in prayer, but often stretch out thy hands and say, "Lord, as Thou wilt and Thou knowest, have mercy upon me." But if there is war in thy soul, add, "Help me." And because He knoweth what we have need of, he showeth us His mercy.

—Abbot Macarius, *saying*

When your prayer is ended gather together the essence of your devout meditations, as it were in a little nosegay, and keep it before you through the day.

—Francis de Sales, *The Devout Life*

Devote one hour daily to mental prayer—if you can, let it be early in the morning, because then your mind is less cumbered and more vigorous after the night's rest.

—Francis de Sales, *The Devout Life*

To profit from prayer, we must not pour out our attention on externals when we leave it, but remain with the thoughts that we have retained from our meditation, not speaking except through necessity and for the edification of our neighbor.

—Marguerite Bourgeoys, *Autographic Writings*

It seems to me that we do not pay enough attention to prayer, for unless it arises from the heart which ought to be its center, it is no more than a fruitless dream. Prayer ought to carry over into our words, our thoughts and our actions. We must strive as much as we can to reflect on what we ask or promise. We do not do this if we do not pay attention to our prayers.

—Marguerite Bourgeoys, *Autographic Writings*

We don't pray in order to change God's arrangements, but in order to obtain effects that God has arranged will be achieved through the prayers of his chosen people. God arranges to give us certain things in answer to requests so that we may confidently have recourse to him, and acknowledge him as the source of all our blessings, and this is all for our good.

—Thomas Aquinas, *Summa Theologica*

Moreover, although the apostle bids us to pray without ceasing and although to the saints their very sleep is an orison, yet we ought to have fixed hours for prayer, so that if perchance we are occupied with any business the time itself may remind us of our duty.

—Jerome, *letter, 384*

Let prayer arm us when we leave our lodging: when we return from the streets let us pray before we sit down, nor give our miserable body rest until our soul is fed.

—Jerome, *letter, 384*

It is however to be noted that four things are required if a person is to obtain what he requests through the power of the Holy Name. First that he ask for himself; second, that whatever he asks be necessary for salvation; third, that he asks in a pious manner; and fourth, that he ask with perseverance—and all these things concurrently. If he asks in this manner, he will always be granted his request.

—Bernadine of Siena, *Palm Sunday sermon*

Some in their prayers ask for a wife, others for a country estate; some ask for clothing, others for food. And almighty God is asked for similar things. But we should always bear in mind that in accordance with his teaching, we should always desire our redemption. Seek ye first the kingdom of God and his justice, and all these things shall be added unto you.

—Gregory the Great, *sermon*

Inner prayer, if it comes to a man's spirit, when he is with other people, demands no use of the lips or of books, no movement of the tongue or sound of the voice: and the same is true when you are alone. All that is necessary is to raise your mind to God, and descend deep into yourself, and this can be done everywhere.

—Dimitri of Rostov, *The Inner Closet of the Heart*

Prayer is turning the mind and thoughts towards God. To pray means to stand before God with the mind, mentally to gaze unswervingly at Him, and to converse with Him in reverent fear and hope.

—Dimitri of Rostov, *The Inner Closet of the Heart*

You should not make long prayers, for it is better to pray little but often.

—Theophylact, *The Art of Prayer*

Outward prayer alone is insufficient. God harkens to the mind; and those monks who do not combine inner with exterior prayer are no monks, but are like firewood that is burnt out.

—Theophan the Recluse, *letter*

It is necessary to invoke His Name with a full and unwavering faith—with a deep certainty that He is near, sees and hears, pays a whole-hearted attention to our petition, and is ready to fulfil it and to grant what we seek. There is nothing to be ashamed of in such hope. If fulfilment is sometimes delayed, this may be because the petitioner is still not yet ready to receive what he asks.

—Theophan the Recluse, *letter*

Pray about everything to the Lord, to our most pure Lady, and to your Guardian Angel; and they will teach you everything, either directly or through others.

—Theophan the Recluse, *letter*

The essential, indispensable element in prayer is attention. Without attention there is no prayer. True attention, given by grace, comes when we make our heart dead to the world.

—Ignatius of Antioch, in *The Art of Prayer*

If you pray with your lips but your mind wanders, how do you benefit?

—Gregory of Sinai, *The Philokalia*

I would advise those who practice prayer, especially at first, to cultivate the friendship and company of others who are working in the same way. This is a most important thing, because we can help one another by our prayers, and all the more so because it may bring us even greater benefits.

—Teresa of Ávila, *Life*

I can say what I know from experience, namely that however sinful a man may be, he should not abandon prayer once he has begun it. It is the means by which all may be repaired again, and without it amendment would be much more difficult.

—Teresa of Ávila, *Life*

We must shorten our time of prayer, however much joy it gives us, if we see our bodily strength waning or find that our head aches: discretion is most necessary in everything.

—Teresa of Ávila, *The Way of Perfection*

It has already been said that it is impossible to speak to God and to the world at the same time; yet this is just what we are trying to do when we say our prayers and at the same time listening to the conversation of others or letting our thoughts wander on any matter that occurs to us, with making an effort to control them.

—Teresa of Ávila, *The Way of Perfection*

Listen readily to holy reading, and devote yourself often to prayer. Every day with tears and sighs confess your past sins to God in prayer and change from these evil ways in the future.

—Benedict, *Rule*

We ought always to pray, and not to faint.

—Robert Bellarmine, *The Art of Dying Well*

The soul finds its joy, therefore, in spending lengthy periods in prayer, perhaps even entire nights; its penances are pleasures; its fasts, happiness; and the sacraments and spiritual conversations are its consolations.

—John of the Cross, *The Dark Night of the Soul*

Let us beg pardon for all our sins and contrition against them, and especially let us ask for help against all those passions and vices towards which we incline the most and are most tempted, discovering all our wounds to the heavenly Physician that he may heal and cure them with the unction of his grace.

—Peter of Alcántara, *Treatise on Prayer & Meditation*

Let us ask for those very lofty and noble virtues in which is contained the sum of all Christian perfection—viz., faith, hope, love, fear, humility, patience, obedience, courage to face every toil, poverty of spirit, contempt of the world, discretion, purity of intention, and other similar virtues which lie at the summit of this spiritual edifice.

—Peter of Alcántara, *Treatise on Prayer & Meditation*

In determining the length of time . . . it seems to me that anything less than an hour and a half or two hours is a short time to assign to prayer. . . . He, however, who is pressed for time, on account of his many duties, should not cease to offer his mite, like the poor widow in the Temple, for, where there is no negligence, he who provides for all created things according to their needs and nature, will equally also provide for such a one as that.

—Peter of Alcántara, *Treatise on Prayer & Meditation*

Perfect prayer is that wherein he who prays is not conscious that he is praying.

—John Cassian, *Collations of Cassian*

But one thing is certain. Anyone who prays and who doubts that he will be heard will not be listened to at all.

—John Cassian, *Conferences*

Before the time of prayer we must put ourselves in the state of mind we would wish to have in us when we actually pray. It is an inexorable fact that the condition of the soul at the time of prayer depends upon what shaped it beforehand. The soul will rise to the heights of heaven or plunge into the things of earth, depending upon where it lingered before the time of prayer.

—John Cassian, *Conferences*

We should ask of God things worthy of God. He who asks evil things of God judges and supposes that God is the author of evil. And he who asks for cheap and unworthy things is an ignoble petitioner and ignores the power and might of the Giver. Consequently, we should always ask from such a Giver not unholy gifts, but holy ones; not earthly, but heavenly ones; gifts compatible with virtues, not dangerous attractions; not things likely to stir up hatreds, but those consonant with virtue.

—Peter Chrysologus, *sermon*

Some people pray with their bodies only, saying the words with their mouths, while their minds are far away; in the kitchen, in the marketplace, in the inn. We pray in the spirit when the mind reflects on the words that the mouth utters. . . . To this end, the hands should be joined, to signify the union of heart and lips; that is the prayer of the spirit.

—Vincent Ferrer, *sermon*

Fervent prayer is warm with devotion, and humid when God gives tears. As fresh breath is drawn in, so is the Holy Ghost, who, with his might, cools the soul from the fever of sin—pride, lust and the rest.

—Vincent Ferrer, *sermon*

Thus when we practice faith, hope, and charity with continual desire, we pray always.

—Augustine, *letter to a noblewoman, 411*

When you pray to God in psalms and hymns, meditate in your heart on that which you utter with your lips.

—Augustine, *Rule*

To possess Wisdom we must pray. But how should we pray? First, we should pray for this gift with a strong and lively faith, not wavering, because he who wavers in his faith must not expect to receive any gift from the Lord (James 1:6, 7). Secondly, we must pray for it with a pure faith, not counting on consolations, visions or special revelations. Although such things may be good and true, as they have been in some saints, it is always dangerous to rely on them.

—Louis de Montfort, *The Love of Eternal Wisdom*

To vocal prayer we must add mental prayer, which enlightens the mind, inflames the heart and disposes the soul to listen to the voice of Wisdom, to savor his delights and possess his treasures. For myself, I know of no better way of establishing the kingdom of God, Eternal Wisdom, than to unite vocal and mental prayer by saying the holy Rosary and meditating on its fifteen mysteries.

—Louis de Montfort, *The Love of Eternal Wisdom*

Frequent prayer also commends us to God.

—Ambrose, *Concerning Virgins, to Marcellina, His Sister*

So ought we always to pray for everyone who grieves or reviles us for whatever cause, and for all who are hostile toward us because of an evil disposition, and, indeed, for all the faithful and unfaithful, in order that we may attain to perfection and they be delivered from error and draw near the truth.

—Symeon the New Theologian, *Ethical Discourses*

Your prayer cannot stop at mere words. It has to lead to deeds and practical consequences.

—Josemaría Escrivá, *The Forge*

You should pray at all times—always.

—Josemaría Escrivá, *The Forge*

Pray for everyone, for people of every race and tongue and of every creed, for those who have only a vague idea about religion and for those who do not know the faith at all.

This zeal for souls, which is a sure and a clear sign that we love Jesus, will make Jesus come.

—Josemaría Escrivá, *The Forge*

We always have need of God, therefore we must always pray. The more we pray, the more we please him and the more we obtain.

—Claude de la Colombière, *retreat notes*

If you only pray when you are obliged or because you are obliged, you will never succeed in prayer, nor will you ever love it, nor ever take pleasure in intimate converse with God.

—Claude de la Colombière, *letter*

Unceasing prayer means to have the mind always turned to God with great love, holding alive our hope in him, having confidence in him whatever we're doing and whatever happens to us.

—Maximus the Confessor, *Ascetics*

The whole of our life should be a season of prayer.

—Basil the Great, *On Ascetic Discourse*

The best form of prayer is one that implants the clearest idea of God in the soul and thus makes space for the presence of God within us.

—Basil the Great, *letter to St. Gregory of Nyssa*

JESUS PRAYER

If you truly wish to put your thoughts to shame, to be serenely silent, and to live in the effortless employment of a sober and quiet heart, let the Jesus Prayer cleave to your breathing, and in a few days you will see all this realized.

—Hesychius of Sinai, *The Art of Prayer*

When the Jesus Prayer is absent, all manner of harmful things assail us, leaving no room for anything good in the soul. But when Our Lord is present in the prayer, everything alien is banished.

—Gregory Palamas, *The Art of Prayer*

LORD'S PRAYER

The Lord's Prayer is the best of all prayers. All prayer requires five excellent qualities, which are found here. A prayer should be *confident, ordered, suitable, devout, and humble*.

—Thomas Aquinas, *Exposition of the Lord's Prayer*

If you run through the petitions of all holy prayers, I believe you will find nothing that is not summed up and contained in the Lord's Prayer.

—Augustine, *letter to a noblewoman, 411*

NATURE OF PRAYER

We can tell him all the secrets of our heart, disclosing our want and misery to him who alone can remedy them, and saying: O friend of my heart, she whom thou lovest is sick. Visit and heal me, for I well know that thou canst not love me and yet leave me alone in my distress.

—Margaret Mary, *Life and Writings of St. Margaret Mary*

Then I used to think very deeply, and even though I know nothing of meditation, my soul entered into a true state of prayer. I heard the murmur of the breeze and sounds from far away. The faint music from the band of soldiers garrisoned in the town reached me and filled me with a gentle melancholy. Earth seemed a place of exile and I dreamt of heaven.

—Thérèse of Lisieux, *The Story of a Soul*

The power of prayer is really tremendous. It makes one like a queen who can approach the king at any time and get whatever she asks for. To be sure of an answer, there is no need to recite from a book a formula composed for the occasion. If there were, I should have been pitied.

—Thérèse of Lisieux, *The Story of a Soul*

My whole strength lies in prayer and sacrifice, these are my invincible arms; they can move hearts far better than words, I know it by experience.

—Thérèse of Lisieux, *The Story of a Soul*

Prayer is, for me, an outburst from the heart; it is a simple glance darted upwards to Heaven; it is a cry of gratitude and of love in the midst of trial as in the midst of joy! In a word, it is something exalted, supernatural, which dilates the soul and unites it to God. Sometimes when I find myself, spiritually, in dryness so great that I cannot produce a single good thought, I recite very slowly a *Pater* or an *Ave Maria*; these prayers alone console me, they suffice, they nourish my soul.

—Thérèse of Lisieux, *The Story of a Soul*

To my mind there is no labor so great as praying to God: for when a man wishes to pray to his God, the hostile demons make haste to interrupt his prayer, knowing that their sole hindrance is in this, a prayer poured out to God. With any other labor that a man undertakes in the life of religion, however instant and close he keeps to it, he hath some rest: but prayer hath the travail of a mighty conflict to one's last breath.

—Abbot Agatho, *saying*

Certainly the greatest defect we have in our prayers and in all that happens to us, particularly in that which concerns tribulations, is our lack of confidence. Because of that lack we do deserve to receive the help we desire and ask for.

—Francis de Sales, *Oeuvres*

We are angels in prayer and often devils in conversation and action, offending this same God whom we have recognized as being so lovable and so worthy of being obeyed.

—Francis de Sales, *Oeuvres*

If we remain attentive to the truth of the mysteries which our Lord teaches us in prayer, how happy we will be!

—Francis de Sales, *Oeuvres*

Prayer brings our mind into the brightness of divine light, and exposes our will to the warmth of divine light, and exposes our will to the warmth of divine love. Nothing else can so purge our mind from its ignorance, and our will from its depraved affections. It is a blessed fountain which, as it flows, revives our good desires and causes them to bring forth fruit, washes away the stains of infirmity from our soul, and calms the passions of our hearts.

—Francis de Sales, *The Devout Life*

We shall never return to God if we do not have recourse to prayer. Yes, my dear children, with a prayer well said, we can command Heaven and earth, and all will obey us.

—John Baptiste Marie Vianney, *sermon*

My dear brethren, not only is prayer very efficacious, but, even more, it is of the utmost necessity for overcoming the enemies of our salvation.

—John Baptiste Marie Vianney, *sermon*

Prayers succeeding to lecture rejuvenate and invigorate the soul, which is moved toward God by desire, for beautiful is the prayer that impresses into the mind a clear notion of God. This is properly the "inhabitation" of God, to have God seated in oneself through memory. Thus we become a temple of God, when earthly cares do not interrupt the continuity of memory, when the mind is not disturbed by unforeseen passions, and when, fleeing from all things, the friend of God withdraws unto God, drives out all incitements to evil, and holds fast to those practices that lead to virtue.

—Basil the Great, *letter to Gregory of Nazianzus*

God knows the prayer of each person. So he knows very well who is seeking heavenly things only in appearance and who is seeking them from the depths of his being. He sees quite clearly who says the words of his prayer merely with his lips while his heart is elsewhere. He sees who asks for physical health, earthly riches, or the praise of others.

—Basil the Great, *Commentary on Psalm 28*

Praying for others is a sign of love; and the more love the saints in heaven have, the more they pray for those on earth who can be helped by their prayers. And the closer they are to God, the more effective their prayers are.

—Thomas Aquinas, *Summa Theologica*

Prayer is the raising of the mind to God. We must always remember this. The actual words matter less.

—Pope John XXIII, *letter to niece Giuseppina, Oct. 3, 1948*

How often has prayer taken me to the brink of despair and restored me to the state of soul of one exulting in joy and confident of forgiveness.

—Bernard of Clairvaux, *On the Canticle of Canticles*

All prayers are good, when these are accompanied by the right intention and good will.

—Padre Pio, *Spiritual Maxims*

Prayer is the best armor we have, it is the key which opens the heart of God.

—Padre Pio, *Spiritual Maxims*

Prayer maintains the equilibrium of the world, reconciles people to God, produces holy tears, forms a bridge over temptations, and acts as a buttress between us and affliction.

Prayer drives away the struggles of the spirit. It is the blessedness to come. It is an action that will never come to an end.

—John Climacus, *The Ladder of Divine Ascent*

Everyone can pray in a crowd. For some it is a good thing to pray with a single kindred soul. But solitary prayer is only for the very few.

—John Climacus, *The Ladder of Divine Ascent*

Prayer is by nature a dialogue and a union of man with God. Its effect is to hold the world together. It achieves a reconciliation with God.

—John Climacus, *The Ladder of Divine Ascent*

Prayer is the test of everything; prayer is also the source of everything; prayer is the driving force of everything; prayer is also the director of everything. If prayer is right, everything is right. For prayer will not allow anything to go wrong.

—Theophan the Recluse, *letter*

Whoever has passed through action and thought to true feeling, will pray without words, for God is God of the heart. So that the end of apprenticeship in prayer can be said to come when in our prayer we move only from feeling to feeling.

—Theophan the Recluse, *letter*

The essence of prayer is therefore the spiritual lifting of the heart toward God. The mind in the heart stands consciously before the face of God, filled with due reverence, and begins to pour itself out before Him. This is spiritual prayer, and all prayer should be of this nature

—Theophan the Recluse, *letter*

Our prayer reflects our attitude to God, and our attitude to God is reflected in prayer.

—Theophan the Recluse, *letter*

You must pray not only with words but with the mind, and not only with the mind but with the heart, so that the mind understands and sees clearly what is said in words, and the heart feels what the mind is thinking. All these combined together constitute real prayer, and if any of them are absent your prayer is either not perfect, or is not prayer at all.

—Theophan the Recluse, *letter*

Only perfunctory prayer is displeasing to Him, when someone reads the prayers at home or stands in church at the service without attending the meaning of the words: the tongue reads or the ear listens, but the thoughts wander who knows where. There is no prayer here.

—Theophan the Recluse, *letter*

Prayer is called "of the mind," when it is recited by the mind with profound attention, and with the sympathy of the heart. Prayer is called "of the heart," when it is recited by the mind united with the heart, and send up the prayer from its depths. Prayer is called "of the soul," when it comes from the whole soul, with the participation of the body itself—when it is offered by the whole being, which becomes so to speak the mouthpiece of the heart.

—Ignatius of Antioch, *The Art of Prayer*

Mindfulness of God, or noetic prayer, is superior to all other activities. Indeed, being love for God, it is the chief virtue.

—Gregory of Sinai, *The Philokalia*

Mental prayer is, as I see it, simply a friendly intercourse and frequent solitary conversation with Him who, as we know, loves us.

—Teresa of Ávila, *Life*

The security of a soul that applies itself to prayer lies in its ceasing to be anxious for anything or anybody, in its watching itself and pleasing God. This is very important.

—Teresa of Ávila, *Life*

For there is no state of prayer so high that it is not necessary often to return to the beginning, and the questions of sin and self-knowledge are the bread which we must eat with even the most delicate dish on this road to prayer.

—Teresa of Ávila, *Life*

Those who take the path of prayer have great need of learning; and the more spiritual they are, the greater the need.

—Teresa of Ávila, *Life*

As I say, it is dangerous to keep counting the years that we have practiced prayer. For even though it may be done in humility, it always seems liable to leave us with the feeling that we have earned some merit by our service. I do not say that we deserve nothing or that we shall not be well rewarded. But any spiritual person who believes that by the mere number of years during which he has practiced prayer he has earned these spiritual consolations, will, I am sure, fail to reach the peak of spirituality.

—Teresa of Ávila, *Life*

We must always watch and pray, for there is no better way than prayer of revealing these hidden wiles of the devil and making him declare his presence.

—Teresa of Ávila, *The Way of Perfection*

Prayer coming forth from a clean conscience is like the incense of sweetness in heaven.

—Elisabeth of Schönau, *The Book of the Ways of God*

Where there is prayer, the Word is present, desire is put to flight, lust departs.

—Ambrose, *Concerning Widowhood*

Holy prayer puts down all pride and casts down all vanity.

—Maximus of Turin, *sermon*

Prayer is the foundation of the spiritual edifice. Prayer is all-powerful.

—Josemaría Escrivá, *The Way*

Prayer is the most powerful weapon a Christian has. Prayer makes us effective. Prayer makes us happy. Prayer gives us all the strength we need to fulfill God's commands.

Yes, indeed, your whole life can and should be prayer.

—Josemaría Escrivá, *The Forge*

How can we help our neighbor? By prayer and good works. Preaching is useless without grace, and grace is only obtained by prayer. If conversions are few, it is because few pray. Prayer for souls is so pleasing to God, it is as though we asked a mother to forgive her son.

—Claude de la Colombière, *retreat notes*

What is prayer? It is the mind detached from earthly things and the whole heart pointed to that in which it hopes.

—Isaac of Nineveh, *The Philokalia*

Prayer raises human nature above all the excitements that are stirred up in the heart by the thought of earthly things.

—Isaac of Nineveh, *The Philokalia*

Even if we speak with a low voice, even if we whisper without opening the lips, even if we call to him only from the depths of the heart, our unspoken word always reaches God and God always hears.

—Clement of Alexandria, *Miscellaneous Studies*

The necessity of prayer is so often insisted upon in Holy Scripture that nothing is more clearly commanded than this duty. For although the Almighty knows what we stand in need of, as our Lord Himself tells us in St. Matthew's Gospel, yet He wishes that we should ask for what we require, and, by prayer, grasp it, as if by spiritual hands or some suitable instrument.

—Robert Bellarmine, *The Art of Dying Well*

The fruits of prayer are three especial advantages: merit, satisfaction, and receiving what we pray for.

—Robert Bellarmine, *The Art of Dying Well*

Prayer enlightens the mind: man cannot directly fix the eye of his soul upon God, who is the light, without being enlightened by Him.

—Robert Bellarmine, *The Art of Dying Well*

In all our necessities, trials and difficulties, no better or safer aid exists for us than prayer and hope that God will provide for us by the means he desires.

—John of the Cross, *The Ascent of Mount Carmel*

A soul arms itself by prayer for all kinds of combat.

—Faustina Kowalska, *Divine Mercy in My Soul*

There is no soul which is not bound to pray, for every single grace comes to the soul through prayer.

—Faustina Kowalska, *Divine Mercy in My Soul*

Virtues are the prerequisite foundation of prayer and cannot be effected without it.

—John Cassian, *Conferences*

Prayer comes of the fidelity to promises and the fulfillment of what we have undertaken for the sake of a pure conscience.

—John Cassian, *Conferences*

When the soul, during prayer or outside of it, is visited in any special manner by our Lord, she let it not slip by in vain, but profit by the occasion offered; for it is certain, with such a breeze, that a man will sail further in an hour than he otherwise would in many days.

—Peter of Alcántara, *Treatise on Prayer & Meditation*

Let prayer, mercy, and fasting be one petition for us before God. Let them be one legal aid on our behalf. Let them be a threefold prayer for us. These are the things, brethren, these are the things which hold fast the citadel of heaven, knock at the private chamber of God our Judge, follow up the cases of men before the tribunal of Christ, beg indulgence for the unjust, win pardon of the guilty.

—Peter Chrysologus, *sermon*

Perseverance in Prayer

Never give up prayer, and should you find dryness and difficulty, persevere in it for this very reason. God often desires to see what love your soul has, and love is not tried by ease and satisfaction.

—John of the Cross, *Degrees of Perfection*

Do not be either astonished or discouraged at the difficulties you find in prayer. Only be constant and submissive and God will be pleased with you.

—Claude de la Colombière, *letter*

For if you persevere in asking, without doubt you will receive what you ask for.

—Bede the Venerable, *homily on the Gospels*

Let us persevere in prayer at all times. For if our Lord seems not to hear us, it is not because he wants to refuse us. Rather, his purpose is to compel us to cry out louder and to make us more conscious of the greatness of his mercy.

—Francis de Sales, *Oeuvres*

It is, above all, necessary to persevere in prayer till death, and never cease to pray.

—Alphonsus Liguori, *sermon*

There are times in life when the soul finds comfort only in profound prayer. Would that souls knew how to persevere in prayer at such times. This is very important.

—Faustina Kowalska, *Divine Mercy in My Soul*

We must persist in our prayers, and our persistence will quite certainly win us, as God has told us, everything we ask for. No doubts about this at all!

—John Cassian, *Conferences*

We must never let up in the zeal of our prayers, even when the Lord seems to us to be slow to answer. It may well be that the Lord wishes this delay for our own good. It may be that the angel bringing our divine gift has indeed left the presence of God but has been delayed by the devil, and he will certainly not be able to hand over to us the favor we asked if he finds us to have cooled off in our praying.

—John Cassian, *Conferences*

We ought not to act as so many do when praying for some grace: after they have prayed for a long time, perhaps for years, and God has not granted their request, they become discouraged and give up praying, thinking that God does not want to listen to them. Thus they deprive themselves of the benefit of their prayers and offend God, who loves to give and who always answers, in some way or another, prayers that are well said.

—Louis de Montfort, *The Love of Eternal Wisdom*

Pride

There are very few people, even in the lowliest conditions, who do not have a good opinion of themselves. They regard themselves as far superior to their equals, and their detestable pride urges them to believe that they are worth a great deal more than most other people. From this I conclude that pride is the source of all the vices and the cause of all the evils which have occurred, and are still to come, in the course of the centuries.

—John Baptiste Marie Vianney, *sermon*

Some derive a great deal of pride because they believe that they have more intelligence than others; others because they have a few more inches of land or some money, when in fact they should be in dread of the formidable account which God will demand of them one day.

—John Baptiste Marie Vianney, *sermon*

The door by which pride enters with the greatest strength and ease is the door of wealth. Just as soon as someone improves his possessions and his sources of wealth, you will observe him change his life.

—John Baptiste Marie Vianney, *sermon*

No, my dear brethren, there is nothing that is quite as ridiculous or stupid as to be forever talking about what we have or what we do. . . . This sin is even more to be feared in people who put on a good show of piety and religion.

—John Baptiste Marie Vianney, *sermon*

A great many people slander others because of pride. They think that by deprecating others they will increase their own wealth.

—John Baptiste Marie Vianney, *sermon*

Ignorance is brutal, arrogance is devilish. Pride only, the chief of all iniquities, can make us treat gifts as if they were rightful attributes of our nature, and while receiving benefits, rob our Benefactor of his due glory.

—Bernard of Clairvaux, *On Loving God*

For where there is self-interest there is isolation; and such isolation is like the dark corner of a room where dust and rust befoul.

—Bernard of Clairvaux, *On Loving God*

Man is so full of pride that when he has everything he needs and good health, he believes himself a god, and superior to God himself, but when something happens and he can do nothing, and others can't do anything about it either, only then will he remember that there is a Supreme Being.

—Padre Pio, *Spiritual Maxims*

Oh, whenever the tempter wants you to be puffed up with pride, say to yourself: all that is good in me I have received from God on loan and I should be a fool to boast of what is not mine.

—Padre Pio, *letter, 1915*

Pride is a denial of God, an invention of the devil, contempt for men. It is the mother of condemnation, the offspring of praise, a sign of barrenness. It is a flight from God's help, the harbinger of madness, the author of downfall. It is the cause of diabolical possession, the source of anger, the gateway of hypocrisy. It is the fortress of demons, the custodian of sins, the source of hardheartedness. It is the denial of compassion, a bitter pharisee, a cruel judge. It is the foe of God. It is the root of blasphemy.

—John Climacus, *The Ladder of Divine Ascent*

I thank you that you have taken all earthly riches from me, for since then, you have clothed and fed me through the goodness of others. Because of this, I no longer can clothe my heart in the pride of possessing such things.

—Mechtilde of Magdeburg, *The Flowing Light of the Godhead*

People often show false pride in themselves when they perform the sins which they unsuitably desired.

—Hildegard of Bingen, *Scivias*

The good things of this life, therefore—its riches, honors, and pleasures—are not entirely forbidden to Christians, but only an *immoderate* love of them, which St. John calls "the concupiscence of the flesh, the concupiscence of the eyes, and the pride of life."

—Robert Bellarmine, *The Art of Dying Well*

If the swelling of pride is taking place in anyone, let him repress it, lest he draw the arms of heavenly justice against himself.

—Valerian, *homily*

Pride is a vice of cheapness and an indication of ignobility; nobility of soul does not know how to be puffed up.

—Valerian, *homily*

The vices which spring from pride can scarcely be counted. If a man could overcome or guard against them, he would not get caught in any snare which the Devil sets to bring on damnation.

—Valerian, *homily*

A sure sign of a lukewarm and proud soul is to listen carelessly and negligently to the saving medicine of words which are too zealously and too constantly uttered to it.

—John Cassian, *Conferences*

Pride could not last even for a moment in heaven, nor will it ever be able to get close to it.

—Elisabeth of Schönau, *Third Book of Visions*

You are burning lamps whom the Lord has established on his sacred mountain to illuminate the darkness of the world by your word and example. Take care lest the light that is in you be extinguished by the wind of pride and cupidity, which snuffed out the life of your parents in paradise.

—Elisabeth of Schönau, *The Book of the Ways of God*

For none of us is so puffed up, so proud, so impatient that we would not become humble and meek on seeing and contemplating such great profound love as to see God stoop down to our humanity. That is why God's true holy servants, wanting to reciprocate, always humble themselves and give God all the praise and glory.

—Catherine of Siena, *letter to Cardinal Pietro Corsini of Florence, at Avignon, 1376*

Friend, man's pride is long tolerated out of my patience in order that my humility may be exalted and my virtue may be manifested. And because pride was not created by me but was invented by the devil, it therefore must be fled because it leads to hell. But humility must be practiced because it leads to heaven. And I, God, have taught it by my word and my example.

—Bridget of Sweden, *Book of Questions*

There are some who aim at the credit of generosity for pride alone, because they wish thereby to gain the good opinion of the multitude for leaving nothing to themselves; but while they are seeking rewards in this life, they are laying up none for the life to come, and having received their reward here they cannot hope for it there.

—Ambrose, *Concerning Repentance*

Pride is a terrible rock where wild beasts lurk that would tear you to pieces every day.

—John Chrysostom, *On Priesthood*

Providence

Now, when God sees that man distrusts himself, and places his whole confidence in Providence, he immediately stretches forth his holy hand to help him. He stands ever at our side, he knocks, and, if we open to him, he enters; he drives forth our enemies one after another, and restores to the Soul its baptismal robe of innocence; and all this God does in different modes and ways, operating according to the state in which he finds his creature.

—Catherine of Genoa, *Life and Doctrine*

God in his providence orders all things, even the slightest, through the eternal forethought of his wisdom, and all things that act do so as instruments moved by him, serving him obediently in order to bring forth into the world the order of providence meditated, so to speak, from eternity. And if everything capable of acting must act as his minister, no agent can prevent the realization of divine providence by acting in opposition.

—Thomas Aquinas, *Summa Theologica*

What God wants of you, my dear sister, is that you should live each day as comes, like a bird in the trees, without worrying about tomorrow. Be at peace and trust in divine Providence and the Blessed Virgin, and do not seek anything else but to please God and love Him.

—Louis de Montfort, *letter*

That nothing happens without God we know from many sources; and reversely, that God's dispensations have no element of chance and confusion in them every one will allow, who realizes that God is Reason, and Wisdom, and Perfect Goodness, and Truth, and could not admit of that which is not good and not consistent with His Truth.

—Gregory of Nyssa, *On Infants' Early Death*

It belongs to God to give life to men, to uphold by His providence all things that exist. It belongs to God to bestow meat and drink on those who in the flesh have received from Him the boon of life, to benefit the needy, to bring back to itself, by means of renewed health, the nature that has been perverted by sickness. It belongs to God to rule with equal sway the whole of creation; earth, sea, air, and the realms above the air. It is His to have a power that is sufficient for all things, and above all to be stronger than death and corruption.

—Gregory of Nyssa, *The Great Catechism*

God imparts his benevolence to all those in need.

—Gregory of Nyssa, *Commentary on the Inscriptions of the Psalms*

We know that providence plays a part in our lives, for in the Bible it says that not even the fall of a single sparrow happens without our Father's wish. And so anything that takes place does so according to the will of our Creator. Who can oppose the will of God? And so let us accept what happens, for if we react with anger we will be unable to cope with whatever happens and will ourselves be destroyed.

—Basil the Great, *letter*

To those who have preferred spiritual welfare, He will give health of body, keenness of mind, success in business, and unbroken prosperity. And, even if in this life our efforts should not realize our hopes, the teachings of the Holy Spirit are nonetheless a rich treasure for the ages to come deliver your heart, then, from the cares of this life and give close heed to my words.

—Basil the Great, *homily on the Hexaemeron*

But God in His good Providence allows so many terrors, sorrows, and dangers to be put in our way by our enemy, that He may break down our spirit, give us lowly hearts, and train us to submissiveness of mind and humility, so that we may never in the future feel any trust in our own prudence, but all entire trust in His Divine Protection.

—Francis Xavier, *letter*

God nurtures and caresses the soul, after it has been resolutely converted to his service, like a loving mother who warms her child with the heat of her bosom, nurses it with good milk and tender food, and carries it and caresses it in her arms.

—John of the Cross, *The Dark Night of the Soul*

Of those benefits and good things which God does for his servants there is neither measure nor comprehension; and He bestows some on them now, and others He will grant them later.

—Symeon the New Theologian, *Ethical Discourses*

Just as the wealthy of this world squander their money on whatever needs and lusts and enjoyments they may wish, so, too, our good Master gives Himself to His true servants and fills their every desire and longing, as much as they want and beyond, and fills them with every good thing, keeping nothing back, and generously provides them unceasingly with incorruptible and everlasting delight.

—Symeon the New Theologian, *Ethical Discourses*

God's ordinary providence is a continual miracle; but he will use extraordinary means when they are required.

—Josemaría Escrivá, *The Forge*

Today human beings till the earth and know how to make use of beasts of burden. But even if they paid all possible attention to the earth, even if the weather were always favorable, without God it would all be in vain.

—John Chrysostom, *On Genesis*

Still less should we try to know when we will die and in what place; whether it will be in the country or in the city; on horseback or at the foot of a mountain; or by some stone crushing us; or whether we will die in bed assisted by someone, or alone. What does it matter? Leave the care of it to divine providence, which looks after even the birds in the sky.

—Francis de Sales, *Oeuvres*

We must not think that God tests us in order to lead us to evil, for that simply cannot be. He tests his most beloved servants so that they might prove their love and fidelity for him, and that they might accomplish great and shining works, as he did with Abraham when he commanded him to sacrifice his beloved son Isaac.

—Francis de Sales, *Oeuvres*

For God, under whose guidance we have embarked, will always be attentive to provide us with whatever is necessary. When all shall fail us, then God will take care of us, and then all will *not* fail us since we shall have God, who must be our all.

—Francis de Sales, *Oeuvres*

He lights you by the light of day; he nourishes you with the productions of the earth; in a word, he serves you by each one of the creatures that you use; so that it is true to say that every moment the bounty, the wisdom, and the power of God are at your service, and are exercised in the world for your wants or pleasures.

—Ignatius of Loyola, *Spiritual Exercises*

Prudence

Be prudent in everything that you do and you will have peace and tranquillity wherever you go; on the other hand, there is nothing but disorder without it.

—Vincent de Paul, *Conferences to the Daughters of Charity*

Prudence consists in seeing the means, the times, and the places when we should give admonitions and also how we should comport ourselves in all circumstances.

—Vincent de Paul, *Conferences to the Daughters of Charity*

Prudence consists in speaking about important matters only and not relating a lot of trifles that are not worth saying. That which you feel obliged to say should be expressed in as gentle a manner as possible, remembering that what seems evil is often so only in our feelings and opinions.

—Louise de Marillac, *instructions to sisters*

Human prudence says that we must serve God but that he is quite willing to have us put something aside for old age and illness; He wishes us to have what we need. Our health is better when we are well fed; we pray better when we are comfortable; to sleep on a hard bed causes infirmity; to suffer contempt often causes much harm and it gives others too much freedom to commit sin.

—Marguerite Bourgeoys, *Autographic Writings*

Prudence is knowing what to want and what not to want.

—Thomas Aquinas, *Summa Theologica*

A prudent person does not throw aside his interior life for external things, nor does he reject internal things because of his interior life. He should diligently perform external works with holy zeal in order to return what is within. And within himself he should be so detached that he can do justice to external things when it is timely and proper. Thus does he within and without find peace in all things according to the teachings of Wisdom, which nourishes the soul, as Christ said.

—Henry Suso, *letter*

True prudence implies that we who are always in need of God's help should always be asking for it. True, our Father knows what we need and is prepared to supply it generously, especially everything that relates to our eternal salvation. But he wants to give it to us by means of prayer, since this does him more honor and is more useful for us than if he were to give everything to us while we slept and did nothing.

—Robert Bellarmine, *The Mind's Ascent to God by the Ladder of Created Things*

To reflect on Wisdom is the highest prudence and he who forgoes sleep to possess her will so be given repose.

—Louis de Montfort, *The Love of Eternal Wisdom*

The usual way for prudent persons to learn the virtue of prudence is not only from things that they recognize have been done or said properly and prudently, but also from the things that have been done or said otherwise.

—Bede the Venerable, *homily on the Gospels*

Punishment

The reason for God punishing us is twofold: he punishes the just to improve them for the future and to reprove them for their previous actions.

—Basil the Great, *Consolation in Adversity*

The punishments of sinners in hell will be many, terrible, and pure, that is, unmixed with any consolations, and what infinitely increases their misery, they will be everlasting.

—Robert Bellarmine, *The Mind's Ascent to God by the Ladder of Created Things*

It is quite right that those whose sin will last forever should be punished forever. The nature and amount of punishment in hell is terrible even to think about.

—Robert Bellarmine, *The Mind's Ascent to God by the Ladder of Created Things*

Man has shown himself ungrateful for the gifts he received, has followed the devil in pride and disobedience and should therefore follow him in his punishment, for sin must necessarily be punished.

—Louis de Montfort, *The Love of Eternal Wisdom*

Purgatory

It is most certain that, as we share here below in the prayers of one another, so these same prayers and good works profit the souls in Purgatory, who can be helped by them.

—Francis de Sales, *Oeuvres*

I see that as far as God is concerned, paradise has no gates, but he who will may enter. For God is all mercy, and his open arms are ever extended to receive us into his glory. But I see that the divine essence is so pure—purer than the imagination can conceive—that the soul, finding in itself the slightest imperfection, would rather cast itself into a thousand hells than appear, so stained, in the presence of divine majesty. Knowing then, that purgatory was intended for her cleaning, she throws herself therein, and finds there that great mercy, the removal of her stains.

—Catherine of Genoa, *Life and Doctrine*

\I saw my Guardian Angel, who ordered me to follow him. In a moment I was in a misty place full of fire in which there was a great crowd of suffering souls. They were praying fervently, but to no avail, for themselves; only we can come to their aid. The flames which were burning them did not touch me at all. My Guardian Angel did not leave me for an instant. I asked these souls what their greatest suffering was. They answered me in one voice that their greatest torment was longing for God.

—Faustina Kowalska, *Divine Mercy in My Soul*

Notice, dear children, how lovingly eternal Wisdom knows how to order all things so that people imagine that they have suffered a great loss, but God has turned it to their great advantage. It also diminishes their purgatory and garners them a great reward.

—Henry Suso, *sermon*

We can infer the manner in which souls suffer in purgatory. The fire, when applied, would be powerless over them if they did not have imperfections from which to suffer. These imperfections are the fuel that catches on fire, and once they are gone there is nothing left to burn. So it is here on earth; when the imperfections are gone, the soul's suffering terminates, and joy remains.

—John of the Cross, *The Dark Night of the Soul*

The holy souls in purgatory. Out of charity, out of justice, and out of excusable selfishness—they have such power with God!—remember them often in your sacrifices and in your prayer.

May you be able to say when you speak of them, "My good friends the souls in purgatory."

—Josemaría Escrivá, *The Way*

In the face of suffering and persecution, a certain soul with supernatural sense said, "I prefer to take a beating down here rather than get it in purgatory."

—Josemaría Escrivá, *The Forge*

Purification

The discipline of purification can and must cease only with our life, therefore be not discouraged by infirmities; our perfection consists in struggling against them, which we cannot do unless we perceive them, neither can we conquer unless we come into collision with them. Victory does not lie in ignoring our infirmities, but in resisting them.

—Francis de Sales, *The Devout Life*

There is no disposition so good by nature that it cannot acquire bad habits, neither is there any disposition naturally so perverse that by the grace of God, united to diligence and industry, it may not be conquered and subdued.

—Francis de Sales, *The Devout Life*

Men cannot unite themselves with this divine and incomprehensible light and see it unless they purify themselves by the fulfillment of the commandments and consecrate themselves to spiritual and purifying prayer in order to receive the supernatural powers of contemplation.

—Gregory Palamas, *A Study of Gregory Palamas*

Purify your hearts that they may appear to Him like bright little stars at the bottom of a fountain.

—Elizabeth Seton, *Collected Writings*

To undertake the journey to God the heart must be burned with the fire of divine love and purified of all creatures. Such a purgation puts the devil to flight, for he has power over people through their attachment to temporal and bodily things.

—John of the Cross, *The Ascent of Mount Carmel*

There were six stone jars in Cana of Galilee containing water used for ritual ablutions; there are also "six stone jars" of purification found in a soul which, motivated by love, converts from vice to virtue: contrition, confession, prayer, fasting, almsgiving, and sincere forgiveness.

—Anthony of Padua, *Sermones*

Purification consists in driving out everything that is creature or smacks of creature and that one wrongly desires, worries about or is attached to; anything that is in some way an obstacle for man. Even if this were the highest spirit of the

Seraphim, St. John himself, or anything whatever that is creature, one must abandon it.

—Henry Suso, *letter*

These things purify the eyes of the heart so that they can be lifted up to the true light: rejection of worldly concern, affliction of the flesh, contrition of the heart, frequent and pure confession of sin, and the washing of tears.

—Elisabeth of Schönau, *The Book of the Ways of God*

O my God, I will try so to prepare my heart that you may take pleasure and delight in it, and so that I may not place any obstacle to the immense graces I shall receive if I purify myself and realize what great good I shall lose if I do not do so.

—Claude de la Colombière, *spiritual notes*

When souls undergo purification through penitence and the practice of the commandments, they receive grace to discover themselves completely and to know what is beyond their reach. By intensifying their purification, by deepening their humility, they begin gradually to understand, albeit in obscure fashion, the things of God and what belongs to God.

—Symeon the New Theologian, *Ethical Discourses*

Not that everyone is capable of discussing God, but only those who have purified their souls and their bodies, or at least are striving to purify them.

—Gregory of Nazianzus, *oration*

Our greater impurity needs to be purified by a greater practice of prayers, vigils and fasting, of tears and almsgiving.

—Bede the Venerable, *homily on the Gospels*

Once the mind has been purified of all desire for this world and has left behind every form of sentient life, rising up like a fish from the depths to the surface, it will not in the purity of its creation be able to see the Holy Spirit, the Father and the Son, who in the same nature in essence possess the same goodness, righteousness, holiness and life.

—Basil the Great, *On Faith*

Purity

Purity of conscience can endure nothing but God only; for he alone is spotless, simple, pure: of all things else, that is, of what is evil, it cannot endure even the smallest spark; this neither be understood nor appreciated, if it be not felt.

—Catherine of Genoa, *Life and Doctrine*

For pure is the soul that is humble; pure is the soul that has abandoned itself; and pure is the soul that wants nothing, knows nothing, and understands nothing. In a word, purity exclusively, absolutely lies in seeking God's honor and glory, and in enjoying it.

—Maria Maddalena de' Pazzi, *Probation*

But the atmosphere of the soul is not purified until a small spiritual flame is kindled in the soul. This flame is the work of the grace of God; not a special grace, but one common to all. This flame appears when a man has attained a certain measure of purity in the general moral order of his life.

—Theophan the Recluse, *letter*

You cannot be or become spiritually intelligent in the way that is natural to man in his pre-fallen state unless you first attain purity and freedom from corruption.

—Gregory of Sinai, *The Philokalia*

Alas, my dear brethren, how little purity is known in the world; how little we value it; what little care we take to preserve it; what little zeal we have in asking God for it, since we cannot have it of ourselves.

—John Baptiste Marie Vianney, *sermon*

Purity! No, my dear brethren, this beautiful virtue is not unknown by such a person whose lips are but an opening and a supply pipe which hell uses to vomit its impurities upon the earth and who subsists in these as upon his daily bread. Alas! That poor soul is only an object of horror in heaven and on earth!

—John Baptiste Marie Vianney, *sermon*

Holy purity is given by God when it is asked for with humility.

—Josemaría Escrivá, *The Way*

Without charity, purity is barren, and its sterile water turns the soul into a swamp, into a cesspool from which rises the stench of pride.

—Josemaría Escrivá, *The Way*

To defend his purity, Saint Francis of Assisi rolled in the snow, Saint Benedict threw himself into a thorn bush, Saint Bernard plunged into an icy pond. . . . You . . . what have you done?

—Josemaría Escrivá, *The Way*

We must know that God regards our purity of heart and tears of compunction, not our many words.

—Benedict, *Rule*

The truly pure of heart are those who despise the things of earth and seek the things of heaven, and who never cease to adore and behold the Lord God living and true with a pure heart and soul.

—Francis of Assisi, *saying*

Purity is corrupted more speedily than corruption is made pure. So it goes with the container which is our heart. If it has not first been cleansed of all the foulest contagion of sin it will not deserve to receive that perfume of benediction about which the prophet speaks, "Like the oil poured over the head, comes down on to the beard of Aaron, comes down on to the edges of his clothing." (Psalms 132:2)

—John Cassian, *Conferences*

Perfect purity brings one closer to God.

—Louis de Montfort, *The Love of Eternal Wisdom*

For with God, no one who is unjust is pure.

—Ambrose, *Concerning Repentence*

R

Rape

When a woman is violated while her soul admits no consent to the iniquity, but remains inviolately chaste, the sin is not hers, but his who violates her.

—Augustine, *The City of God*

Rapture

Rapture means the total elevation of the soul's powers towards the majesty of divine glory, disclosed as undivided unity. Or again rapture is a pure and all-embracing ascent toward the limitless power that dwells in the light.

—Gregory of Sinai, *The Philokalia*

I wish that I could explain, with God's help, the difference between union and rapture, or elevation, or flight of the spirit or transport—for they are all one. I mean that these are all different names for the same thing, which is also called ecstasy.

—Teresa of Ávila, *Life*

The effects of rapture are great. One is that the mighty power of the Lord is made manifest. We see that against His Majesty's will we can do nothing to control either the soul or the body. We are not the masters; whether we like it or not, we see that there is One mightier than we, that these favors are given by Him, and that, of ourselves we can do absolutely nothing. This imprints a deep humility upon us.

—Teresa of Ávila, *Life*

Rapture leaves behind a certain strange detachment also, the real nature of which I shall never be able to describe. All that I can say is that it is somewhat different from that caused by purely spiritual graces.

—Teresa of Ávila, *Life*

Redemption

For Christ granted to His Church that one should be redeemed by means of all, as she herself was found worthy of the coming of the Lord Jesus, in order that through One all might be redeemed.

—Ambrose, *Concerning Repentance*

If pride turned some of the angels into demons, then humility can doubtless make angels out of demons. So take heart, all you sinners.

—John Climacus, *The Ladder of Divine Ascent*

Repentance

Repentance is the renewal of baptism and is a contract with God for a fresh start in life.

—John Climacus, *The Ladder of Divine Ascent*

In my meditation, or more accurately, in my acts of repentance, a fire of prayer will burn and will consume everything material.

—John Climacus, *The Ladder of Divine Ascent*

Total contrition is necessary for everyone, but particularly for those who have come to the King to obtain forgiveness of their sins.

—John Climacus, *The Ladder of Divine Ascent*

Forgetting offenses is a sign of sincere repentance. If you keep the memory of them, you may believe you have repented but you are like someone running in his sleep.

—John Climacus, *The Ladder of Divine Ascent*

He who commits sin does what is not pleasing to God; but he who repents of his sins, does what is most pleasing to Him.

—Robert Bellarmine, *The Art of Dying Well*

Repentance destroys all sin. But if the sinner is incapable of repentance, for instance, the demons and men after this life, then the divine wrath turns against these sinners.

—Robert Bellarmine, *The Mind's Ascent to God by the Ladder of Created Things*

Thus, beloved Christians, God has spoken to you, and, seeing that you disregarded his words, he has had recourse to scourges: he has called you to repentance by such a persecution, by temporal losses, by the death of a relative, by sickness which has brought you to the brink of the grave.

—Alphonsus Liguori, *sermon*

He who has repented travels towards the Lord.

—Theophan the Recluse, *letter*

If, then, the time of this life is time for repentance, the very fact that a sinner still lives is a pledge that God will accept whoever desires to return to him.

—Gregory Palamas, *To the Most Reverend Nun Xenia*

If you repent at the inception of sin you will not commit the sin itself; but if you feel no pang in committing minor offences you will through them fall into major transgressions.

—Gregory Palamas, *A New Testament Decalogue*

I shall not die in my sins if I rise up in daily repentance. Instead, I shall live forever through the true, pure attitude of remorse I feel toward God.

—Hildegard of Bingen, *Book of Divine Works*

Sin then is, as we have said, a fearful evil, but not incurable; fearful for him who clings to it, but easy to cure for him who by repentance puts it from him.

—Cyril of Jerusalem, *Catecheses*

For it is a fearful thing not to believe in a hope for repentance.

—Cyril of Jerusalem, *Catecheses*

The robber who looks not for pardon grows desperate; but, if he hopes for forgiveness, often comes to repentance.

—Cyril of Jerusalem, *Catecheses*

Look very closely into what you have from negligence omitted to do, or what you have done badly, and resolve seriously on the necessary amendment, which you must then carry out with great fidelity. For if as soon as you have perceived your fault you strive to correct it, our merciful Lord will not fail to accompany your repentance with His voluntary gifts, and to turn even your past errors to your great profit by loading you with His graces.

—Francis Xavier, *letter*

All the angels rejoice, for in heaven there is greater joy over the sinner that repents, than over ninety and nine just persons who need not repentance.

—Ambrose, *Concerning Repentance*

If you were to see a blind man about to fall into a pit or over a precipice, would you not warn him? Behold, I do the same, and do it I must, for this is my duty. I must warn sinners and make them see the precipice which leads to the unquenchable fires of Hell, for they will surely go there if they do not amend their ways.

—Anthony Mary Claret, *autobiography*

True repentance through confession and tears, like a kind of medicine and dressing, cleanses and clears away the wound of the heart and the scar which the sting of spiritual death has opened in it. Next, it casts out and puts to death the worm which had nestled there, and restores the wound to complete healing and perfect health.

—Symeon the New Theologian, *Ethical Discourses*

The Lord does not want the sinner to die but wishes him to repent and find life. . . . If you have fallen then pick yourself up, if you have sinned, then you must repent. Do not remain on the path of sin, but get off it. Once you have corrected and have groaned in pain, then you will be saved, for it is only after sweat and toil that you can be restored to health and find salvation.

—Basil the Great, *letter*

Contrition is for the soul which discovers the many and different kinds of its sins. The fire of repentance gathers them together, piles them up and grinds them into the mortar of conscience. She melts them down over the fire of repentance and sorrow.

—Bernard of Clairvaux, *On the Canticle of Canticles*

For the first sacrifice that must be offered to God is a contrite and humble heart. The soul will be less contemptible in the eyes of God the more contemptible she becomes in her own eyes.

—Bernard of Clairvaux, *On the Canticle of Canticles*

God cannot turn away his face from those who cast themselves at his feet with a humble and contrite heart.

—Alphonsus Liguori, *sermon*

Oh! with what tenderness does God embrace a sinner that returns to him!

—Alphonsus Liguori, *sermon*

Contrition and looking on oneself as the least of all bring about the perfect humility that is the gift of God, a power rightly regarded as the perfection of all virtues.

—Gregory of Sinai, *The Philokalia*

By [the] water pot of contrition the soul is washed and purified, especially when the pot contains the water of tears.

—Vincent Ferrer, *sermon*

The sinner is always at war with God; but contrition for sin makes peace between God and sinner, therefore he says: "In peace is my bitterness most bitter," for peace is brought about by bitterness, that is, by contrition.

—Vincent Ferrer, *sermon*

When feelings of repentance arise in your heart, God looks upon you with pity.

—Ignatius of Loyola, *Spiritual Exercises*

Resolutions

Make few resolutions. Make them definite.—And fulfil them with the help of God.

—Josemaría Escrivá, *The Way*

Resurrection

Faith in the resurrection of Christ never misleads us, and hope in our own resurrection never deceives us, because God the Father both restored our Lord to life and will restore us to life too by virtue of his power.

—Bede the Venerable, *homily on the Gospels*

Do not believe those stupid people who think they will be reborn in their present bodily form on the day of resurrection, since this is merely a vain and baseless piece of superstition. Indeed I challenge anyone who believes that to show me the page in the Bible where it is written. I have certainly never seen it and I am sure that, if they had taken the trouble to study this matter carefully, they would not have committed such a lie and blunder.

—Basil the Great, *Consolation in Adversity*

The Word perceived that corruption could not be got rid of otherwise than through death; yet He Himself, as the Word, being immortal and the Father's Son, was such as could not die. For this reason, therefore, He assumed a body capable of death, in order that it, through belonging to the Word Who is above all, might become in dying a sufficient exchange for all, and, itself remaining incorruptible through His indwelling, might thereafter put an end to corruption for all others as well, by the grace of the resurrection.

—Athanasius, *On the Incarnation*

For by the sacrifice of His own body He did two things: He put an end to the law of death which barred our way; and He made a new beginning of life for us, by giving us the hope of resurrection.

—Athanasius, *On the Incarnation*

Had the interval between His death and resurrection been but two days, the glory of His incorruption might not have appeared. He waited one whole day to show that His body was really dead, and then on the third day showed it incorruptible to all.

—Athanasius, *On the Incarnation*

The body is a help to the soul that loves God, even when it is ill, even when it is dead, and all the more when it is raised again from the dead: for illness is aid to penitence; death is the gate of rest; and the resurrection will bring consummation.

—Bernard of Clairvaux, *On Loving God*

Revelation

If you say: "Master, it is doubtful how a man can have sufficient command over himself to determine whether it is a dream or a revelation," the answer is: "When it is a revelation from God, it comes with such brightness and certitude that it is as if it were actually seen." So the Apostle says of a certain revelation which he received: "For I know what I have believed and I am certain." (2 Timothy 1:12)

—Vincent Ferrer, *sermon*

I tell you that, as by the brightness of the sunrise you know that is the day, so Divine revelation is known by the brightness of illumination given it by God. But if it is doubtful whether or not it is a revelation, then it is not a perfect revelation from God.

—Vincent Ferrer, *sermon*

The devil is most pleased when he sees that people desire to accept revelations and are inclined toward them. For then he has an excellent opportunity to inject errors and disparage faith as much as possible.

—John of the Cross, *The Ascent of Mount Carmel*

Rewards

If the day of reward or of persecution comes upon us ready and swift as we run in this contest of good works, the Lord will never fail to give a reward for our merits; in peace He will give to those who conquer a white crown for their good works; in persecution He will give a second crown, a purple one, for our passion.

—Cyprian of Carthage, *Works and Almsgiving*

Riches

Clearly, it is better to carry the gold to the abode of the soul than to bury the soul in the mine of the gold. That is why God orders those who will serve in His army here below to fight as men stripped of concern for riches and unencumbered by anything. To these He has granted the privilege of reigning in heaven.

—Peter Chrysologus, *sermon*

For it is not earthly riches which make us or our sons happy; for they must either be lost by us in our lifetime, or be possessed when we are dead, by whom we know not, or perhaps by whom we would not. But it is God who makes us happy, who is the true riches of our minds.

—Augustine, *The City of God*

Lord, when I came into this world, I did not bring anything with me, and when I leave it, I shall not take anything out. So long as I have something to eat and clothes to wear, I am happy.

—Augustine, *sermon*

Rich people may become poor, owing to accidents which frequently occur, but those who are resolved to depend utterly on God shall never be poor.

—Vincent de Paul, *Conferences to the Daughters of Charity*

The world's riches are yours only for your necessary nourishment and clothing.

—Bridget of Sweden, *Book of Questions*

To gain eternal life it is more useful to spurn riches than to possess them, because the rich have difficulty in entering the kingdom of heaven due to the fact that it is difficult not to be held fast by the love of riches, and it is that which makes it impossible to enter the kingdom of heaven. Consequently, it was with an eye to our advantage that Our Lord counseled it as being more useful that riches be abandoned.

—Thomas Aquinas, *On the Perfection of the Spiritual Life*

For they who in appearance are rich, and have many possessions, are poor in soul: since the more they gather, the more they pine with longing for what is still lacking.

—Cyril of Jerusalem, *Catecheses*

Be a lover of the ordinary man, and don't wish for riches, but cool down excitement and don't speak your mind.

—Columban, *letter, c. 610*

If you are a man of God, you will seek to despise riches as intensely as men of the world seek to possess them.

—Josemaría Escrivá, *The Way*

We must hurry therefore to make a total effort to ensure that the inner man shall reject and scatter those sinful riches which he gathered during his earlier way of life. These riches belong to us and hold fast to us in body and soul and if we do not cut them out and throw them away while we are still alive they will continue to be our companions after death.

—John Cassian, *Conferences*

To use riches according to one's state and condition, when it is done as it should be, is permissible. But to make idols of them is to be condemned and damned.

—Francis de Sales, *Oeuvres*

Righteousness

He is Righteousness, because He distributes according to that which we deserve, and is a righteous Arbiter both for those who are under the Law and for those who are under Grace, for soul and body, so that the former should rule, and the latter obey, and the higher have supremacy over the lower; that the worse may not rise in rebellion against the better.

—Gregory of Nazianzus, *theological oration*

The truly righteous are set apart from the world because they produce the fruits of grace in their actions.

—Clement of Alexandria, *Miscellaneous Studies*

It is clear that the word "righteousness" means the sum total of the virtues. It means that the person is blessed who possesses prudence, courage, moderation, temperance, self-control, who is hungry, in short, for all included in the definition of virtue.

—Gregory of Nyssa, *On the Beatitudes*

The good should always rejoice in their performance of works of righteousness, and in what they suffer for righteousness' sake, since for those "who love God, all things work together for good." (Romans 8:28)

—Bede the Venerable, *homily on the Gospels*

Rosary

The holy Rosary is a powerful weapon. Use it with confidence and you will be amazed at the results.

—Josemaría Escrivá, *The Way*

S

Sacrifice

What regret would be yours at the hour of death, should you see yourself deprived of the crown which awaits you if you are faithful in generously following the light that our Lord gives you. And, to tell the truth, you will only find peace and rest when you have sacrificed all for God.

—Margaret Mary, *Life and Writings of St. Margaret Mary*

Our divine Lord wishes to have his court here below as on high, he desires angel-martyrs and angel-apostles.

—Thérèse of Lisieux, *letter to Her Sister Celine*

True love grows by sacrifice and that the more thoroughly the soul rejects natural satisfaction, the stronger and more detached its tenderness becomes.

—Thérèse of Lisieux, *The Story of a Soul*

One sweet sacrifice will unite my soul with our All who offers it.

—Elizabeth Seton, *Collected Writings*

The reward of sacrifice is peace.

—Elizabeth Seton, *Collected Writings*

You think you make sacrifices. Look at the sacrifice of Calvary and compare yours with it.

—Elizabeth Seton, *Collected Writings*

To enjoy we must love, and to love, we must sacrifice.

—Elizabeth Seton, *Collected Writings*

Thus a true sacrifice is every work which is done that we may be united to God in holy fellowship, and which has a reference to that supreme good and end in which alone we can be truly blessed.

—Augustine, *The City of God*

The more you give yourself, the more God will give himself to you.

—Louis de Montfort, *letter*

If there is sacrifice when you sow love, you will also reap Love.

—Josemaría Escrivá, *The Forge*

The way of Love has a name: it is *Sacrifice.*

—Josemaría Escrivá, *The Forge*

No matter what price I have to pay, God must be pleased with me.

—Claude de la Colombière, *spiritual notes*

Sadness and sorrow

Sadness . . . is the slow death of the soul, and serves no purpose.

—Padre Pio, *The Time-Piece of the Passion of Our Lord Jesus Christ*

Learn how to profit by your sorrows, for they bring great riches to the soul. They cleanse it from past sin; what fire is to gold, that tribulation is to the just man, whose heart it purifies.

—John of Ávila, *letter to a disciple, 1563*

Learn to give sorrow no long dominion over you.

—Robert Southwell, *letter to a friend, 1591*

All other sorrow is pleasure compared with this worst of sorrows—the offending my gracious Lord.

—Elizabeth Seton, *Collected Writings*

Can there be any actual sorrow in that soul which confidently says: "My God and My All?"

—Elizabeth Seton, *Collected Writings*

Sorrow is a virtue that, when practiced with full awareness, takes away a person's sin.

—Henry Suso, *sermon*

Love stirs itself from sorrow; and love itself is in equal measure lanced with sorrow. Out of great love great sorrow is extorted. Who loves greatly, sorrows greatly when what was loved is taken away.

—Lawrence of Brindisi, *sermon*

Don't forget that Sorrow is the touchstone of Love.

—Josemaría Escrivá, *The Way*

Unholy sorrow disturbs the soul, disquiets her, arouses vain fears, disgusts her with prayer, overpowers the brain and makes it drowsy, deprives the soul of wisdom, resolution, judgment and courage, and crushes her strength: in short, it resembles a hard winter, which withers the beauty of the earth and numbs all life, for it deprives the soul of all suppleness, rendering all her faculties of no avail and powerless.

—Francis de Sales, *The Devout Life*

Saints

We are all called to be saints. Every one of us has heard, and still hears, ringing in his conscience, the command: "Climb higher"; higher, ever higher, until while we are on this earth we can reach up to grasp the heavens, until we can join our saints, whether they be the venerable saints of old or the wonderful saints of modern times, who were our own contemporaries, and in whom our Mother the Church already rejoices.

—Pope John XXIII, *Writing and Addresses While Patriarch of Venice*

We should not only want to be with the saints, we should also hope to possess their happiness. While we desire to be in their company, we must also earnestly seek to share in their glory. Do not imagine that there is anything harmful in such an ambition as this; there is no danger in setting our hearts on such glory.

—Bernard of Clairvaux, *sermon*

It is difficult to become a saint. Difficult, but not impossible. The road to perfection is long, as long as one's lifetime. Along the way, consolation becomes rest; but as soon as your strength is restored, you must diligently get up and resume the trip.

—Padre Pio, *Archives of Padre Pio*

If you consider all the saints, you will see that all of them had a devotion to the Blessed Virgin; her intercession is most powerful, she is the Mother of God and the Mother of men.

—Brother André, *Brother André According to Witnesses*

I do not think anyone should be classed as a saint until he has made holy his body, if indeed that is possible.

—John Climacus, *The Ladder of Divine Ascent*

Scripture tells us that the Name of the Father and the Son, written on the foreheads and minds of the saints, is written there by the finger of the Living God, which, as explained in Exodus 32, is the Holy Spirit. Thus, through the testimony of these first two, we come, in glory, to one Name in three persons, which constitutes the glory of the saints.

—Bernadine of Siena, *sermon*

He who wishes to share in the glory of the saints, must suffer in this life as the saints have suffered. None of the saints has been esteemed or treated well by the world—all of them have been despised and persecuted.

—Alphonsus Liguori, *sermon*

The saints, represented by the stars, not only do not pity the damned, but they even rejoice in the vengeance inflicted on the injuries offered to their God.

—Alphonsus Liguori, *sermon*

The saint is not afflicted, like worldlings, at the thought of being obliged to leave the goods of this Earth, because he has kept his soul detached from them. During life, he always regarded God as the Lord of his heart, and as the sole riches which he desired.

—Alphonsus Liguori, *sermon*

I find that the saints have trembled at the hour of death; how much more ought I to tremble! I answer: It is true that Hell does not cease to assail even the saints at death, but it is also true that God does not cease to assist his servants at that moment; and when the dangers are increased, he multiplies his help.

—Alphonsus Liguori, *sermon*

Hence the saints continually seek light from God; for they know that, should he withdraw his light, they may become the greatest of sinners.

—Alphonsus Liguori, *sermon*

Devout souls, if you love God and desire to become saints, you must seek his will and wish what he wishes.

—Alphonsus Liguori, *sermon*

The saints in Heaven love God perfectly. In what, I ask, does the perfection of their love consist? It consists in an entire conformity to the divine will.

—Alphonsus Liguori, *sermon*

The jewels which give the greatest splendor to the crown of the saints in Heaven, are the tribulations which they bore with patience, as coming from the hands of the Lord.

—Alphonsus Liguori, *sermon*

The saints are in Heaven; but the saints that are on Earth are flesh, and by proximate occasions, they may become devils.

—Alphonsus Liguori, *sermon*

At the time of the passage of their souls from this life to eternity, the sight of their past sins, the rigor of God's judgment, and the uncertainty of their eternal salvation, have made the saints tremble.

—Alphonsus Liguori, *sermon*

Even the saints have been tormented by temptations. The Devil labors harder to make the saints fall, than to make the wicked sin: he regards the saints as more valuable prey.

—Alphonsus Liguori, *sermon*

The saints have buried themselves alive in this life, that, after death, they may not find themselves buried in Hell for eternity.

—Alphonsus Liguori, *sermon*

I give thanks to God that I am worthy to be hated by the world.

—Jerome, *letter*

Only those who through their purity have become saints are spiritually intelligent in the way that is natural to man in his pre-fallen state. Mere skill in reasoning does not make a person's intelligence pure, for since the fall our intelligence has been corrupted by evil thoughts.

—Gregory of Sinai, *The Philokalia*

Make icons of the saints and venerate them, not as gods—for this is forbidden—but because of the attachment, inner affection and sense of surpassing honor that you feel for the saints when by means of the icons the intellect is raised up to them.

—Gregory Palamas, *A New Testament Decalogue*

The Saints in heaven worship the mercy of the Lord.

—Faustina Kowalska, *Divine Mercy in My Soul*

The honor and glory of the saints surpass all eloquence, for God himself will praise all the saints with the whole world, all men and angels as an audience, and he will crown them like victors, and they will be seated on the throne of Christ as participants in his kingdom, something that surpasses every dignity.

—Robert Bellarmine, *The Mind's Ascent to God by the Ladder of Created Things*

There is in man's very nature a continual drive to perfect himself physically, mentally and also morally. In the history of man we find individuals everywhere whom we consider to be in a class above the ordinary crowd, above even the well-educated. These persons we call "saints."

—Maximilian M. Kolbe, *article on saintliness, 1922*

And if we ask who the saints are who are gathered unto Him by the angels, we are told, "They who make a covenant with Him over sacrifices." This is the whole life of the saints, to make a covenant with God over sacrifices.

—Augustine, *The City of God*

Therefore it is a great shame for us, the servants of God, that the saints have accomplished great things and we want only to receive glory and honor by recounting them.

—Francis of Assisi, *saying*

For the saint who's gone up to heaven has no need of acclamation from human beings in order to arrive at a greater and more blessed lot. We, on the other hand, who are meanwhile engaged in matters on earth and crave a great deal of consolation from all quarters, need to hear the saint praised in order to be galvanized to emulate him.

—John Chrysostom, *homily on Blessed Philogonius*

One cannot possibly understand the teaching of the saints unless one has a pure mind and is trying to imitate their life.

—Athanasius, *On the Incarnation*

But not only, O my God, do I wish to be all Thine; I wish to become a saint, and as I do not know whether my life will be long or short, I protest to Thee that I wish to make myself a saint soon. Let the people of the world seek the vanity and pleasures and dignities of this earth; I wish and desire and seek only to become a saint, and I shall be the happiest of men if I make myself a saint soon—a great saint.

—Joseph Cafasso, *second panegyric on St. Joseph Cafasso by St. John Bosco*

Without great sobriety it is impossible for us to become saints.

—Joseph Cafasso, *second panegyric on St. Joseph Cafasso by St. John Bosco*

Just as we recognize the different nations by their clothing and most people by their voice and speech, just so then do we recognize the saints by, on the one hand, their decency and attractive behavior and other outward signs; but it is their speech, on the other hand, which truly and accurately reveals their real identity. What the heart does not have, the mouth is unable to produce.

—Symeon the New Theologian, *Ethical Discourses*

The saints were not abnormal beings: cases to be studied by a "modernistic" doctor. They were—they are—normal: of flesh, like yours. And they won.

—Josemaría Escrivá, *The Way*

Each day be conscious of your duty to be a saint. A saint! And that doesn't mean doing strange things. It means a daily struggle in the interior life and in heroically fulfilling your duty right through to the end.

—Josemaría Escrivá, *The Forge*

The saints are those who struggle right to the end of their lives, who always get up each time they stumble, each time they fall, and courageously embark on their way once more with humility, love, and hope.

—Josemaría Escrivá, *The Forge*

It is possible to be a saint anywhere and everywhere when one really wishes to become one.

—Claude de la Colombière, *letter*

The victories of the saints give our spirits wings through the joy they cause; their failures give us pause through fear.

—Gregory the Great, *Commentary on the Book of Job*

The saints are precisely lords, kings and gods, not in their own nature but because they have become lords over themselves, they have ruled their passions, they have kept intact that image of God in which they were created.

—John Damascene, *On the Orthodox Faith*

It is of the saints that Scripture says: "The souls of the righteous are in the hand of God and the torment of death shall not touch them." (Wisdom 3:1) In fact, their death is more like dreaming than dying. God is life and light, and those who are in the hand of God are themselves life and light.

—John Damascene, *On The Orthodox Faith*

When the saints are received into eternal peace, there will be no need for anything to be prayed on their behalf, since they will have been endowed with such great happiness that it could not be greater.

—Bede the Venerable, *homily on the Gospels*

Those who seek to perfect themselves in every aspect of virtue should look to the lives of the saints, which are like living and breathing works of art, and thus by imitation try to reproduce their virtues in their own life.

—Basil the Great, *letter to St. Gregory of Nyssa*

Salvation

Be mindful of God, so that in every moment he may be mindful of you. If he is mindful of you, he will give you salvation.

—Isaac of Nineveh, *The Philokalia*

We cannot be saved by seeking just our own individual salvation; we need to look first to the good of others.

—John Chrysostom, *On the Gospel of Matthew*

We are incapable of enduring the greatness of God's wrath due to the weakness of our human nature against which sin militates, and we thus stand in need of instruction. Let salvation instruct us through conversion rather than by the punishment due to our sins.

—Gregory of Nyssa, *Commentary on the Psalms*

Both the good and salvation for mankind come from God, for all things come through his grace and goodness. We are not the cause of this goodness; on the contrary, we have committed every kind of evil, while God has never been divested of his nature, for he acts according to this nature.

—Gregory of Nyssa, *Commentary on the Psalms*

Salvation admits of no differences between the sexes; rather, the salvation of each one and their relationship to one another both depend on the same close personal union with Christ.

—Edith Stein, *Essays on Woman*

Christ sowed the seed of salvation in humanity in order that it might grow especially in each individual soul.

—Edith Stein, *Essays on Woman*

Let us believe in him who saves not only the body, but also the soul from death, and let us observe in our works what we believe, so that by believing we may have eternal life in his name, for he lives and reigns with the Father and the Holy Spirit throughout all ages of ages.

—Bede the Venerable, *homily on the Gospels*

For everyone who calls upon the name of the Lord will be saved.

—Bede the Venerable, *homily on the Gospels*

Beyond all doubt, he does listen to our prayers and is ready to console us, but he sees things in a different way. He views them as a whole, we merely in part; he in the light of eternity, we in time only; he puts the well-being of the soul before that of the body, looks to our eternal salvation even at the cost of this life.

—Placid Riccardi, *letter to his brother, 1906*

When there is a question of salvation, we must do and suffer everything, sacrifice and give up everything.

—Margaret Mary Alacoque, *Life and Writings of St. Margaret Mary*

We cannot be saved without a struggle, for this life is a continual warfare. But be of good courage, do not be disheartened or troubled about your faults, but always try to draw from them a love of abjection, which must never for a moment be absent from your heart.

—Margaret Mary Alacoque, *Life and Writings of St. Margaret Mary*

Few things are really necessary for salvation: believe all the mysteries of our religion and keep the commandments of God.

—Francis de Sales, *Oeuvres*

Oh, how we could merit heaven every day, my dear brethren, by doing just our ordinary duties, but by doing them for God and the salvation of our souls.

—John Baptiste Marie Vianney, *sermon*

Keep in view this truth: my end is, in glorifying God, to save myself.

—Ignatius of Loyola, *Spiritual Exercises*

Remember then, that although you were made from nothing, you were not redeemed with nothing. In six days God created all things, including you, but for thirty years he worked out your salvation including the ignominy of dying on the cross.

—Bernard of Clairvaux, *On the Canticle of Canticles*

Time spent in honor of God and for the salvation of souls is never badly spent.

—Padre Pio, *Spiritual Maxims*

Let us fix our thoughts on the Blood of Christ; and reflect how precious that Blood is in God's eyes, inasmuch as its outpouring for our salvation has opened the grace of repentance to all mankind. For we have only to survey the generations of the past to see that in every one of them the Lord has offered the chance of repentance to any who were willing to turn to him.

—Clement of Rome, *first epistle to the Corinthians*

All that God has ordained for the salvation of mankind is encompassed and comprehended in the Name of Jesus.

—Bernadine of Siena, *sermon*

All would wish to be saved and to enjoy the glory of Paradise; but to gain Heaven, it is necessary to walk in the straight road that leads to eternal bliss. This road is the observance of the divine commands.

—Alphonsus Liguori, *sermon*

It is not necessary to become rich on this Earth—to acquire honors and dignities; but it is necessary to save our souls; because, unless we gain Heaven, we shall be condemned to Hell: there is no middle place; we must either be saved or damned.

—Alphonsus Liguori, *sermon*

Awaken in your soul the thirst for salvation, and the assurance that Our Lord alone can bring it.

—Theophan the Recluse, *letter*

Nothing can be imagined more useful than for those who value their salvation to examine their consciences diligently twice every day, morning and night. . . . And if they discover any mortal sin, let them not defer seeking the remedy of true contrition, but resolve to approach the sacrament of Penance at the very first opportunity.

—Robert Bellarmine, *The Art of Dying Well*

Since our supreme legislator is God, our salvation depends on carrying out his will.

—Maximilian M. Kolbe, *article, 1938*

I know what I will do; I will take the chalice of salvation. I will place Jesus' chalice on the empty scales of Truth. Thus, I will make amends for everything I lack. Thus, I will fully cover over all my sins. With this chalice I will fill all my ruins. With this chalice I will make amends even more than adequate for all my imperfection.

—Gertrude the Great, *Spiritual Exercises*

Salvation, such as it shall be in the world to come, shall be our final happiness.

—Augustine, *The City of God*

How can a soul that knows not God, nor what God has done for love of it, how can that soul believe, hope, and love? And how can it be saved without faith, hope and love?

—Vincent de Paul, *Conferences*

The salvation of the world began through Mary and through her it must be accomplished. Mary scarcely appeared in the first coming of Jesus Christ so that men, as yet insufficiently instructed and enlightened concerning the person of her Son, might not wander from the truth by becoming too strongly attached to her. . . . But in the second coming of Jesus Christ, Mary must be known and openly revealed by the Holy Spirit so that Jesus may be known, loved, and served through her.

—Louis de Montfort, *Treatise on True Devotion to the Blessed Virgin*

Is it not evident that the Lord Jesus is angry with us when we sin in order that He may convert us through fear of His indignation? His indignation, then, is not the carrying out of vengeance, but rather the working out of forgiveness, for these are His words: "If thou shalt turn and lament, thou shall be saved." He waits for our lamentations here, that is, in time, that He may spare us those which shall be eternal. He waits for our tears, that He may pour forth His goodness.

—Ambrose, *Concerning Repentence*

The sole reason why society is perishing is because it has refused to hear the word of the Church, which is the word of life, the word of God. All plans for salvation will be sterile if the great word of the Catholic Church is not restored in all its fullness.

—Anthony Mary Claret, *autobiography*

I can sin, but I cannot rise from my sins without the help of God and the merits of Jesus Christ. I can condemn myself, but I cannot save myself except by the goodness and mercy of God.

—Anthony Mary Claret, *autobiography*

Sanctity

Sanctity does not consist in great concerns. It consists in struggling to ensure that the flame of your supernatural life is never allowed to go out; it consists in letting yourself to be burned down to the last shred, serving God in the lowest place, or in the highest: wherever the Lord may call you.

—Josemaría Escrivá, *The Forge*

The great secret of sanctity comes down to becoming more and more like him, the only and most lovable Model.

—Josemaría Escrivá, *The Forge*

Sanctity consists precisely in this: in struggling to be faithful throughout your life and in accepting joyfully the Will of God at the hour of death.

—Josemaría Escrivá, *The Forge*

It is only God who can sanctify us, and it is no small thing to desire sincerely that he may do all that is necessary for this, for of ourselves we have neither sufficient light nor sufficient strength.

—Claude de la Colombière, *letter*

Self-denial

Where there is no self-denial, there is no virtue.

—Josemaría Escrivá, *The Way*

How little value is penance without constant self-denial!

—Josemaría Escrivá, *The Way*

Selfishness

The majority of people who have personal problems "have them" because they selfishly think about themselves.

—Josemaría Escrivá, *The Forge*

Earthly affections, even when they aren't just squalid concupiscence, usually involve some element of selfishness.

So, though you must not despise those affections—they can be very holy—always make sure you purify your intention.

—Josemaría Escrivá, *The Forge*

Self-knowledge

We shall never completely know ourselves if we don't strive to know God. By gazing at His grandeur, we get in touch with our own lowliness; by looking at His purity, we shall see our own filth; by pondering His humility, we shall see how far we are from being humble.

—Teresa of Ávila, *The Interior Castle*

My beloved in the Lord, know yourselves! Those who know themselves know their time, and those who know their time are able to stand upright without being moved by shifty tongues.

—Anthony, *letter*

Self-knowledge is the swelling in which we discover our own lowliness, and this makes us humble. There we find the knowledge of God's goodness, too, and in this light a warmth, a fire of love, is born in us—so gentle that all the bitterness becomes sweet, everything weak grows strong, and all the ice of selfish love melts away.

—Catherine of Siena, *letter to a nobleman, c. 1375*

You cannot put straight in others what is warped in yourself.

—Athanasius, *On the Incarnation*

Self-knowledge leads us by the hand, as it were, to humility.

—Josemaría Escrivá, *The Way*

Self-love

Self-love, which destroys charity and affection towards the neighbor, is the principle and foundation of every evil.

—Catherine of Siena, *Dialogue*

Thou knowest that every evil is founded in self-love, and that self-love is a cloud that takes away the light of reason, which reason holds in itself the light of faith, and one is not lost without the other.

—Catherine of Siena, *Dialogue*

Self-love is a tree on which grows nothing but fruits of death, putrid flowers, stained leaves, branches bowed down, and struck by various winds.

—Catherine of Siena, *Dialogue*

For those who love themselves—whether they are rulers or the ruled—harbor within themselves the evil pride that is the head and origin of all evil. For those who are isolated in their self-centeredness, loving themselves selfishly and not for God, can do nothing but evil; all virtue is dead in them.

—Catherine of Siena, *letter to Pope Gregory XI at Avignon, c. 1376*

When God wills to purify a soul from self-love, he first sends her his divine light, that by it she may discern a spark of love; for he has need of us in nothing, not even the least thing. We are his enemies, not only by our nature, which is inclined to evil, but by our manifold offenses, which we are ever ready to repeat.

—Catherine of Genoa, *Life and Doctrine*

Do not let your life be precious in your own eyes; instead, always consider it worthless and despicable. Indeed, those who love themselves and consider themselves great are not able to endure the abuse of persecution and are not fit for the contest of the saints.

—Elisabeth of Schönau, *The Book of the Ways of God*

He, then, who sets his mind on doing wrong things, and yet wishes all other men to hold their peace about them, is himself a witness to himself that he desires to be loved himself more than the truth, which he is unwilling should be defended against him.

—Gregory the Great, *The Book of Pastoral Rule*

A person who exalts himself debases God, and a person who humbles himself exalts God.

—Louis de Montfort, *Treatise on True Devotion to the Blessed Virgin*

Who of us, if we do not love ourselves, can love our neighbor, for as we love ourselves so are we to love our neighbor.

—Aelred of Rielvaux, *Spiritual Friendship*

Senses

Let us live soberly, for through the senses of our body, even though it be against our will, thieves do enter in: for how shall the house not be darkened, if the smoke rising without shall find the windows open?

—Abbot Syncletica, *saying*

The perfect spirit pays no attention to the senses. It neither receives anything through them, nor uses them principally, nor judges them to be requisite in its relationship with God, as it did before its spiritual growth.

—John of the Cross, *The Ascent of Mount Carmel*

To conquer oneself for one's own good is to make use of the senses in the service of the interior life.

—Teresa of Ávila, *The Way of Perfection*

Consider attentively the common deception of mortals and the woeful damage they suffer. For in the decisions of their will they ordinarily are moved solely by what they perceive through the senses, and they immediately proceed to act upon their choice without further consideration or counsel. Since the sensible impressions immediately move the animal passions and inclinations, it is evident that men do not act according to right reason, but according to the impulse of passion, excited by the senses and their objects.

—Mary of Agreda, *The Mystical City of God*

Strive to give your reason prominence in your actions because all evil comes from the overhasty impulsiveness of the senses.

—Henry Suso, *The Life of the Servant*

The defeat of the senses means the ascent of truth.

—Henry Suso, *The Life of the Servant*

Do not imagine that incarnate Wisdom, who is purer than the rays of the sun, will enter a soul and a body soiled by the pleasures of the senses. Do not believe that he will grant his rest and ineffable peace to those who love worldly company and vanities.

—Louis de Montfort, *The Love of Eternal Wisdom*

In order to empty ourselves of self, we must die daily to ourselves. This involves our renouncing what the powers of the soul and the senses of the body incline us to do. We must see as if we did not see, hear as if we did not hear and use the things of this world as if we did not use them.

—Louis de Montfort, *Treatise on True Devotion to the Blessed Virgin*

When the sensory appetites, gratifications, and supports are quenched, the intellect is left clean and free to understand the truth, for even though these appetites and pleasures concern spiritual things, they blind and impede the spirit.

—John of the Cross, *The Dark Night of the Soul*

Oh, what a sheer grace it is for the soul to be freed from the house of its senses! This good fortune, in my opinion, can only be understood by the ones who have tasted it. For then such persons will become clearly aware of the wretched servitude and the many miseries they suffered when they were subject to the activity of their faculties and appetites. They will understand how the life of the spirit is true freedom and wealth and embodies its inestimable goods.

—John of the Cross, *The Dark Night of the Soul*

Sensuality

Bear yourselves with manful courage, and make yourselves dead to all your own sensuality.

—Catherine of Siena, *Dialogue*

An evil man will love sensual pleasure so much and consider it so precious that he will not quit the delight that he takes in it for all the wealth and honors in the world.

—Francis de Sales, *Oeuvres*

Serenity

Complete serenity of mind is a gift of God; but this serenity is not given without our own intense effort. You will achieve nothing by your own efforts alone; yet God will not give you anything, unless you work with all your strength. This is an unbreakable law.

—Theophan the Recluse, *The Fruits of Prayer*

Don't confuse serenity with being lazy or careless, with putting off decisions or deferring the study of important matters.

Serenity always goes hand in hand with diligence, which is a virtue we need in order to consider and solve outstanding problems without delay.

—Josemaría Escrivá, *The Forge*

Service

One refuge and solace alone remains, which is that we who are bound to one another by charity's beautiful engagements should graft and establish our souls in Christ, serve him with a freeman's service, drink of his spirit, win him in our sufferings and our dying, and possess him in everlasting beatitude.

—Peter Canisius, *letter to Jesuit novices, 1548*

Extensive learning or great wealth are not at all necessary for the service of God. On the contrary, they are often a very big obstacle to it.

—John Baptiste Marie Vianney, *sermon*

God generally gives those who enter his service some foretaste of heavenly joy, in order to lead them from earthly delights, and to encourage them in the pursuit of divine love.

—Francis de Sales, *The Devout Life*

A heart enamored of God is unconquerable, for God is its strength; hell does not affright it nor heaven allure it, for it is so disposed that it receives all that befalls us from the hand of God, remaining with him in immoveable peace, and inwardly strengthened and fortified by him.

—Catherine of Genoa, *Life and Doctrine*

Thou are that great most high God of whom we can neither speak nor think, because of the ineffable supereminence of thy glory, wisdom, power, and infinite goodness: and all these thou employed in the service of man, who is so vile, but whom thou wouldst make so great and worthy, and therefore thou art unwilling to force the free-will which thou hast given him.

—Catherine of Genoa, *Life and Doctrine*

We must draw fresh strength with which to serve Him and manage not to be ungrateful, for the Lord's gifts are made on one condition, that if we do not make good use of His treasures and of the estate to which He raises us, He will take them away again, and we shall be left poorer than before. Then His Majesty will give those jewels to one who will display them, and profit himself and others by their use.

—Teresa of Ávila, *Life*

Still, the sick must be patiently borne with, because serving them leads to a greater reward.

—Benedict, *Rule*

Only those who set aside their own knowledge and walk in God's service like unlearned children receive wisdom from God.

—John of the Cross, *The Ascent of Mount Carmel*

The man who gives a reluctant service brings a state of slavery upon himself. For, if you should make your service a willing one, you would find yourself to be not God's servant but his Son.

—Valerian, *homily*

Surely the great secret of the spiritual life is to abandon to him all that we love by abandoning ourselves to all that he wishes, in perfect confidence that all will be for the best; and hence it has been said that all things turn to good for those who serve God.

—Vincent de Paul, *letter to a sister, 1660*

We can conceive of no higher calling than that of being in the service of God and we believe that the least of God's servants is richer, stronger, and nobler than any earthly monarch who does not serve God. How rich and strong and noble then must the good and faithful servant be, who serves God as unreservedly and as completely as he possibly can!

—Louis de Montfort, *Treatise on True Devotion to the Blessed Virgin*

Only in prayer, and through prayer, do we learn to serve others.

—Josemaría Escrivá, *The Forge*

We must serve God with our whole heart and do all in our power to prevent ourselves from sinning, but all that is to be done with joy, liberty of heart, and entire confidence, in spite of all the weakness that we feel and the faults we commit.

—Claude de la Colombière, *retreat notes*

A human being's true glory is to persevere in the service of God.

—Irenaeus, *Against Heresies*

Sex

see ADULTERY; CHASTITY; LUST; MARRIAGE; PASSIONS; VIRGINITY

Shame

Let us not then be ashamed to confess our sins unto the Lord. Shame indeed there is when each makes known his sins, but that shame, as it were, ploughs his land, removes the ever-recurring brambles, prunes the thorns, and gives life to the fruits which he believed were dead.

—Ambrose, *Concerning Repentance*

For he whose sin is forgiven has nothing whereof to be ashamed.

—Ambrose, *Concerning Repentance*

Sickness

see ILLNESS

Silence

Let us be silent when we should, and speak when the time for it comes.

—Francis de Sales, *Oeuvres*

Little love for silence leads to a lax and easy life.

—Marguerite Bourgeoys, *Autographic Writings*

You ask what our silence means? It means a right balance between talking and being silent, for he who masters it whole shall master part of it [by speaking only when it is appropriate]. Moreover, silence makes wise the heart that does not chatter, but spends only what it contains.

—Gregory of Nazianzus, *letter to Kledonios*

We do not talk, we observe silence, learning to tell only what is necessary, and training ourselves to conquer the passions. If someone chooses to do this, good! Anyhow, the advantage of being silent is that we need not answer to many.

—Gregory of Nazianzus, *letter to Kledonios*

The lover of silence draws close to God. He talks to him in secret and God enlightens him.

—John Climacus, *The Ladder of Divine Ascent*

Intelligent silence is the mother of prayer, freedom from bondage, custodian of zeal, a guard on our thoughts, a watch on our enemies, a prison of mourning, a friend of tears, a sure recollection of death, a painter of punishment, a concern with judgment, servant of anguish, foe of license, a companion of stillness, the opponent of dogmatism, a growth of knowledge, a hand to shape contemplation, hidden progress, the secret journey upward.

—John Climacus, *The Ladder of Divine Ascent*

The silence of death will tell us so plainly that our life is but a vapor, the world a passing scene, its dearest hopes illusive; that God and eternity are our all and all forever.

—Elizabeth Seton, *Collected Writings*

In order to hear the voice of God, one has to have silence in one's soul and to keep silence; not a gloomy silence, but an interior silence; that is to say, recollection in God. One can speak a great deal without breaking silence and, on the contrary, one can speak little and be constantly breaking silence.

—Faustina Kowalska, *Divine Mercy in My Soul*

A soul that has never tasted the sweetness of inner silence is a restless spirit which disturbs the silence of others.

—Faustina Kowalska, *Divine Mercy in My Soul*

Silence is a sword in the spiritual struggle. A talkative soul will never attain sanctity. The sword of silence will cut off everything that would like to cling to the soul. . . . A silent soul is strong. No adversities will harm it if it perseveres in silence. The silent soul is capable of attaining the closest union with God. It lives almost always under the inspiration of the Holy Spirit. God works in a silent soul without hindrance.

—Faustina Kowalska, *Divine Mercy in My Soul*

The more I feel that God is transforming me, the more I desire to immerse myself in silence. The love of God is doing its work in the depths of my soul.

—Faustina Kowalska, *Divine Mercy in My Soul*

Sometimes the soul lies low, hidden in the depths of silence. The stunning onset of sudden light takes all sound of voice away. All its senses are withdrawn into its own depths or else are let go and with unspeakable groanings it pours out its longings to God.

—John Cassian, *Conferences*

Be silent with others, so as to converse with divine Wisdom. "He who knows how to keep silent is a wise man." (Sirach 20:5)

—Louis de Montfort, *The Love of Eternal Wisdom*

The virtue of silence, especially in Church, is very great. Let no sentence of the divine lessons escape you; if you give ear, restrain your voice, utter no word with your lips which you would wish to recall, but let your boldness to speak be sparing. For in truth in much speaking there is abundance of sin.

—Ambrose, *Concerning Virgins, to Marcellina, His Sister*

When anything disagreeable and displeasing happens to you, remember Christ crucified and be silent.

—John of the Cross, *letter to a Carmelite nun, c. 1589*

The soul that is quick to turn to speaking and conversing is slow to turn to God. For when it is turned toward God, it is then strongly and inwardly drawn toward silence and flight from all conversation. For God desires a soul to rejoice with him more than with any other person, however advanced and helpful the person may be.

—John of the Cross, *letter*

Our greatest need is to be silent before this great God with the appetite and with the tongue, for the only language he hears is the silent language of love.

—John of the Cross, *letter*

If, as we have said, you honor and accept Him, and give Him a place and provide Him with silence, know well that you will hear ineffable things from the treasuries of the Spirit.

—Symeon the New Theologian, *Ethical Discourses*

Silence is the door-keeper of the interior life.

—Josemaría Escrivá, *The Way*

Simplicity

If you do not want to bear yourself in simplicity, you will have to bear yourself in multiplicity.

—Henry Suso, *The Life of the Servant*

Jesus, the Lord, expects us to have the simplicity of a dove. This means giving a straightforward opinion about things in the way we honestly see them, without needless reservations. It also means doing things without double-dealing or manipulation, our intention being focused solely on God.

—Vincent de Paul, *Common Rules or Constitutions of the Congregation of the Mission*

If you wish to draw the Lord to you, approach him as disciples to master, in all simplicity, openly, honestly, without duplicity, without idle curiosity. He is simple and uncompounded. And he wants the souls that come to him to be simple and pure. Indeed you will never see simplicity separated from humility.

—John Climacus, *The Ladder of Divine Ascent*

Simplicity is an enduring habit within a soul that has grown impervious to evil thoughts.

—John Climacus, *The Ladder of Divine Ascent*

Sin

If the man has sinned and denies it not, but says, "I have sinned," scold him not, for thou wilt break the purpose of his heart. But rather say to him, "Be not sad my brother, but watch thyself hereafter," and thou will rouse his heart to repentance.

—Abbot Pastor, *saying*

The nearer a man approaches to God, the greater sinner he sees himself to be. For the prophet Isaiah saw God, and said that he was unclean and undone.

—Abbot Mathois, *saying*

That with our neighbor there is life and death: for if we do good to our brother, we shall do good to God: but if we scandalize our brother, we sin against Christ.

—Abbot Anthony, *saying*

With the imagination of lust and the disparaging of thy neighbor, with these two speak not in thy heart, or consent to any of their befouling in thy soul. For if thou hast suffered thy heart to dwell on these, thou shalt soon feel their poisoning: it is the stirring of perdition: but by prayer and good actions bring the malignant spirit to naught, and to fight them off more hardily, and thou shalt have quiet.

—Abbot Poemon, *saying*

We have all been soiled by original and actual sin; we all shall die.

—Francis de Sales, *Oeuvres*

If we are truly humble, we shall grieve bitterly over our sin because it offends God, but we shall find sweetness in accusing ourselves, because in so doing we honor him; and we shall find relief in fully revealing our complaints to our physician.

—Francis de Sales, *The Devout Life*

There are three steps downward towards sin—temptation, delight, and consent.

—Francis de Sales, *The Devout Life*

It is sin that has brought discord into the beautiful order of the world. Man, created in the image of God and endowed with free will, can always be saved by developing the talent which has been given to him. Through malice, he often refuses; through cowardice, he fails to make any effort to possess the place in heaven which has been destined for him.

—Marguerite Bourgeoys, *Autographic Writings*

When anyone has really given up his sins, he must not be content simply with bewailing them. He must give up, leave far behind, and fly from anything which is capable of leading him in the direction of them again. In other words, my dear brethren, we must be ready to suffer anything rather than fall back into those sins which we have just confessed.

—John Baptiste Marie Vianney, *sermon*

By sin you reverse the order of his providence; you turn creatures away from their end, and you destroy the harmony of the universe.

—Ignatius of Loyola, *Spiritual Exercises*

If sin could destroy your fortune or your reputation, you would not commit it; and because it exposes you only to the anger of God, to the rigor of his judgment, you commit it without fear, and as if you had nothing to dread from his justice.

—Ignatius of Loyola, *Spiritual Exercises*

Even if you united in yourself all the merits of all the saints together, all their alms, all their prayers, all their austerities, all their sacrifices—a single mortal sin would be enough to destroy all.

—Ignatius of Loyola, *Spiritual Exercises*

The soul is the life of the body, and God is the life of the soul. Thus sin kills our soul in separating it from God.

—Ignatius of Loyola, *Spiritual Exercises*

A corpse, if not placed in the grave, spreads around it a fatal contagion. The sinner exhales an odor of corruption; the contagion of his scandals spreads death around him, and the infection of his vices makes him an object of horror to just men, to angels, and to God.

—Ignatius of Loyola, *Spiritual Exercises*

The understanding of the reprobate never ceases to show him the deformity of sin, the greatness and beauty of God, the justice of the punishment of hell.

—Ignatius of Loyola, *Spiritual Exercises*

The repetition of venial sins insensibly weakens the fear of God, hardens the conscience, forms evil attachments and habits, gives fresh strength to the temptations of the enemy of our salvation, nourishes and develops the passions.

—Ignatius of Loyola, *Spiritual Exercises*

Mortal sin is committed by thought, first, when thought is consented to; and secondly, when the thought is acted upon, which is a more grievous sin: 1, because it is entertained longer; 2, because we give ourselves up to it more ardently; 3, because we generally injure others by scandalizing them.

—Ignatius of Loyola, *Spiritual Exercises*

Alas! my God! what will become of me? I know not where to hide myself: I wander on, lamenting, and find no place of rest, for I am so stained with sin that I cannot appear where thou art, and yet I find thee everywhere.

—Catherine of Genoa, *Life and Doctrine*

O Lord my God, how deep are your secret places, and how far from them have the consequences of my sins cast me! Heal my eyes, and let me share in the joy of your light.

—Augustine, *Confessions*

Sin is a sticking to something against the light of reason and divine law. The tarnished brightness resulting from such contact is metaphorically described as a stain of soul. As long as the sinner stays away from the lights, the stain of sin persists, but when he returns by grace to the light of reason and God, the stain disappears.

—Thomas Aquinas, *Summa Theologica*

Every sin arises from disordered desire for some temporal good and that arises from disordered love of self.

—Thomas Aquinas, *Summa Theologica*

If a sin so disorders our life as to turn it away from its ultimate goal in God, to whom we are joined by charity, then the sin is fatal or mortal; in its nature it is irreparable and brings with it eternal penalty. But if the disorder stops short of such turning away, then the sin is non-fatal or venial, reparable in its nature and undeserving of eternal penalty.

—Thomas Aquinas, *Summa Theologica*

A man sins not only by willing bad ends but by willing bad actions.

—Thomas Aquinas, *Summa Theologica*

Remember: the sinner who is sorry for his sins is closer to God than the just man who boasts of his good works.

—Padre Pio, *Advice and Exhortations of Padre Pio of Petrelcina*

I lie in the tomb of my sins, bound in the chains of iniquity, and wait for the Lord's gospel cry: "Jerome, come forth."

—Jerome, *letter*

I would not like you ever to go to bed at night without first seeing in yourself whether you are conscious of offense against God, so that if you feel guilty of mortal sin, from which God preserves you, you may resolve to cancel it so soon as possible by means of the sacrament of penance. You must recall that this is always necessary if you have to be sorry for anything, but you must never, for that, wait for a fixed time such as Easter, because no one can promise that you will live till then.

—Aloysius Gonzaga, *letter to his father, 1737*

A man suffering from a wound needs a remedy. The wound is our being slaves to sin; and the remedy? The heavenly and adorable sacrament.

—Pope Gregory VII, *letter to his daughter Matilda, 1074*

If as often as the Lord's Blood is shed, it is poured forth for the remission of sins, I ought to receive it always, so that my sins may always be forgiven. I who am always committing sin ought always to have a remedy.

—Pope Gregory VII, *letter to his daughter Matilda, 1074*

But miserable the sinner whom the Lord does not punish in this life! For those whom he does not chastise here, he treasures up his wrath, and for them he reserves eternal chastisement.

—Alphonsus Liguori, *sermon*

God cannot but hate sin, which is his enemy and diametrically opposed to his will; and therefore, in hating sin, he necessarily hates the sinner who is united with his sin.

—Alphonsus Liguori, *sermon*

And do you not know that God has fixed for each of us the number of sins which he will pardon? . . . God has patience, and waits for a while; but when the measure of sins which he has determined to pardon is filled up, he pardons no more, but chastises the sinner by suddenly depriving him of life in the miserable state of sin, or by abandoning him in his sin.

—Alphonsus Liguori, *sermon*

God pardons sins, but he cannot pardon those who are determined to offend him.

—Alphonsus Liguori, *sermon*

They who sow sins, can hope for nothing but the hatred of God and Hell.

—Alphonsus Liguori, *sermon*

And how does God abandon the sinner? He either sends him a sudden death, and cuts him off in sin, or he deprives him of the graces which would be necessary to bring him to true repentance: he leaves him with the sufficient graces with which he can, but will not, save his soul.

—Alphonsus Liguori, *sermon*

Sins chain the sinner, and make him their slave, so that he knowingly brings himself to destruction.

—Alphonsus Liguori, *sermon*

Whoever sins against his neighbor sins against himself, and whoever does evil to his neighbor does evil to himself.

—Anthony, *letter*

What is more, as my sins increased I began to lose my joy and pleasure in virtuous things. I saw very clearly, my Lord, that this departed from me because I departed from you.

—Teresa of Ávila, *Life*

It is a dangerous thing indeed for a soul to follow its own pleasure, or to be calm and complacent when at every step it is falling into mortal sin. For the love of God, let us avoid occasions for sin, and the Lord will help us all as He helped me.

—Teresa of Ávila, *Life*

While we guard ourselves at every moment from sins and vices of thought or tongue, of hand or foot, of self-will or bodily desire, let us recall that we are always seen by God in the heavens, that our actions everywhere are in God's sight and are reported by angels at every hour.

—Benedict, *Rule*

Sin arises simply from loving what God hates and hating what God loves. So if you love the passing things of this world and love yourself with a sensual love, you sin. For this is what God hates; in fact, it so displeases him that he willed to work out vengeance and punishment for it upon his own body. He made himself an anvil, and on this anvil hammered out our sins.

—Catherine of Siena, *letter to a nobleman's wife*

Sin is nothing. Thou, then, hast become nothing; it has deprived thee of life, and given thee death.

—Catherine of Siena, *Dialogue*

Nothing should upset the servant of God except sin.

—Francis of Assisi, *saying*

A person sins who wishes to receive more from his neighbor than what he wishes to give of himself to the Lord.

—Francis of Assisi, *saying*

Three things keep men from giving themselves over to sin. There is the fear either of hell or of earthly laws. There is the hope and the desire for the kingdom of heaven. Or there is the attraction of good itself and the love of virtue.

—John Cassian, *Conferences*

He that is wounded requires medicine; we are wounded, because we are under sin; and the medicine is the sacred and heavenly sacrament.

—Robert Bellarmine, *The Art of Dying Well*

Water washes away physical stains, God washes away spiritual stains.

—Robert Bellarmine, *The Mind's Ascent to God by the Ladder of Created Things*

Had he not sinned, man would have at most obtained equality with the angels; now through the redemption which is in Christ Jesus the human race has obtained that one man, raised above all the angels, sits at God's right hand, and is head and Lord of angels and men.

—Robert Bellarmine, *The Mind's Ascent to God by the Ladder of Created Things*

God often makes the wicked abound in temporal goods so that he may reward their few good moral acts since he is not going to give them eternal life or so that he may coax them by temporal benefits to the conversion from their sins and lead them to hope for and desire eternal benefits. Sometimes he does not punish their sins in this life since he will punish them enough in hell.

—Robert Bellarmine, *The Mind's Ascent to God by the Ladder of Created Things*

Not only will all sins be punished, but they will be punished with horrible punishments which will be so massive that only a few can now imagine them.

—Robert Bellarmine, *The Mind's Ascent to God by the Ladder of Created Things*

A root of all sin and a clouding of all truth is transitory love.

—Henry Suso, *The Life of the Servant*

Be favorable toward my sins and thoughtlessness, Lord, and deign to make amends for all errors of my wasted way of life by your most perfect way of life.

—Gertrude the Great, *Spiritual Exercises*

For he who sins is still worse if he rejoices in his loss of righteousness.

—Augustine, *The City of God*

Since God is so near us, we ought to stand in awe of him and beware of sinning against him.

—Vincent Ferrer, *sermon*

For sinning in private and in secret isn't the same thing as sinning in public.

—John Chrysostom, *homily*

If any here is a slave of sin, let him promptly prepare himself through faith for the new birth into freedom and adoption; and having put off the miserable bondage of his sins, and taken on him the most blessed bondage of the Lord, so may he be counted worthy to inherit the kingdom of heaven.

—Cyril of Jerusalem, *Catecheses*

A fearful thing is sin, and the sorest disease of the soul is transgression, secretly cutting its sinews and becoming also the cause of eternal fire; and evil of man's own choosing, an offspring of the will.

—Cyril of Jerusalem, *Catecheses*

For sin burns the sinews of the soul, and breaks the spiritual bones of the mind, and darkens the light of the heart.

—Cyril of Jerusalem, *Catecheses*

He, therefore, who bestows meat or raiment on the poor, and yet is polluted by iniquity of soul or body, has offered the lesser thing to righteousness, and the greater thing to sin; for he has given his possessions to God, and himself to the devil.

—Gregory the Great, *The Book of Pastoral Rule*

Those who transgress frequently in very little things are to be admonished to consider anxiously how that sometimes there is worse sin in a small fault than in a greater one. For a greater fault, in that it is the sooner acknowledged to be one, is by so much the more speedily amended; but a smaller one, being reckoned as though it were none at all, is retained in use with worse effect as it is so with less concern.

—Gregory the Great, *The Book of Pastoral Rule*

Still, man should be pitied because he sinned more through ignorance and weakness than through malice.

—Louis de Montfort, *The Love of Eternal Wisdom*

Sinners sell their birthright, that is, the joys of paradise, for a dish of lentils, that is, the pleasures of this world. They laugh, they drink, they eat, they have a good time, they gamble, they dance and so forth, without taking any more trouble than Esau to make themselves worthy of their heavenly Father's blessing.

—Louis de Montfort, *Treatise on True Devotion to the Blessed Virgin*

Sinners, on the other hand, put all their confidence in themselves. Like the prodigal son, they eat with the swine. Like toads they feed on earth. Like all worldlings, they love only visible and external things. They do not know the sweetness of Mary's bosom.

—Louis de Montfort, *Treatise on True Devotion to the Blessed Virgin*

There is only one kind of wound at all that is to be feared, and that is when the mind is wounded by giving consent to sin.

—Francis Xavier, *letter*

For he who thinks on sins endeavors to shut himself up within his own consciousness.

—Ambrose, *Concerning Repentance*

But nothing causes such exceeding grief as when any one, lying under the captivity of sin, calls to mind whence he has fallen, because he turned aside to carnal and earthly things, instead of directing his mind in the beautiful ways of the knowledge of God.

—Ambrose, *Concerning Repentance*

I see how people live, how many of them live habitually in mortal sin, so that a day never passes without their increasing the number of their iniquities. They commit sin as easily as they drink a glass of water, just for diversion, or for a laugh. These disgraceful people run to Hell on their own accord, blind as bats.

—Anthony Mary Claret, *autobiography*

Sin is unstable and transitory; he who brought all things into existence and invested them with being did not create sin along with creation at the beginning, nor does sin always remain with created beings. Those things which are in him who exists always continue in being. If anything lies outside him who exists, it does not have the existence but exists in what is not good.

—Gregory of Nyssa, *Commentary on the Inscriptions of the Psalms*

To return to heaven there is only one route and that is to admit one's sinfulness and seek to avoid it. To make the decision to avoid it is already to be perfecting one's likeness to God.

—Gregory of Nyssa, *On the Lord's Prayer*

If sin is nothing other than transgression of a commandment, and if it is a commandment not to lie, not to covet, not to steal, not to talk idly, not to speak harshly to one's brother, then everyone who does any of these things has been pricked by the sting of death which is sin, and into the wound left by the bite of sin the devil, like a worm, slips immediately and is found to dwell.

—Symeon the New Theologian, *Ethical Discourses*

And so if you see anyone committing great sins and yet never being punished for them and whose body is never afflicted by illness or misfortune, you may be sure that they have been abandoned by God because of the magnitude of their sins. Such a person is not punished because they are not worth saving; while you are rebuked so that you are not consigned to eternal death.

—Basil the Great, *Consolation in Adversity*

And if you are a sinner, you should be pleased if you are afflicted, for in this way you will be cleansed of your sins and will find consolation in the time to come.

—Basil the Great, *Consolation in Adversity*

Sincerity

A small gift given with true sincerity is often worth more than a valuable gift without it.

—Henry Suso, *Little Book of Eternal Wisdom*

But there is nothing safer for defense than sincerity, nothing easier to say than truth. For, when obliged to defend its deceit, the heart is wearied with hard labor.

—Gregory the Great, *The Book of Pastoral Rule*

Slander

The more you pray with all your heart for the one who has slandered you, the more readily God reveals the truth to those whom the slander has scandalized.

—Maximus the Confessor, *Centuries on Charity*

If you are slandered then respond with gentleness.

—Basil the Great, *letter*

If you have calumniated your neighbor, you must go and find the people to whom you have said false things about him and tell them that what you have been saying is not true, that you are very grieved about it, and that you beg them not to believe it.

But if you have done him harm in his soul, it is still a more difficult thing to repair, and yet it must be done as fast as possible; otherwise God will not pardon you.

—John Baptiste Marie Vianney, *sermon*

Whoever unjustly deprives his neighbor of his good name is guilty of sin, and is further bound to make reparation, according to his slander: no man can enter heaven with another's goods, and of all worldly goods none is equal to a good reputation.

—Francis de Sales, *The Devout Life*

Slander is a kind of murder, for we have three lives—the spiritual life, which consists of the grace of God, the corporal life, which is the soul, and the civil life, which consists of our reputations. Sin destroys the first, death the second, and slander the third; but the slanderer is guilty of a triple murder with his tongue. He destroys his own soul and that of his hearer by a spiritual homicide, and deprives the object of his slander of civil existence.

—Francis de Sales, *The Devout Life*

Beware of falsely imputing crimes and sins to your neighbor, of disclosing his secret faults, of exaggerating those which are obvious, of interpreting good actions ill, of denying the good which you know to be in any, or of maliciously concealing it or lessening it, for all these things grievously offend God.

—Francis de Sales, *The Devout Life*

The most refined and venomous slanderers are those who pretend to mean well, or craftily insinuate their poison by means of jests and banter.

—Francis de Sales, *The Devout Life*

Slander in the shape of a jest is worse than all, for as hemlock is not in itself a quick poison and an antidote may easily be found, yet when taken in wine it is incurable; and so slander, which by itself would go in at one ear and out the other, remains in the mind of the listeners when it is dressed up in some clever and witty saying.

—Francis de Sales, *The Devout Life*

If you come in the way of a downright slanderer, do not defend him by calling him frank and honest-spoken . . . do not fly from slander into flattery and indulgence of vice, but call evil evil without hesitation, and blame that which is blamable.

—Francis de Sales, *The Devout Life*

If you have done wrong to your neighbor in his honor, as, for instance, by scandalous talk, you are obliged to make up by favorable and beneficent talk for all the harm you have done to his reputation, saying all the good of him which you know to be true and concealing any faults which he may have and which you are not obliged to reveal.

—John Baptiste Marie Vianney, *sermon*

Slander is the offspring of hatred, a subtle and yet crass disease, a leech in hiding and escaping notice, wasting and draining away the lifeblood of love. It puts on the appearance of love and is the ambassador of an unholy and unclean heart. And it is the ruin of chastity.

—John Climacus, *The Ladder of Divine Ascent*

As they who always speak well of others are loved by all, so he who detracts his neighbor is hateful to all—to God and to men, who, although they take delight in listening to detraction, hate the detracter, and are on their guard against him.

—Alphonsus Liguori, *sermon*

The most common sins of the tongue are lying, false testimony and detraction. As to this last, it is a mortal sin to make known a serious fault which is not public, if done with a bad intention or with a notable prejudice to our neighbor's reputation. If the fault revealed be less serious, the sin is only venial.

—Ignatius of Loyola, *Spiritual Exercises*

Sleep

Excessive sleep is a bad companion, stealing half a lifetime or more from the lazy man.

—John Climacus, *The Ladder of Divine Ascent*

Go to bed modestly and sleep with a good thought in your mind. This will be a useful means of remembering God when you waken and, in the morning, your mind will be better prepared for prayer.

—Vincent de Paul, *Conferences to the Daughters of Charity*

In your bed-chamber itself, I would have you join psalms in frequent interchange with the Lord's prayer, either when you wake up, or before sleep bedews your body, so that at the very commencement of rest sleep may find you free from the care of worldly matters, meditating upon the things of God.

—Ambrose, *Concerning Virgins, to Marcellina, His Sister*

At night, before you go to sleep, you must examine your conscience, enquiring into the thoughts, words, and deeds of the whole day, and also whether you have left out anything of what you ought to have done. Examine all these thing as if you were presently going to cleanse your soul in sacramental confession to a priest, and then conceive deep contrition for what you have done amiss, and for what you have omitted, out of regard to God, Whom you have offended thereby, and Whom you love above all things, and then pray Jesus Christ earnestly to prosper you, and promise amendment.

—Francis Xavier, *letter*

I have always preached that every Christian should before retiring leave his affairs settled as if it were the last night of his life.

—Joseph Cafasso, *second panegyric on St. Joseph Cafasso by St. John Bosco*

Sleep is like the tax-collector; it robs us of half our life.

—Clement of Alexandria, *The Teacher*

Night sets you free from sorrow and relieves your worries.

—John Chrysostom, *On Providence*

The death of the saints is called a sleep;—that is, the repose which God gives to his servants as the reward of their toil.

—Alphonsus Liguori, *sermon*

Solitude

Solitude offers us an excellent opportunity for calming our passions and giving our reason time to remove them thoroughly from our soul. For just as wild animals can be soothed by being stroked, so all our anger, fear and stress, which poison and disrupt our soul, can be soothed by an atmosphere of peace where the freedom from constant disturbance ensures that our soul can be brought more easily under the power of reason. We should look for a place we can make entirely our own, away from contact with other people, so that our spiritual training may progress on an uninterrupted path, feeding our soul with thoughts of God.

—Basil the Great, *letter to Gregory of Nyssa*

Each day try to find a few minutes of that blessed solitude which you so much need to keep your interior life going.

—Josemaría Escrivá, *The Way*

Who sits in solitude and is quiet hath escaped from three wars: hearing, speaking, seeing: yet against one thing shall he continuously battle: that is, his own heart.

—Abbot Anthony, *saying*

Invulnerable from the arrows of the enemy is he who loves quiet: but he who mixeth with the crowd hath often wounds.

—Nilus, *saying*

It is better to have many about thee, and to live the solitary life in thy will, than to be alone, and the desire of thy mind be with the crowd.

—Matrona of Thessalonica, *saying*

Incline towards a solitary life, for not merely does it remove from the senses occasions of distraction, and from the heart occasions of sin, but it also invites a man to enter more into himself, and to occupy himself alone with God, for to this one is, indeed, much drawn by circumstances of place, when no alien company finds admittance there.

—Peter of Alcantara, *Treatise on Prayer & Meditation*

Sinners have no liking for solitude or the spiritual life or interior devotion. They consider those who live an exterior life, secluded from the world, and who work more interiorly than exteriorly, as narrow-minded, bigoted and uncivilized.

—Louis de Montfort, *Treatise on True Devotion to the Blessed Virgin*

Soul

Consider the nobility and excellence of your soul, which has an understanding capable not only of knowing the things of this visible world, but knows that there are angels and a paradise; knows that there is an all-mighty, all-good, and ineffable God, knows that there is an eternity, and further knows that which is required to lead a good life here, to be numbered with the angels in paradise and to rejoice forever in God.

—Francis de Sales, *The Devout Life*

Contrition, confession, and satisfaction, are the first works of the Soul after it has been enlightened by God. By this means she is freed from her sins and imperfections, clothed with virtue, and remains thus until she has formed the habit of virtue.

—Catherine of Genoa, *Life and Doctrine*

The state of the soul is this: she is very sensitive, so that her mind cannot endure the least suspicion of defect, because pure love cannot remain where there is even the slightest fault, and the loving Soul, unable to endure it, would be thrown into intolerable pain. In this world man cannot be wholly free from imperfections, but at times God keeps him in ignorance of them, because he could not support the sight; at other times he reveals them all; and in this way man is purified.

—Catherine of Genoa, *Life and Doctrine*

The soul was created by God for himself, and is governed by him, and it can find no repose but in him alone. The condemned in hell are in the order of God through justice.

—Catherine of Genoa, *Life and Doctrine*

A local change will not bring you closer to God, but no matter where you are, God will come to you, if only your soul is found a proper resting place where God can dwell and converse.

—Gregory of Nyssa, *letter*

Because there is nothing above to break the impetus of the soul, and because the very nature of the good is that it attracts those who look upward toward it, the soul rises always, extending itself forward through the desire of heavenly things . . . and its flight will always lead it higher.

—Gregory of Nyssa, *Life of Moses*

The soul's exalted and royal nature is shown to be far removed from submissiveness by the fact that it is free and independent and acknowledges no master: it has been provided with its own unchallenged power of choice.

—Gregory of Nyssa, *The Creation of Man*

The true and perfect life, however, is that of the soul. In the soul is found the beauty of the likeness of God, who created humanity with the words, "Let us make human beings in our own image, after our own likeness."

—Gregory of Nyssaa, *The Creation of Man*

Now the human soul is the lowest grade of mind in nature's hierarchy, since its knowledge of truth is not inborn (like angels) but gathered from sense-experience of things spatially outside it. As such, it needs a body suited to sensing.

—Thomas Aquinas, *Summa Theologica*

God enriches the soul which empties itself of everything.

—Padre Pio, *Spiritual Maxims*

It is in fact absolutely necessary that the world should be transformed if our souls are due to be transformed in a different kind of life.

—Basil the Great, *homily on the Hexaemeron*

Even if I am imperfect in so many ways, nonetheless I want my brothers and my family to know my mettle, so that they may clearly recognize the set of my soul.

—Patrick, *letter to the soldiers of Coroticus*

If anyone has been stripped of the heavenly garment of the new life, which is the Spirit of Truth and the power which comes from Him, he must go on pleading tearfully with the Lord until He clothes his soul in the power which comes from above in place of the shame and confusion with which it is now covered. For just as bodily nakedness is a source of confusion and dishonor for me, so, too, do God and his saints turn their faces away from those who are not clothed in the Holy Spirit.

—Ammonas the Hermit, *letter to disciples, c. 340*

Once the soul has seen the true light, it will never again be blind; once it has been healed of its wounds, it will never again have to suffer from its evil passions.

—Ammonas the Hermit, *letter to disciples, c. 340*

A soul that loves God is loved by him, and God himself comes to dwell in her. . . . The Lord, then, never departs from a soul, unless he is driven away, even though he should know that she will soon banish him from her heart.

—Alphonsus Liguori, *sermon*

The vines of the Lord are our souls, which he has given us to cultivate by good works, that we may one day be admitted into eternal glory.

—Alphonsus Liguori, *sermon*

If, from being created by God to his own image, you do not comprehend the value of your soul, learn it from Jesus Christ, who has redeemed you with his own blood.

—Alphonsus Liguori, *sermon*

Every sin, though pardoned, always leaves a wound on the soul. When to this wound a new one is added, the soul becomes so weak that, without a special and extraordinary grace from God, it is impossible for her to conquer temptations.

—Alphonsus Liguori, *sermon*

Those who are pure and simple in their hearts extol the beauty of the soul.

—Maria Maddalena de' Pazzi, *The Dialogues*

With the achievements and efforts of the Word the soul acquires its copiousness. Its beauty will be its vision of God, who is so beautiful and precious that the soul, by participating in this beauty, becomes beautiful itself.

—Maria Maddalena de' Pazzi, *The Dialogues*

God greets the soul in the language of the court of heaven, which is not understood by us on earth. The soul is clothed with such heavenly garments and surrounded by such strength that it may ask whatever it wishes and be sure that the wishes shall be granted.

—Mechtilde of Magdeburg, *The Flowing Light of the Godhead*

The faithful soul walks in a wondrous and lofty way! The soul leads the senses as someone with sight might lead a blind person. In this way, the soul is free and travels without any grief in the heart. Now the soul sees that it wishes nothing other than what the Lord wills, for the Lord wills only what is best for the soul.

—Mechtilde of Magdeburg, *The Flowing Light of the Godhead*

I cannot dance, O Lord, unless you lead me.

—Mechtilde of Magdeburg, *The Flowing Light of the Godhead*

God is closer to us than our own soul, for God is the foundation on which the soul stands. Our soul sits in God and in true rest, and our soul stands in God in sure strength, and our soul is naturally rooted in God in endless love. Therefore, if we want to have knowledge of our soul, and communion and discourse with it, we must seek in our Lord God in whom it is enclosed.

—Julian of Norwich, *Showings*

The center and final purpose of the soul, which God created, must be God Himself alone, and nothing else—God from whom the soul has received its life and its nature, and for whom it must eternally live.

—Dimitri of Rostov, *The Inner Closet of the Heart*

For the soul provides life to the body, just as fire pours its light into the darkness.

—Hildegard of Bingen, *Scivias*

The soul has not only earthly but heavenly powers when it knows God wisely.

—Hildegard of Bingen, *Scivias*

O my Jesus, how much can a soul do when ablaze with Your love! What a high value we ought to set on it, and how we ought to pray the Lord to leave it with us for this life!

—Teresa of Ávila, *Life*

Everything seems to me like a dream. That which I see with the eyes of the body is a mockery, and that which I have seen with the eyes of the soul is what the soul desires.

—Teresa of Ávila, *Life*

When God takes possession of the soul, he gives it more and more dominion over created things, and even if his presence is withdrawn and the satisfaction which the soul was enjoying disappears, he does not withdraw himself from the soul, nor does it fail to grow very rich in graces, and, as time goes on, that becomes evident in the affections.

—Teresa of Ávila, *letter to her brother Toledo, 1577*

Enter into yourself, then, and see that your soul loves itself most fervently; that it could not love itself unless it knew itself, nor know itself unless it remembered itself, because our intellects grasp only what is present to its memory.

—Bonaventure, *The Soul's Journey Into God*

Merit consists in the virtue of love alone, flavored with the light of true discretion, without which the soul is worth nothing.

—Catherine of Siena, *Dialogue*

God nurtures and caresses the soul, after it has been resolutely converted to his service, like a loving mother who warms her child with the heat of her bosom, nurses it with good milk and tender food, and carries it and caresses it in her arms.

—John of the Cross, *The Dark Night of the Soul*

The Lord has inclined himself to my misery like a ray of the sun upon a barren and rocky desert. And yet, under the influence of His rays, my soul has become covered with verdure, flowers, and fruit, and has become a beautiful garden for His repose.

—Faustina Kowalska, *Divine Mercy in My Soul*

The human soul has so much likeness to God its Creator that I surely know of no other way by which one can more easily mount to a knowledge of God than from reflection on one's own soul.

—Robert Bellarmine, *The Mind's Ascent to God by the Ladder of Created Things*

At one time the human soul did not exist, and it came to exist only through God's will, and it could also be reduced to nothing by God's will, even though it does not have of itself a principle of corruption.

—Robert Bellarmine, *The Mind's Ascent to God by the Ladder of Created Things*

The house of our soul ought to be adorned with all kind of virtues, especially with faith, hope, charity, devotion, and the fruits of good works, such as prayer, fasting, and almsgiving.

—Robert Bellarmine, *The Art of Dying Well*

Truly, the soul is more worthy and more noble than the whole world and more stable than all things. It is more worthy because it is spiritual and equal to the angels and created for eternal joy.

—Bridget of Sweden, *Book of Questions*

A soul is that which all living things have in common; in this we are all alike.

—Thomas Aquinas, *Commentary on the Soul*

For our bodies are begotten by parents who are seen, but our souls are begotten anew through faith: "for the Spirit bloweth where it listeth" (John 3:8): and then, if thou be found worthy, thou mayest hear, "Well done, good and faithful servant" (Matthew 25:21), when thou art found to have no defilement of hypocrisy in thy conscience.

—Cyril of Jerusalem, *Catecheses*

For the first exercise in training the soul is to turn away sin, the second to implant virtue.

—Ambrose, *Concerning Widowhood*

The soul finds its joy, therefore, in spending lengthy periods of prayer, perhaps even entire nights; its penances are pleasures; its fasts, happiness, and the sacraments and spiritual conversations are its consolations.

—John of the Cross, *The Dark Night of the Soul*

The human soul is not a complete, static, unchanging, monolithic existence. It is being in the state of becoming and in the process of becoming; the soul must bring to fruition those predispositions with which it was endowed when coming into the world; however, it can develop them only through activation.

—Edith Stein, *Essays on Woman*

The mind is the rational part of the soul. Conclusion: the soul is rational.

The dignity of the soul consists in doing everything according to reason.

—Maximus the Confessor, *Treatise on the Soul*

Spiritual path

God leads souls along many roads and paths, as He has led mine.

—Teresa of Ávila, *Life*

For our part, we were created and put into the world to love God and his glory. We are in the world for a short time and we hope for an eternity. It will arrive, if we take the Way, the Truth and the Life which is the One who opened the way for us.

—Marguerite Bourgeoys, *Autographic Writings*

Whoever wishes to ascend to God must first avoid sin, which deforms our nature, then exercise his natural powers . . . : by praying, to receive restoring grace; by a good life, to receive purifying justice; by meditating, to receive illuminating knowledge; and by contemplating, to receive perfecting wisdom.

—Bonaventure, *The Soul's Journey Into God*

As ye have entered upon a good and most glorious path, run with reverence the race of godliness.

—Cyril of Jerusalem, *Catecheses*

Wrestle for thine own soul, especially in such days as these.

—Cyril of Jerusalem,*Catecheses*

The journey to God follows many routes. So let each person take to the end and with no turning back the way he first chose so that he may be perfect, no matter what his profession may be.

—John Cassian, *Conferences*

For if you seek God in truth, and enter vigorously the path which leads to Him, you will certainly find so much delight proceed from His service, as will easily mitigate and soften whatever sharpness or bitterness there is in conquering yourself.

—Francis Xavier, *letter*

But for the searching and right understanding of the Scriptures there is need of a good life and a pure soul, and for Christian virtue to guide the mind to grasp, so far as human nature can, the truth concerning God the word.

—Athanasius, *On the Incarnation*

For the human mind, after the manner of water, when closed in, is collected unto higher levels, in that it seeks again the height from which it descended; and, when let loose, it falls away in that it disperses itself unprofitably through the lowest places.

—Gregory the Great, *The Book of Pastoral Rule*

Dearest brother, let not our feet be diverted from the ways of the Lord or from treading the narrow path, should the wicked or foolish voices of worldly men from time to time bark around us.

—Paulinus of Nola, *letter*

Before all things, devote your first and principal care to cleansing your own conscience and keeping it without stain. Let your diligence in preserving or cleansing the consciences of others come after this of your own; for how can a man be of use to others who takes no care for himself?

—Francis Xavier, *letter*

Choose now what you would wish to have chosen at life's end.

—Anthony Mary Claret, *autobiography*

Heroism, sanctity, daring, require a constant spiritual preparation. You can only ever give to others what you already have.

—Josemaría Escrivá, *The Forge*

You should make sure that wherever you are, there is that *good humor*—that cheerfulness—which is born of an interior life.

—Josemaría Escrivá, *The Forge*

Thus in our moral development we can distinguish three very important stages:
firstly, never to commit a sin in our acts;
secondly, never to pause at a passionate thought;
and thirdly, to keep our peace of soul in the face of impure pictures or memories of offenses received.

—Maximus the Confessor, *Centuries on Charity*

Whoever follows the Word is no longer attached to earthly bread, because he receives the bread of heaven and knows the divine is better than the human, the spiritual is better than the physical. Therefore, because such a person desires the true life, he looks for that which fortifies the heart by means of its invisible substance.

—Ambrose, *On the Gospel of St. Luke*

The gate of the kingdom must be asked for by praying; it must be sought after by living properly; it must be knocked at by persevering. It is not sufficient to ask in words only if we do not also seek diligently how we ought to be living, so that we may be worthy to obtain that for which we plead, as he bears witness when he says: "Not everyone who says to me, 'Lord, Lord,' will enter the kingdom of heaven; but he who does the will of my Father who is in heaven, he will enter the kingdom of heaven." (Matthew 7:21)

—Bede the Venerable, *homily on the Gospels*

Spiritual study

Don't neglect your spiritual reading. Reading has made many saints.

—Josemaría Escrivá, *The Way*

An hour of study, for a modern apostle, is an hour of prayer.

—Josemaría Escrivá, *The Way*

Then indeed do we usefully direct our minds to the sacred scriptures, when we put before [us] as a motive for doing good not only the virtues and the rewards of the just, but also the vices and punishment of the damned.

—Bede the Venerable, *homily on the Gospels*

Make a practice of reading spiritual and devout books. They serve to feed the imagination and to keep the heart recollected, and they lead men of good will to occupy their minds with what has appealed to them, for what the heart is full of is always the first to suggest itself to the mind.

—Peter of Alcántara, *Treatise on Prayer & Meditation*

The best guide you can find to the correct path is the serious study of the Bible. There we can find rules for the conduct of our life and, in the lives of great figures, living images of a life with God whose actions we are encouraged to copy. Each person can concentrate on the area where they feel themselves to be lacking and find, as in a hospital, a cure for their particular trouble.

—Basil the Great, *letter to Gregory of Nyssa*

Give some time, if it is only half an hour in every day, to devotional reading, which is as necessary to the well ordering of the mind as the hand of the gardener is to prevent weeds destroying your favorite flowers.

—Elizabeth Seton, *Collected Writings*

Stillness

He who has achieved stillness has arrived at the very center of the mysteries, but he would never have reached these depths if he had not first seen and heard the sound of the waves and of the evil spirits, if he had not even been splashed by those waters.

—John Climacus, *The Ladder of Divine Ascent*

To occupy the powers of the mind and at the same time to imagine that we can keep them quiet is a folly.

—Teresa of Ávila, *Life*

Stinginess

I'm acutely ashamed when I see many of the rich riding horses with golden bridles, with a train of servants clad in gold. They have silver couches and an excessive amount of other ostentation, and when they're asked to give an offering to a poor person, they become poorer than the extremely poor.

—John Chrysostom, *homily*

Strength

But how good God is! How well he fits our trials to our strength!

—Thérèse of Lisieux, *The Story of a Soul*

Recommend yourself to the Blessed Virgin Mary, and she will obtain for you strength to overcome all repugnance.

—Alphonsus Liguori, *letter to Redemptoristien nuns, 1773*

Our Lord is so good and so powerful that he gives strength to those he sees to be doing their best. Sometimes he bestows more favors on people who lie ill in bed and are unable to pray, than on others who spend hours in prayer.

—John of Ávila, *letter to a layman, 1560*

God is faithful: he will never permit us to be tempted above our strength.

—Alphonsus Liguori, *sermon*

When you see you have not sufficient strength to resist temptation with the ordinary assistance of God, ask of him the additional help which you require, and he will give it to you; and thus you shall be able to conquer all temptations, however violent they may be.

—Alphonsus Liguori, *sermon*

God has strengthened us with all the power of nature. God buckled upon us the armor of creation so that we can know the whole world through our sight, understand it through our hearing, and distinguish it through our sense of smell. As a result, we will be nourished by the world and dominate it by our sense of touch. And, in this way, we come to know the true God, who is the author of all creation.

—Hildegard of Bingen, *Book of Divine Works*

I want to be like the strongest of swords, and I want to make all the arms most unconquerable and suitable for the wars of God.

—Hildegard of Bingen, *Scivias*

I can do all things through Christ which strengtheneth me.

—Paul, *Philippians 4:13*

First strengthen my soul, and prepare it, O Jesus, my Supreme Good, and then ordain the means whereby I may do something for You.

—Teresa of Ávila, *Life*

Walk carefully with the Lord your God and he will take good care of you. Guard with all your strength against offending his justice, and his mercy will always protect you, and you will not fear what man or devil may do to you.

—Robert Bellarmine, *The Mind's Ascent to God by the Ladder of Created Things*

But the Church does not overcome the powers of the enemy with weapons of this world, but with spiritual arms, "which are mighty through God to the destruction of strongholds and the high places of spiritual wickedness."

—Ambrose, *Concerning Widowhood*

The weapons of the Church are faith, the weapons of the Church are prayer, which overcomes the enemy.

—Ambrose, *Concerning Widowhood*

When the brave suffer in weakness, it is for the weak a stimulus to strength; for the strong man is weakened so that the weak may be strengthened and, by imitation of the strong, learn to prevail in the fight.

—Paulinus of Nola, *letter*

Be strong in trials, weak in dissentions.

—Columban, *letter, c. 610*

Those wounded in battle and taken off the field get up again and, having learned with experience, fight against their enemies more vigorously.

—Symeon the New Theologian, *Ethical Discourses*

A man who leans on God is immovable and cannot be overthrown.

—Claude de la Colombière, *spiritual notes*

One who is anchored firmly in God does not suffer any loss, even if attacked by a thousand waves and a thousand storms. On the contrary, he emerges stronger.

—John Chrysostom, *On Providence*

Success

If I succeed, I bless God; if I do not succeed, I bless God, for then it will be right that I should not succeed.

—Elizabeth Seton, *Collected Writings*

Suffering

Your sufferings press hard. But look at your sins.

—Elizabeth Seton, *Collected Writings*

I do not know if your troubles continue, but I know very well that to a heart that is pure and detached from creatures there is no suffering that prevents it from being united to its Creator.

—Claude de la Colombière, *letter*

Love thrives on suffering; and suffering is to be found everywhere.

—Claude de la Colombière, *letter*

It is more through suffering and persecution than through eloquent preaching, that God wills to establish his kingdom in souls.

—Thérèse of Lisieux, *letter to missionary brothers*

In the world, on awakening in the morning I used to think over what would probably occur either pleasing or vexatious during the day; and if I foresaw only trying events I arose dispirited. Now it is quite the other way: I think of the difficulties and the sufferings that await me, and I rise more joyous and full of courage the more I foresee opportunities of proving my love for Jesus, and *earning the living of my children*—seeing that I am the *mother* of souls. Then I kiss my crucifix and lay it tenderly on the pillow while I dress, and I say to him: "My Jesus, thou hast worked enough and wept enough during the three-and-thirty years of thy life on this poor earth. Take now thy rest. . . . My turn it is to suffer and to fight."

—Thérèse of Lisieux, *Counsels and Reminisces*

Lord, with thee, and for thee, I am ready to endure every suffering.

—Gertrude the Great, *Love, Peace and Joy*

Know that God, by the decree of his goodness, never allows man to suffer beyond his strength. If we regarded our own proper good, it would seem better for us to suffer here for a little than to remain in torments forever; better to suffer for a thousand years every woe possible to this body in this world than to remain one hour in purgatory.

—Catherine of Genoa, *Life and Doctrine*

For whoever suffers purgation in this life pays but a small portion of what is due, by reason of the liberty of his free-will cooperating with infused grace. God never subjects man to this discipline until he has obtained from him his free consent. For a moment it is put before him, and accepting it of his own free-will, he puts himself into the hands of God to be dealt with according to his pleasure.

—Catherine of Genoa, *Life and Doctrine*

The source of all suffering is either original or actual sin. God created the soul pure, simple, free from every stain, and with a certain beatific instinct toward himself. It is drawn aside from him by original sin, and when actual sin is afterwards added, this withdraws it still farther, and ever as it removes from him its sinfulness increases because its communication with God grows less and less.

—Catherine of Genoa, *Life and Doctrine*

Everyone of us has his own service to render—some serve by working and some by suffering. The reward of suffering is even more generous and certain.

—Pope John XXIII, *letter to his brother Saverio, Apr. 6, 1947*

Many suffer, but few know how to suffer well. Suffering is a gift from God; blessed is he who knows how to profit by it.

—Padre Pio, *Archives of Padre Pio*

When you suffer a lot, have you ever thought of the sufferings which Our Lord Jesus endured for us during his passion? The time has now come to offer your share in his sufferings. Today, the Lord has heard your prayers and he is sending you something to suffer. God never forgets us. He knows your needs. Show that you are generous in accepting whatever he may send you in the future. Nothing will happen to you without him knowing it.

—Brother André, *Brother André According to Witnesses*

An unpitied pain wins greater merit before God. Never say to God: "Enough," simply say: "I am ready!" When it is all over, you will not regret having suffered; rather you will regret having suffered so little and suffered that little so badly.

—Sebastian Valfrè, *letter to an invalid, 1690*

Your holy Paternity knows perfectly well that as the flesh fails, the soul advances; out of the body's infirmity springs the soul's health; where vengeance is due, pardon is meted out; the very suffering gives birth to consolation, the very grief to joy.

—Anselm, *letter to a friend and monk, c. 1076*

To test our obedience, and to teach us what great things we are bound to do and to suffer for so great a Master, God is accustomed to deprive us of what is as dear to us as the light of our eyes.

—John of Ávila, *letter to a widow, 1568*

But if God dwells in us, we must restrain our feelings, and make them subservient to reason and to his will. Whatever our suffering may be, we must not let it overwhelm us.

—John of Ávila, *letter to a widow, 1568*

The man whom the Lord afflicts in this life has a certain proof that he is dear to God.

—Alphonsus Liguori, *sermon*

Let us, then, brethren, courageously resolve to bear patiently with all the sufferings which shall come upon us during the remaining days of our lives: to secure Heaven they are all little and nothing.

—Alphonsus Liguori, *sermon*

A soul that loves God is not disturbed by any misfortune that may happen to her.

—Alphonsus Liguori, *sermon*

I shall dare to say that it is better to suffer for you [God] than to have you, because when we have you we can lose you, but if we suffer for your sake you write it in the book of life, where it can't get lost.

—Maria Maddalena de' Pazzi, *The Dialogues*

Pain and suffering cannot refresh unless Love rules over all.

—Mechtilde of Magdeburg, *The Flowing Light of the Godhead*

Every struggle in the soul's training, whether physical or mental, that is not accompanied by suffering, that does not require the utmost effort, will bear no fruit.

—Theophan the Recluse, *letter*

The life of a Christian on earth is a chain of suffering. It is necessary to fight against our own body, against passions and evil spirits. Our hope lies in this fight. Our salvation is from God.

—Ignatius of Antioch, *The Art of Prayer*

Persistently suffer hardships in order to avoid the hardship of vain suffering.

—Gregory of Sinai, *The Philokalia*

The lot of humanity is to suffer. Bow with me in patient submission to our All-wise Director.

—Elizabeth Seton, *Collected Writings*

Suffering is a great grace; through suffering the soul becomes like a Savior; in suffering love becomes crystallized; the greater the suffering, the purer the love.

—Faustina Kowalska, *Divine Mercy in My Soul*

Suffering is the greatest treasure on earth; it purifies the soul. In suffering, we learn who our true friend is.

—Faustina Kowalska, *Divine Mercy in My Soul*

True love is measured by the thermometer of suffering.

—Faustina Kowalska, *Divine Mercy in My Soul*

My soul is in a sea of suffering. Sinners have taken everything away from me. But that is all right; I have given everything away for their sake that they might know that You are good and infinitely merciful.

—Faustina Kowalska, *Divine Mercy in My Soul*

Learn to suffer a little for the love of God without telling everyone about it.

—Teresa of Ávila, *The Way of Perfection*

Let us keep our spirits up and suffer in patience, because after this there follows joys in the beautiful kingdom of heaven.

—Henry Suso, *letter*

It seems more possible for me to endure death than, heavenly Father, that you should ever again be seriously angry with me. Any suffering and oppression—be it hell or purgatory—there is nothing I lament so much or that causes my heart such pain as that I might anger you, my Creator, my Lord, my God, my Redeemer, all my joy and heart's delight, or that I might cause you dishonor.

—Henry Suso, *Little Book of Eternal Wisdom*

Here on earth, suffering is the salt of life.

—Josemaría Escrivá, *The Way*

I want you to be happy on earth. And you will not be happy if you don't lose that fear of suffering. For, as long as we are "wayfarers," it is precisely in suffering that our happiness lies.

—Josemaría Escrivá, *The Way*

You suffer in this present life, which is a dream, a short dream. Rejoice, because your Father-God loves you so much, and if you put no obstacles in his way, after this bad dream he will give you a good awakening.

—Josemaría Escrivá, *The Way*

The cheerful love that fills the soul with happiness is founded on suffering. There is no love without renunciation.

—Josemaría Escrivá, *The Forge*

The merit of good work increases when someone does or suffers for God what he would not will for its own sake; for we can recognize that a will is more kindled by the fire of divine love, the more opposed to our will are the things we do or suffer for God.

—Thomas Aquinas, *On the Perfection of the Spiritual Life*

But different kinds of sufferings are imposed on us to test and prove us, and many forms of temptations are inflicted upon us by loss of wealth, burning fevers, torments of wounds, by the death of dear ones. Nothing else distinguishes the unjust and the just the more than this, that in adversities the unjust man complains and blasphemes because of impatience, while the just man is proved by patience, as it is written: "I thy sorrow endure and in thy humiliation keep patience, for gold and silver are tried in fire."

—Cyprian of Carthage, *The Good of Patience*

God's will in my regard is that I suffer with patience and for the love of him all pains of body and of soul, as well as those persecutions directed against my honor. It is my firm belief that I shall thus be doing what will be for the greater glory of God, for I shall then be suffering in silence, like Jesus, who died on the Cross abandoned by all.

—Anthony Mary Claret, *autobiography*

To labor and to suffer for the one we love is the greatest proof of our love.

—Anthony Mary Claret, *autobiography*

If suffering did not occur, how would endurance be achieved? Suffering plants the vine of endurance, endurance brings forth the grape of proof that we have stood the test, and this proof produces the wine of hope, and hope makes the heart rejoice because it beholds the happiness that is to come as if it were at hand.

—Theoleptos of Philadelphia, *letter*

To be in good spirits while suffering and rejoice within in the Lord while being tempted from without is the sign of a soul which is moved by the abundant grace of the Comforter.

—Theoleptos of Philadelphia, *letter*

All the pains in a hundred thousand million Hells suffered with the greatest perfection possible to a human creature would have been nothing compared to the smallest sigh of Our Lord, to the smallest drop of blood that he shed for love of us.

—Francis de Sales, *Oeuvres*

Suffering is greatly purified by a whole-hearted acquiescence in God's will.

—Francis de Sales, *The Devout Life*

Suicide

Suicide is altogether wrong for three reasons. Firstly, it runs counter to the inclinations of nature and charity to love and cherish oneself. . . . Secondly, it does injury to the community to which each man belongs as part of a whole. And thirdly, it wrongs God whose gift life is and who alone has power over life and death. What gives man mastery of himself is free will. So he may licitly manage his own life in respect of everything that contributes to it, but his passage out of this life to a happier one is not subject to his own free will but to the authority of God.

—Thomas Aquinas, *Summa Theologica*

For it is not lawful to take the law into our own hands, and slay even a guilty person, whose death no public sentence has warranted, then certainly he who kills himself is a homicide, and so much guiltier of his own death, as he was more innocent of that offence for which he doomed himself to die.

—Augustine, *The City of God*

He, then, who knows it is unlawful to kill himself, may nevertheless do so if he is ordered by Him whose commands we may not neglect. Only let him be very sure that the divine command has been signified.

—Augustine, *The City of God*

No man should put an end to this life to obtain that better life we look for after death, for those who die by their own hand have no better life after death.

—Augustine, *The City of God*

Sun

Think not that the sun is brighter than He, or equal to Him: for He who at first formed the sun needs be incomparably greater and brighter.

—Cyril of Jerusalem, *Catecheses*

The sun is a work of God, which, great though it may be, is but a spot in comparison with the whole heaven; first gaze steadfastly upon the sun, and then curiously scan the Lord of the sun.

—Cyril of Jerusalem, *Catecheses*

And let them be silenced who say that the sun is God: God is the maker of the sun than shines.

—Cyril of Jerusalem, *Catecheses*

It looks small, the sun, but it possesses enormous power. It appears in the east and scatters its rays as far as the west. Indeed, describing the dawn, the Psalmist says: "The sun comes forth like a bridegroom leaving his chamber and like a strong man runs its course with joy." (Psalms 19:6) Yes, triumphant, and yet lovely and gentle, exactly like a bridegroom, it shows itself to everyone. Then, at midday, we very often have to take shelter, because it is burning hot. But at its rising it is like a bridegroom and it fills us with joy.

—Cyril of Jerusalem, *Catecheses*

We must imitate our attendant and servant, the sun. For just as the latter never stop shining and shedding light, but fulfills the Master's command without ceasing, so should we, too, not will to sit inattentively in the darkness of pleasure and the passions, but instead keep the commandments of Him Who said: "Repent, for the Kingdom of God is at hand." (Matthew 3:2)

—Symeon the New Theologian, *Ethical Discourses*

Supplication

My advice is that supplication should be offered up for everyone. A supplication is a plea or petition made on account of present and past sin by someone who is moved by contrition to seek pardon.

—John Cassian, *Conferences*

Devoted prayer is when a man on bended knees with hands, eyes and heart raised to heaven, makes supplication, just as it is made to the Pope or the King.

—Vincent Ferrer, *sermon*

Surrender

Jesus does not demand great deeds. All he wants is self-sacrifice and gratitude.

—Thérèse of Lisieux, *The Story of a Soul*

To be truly a victim of Love requires absolute self-surrender. *The soul is consumed by love only insofar as she surrenders herself to Love.*

—Thérèse of Lisieux, *Counsels and Reminisces*

Let God strip you to the skin, yea to the soul, so he stay with you himself: let his reproach be your honor, his poverty your riches, and he in lieu of all other friends. Think him enough for this world that must be your possession for a whole eternity.

—Robert Southwell, *letter to a friend, 1591*

Keep your eye on God's pleasure and the eternal plan for you. Surrender all the remaining days of your life to God, and let the Lord use these for such activities and services as will be pleasing to God and not to yourself.

—Jane Frances de Chantal, *letter to a superior*

When people subject themselves to God on the height of triumphant subservience and overcome Satan, they will advance and enjoy the bliss of divine protection.

—Hildegard of Bingen, *Book of Divine Works*

Therefore, a person who submits himself or herself to God with devotion and humility may work out his or her own salvation. This salvation flows from the highest good.

—Hildegard of Bingen, *Scivias*

Yes, we must learn the hard lesson of submission; and once this has been accomplished, everything that comes after will be rendered easy.

—Elizabeth Seton, *Collected Writings*

Submission to God's free will frees us from all other yokes.

—Claude de la Colombière, *sermon*

I firmly believe, and in this I find joy, that God guides those who give themselves up to his leading and that he takes care of the least things that concern him.

—Claude de la Colombière, *retreat notes*

In all our actions and in all our circumstance we ought to hold submission to God before our eyes.

When that is rooted in the soul, not only comfort, honors and rank, but also slanders, injuries, tortures, in fact everything, will produce in us fruits of joy.

—John Chrysostom, *To the People of Antioch*

My Lord,
I am all yours.
You know
I have nothing
besides my tunic, cord and underpants.
And even these three things are yours.
So what can I give you?

—Francis of Assisi, *Third Consideration on the Sacred Stigmata*

Swearing and cursing

There are many ways of offending God by words; for example, by swearing and blaspheming. We must not swear by the Creator, nor by any creature, except with these three conditions—truth, necessity, respect.

—Ignatius of Loyola, *Spiritual Exercises*

In a word, obscene tongues are the ruin of the world. One of them does more mischief than a hundred devils; because it is the cause of the perdition of many souls.

—Alphonsus Liguori, *sermon*

Those who curse themselves are like insane people who die by their own hands.

—John Baptiste Marie Vianney, *sermon*

If something irritating or troublesome happens, instead of loading with curses whatever is not going the way we want it to, it would be just as easy and a great deal more beneficial for us to say: "God bless it!"

—John Baptiste Marie Vianney, *sermon*

We ought, you see, my dear brethren, to have a great respect for the name of God and pronounce it only with tremendous veneration and never in vain.

—John Baptiste Marie Vianney, *sermon*

People never believe someone who swears because swearing presupposes someone who has no religion, and a person without religion is not worthy of being believed.

—John Baptiste Marie Vianney, *sermon*

There is another kind of swearing and cursing to which people give little thought—these are the oaths which are uttered by the heart. There are those who believe that because they are not actually said by the mouth, there is no harm in them. You are greatly mistaken in that, my friends.

—John Baptiste Marie Vianney, *sermon*

Do not ever forget that the Holy Ghost tells us that a curse uttered irresponsibly or carelessly will fall upon someone.

—John Baptiste Marie Vianney, *sermon*

I tell you yet again that you must never curse your children, your animals, your work, or the weather, because in cursing all these things, you are cursing what Almighty God has done by his holy will.

—John Baptiste Marie Vianney, *sermon*

Children should take care never to give occasion to their parents to curse them, which is the greatest of all evils. Often a child who is cursed by his parents is cursed by Almighty God.

—John Baptiste Marie Vianney, *sermon*

When someone has done something to you which has angered you very much, now instead of wishing him to the Devil, you would do far more good by saying to him: "May God bless you!" Then you would be a genuinely good servant of God who returns good for evil.

—John Baptiste Marie Vianney, *sermon*

T

Temperance

Temperance, indeed, is the virtue of women.

—Ambrose, *Concerning Widowhood*

Temperance is the bridle of intentional passions; it checks the soul's willing inclinations to pleasure, because it separates the soul from the desire of things of this world and unites it with God through love.

—Theoleptos of Philadelphia, *letter*

Temperance destroys the pleasure-seeking will, while patience does away with conceit. Temperance and patience make war on anger and desire. If you do not have temperance, the desire of the body prevails over your soul; if you do not have patience, anger gains the mastery over your mind.

—Theoleptos of Philadelphia, *letter*

Temptation

The world entices the wealthy with its enchanting song of worldly delights. While the person is entranced by the promise of these delights, he is killed by the devil and taken to hell's kitchen to be roasted and boiled.

—Anthony of Padua, *Sermones*

Note that just as the devil tempted our Lord with gluttony during His fast in the desert, with pride on the parapet of the Temple, and with greed on a very high mountain, so too he tempts us with gluttony when we fast, with pride when we pray in church, and with many forms of greed on the mountain of our successes.

—Anthony of Padua, *Sermones*

Therefore, daughter, you are not to marvel if even in old age temptations increase. For as long as life is permitted, temptation too is possible. The devil never sleeps, because temptation is an opportunity for perfection so that man may not presume.

—Bridget of Sweden, *Book of Questions*

Temptations are granted as a training for the will.

—Theoleptos of Philadelphia, *letter*

If you fall under the stress of temptation, rise promptly, ask God's pardon, hope in him in spite of your fall, and with all your heart welcome the humiliation and detest the sin.

—Claude de la Colombière, *letter*

We ought never to trust in our own strength or in our courage and go out to seek temptation, thinking to confound it; but if in that place where the Spirit of God had led us we encounter it, we must remain firm in the confidence which we ought to have that he will strengthen us against the attacks of our enemy, however furious they may be.

—Francis de Sales, *Oeuvres*

There is no place where temptation does not have access.

—Francis de Sales, *Oeuvres*

For whether we desire it or not we shall be tempted. If we do nor struggle, we shall not be victorious, nor shall we merit the crown of immortal glory which God has prepared for those of us who are victorious and triumphant.

Let us fear neither the temptation nor the tempter, for if we make use of the shield of faith and the armor of truth, they will have no power whatsoever over us.

—Francis de Sales, *Oeuvres*

Never seek temptations, it is presumptuous and rash to do so; but prepare your heart to await them with courage and to defend itself when they do come.

—Francis de Sales, *The Devout Life*

Whatever temptations, then, assault you, and whatever attraction ensues, so long as your will refuses to consent to either, be not afraid, God is not displeased.

—Francis de Sales, *The Devout Life*

If then you are tempted to sin, reflect whether you have voluntarily brought it on yourself; and when the temptation is in itself sinful, whether you have cast yourself into it; that is, whether you might not have avoided the occasion, or have foreseen the temptation. If you have in no way induced it, then it cannot be imputed to you as sin.

—Francis de Sales, *The Devout Life*

If you seek the flesh of Egypt, you will not receive the manna of heaven.

—Francis de Sales, *The Devout Life*

We are not yet in our Fatherland, and temptation must purify us as gold is purified by the action of fire.

—Thérèse of Lisieux, *letter to her sister Celine*

In the moment of temptation have you not sought to deceive yourself by foolish reasonings on the justice of God, and on his mercy? Have you not sought to persuade yourself that sin is not so great an evil—that God is too good to punish you? And is it not true that it was only after the sin that your blindness ceased, and that your eyes were opened to the light?

—Ignatius of Loyola, *Spiritual Exercises*

But words coming out of man's mouths and deeds known to men contain a most perilous temptation. This arises from love of praise which, to build up a sort of private superiority, begs for and hoards up marks of approval. Even when this is rebuked within myself by myself, it affords temptation by the very fact that it is rebuked.

—Augustine, *Confessions*

We must recognize that wickedness is in us because, although the temptation comes from without, the grace to resist it is entirely at our disposal and is stronger than the temptation.

—Pope John XXIII, *Journal of a Soul*

If you succeed in overcoming temptation, this has the effect of washing on dirty clothes.

—Padre Pio, *Spiritual Maxims*

Don't let temptations frighten you; they are the trials of the souls whom God wants to test when he sees they have the necessary strength to sustain the struggle, thus weaving the crown of glory with their own hands.

—Padre Pio, *letter, 1920*

The place of temptation is the place where we find ourselves having to put up a bitter fight against the enemy, and wherever we are not involved in a struggle is surely the place where the enemy is posing as a friend.

—John Climacus, *The Ladder of Divine Ascent*

So long as you live, never trust that clay of which you are made and never depend on it unto the time you stand before Christ himself. And never imagine that abstinence will keep you from falling. It was a being who never ate that was nevertheless thrown out of heaven.

—John Climacus, *The Ladder of Divine Ascent*

Do not argue with perverse thoughts or evil desires, but when they attack you, occupy your mind vigorously with some profitable meditation and plan until they vanish away. No thought or intention is ever expelled from the heart except by some other thought or intention incompatible with it.

—Anselm, *letter, c. 1095*

Truly we have three adversities in this life; the devil, the flesh and the world.

—Bernadine of Siena, *sermon*

To resist every temptation, it is sufficient to pronounce the names of Jesus and Mary; and if the temptation continues, let us continue to invoke Jesus and Mary, and the Devil shall never be able to conquer us.

—Alphonsus Liguori, *sermon*

If, then, we wish Jesus Christ to dwell within us, we must keep the doors of our senses closed against dangerous occasions, otherwise the Devil will make us his slaves.

—Alphonsus Liguori, *sermon*

When you are tempted by the enemy, the best remedy is to hasten with all speed to the Cross, and to see Christ thereon, covered with wounds, torn, disfigured, streaming with blood. Then reflect that the chief reason why he is there is to destroy sin; and so, with all devotion, beg him not to allow what is so abominable, and what he sought, with such labor, to overthrow, ever to reign in our hearts.

—Peter of Alcántara, *Treatise on Prayer & Meditation*

The temptations we must fear most are those of which we are not conscious.

—John Baptiste Marie Vianney, *sermon*

Temptation is necessary to make us realize that we are nothing in ourselves.

—John Baptiste Marie Vianney, *sermon*

The sign of the cross is the most terrible weapon against the Devil. Thus the Church wishes not only that we should have it continually in front of our minds to recall to us just what our souls are worth and what they cost Jesus Christ, but also that we should make it at every juncture ourselves: when we go to bed, when we awaken during the night, when we get up, when we begin any action, and above all, when we are tempted.

—John Baptiste Marie Vianney, *sermon*

Thanksgiving

Thanksgiving also belongs to prayer. Thanksgiving is a true inward acknowledgment, we applying ourselves with great reverence and in loving fear and with all our powers to the work that our Lord has moved us to, rejoicing and giving thanks inwardly.

—Julian of Norwich, *Showings*

Render thanks to God. O great and good Creator, how much do I owe to thee, since out of my nothingness thou has made me what I am? How can I ever worthily bless thy holy name, and thank thine infinite goodness.

—Francis de Sales, *The Devout Life*

Whatever will come my way, whether good or bad, I may accept it calmly, and always give thanks to God, who has ever shown me how I should believe in him unfailing without end.

—Patrick, *letter to the soldiers of Coroticus*

To thank God in all things that are agreeable to us, is acceptable to him; but to accept with cheerfulness what is repugnant to our inclinations, is still more pleasing to him.

—Alphonsus Liguori, *sermon*

Oh, Fire of Love! Thanks, thanks be to Thee, Eternal Father! I am imperfect and full of darkness, and Thou, Perfection and Light, has shown me to perfection, and the resplendent way of the doctrine of Thy only-begotten Son. I was dead, and Thou has brought me to life.

—Catherine of Siena, *Dialogue*

My spirit engrossed itself in the benefits that God has lavished on me throughout this whole year. My soul trembled at the sight of this immensity of God's graces. From my soul there burst forth a hymn of thanksgiving to the Lord. For a whole hour, I remained steeped in adoration and thanksgiving, contemplating, one by one, the benefits I had received from God and also my own minor shortcomings. All that this year contained has gone into the abyss of eternity. Nothing is lost. I am glad that nothing gets lost.

—Faustina Kowalska, *Divine Mercy in My Soul*

Thanksgiving is generated by the contemplation of God's goodness and greatness and faithfulness.

—John Cassian, *Conferences*

May my heart and soul with all the substance of my flesh and spirit, through the efficacy of the entire universe, be jubilant to you. To you, then, from whom everything, through whom everything, and in whom everything, to you alone [be] honor and glory forever.

—Gertrude the Great, *Spiritual Exercises*

My Lord Jesus Christ, although I know well that your blessed body is unceasingly praised and glorified by the harmonious jubilee of the citizens of heaven above, and yet, because I am bound by a debt to render to you infinite thanksgiving, therefore I, although a person unwise and unworthy, desire nevertheless with all my heart and with all my mouth to offer to all the members of your precious body such thanks as I can and praise and honor.

—Bridget of Sweden, *prayer*

To you be praise indeed, O eternal God, and endless thanksgiving for the fact that you deigned to become a human being and that for us in the world you willed to consecrate your venerable Body out of material bread and lovingly bestow it on us as food for the salvation of our souls!

—Bridget of Sweden, *Book of Questions*

Certainly our customary prayers ought to be said with giving of thanks, when we rise from sleep, when we go forth, when we prepare to receive food, after receiving it, and at the hour of incense, when at last we are going to rest.

—Ambrose, *Concerning Virgins, to Marcellina, His Sister*

Thoughts

Every day keep turning over in your mind some thought which has deeply impressed you and fallen into your heart. Unless you exercise your powers of thought, the soul becomes numb.

—Theophan the Recluse, *letter*

There remains the struggle with thoughts which will often continue to buzz like importunate mosquitoes. You must learn for yourself how to overcome them: experience will teach you.

—Theophan the Recluse, *The Fruits of Prayer*

Keep the thought of God continually before you, and walk always in his presence.

—Peter of Alcantara, *Treatise on Prayer & Meditation*

The Christian ought to have thoughts worthy of his heavenly calling and order his life to be worthy of the Gospel of Christ.

—Basil the Great, *letter to Gregory of Nazianzus*

It is indeed a good thing to keep the thought of God uppermost in our mind and something that a true Christian should never cease doing.

—Basil the Great, *On Faith*

A true friend of God should always keep some good images or thoughts in his soul's mouth and chew on them in order to inflame his heart with love of God. The most perfect thing we can do in this life is to think frequently of God's love, to languish for his love; to speak often about him, to meditate on his words, to do all our actions for him, and to think of him alone.

—Henry Suso, *letter on devotion to the Sacred Name of Jesus*

It is not the bad thought, but the consent to it, that is sinful.

—Alphonsus Liguori, *sermon*

At the hour of death sinful actions cannot be committed; but we may then be guilty of sin of thought; and he who has had a habit of consenting to bad thoughts during life, will be in danger of indulging them at death: for then the temptations of the Devil are most violent.

—Alphonsus Liguori, *sermon*

For those who speak what are simply their own thoughts before they have attained purity are deluded by the spirit of self-conceit.

—Gregory of Sinai, *The Philokalia*

Whenever we believers simply go about our work in life, our thoughts are turned in proper longing toward what is useful and fruitful. And so our thinking affects our greening power to bring forth many fruits of holiness. And our thinking lifts up our minds toward heavenly things so that we turn our desires upward, and in this way our thinking is strengthened.

—Hildegard of Bingen, *Book of Divine Works*

Therefore, Lord, not only are You that which a greater cannot be thought, but You are also something greater than can be thought. For since is it possible to think that there is such a one, then, if You are not this same being something greater than You could be thought—which cannot be.

—Anselm, *Proslogion*

From all sides temptation comes in torrents to drive it along and in no way will it be free of turbulent thoughts. But the workings of zeal and diligence will decide which of those thoughts may be allowed in and cultivated. . . . If we turn to the constant meditation of Scripture, if we lift up our memory to the things of the spirit, to the longing for perfection and to the hope of future blessedness, then the thoughts deriving from all this will of necessity be spiritual and they will hold the mind where the thoughts have been.

—John Cassian, *Conferences*

Above all we should realize that there are three sources for our thoughts—God, the devil, and ourselves.

—John Cassian, *Conferences*

To keep the thought of God always in your mind you must cling totally to this formula for piety: "Come to my help, O God; Lord, hurry to my rescue." (Psalms 69:2)

It is not without good reason that this verse has been chosen from the whole of Scripture as a device. It carries within it all the feelings of which human nature is capable.

—John Cassian, *Conferences*

Saint Paul tells us how much we lose when the first thoughts of our minds are occupied with anything else but God. The devil does his best, when you waken, to inspire you with other thoughts. . . . The first thing you should do when you have risen and put on your clothes is to kneel down and adore God. What do you think it means to adore God? It is to offer him the homage that belongs to him alone, and to acknowledge him as your creator and sovereign lord.

—Vincent de Paul, *Conferences to the Daughters of Charity*

We should be aware that there are three degrees of evil thoughts: one, of those which contaminate the mind by the deliberate choice and purpose of sinning; another, of those which confuse the mind by the delight of sin, yet do not allure it to consent to sin; the third, of those which move across the mind in a natural way yet do not entice it to give in to vices, though they keep it from the good things it ought to reflect on.

—Bede the Venerable, *homily on the Gospels*

Because we cannot totally avoid idle thoughts, we should put them to flight, as far as we can, by stirring up good thoughts, and especially by frequent meditation on the scriptures, according to the example of the psalmist who said, "Oh, how I have loved your law, O Lord; it is my meditation all the day." (Psalms 119:87)

—Bede the Venerable, *homily on the Gospels*

Thrift

see MONEY AND WEALTH

Time

What a pity to be killing time when time is a treasure from God!

—Josemaría Escrivá, *The Forge*

Those who are engaged in business say that the time is money. That seems little to me: for us who are engaged in affairs of soul, time is . . . glory!

—Josemaría Escrivá, *The Way*

Who will see that all past time is driven back by the future, that all the future is consequent on the past, and all past and future are created and take their course from that which is ever present?

—Augustine, *Confessions*

There are three things, the present of things past, the present of things present, and the present of things future. These three are in the soul, but elsewhere I do not see them: the present of things past is in memory; the present of things present is in intuition; the present of things future is in expectation.

—Augustine, *Confessions*

Again and again God gives more in a moment than in a long period of time, for his actions are not measured by time at all.

—Teresa of Ávila, *letter to her brother Toledo, 1577*

There is nothing shorter than time, but there is nothing more valuable. There is nothing shorter than time, because the past is no more, the future is uncertain, and the present is but a moment.

—Alphonsus Liguori, *sermon*

But the time of this life is as precious as it is short; for, in every moment, if we spend it well, we can acquire the treasures of merits for Heaven; but, if we employ time badly, we may in each moment commit sin, and merit Hell.

—Alphonsus Liguori, *sermon*

The Devil regards the whole of our life as very short, and therefore he loses not a moment of time, but tempts us day and night.

—Alphonsus Liguori, *sermon*

Have confidence! Never let the comparison of time and eternity slip in an instant from your mind. I find this cures all sorrow.

—Elizabeth Seton, *Collected Writings*

And when did the Father come into being? There never was a time when he was not. And the same thing is true of the Son and the Holy Ghost.

—Gregory of Nazianzus, *theological oration*

"In the beginning God made." That which was begun in time is condemned to come to an end in time. If there has been a beginning do not doubt of the end.

—Basil the Great, *homily on the Hexaemeron*

Is not this the nature of time, where the past is no more, the future does not exist, and the present escapes before being recognized?

—Basil the Great, *homily on the Hexaemeron*

God who made the nature of time measured it out and determined it by intervals of days; and, wishing to give it a week as a measure, he ordered the week to revolve from period to period upon itself, to count the movement of time, forming the week of one day revolving seven times upon itself: a proper circle begins and ends with itself. Such is also the character of eternity, to revolve upon itself and to end nowhere. If then the beginning of time is called "one day" rather than the "first day," it is because Scripture wishes to establish its relationship with eternity.

—Basil the Great, *homily on the Hexaemeron*

Timidity

But the devil can never hurt any one at all, except as far as God Himself permits it: so that at such times we ought much rather to fear having any distrust in God, than to fear the assault of our enemy. For God does permit our foe to harass and vex those who are led by their own timidity not to trust in their Creator, who do not seek for strength in Him, and do not place their hopes in Him.

—Francis Xavier, *letter*

For in truth no man is really timid and weak who knowingly leans upon the assistance of God.

—Francis Xavier, *letter*

Trials and tribulation

He who suffers tribulations in this world, should, in the first place, abandon sin, and endeavor to recover the grace of God; for as long as he remains in sin, the merit of all his sufferings is lost.

—Alphonsus Liguori, *sermon*

Great indeed are the advantages of tribulations. The Lord sends them to us, not because he wishes our misfortune, but because he desires our welfare. Hence, when they come upon us, we must embrace them with thanksgiving, and must not only resign ourselves to the divine will, but must also rejoice that God treats us as he treated his son Jesus Christ, whose life upon this Earth was always full of tribulation.

—Alphonsus Liguori, *sermon*

They who live in prosperity, and have no experience of adversity, know nothing of the state of their souls. In the first place, tribulation opens the eyes which prosperity had kept shut.

—Alphonsus Liguori, *sermon*

By tribulations we atone for the sins we have committed, much better than by voluntary works of penance.

—Alphonsus Liguori, *sermon*

To teach us to recommend ourselves continually to him who can save us by his grace, the Lord has ordained that, so long as we remain on this Earth, we should live in the midst of a continual tempest, and should be surrounded by enemies. . . . The Lord permits all these apparent evils, that we may take our affections away from fading goods, in which we meet with so many dangers of perdition, and that we may seek to unite ourselves with him who alone can make us happy.

—Alphonsus Liguori, *sermon*

The life of a Christian is nothing but a perpetual struggle against self; there is no flowering of the soul to the beauty of its perfection except at the price of pain.

—Padre Pio, *Spiritual Maxims*

Indeed however many trials and persecutions we undergo, they all contribute to our greater gain, so long as we bear them without offending the Lord, but rejoice that we are suffering for His sake.

—Teresa of Ávila, *Life*

I can say then that if I were asked whether I should prefer to endure all the trials in the world until the world itself ends and gain a little more glory, I would willingly accept every trial in exchange for a little more of the blissful contemplation of God's greatness. For I see that he who best understands Him loves and praises Him best.

—Teresa of Ávila, *Life*

It is clear that, since God leads those whom He most loves by the way of trials, the more He loves them, the greater will be their trials.

—Teresa of Ávila, *The Way of Perfection*

Afflictions are the steps to Heaven.

—Elizabeth Seton, *Collected Writings*

For trials I bless Him most of all. Where should I now be if He had not scourged and bound me? What matters by whose hands? If I get to His kingdom, what matters how? The Captain marches on. Oh, yes we follow; we follow.

—Elizabeth Seton, *Collected Writings*

Gladly endure whatever goes against you and do not let good fortune lift you up: for these things destroy faith.

—Clare of Assisi, *letter to Ermentrude of Bruges*

The darknesses and trials, spiritual and temporal, that fortunate souls ordinarily undergo on their way to the high state of perfection are so numerous and profound that human science cannot understand them adequately. Nor does experience of them equip one to explain them. Only those who suffer them will know what this experience is like, but they won't be able to describe it.

—John of the Cross, *The Ascent of Mount Carmel*

Sin is committed by base indulgence and is repugnant to suffering sorrow, while tribulation earns the pardon of the just judge.

—Mary of Agreda, *The Mystical City of God*

After big storms there follow bright days.

—Henry Suso, *letter*

May I endure fire, the cross, beasts, the breaking of bones, dismemberment, the crushing of the whole body, and all the torments of the devil, if only I can enjoy Christ.

—Ignatius of Antioch, *letter to the Romans*

You must be prepared for periods of darkness, anxiety, doubts, fears, of temptations that are sometimes very, very insistent, of sufferings of the body and, what is a hundredfold more painful, of the soul. For if there were nothing to bear, for what would you go to heaven? If there were no trials, there would be no struggle. Without a struggle, victory would be impossible, and without victory, there is no crown, no reward. . . . So be prepared from now on for everything.

—Maximilian M. Kolbe, *letter to newly invested brothers in Grodno, 1927*

But because the flesh is sometimes imprudently insolent, one must cheerfully tolerate tribulations and all those things by which the flesh may be corrected.

—Bridget of Sweden, *Book of Questions*

We may know with certainty that nothing belongs to us except our vices and sins. We must rejoice, instead, when we fall into various trials and, in this world, suffer every kind of anguish or distress of soul and body for the sake of eternal life.

—Francis of Assisi, *early Rule*

But in the shipwreck of this present life sustain me, I beseech thee, by the plank of thy prayer, that, since my own weight sinks me down, the hand of thy merit may raise me up.

—Gregory the Great, *The Book of Pastoral Rule*

In order to discipline them [souls] and make them more worthy of himself, he [Wisdom] permits them to engage in strenuous conflicts and in almost everything they undertake they encounter contradictions and disappointments. At times, he allows the devil to tempt them, the world to calumniate and scorn them, their enemies to defeat and crush them, their friends and relatives to forsake and betray them. Sometimes they have to suffer illness or loss of possessions, and at other times endure insults, sadness and heartbreak. In short, Wisdom tests them thoroughly in the crucible of tribulation like God is tested in a furnace.

—Louis de Montfort, *The Love of Eternal Wisdom*

For affliction achieves strength of patience, and patience begets proof of faith and bestows the reward of glory. This reward virtue certainly cannot win unless she conquers, and she will not have the opportunity of victory unless she first struggles with some difficulty.

—Paulinus of Nola, *letter*

There is nothing more fruitful of good to the soul in this life of misery than to live in the midst of great dangers of death, the true and only cause for braving which has been the simple love of God and of pleasing Him, and the sincere desire to extend our holy religion. Believe me, it is sweeter for a man to live in labors of this sort, than to pass his time in peace and leisure without them.

—Francis Xavier, *letter*

If you accept difficulties with a faint heart you lose your joy and your peace. And you run the risk of not deriving spiritual profit from the trial.

—Josemaría Escrivá, *The Way*

God is touched by our sorrows and does not allow them to last forever. He takes pleasure in trying our love for a time because he sees that trials purify us and render us worthy to receive his greater graces.

—Claude de la Colombière, *letter*

One who is firmly anchored in God does not suffer any loss, even if attacked by a thousand waves and a thousand storms. On the contrary, he emerges stronger.

—John Chrysostom, *On Providence*

Just as a ship tossed by the waves of a storm will be dashed to pieces unless it has an experienced captain at the helm, so anyone who is in difficulties will find their spirit broken and their hope of salvation dashed unless they are guided by the teaching of the Lord.

—Basil the Great, *Consolation in Adversity*

Trinity

Unity having from all eternity arrived by motion at Duality, found its rest in Trinity. This is what we mean by Father and Son and Holy Ghost. The Father is the Begetter and the Emitter; without passion of course, and without reference to time, and not in a corporeal manner. The Son is the Begotten, and the Holy Ghost the Emission; for I know now how this could be expressed in terms altogether excluding visible things.

—Gregory of Nazianzus, *theological oration*

The Father was the True Light which lighteneth every man coming into the world. The Son was the True Light which lighteneth every man coming into the world. The Other comforter was the True Light which lighteneth every man coming into the world, Was and Was and Was, but Was One Thing. Light thrice repeated; but One Light and One God. This was what David represented to himself long before when he said, "In Thy Light we shall see Light." And now we have both seen and proclaim concisely and simply the doctrine of God the Trinity, comprehending out of Light (the Father), Light (the Son), in Light (the Holy Ghost).

—Gregory of Nazianzus, *theological oration*

But you will never find the Father without the Son and Spirit, neither the Son without the Father and Spirit, nor the Spirit a stranger to union with Him from Whom He proceeds. The Father and Son are in the Spirit, and in the Son there is the Father with the Spirit, and the Son is and abides co-everlastingly in the Father and has the Holy Spirit shining forth together with Himself. Believe it! These are one God and not three.

—Symeon the New Theologian, *Ethical Discourses*

Trust

I trusted in God . . . and suddenly in that moment all my pain left me.

—Julian of Norwich, *Showings*

In all your undertakings rely wholly on God's providence, through which alone they can succeed; but seek steadily on your part to cooperate with it, and then rest satisfied that if you are trusting all to God, whatever happens will be best for you, whether it seems to your own judgment good or bad.

—Francis de Sales, *The Devout Life*

I do not understand how it is possible not to trust in Him who can do all things. With Him, everything; without Him, nothing. He is Lord. He will not allow those who have placed all their trust in Him to be put to shame.

—Faustina Kowalska, *Divine Mercy in My Soul*

Be wise, my soul, and trust in God alone, cling to him alone, and cast all your cares on him alone.

—Robert Bellarmine, *The Mind's Ascent to God by the Ladder of Created Things*

Be trustful, firmly believing that God always provides for souls who trust in him. Then the devil is powerless, because the power of the trust in him.

—Catherine of Siena, *letter to a man, c. 1372–75*

Do you think that he who trusts in this world has greater abundance than he who trusts in God? Or that he who feasts on his own preoccupations is richer than he who feasts on God's? What possessions can the wretch have who does not possess himself? For he who puts greater hopes in himself than in God does not possess himself; he is indeed dead who fears that if he trusts and entrusts himself wholly to God he is not alive.

—Paulinus of Nola, *letter*

Trust fully in God and have a greater desire each day never to run away from Him.

—Josemaría Escrivá, *The Forge*

Truth

If anyone attains the truth which is in accord with their teachings, this person serves to complete the form of one body.

—Gregory of Nyssa, *sermon*

Truth is the object of understanding and love that of the will.

—Francis de Sales, *Oeuvres*

If we want our word to be accepted, it must be the truth. But what is truth? Nothing else, my dear friends, than faith. It is written that our Lord is full of grace and truth (John 1:14), which means that he is full of faith and charity.

—Francis de Sales, *Oeuvres*

So not only is truth to be found in God, but God is the source and highest form of truth.

—Thomas Aquinas, *Summa Theologica*

Truth does not love corners nor does she seek out whisperers.

—Jerome, *letter to Rusticus, 411*

A man drunk on wine unwittingly tells the truth about everything. And a man drunk with compunction cannot lie.

—John Climacus, *The Ladder of Divine Ascent*

For this too I believe, that "unless I believe, I shall not understand." (Isaiah 7:9)

—Anselm, *Proslogion*

I do not try, Lord, to attain Your lofty heights, because my understanding is in no way equal to it. But I do desire to understand Your truth a little, that truth that my heart believes and loves. For I do not seek to understand so that I may believe; but I believe so that I may understand.

—Anselm, *Proslogion*

O whole and blessed truth, how far You are from me who am so close to You! How distant You are from my sight while I am so present to Your sight! You are wholly present everywhere and I do not see You. In You I move and in You I have my being and I cannot come near You. You are within me and around me and I do not have any experience of You.

—Anselm, *Proslogion*

Truths are inscribed in the heart by the finger of God, and remains there firm and indelible. Do not neglect these truths which God inscribes, but write them down.

—Theophan the Recluse, *The Fruits of Prayer*

By knowledge of truth understand above all apprehension of truth through grace. Other kinds of knowledge should be regarded as images of intellections or the rational demonstration of facts.

—Gregory of Sinai, *The Philokalia*

About your names in the flesh there is nothing to say; they will vanish. But if a man knows his true name he will also perceive the name of Truth.

—Anthony, *letter*

While a person dwells in the body, the person will love to be part of the journey of those who run along the way of truth and avoid the error of falsehood.

—Hildegard of Bingen, *Scivias*

For all the harm that befalls the world comes from a failure to understand the truths of Scripture in all their true clarity, of which not one tittle shall fail.

—Teresa of Ávila, *Life*

O Lord! All our trouble comes to us from not having our eyes fixed upon Thee. If we only looked at the way along which we are walking, we should soon arrive; but we stumble and fall a thousand times and stray from the way because, as I say, we do not set our eyes on the true Way.

—Teresa of Ávila, *The Way of Perfection*

If we sometimes possess the truth, we do not realize we have it, and we act like someone who is looking for something that he has in his hand.

—Henry Suso, *letter*

Because a wheel is round, it has nothing by which its progress is impeded. Likewise, sacred teaching, trimmed all around and agreeing with itself, nowhere has the smallest part of untruth slowing it down when it should be rolling toward the mind of its hearers.

—Elisabeth of Schönau, *Third Book of Visions*

May your luminous truth lead me and make me walk in your presence sincerely, with a perfect heart.

—Gertrude the Great, *Spiritual Exercises*

For what can be more true than the mystery of Christ and the Church?

—Ambrose, *Concerning Widowhood*

You will know that you are but ordained to command beings without reason and soul; inferior as regards natural advantages, but, thanks to the privilege of reason, capable of raising yourself to heaven. If we are penetrated by these truths, we shall serve our Master, we shall glorify our Father, we shall love our Sustainer, we shall bless our Benefactor, we shall not cease to honor the Prince of present and future life, Who, by the riches that He showers upon us in this world, makes us believe his promises and uses present good things to strengthen our expectation of the future.

—Basil the Great, *homily on the Hexaemeron*

I had wasted much of my time and devoted almost all of my youth in acquiring knowledge which now appears as just foolishness before God. Then one day I awoke suddenly, as if from some deep sleep. And saw the intense light of divine truth, and realized the absolute worthlessness of all the wisdom taught by the leaders of this world.

—Basil the Great, *letter*

Let us carry out Christ's commands that we may obtain Christ's promises. His truth is with us; let not our faith fail Him.

—Paulinus of Nola, *letter*

As soon as you concentrate your mind's eye on the sanctuary above, Truth will reveal Its face to you and unlock to you your own person, because it is by recognition of the divine truth that we also come to know ourselves.

—Paulinus of Nola, *letter*

Disagree when necessary, but be in agreement about truth.

—Columban, *letter, c. 610*

Don't be afraid of the truth, even though the truth may mean your death.

—Josemaría Escrivá, *The Way*

Never be afraid of telling the truth. But don't forget that sometimes it is better to remain silent out of charity towards your neighbor. However, you should never be silent out of laziness, or love of comfort, or cowardice.

—Josemaría Escrivá, *The Forge*

If our ears are so closed to the truth that we are not able to hear the truth from a friend, our salvation must be despaired of.

—Aelred of Rielvaux, *Spiritual Friendship*

It is one thing to speak about the truth and quite another to see the Truth who teaches us himself. One thing is the copy and the other is the original. The former is given by study, the latter by faith.

—Clement of Alexandria, *Miscellaneous Studies*

True teachers know that they serve their neighbor by the likeness of their own life to their own message. They think the truth and speak it to the advantage of those who hear them and give them their assent. They speak as they think, and they live as they think.

—Clement of Alexandria, *Miscellaneous Studies*

Whoever has been called to eternal life ought to resemble the Incorruptible. For this reason, let our whole life be springtime; let the truth within us never grow old.

—Clement of Alexandria, *The Teacher*

Let us speak the truth in our hearts and not practice treachery with our tongues, so that by pouring forth charity more and more in our hearts, the Spirit of truth may teach us recognition of all truth.

—Bede the Venerable, *homily on the Gospels*

U

Understanding

But in our intention we wait for God, and trust faithfully to have mercy and grace; and this is how in his goodness he opens the eye of our understanding, by which we have sight, sometimes more and sometimes less, according to the ability God gives us to receive.

—Julian of Norwich, *Showings*

Only by names can humanity grasp the essence of a thing, and only by numbers can humanity know the multiplicity of things.

—Hildegard of Bingen, *Book of Divine Works*

He appears to the soul by a knowledge brighter than the sun. I do not mean that any sun is seen, or any brightness, but there is a light, which, though unseen, illumines the understanding so that the soul may enjoy this great blessing, which brings very great blessings with it.

—Teresa of Ávila, *Life*

You must give up human understanding if you want to reach the goal, because the truth is known by not knowing.

—Henry Suso, *Little Book of Truth*

As long as a person understands oneness or something like it as something that can be presented in words, he still has to go "further within."

—Henry Suso, *Little Book of Truth*

Charity does not consist so much in "giving" as in "understanding."

—Josemaría Escrivá, *The Way*

Nobody is so blind or so stupid as to believe that they can reach perfect understanding; indeed, the deeper their understanding, the more they are conscious of their ignorance.

—Basil the Great, *On Faith*

The poverty of man's understanding is spendthrift of words, because searching speaks more than does finding, pleading takes longer than acceptance, and the hand that knocks is busier than the hand that receives.

—Augustine, *Confessions*

Unhappiness

Man is truly unhappy in this world; the only thing capable of consoling him would be if he were able to live without eating and without sleeping in order to labor solely for Heaven.

—Joseph Cafasso, *second panegyric on St. Joseph Cafasso by St. John Bosco*

You are unhappy?—think: there must be an obstacle between God and me. You will seldom be wrong.

—Josemaría Escrivá, *The Way*

Indeed, my dear brethren, man on earth, unless he turns to the side of God, cannot be other than unhappy.

—John Baptiste Marie Vianney, *sermon*

Whoever wants to please both the world and God leads one of the most unhappy of lives.

—John Baptiste Marie Vianney, *sermon*

Unity

Unity exists at the moment when we all believe alike.

—John Chrysostom, *homily*

V

Vanity

When we depart from the truth, we simultaneously and increasingly choose vanity. Vanity is the absence of truth. With it we stumble into hell.

—Francis de Sales, *Oeuvres*

Nothing can be more foolish than to fancy we know more than we do *not* know, and no vanity is more contemptible than that which affects knowledge which it really does not possess. For myself, I would neither boast of what I do know, nor pretend to be more ignorant than I am.

—Francis de Sales, *The Devout Life*

The rich bring with them a miserable garment, which shall rot with them in the grave. And should they, during life, have acquired a great name, they shall soon be forgotten.

—Alphonsus Liguori, *sermon*

The force of God's wrath will prevail while our life lacks substance and resembles a shadow or spider's web. Although the web appears to have substance, it is immediately destroyed as soon as you touch it. Such is human existence with its transitory endeavors. It weaves insubstantial vanity like a web held together by light strings.

—Gregory of Nyssa, *Commentary on the Inscriptions of the Psalms*

Beware of vanity. Remembrance of the past is a good antidote.

—Claude de la Colombière, *letter*

There are those who take enjoyment in vain and ludicrous things, in worldly pomp and mundane spectacles, in the pursuit of vanity and in reveling in falsehood. They do not enjoy themselves in wisdom nor in him who is the strength of God and the wisdom of God.

—Aelred of Rievaulx, *Mirror of Charity*

The Spirit of truth flees from a heart it discerns is subject to vanity, and restores by the light of his coming only those it beholds carrying out the commandments of Truth out of love.

—Bede the Venerable, *homily on the Gospels*

Vices

I have in me the seeds of every vice: there is not one that I am not capable of committing. Only the grace of God prevents me from falling into the abyss.

—Claude de la Colombière, *retreat notes*

We must do away with all mockery and back-biting, with mimicking persons, and with all that is contrary to the love of neighbor. We must not do this even in recreation; we must not scrutinize the actions of others except in strict necessity and then it must be done prudently.

—Marguerite Bourgeoys, *Autographic Writings*

A careless, lax and easy life is a dense cloud which hides our eyes from the boundless treasures of his goodness.

—Marguerite Bourgeoys, *Autographic Writings*

I ought to believe that my faults are greater and do me more harm than anyone else. We must bear with the faults of others so that they may bear with us and God may not condemn us.

—Marguerite Bourgeoys, *Autographic Writings*

Often we take pleasure in having come up so well with words of mockery, jeering or banter spoken with wit and skill. They do not seem to us to oblige us to accuse ourselves of them and confess them. But they are stains which take away all the brilliance of our robe of innocence in which we ought to appear before the Lord. We cannot hope to live a spiritual life if we are attached to these faults. We must not, either, listen to them or approve them.

—Marguerite Bourgeoys, *Autographic Writings*

For those beginning the spiritual life even little things can provide setbacks. Those who are making progress are pursued by crafty little foxes who lie in wait and propose vices under the guise of virtues.

—Bernard of Clairvaux, *On the Canticle of Canticles*

When a young person has lived in evil habits, his bones shall be filled with the vices of his youth, so that he will carry them with him to his death; and the impurities, blasphemies, and hatred to which he was accustomed in his youth, shall accompany him to his grave, and shall sleep with him after his bones shall be reduced to dust and ashes.

—Alphonsus Liguori, *sermon*

There are three principal vices, namely: self-love, whence proceeds the second, that is love of reputation, whence proceeds the third, that is pride, with injustice and cruelty, and with other filthiness and iniquitous sins, that follow upon these.

—Catherine of Siena, *Dialogue*

He who wants to overcome vices should fight with the arms of love, not of rage.

—Peter Chrysologus, *sermon*

When vice is believed to be virtue, guilt is piled up without fear.

—Gregory the Great, *The Book of Pastoral Rule*

No growth of evil had its beginning in the Divine will. Vice would have been blameless were it inscribed with the name of God as its maker and father. But the evil is, in some way or other, engendered from within, springing up in the will at that moment when there is a retrocession of the soul from the beautiful. For as sight is an activity of nature, and blindness a deprivation of that natural operation, such is the kind of opposition between virtue and vice. It is, in fact, not possible to form any other notion of the origin of vice than as the absence of virtue.

—Gregory of Nyssa, *The Great Catechism*

If you want to stay close to God, you must not be sullied by any of the vices of this world.

—Basil the Great, *On Ascetic Discourse*

If you have raised yourself to the order of angels and then cover yourself with ordinary vices, you are like a leopard's skin, whose hair is neither pure white nor pure black, but is spotted with a mixture of both colors, and can be described neither white nor black.

—Basil the Great, *On Ascetic Discourse*

Just as faith is the origin of the virtues, so the basis of the vices is to persevere in unbelief, as the Lord attests in a terrifying way when he says, "But the one who does not believe is already judged, because he does not believe in the name of the only-begotten Son of God." (John 3:18)

—Bede the Venerable, *homily on the Gospels*

Virginity

For virginity is not praiseworthy because it is found in martyrs, but because itself makes martyrs.

—Ambrose, *Concerning Virgins, to Marcellina, His Sister*

Let, then, your work be as it were a honeycomb, for virginity is fit to be compared to bees, so laborious is it, so modest, so continent. The bee feeds on dew, it knows no marriage couch, it makes honey. The virgin's dew is the divine word, for the words of God descend like dew. The virgin's modesty is unstained nature. The virgin's produce is the fruit of the lips, without bitterness, abounding in sweetness. They work in common, and their fruit is in common.

—Ambrose, *Concerning Virgins, to Marcellina, His Sister*

If anyone is able to remain a virgin in honor of the Lord's human nature, let that person be humble: anyone who boasts of virginity is lost in eternity.

—John Chrysostom, *letter to the Ephesians*

For merely refusing to produce children is not true virginity, since you must be a virgin in the whole of your life and character, displaying the purity of the virgin in everything that you do. For it is possible to commit fornication by speaking and adultery by looking, just as we become polluted by what we wear and be defiled in our heart, or pass the limits of moderation by excessive eating or drinking. If you can show self-control within the rule of virginity, then you will find the grace of virginity in all its forms perfected within you.

—Basil the Great, *On Ascetic Discourse*

Virgins have a need of a very simple and tender chastity, banishing all manner of curious thoughts from their hearts, and despising all impure pleasures with absolute contempt.

—Francis de Sales, *The Devout Life*

Far from trumpeting the praises of virginity, I only wish to keep it safe. To know what is good is not enough; when you have chosen it you must guard it with jealous care. The first is a matter of judgment and we share it with many: the second calls for labor and for that few care.

—Jerome, *letter, 384*

Those . . . who have grasped the beauty of virginity, will ascend at dawn to the heavenly mysteries since they have restrained themselves from the delights of their bodies because of their love of my Word.

—Hildegard of Bingen, *Scivias*

Virtues

Unless you strive after virtues and practice them, you'll never grow to be more than dwarfs.

—Teresa of Ávila, *The Way of Perfection*

We all have a zeal for virtue and feel distressed when we see the sins and faults of others.

—Teresa of Ávila, *Life*

When the Lord begins to implant a virtue in us we must attach a high value to it, and on no account run the danger of losing it.

—Teresa of Ávila, *Life*

Whatever virtues God sowed in us in our primal state, therefore, he has commanded us to return to him.

—Columban, *sermon*

No virtue . . . can have life in itself except through charity, and humility, which is the foster-mother and nurse of charity.

—Catherine of Siena, *Dialogue*

There are, therefore, three virtues in which the perfection of the Christian law consists: charity from a pure heart, hope from a good conscience, and faith unfeigned.

—Robert Bellarmine, *The Art of Dying Well*

We must not be wise and prudent according to the flesh; rather, we must be simple, humble, and pure.

—Francis of Assisi, *letter to the Faithful*

The essence of the virtues is the will of God. He who does the will of God faithfully, practices all the virtues.

—Faustina Kowalska, *Divine Mercy in My Soul*

For just as the edifice of all the virtues strives upward toward perfect prayer so will all these virtues be neither sturdy nor enduring unless they are drawn firmly together by the crown of prayer.

—John Cassian, *Conferences*

Thus the servant of God ought not to fix his attention exclusively on one virtue, however great, but upon them all. Just as, in a viol, one string alone cannot produce harmonious music unless the others are made to contribute, so any single virtue is not sufficient to secure this spiritual harmony unless the others join in unison. A single defect destroys the whole value of a clock; so also it is with a spiritual life if but one virtue falters.

—Peter of Alcántara, *Treatise on Prayer & Meditation*

Where does virtue prove itself if not in adversity?

—Henry Suso, *Little Book of Eternal Wisdom*

Fall in love with true virtue: its effect is the opposite of that of vice, because sin brings bitterness while virtue brings sweetness and even in this life foretaste of the next. When the sweet hour of death comes, the virtue we have lived answers for us and shields us from God's judgment.

—Catherine of Siena, *letter to a parish priest*

Plato determined the final good to be to live according to virtue, and affirmed that he only can attain to virtue who knows and imitates God—which knowledge and imitation are the only cause of blessedness.

—Augustine, *The City of God*

Just as a garment is the covering of the body, so is virtue the covering of the soul.

—Vincent Ferrer, *sermon*

If virtue does not exist, life loses its value, reason moves in accordance with fatalism, the praise of moral guardians is gone, sin may be indulged in without risk, and the difference between the courses of life is obliterated.

—Gregory of Nyssa, *The Great Catechism*

I earnestly pray you not to forget your own progress in virtue: for you are well aware that one who does not make progress in virtue, goes backwards.

—Francis Xavier, *letter*

Just as the owner of sparkling stones, sapphires, amethysts, and other such, knows (unless he is inexperienced) the form and size of each of them, so, too, does he who with toil and tears has planted the virtues in himself and has harvested the fruits of the Spirit know both the form and the quality of each of them, and tastes of all their sweetness, and what is greater and more marvelous, he recognizes the same fruit in others.

—Symeon the New Theologian, *On the Mystical Life*

What are the four virtues—temperance, prudence, fortitude and justice—but the weapons with which we wage battle?

—Aelred of Rievaulx, *Mirror of Charity*

There can surely be no better way than this to realize moderation and courage, justice and prudence, and all those other virtues in their various subdivisions which guide decent people in the proper conduct of their life.

—Basil the Great, *letter to Gregory of Nyssa*

Virtue does not consist in making good resolutions, nor in saying fine words, but in keeping one's resolution and carrying out one's good intentions.

—Margaret Mary Alacoque, *Life and Writings of St. Margaret Mary*

A treasure that is known is quickly spent: and even so any virtue that is commented on and made a public show of is destroyed. Even as wax is melted before the face of fire, so is the soul enfeebled by praise, and loses the toughness of its virtues.

—Abbot Syncletica, *saying*

Whatever power thou hast, strive that the life which is within thee may be according to God, and may conquer the passions of the outer man. If we seek God, He will appear to us: and if we hold Him, He will stay with us.

—Abbott Arsenius, *saying*

Faith is the basis and foundation of all the other virtues, but particularly of hope and of charity.

—Francis de Sales, *Oeuvres*

Every action of our daily life should be influenced by gentleness, temperance, humility, and purity.

—Francis de Sales, *The Devout Life*

If we are hindered by some particular vice, we should as far as possible strive to cultivate the opposing virtue, making all things tend to it; for by this means we shall subdue the enemy, and not cease to advance in all virtue.

—Francis de Sales, *The Devout Life*

A really great mind will not waste itself on such empty goods as rank, honor, and form. It has higher pursuits, and leaves these for the weak and vain. He who can procure pearls will not be satisfied with shells, and those who aim at virtue do not trouble themselves about honors.

—Francis de Sales, *The Devout Life*

Charity alone places us in perfection. But the three great means of attaining to it are obedience, chastity, and poverty. Obedience consecrates our heart, chastity our body, and poverty our worldly means to the love and service of God. These are the three branches of the spiritual cross, and all have their foundation in the fourth, which is humility.

—Francis de Sales, *The Devout Life*

I cannot approve of those who in reforming a man would begin with external things—his face, his hair or his dress. On the contrary, we must begin from within.

—Francis de Sales, *The Devout Life*

Reflect that virtue and devotion alone can satisfy your soul in this world; behold how lovely they are; consider the virtues and their opposing vices. How precious is patience compared with revenge, gentleness compared with anger and passion, humility compared with arrogance and ambition, liberality compared with avarice, charity compared with envy, temperance compared with excess! For one admirable property attendant on acts of virtue is, they leave an exceeding sweetness and delight in the soul after their practice, whereas acts of vice leave her injured and enfeebled. Why, then, do we not seek to acquire such satisfaction?

—Francis de Sales, *The Devout Life*

The good God is pleased with little virtues which are practiced for love of him and he ennobles them in the measure that they are exercised with greater love. I must do everything, therefore, for the greater love of God.

—Marguerite Bourgeoys, *Autographic Writings*

All our thoughts, words and actions must have the fulfillment of his commandments as their fitting beginning and purpose.

—Marguerite Bourgeoys, *Autographic Writings*

If a person has true virtue, nothing whatever can change him; he is like a rock in the midst of a tempestuous sea. If anyone scorns you, or calumniates you, if someone mocks you or calls you a hypocrite or a sanctimonious fraud, none of this will have the least effect upon the peace of your soul. You will love him just as much as you loved him when he was saying good things about you. You will not fail to do him a good turn and to help him, even if he speaks badly of your assistance.

—John Baptiste Marie Vianney, *sermon*

It is true that we shall never have the happiness of going to heaven unless we do good works, but let us not be afraid of that, my dear children. What Jesus Christ demands of us are not the extraordinary things or those beyond our powers.

—John Baptiste Marie Vianney, *sermon*

We must practice the little virtues. This is difficult sometimes, but the good God never refuses the first grace, which gives courage to conquer self: if the soul corresponds to it she will find that she immediately receives light. I have ever been struck with those words of praise to Judith: "*Thou hast done manfully, and thy heart has been strengthened.*" (Judith 15:11) We must first act with courage, then the heart is strengthened and we go from victory to victory.

—Thérèse of Lisieux, *Counsels and Reminisces*

It is plain, therefore, that dignity without wisdom is useless and that wisdom without virtue is accursed. But when one possesses virtue, then wisdom and dignity are not dangerous but blessed.

—Bernard of Clairvaux, *On Loving God*

Moderation is a condition characterizing all virtue.

—Thomas Aquinas, *Summa Theologica*

Virtues make men and their actions good.

—Thomas Aquinas, *Summa Theologica*

Virtues are dispositions to act well.

—Thomas Aquinas, *Summa Theologica*

The holy virtues are like the ladder of Jacob and the unholy vices are like the chains that fell off the chief apostle Peter. The virtues lead one from another and carry heavenward the man who chooses them. Vices on the other hand beget and stifle one another.

—John Climacus, *The Ladder of Divine Ascent*

You know that the principal virtues are humility, self-effacement, and a holy simplicity that does away with all kinds of vanity, self-seeking, and self-satisfaction. If you put these virtues into practice, it will become apparent in all that you say, do, and write.

—Jane Frances de Chantal, *letter to a Visitandine*

The virtues are all equal and together reduce themselves to one, thus constituting a single principle and form of virtue. But some virtues—such as divine love, humility and divine patience—are greater than others, embracing and comprising as they do a large number or even all of the rest.

—Gregory of Sinai, *The Philokalia*

No one can learn the art of virtue himself, though some have taken experience as their teacher. For to act on one's own and not on the advice of those who have gone before us is overweening presumption—or, rather, it engenders such presumption.

—Gregory of Sinai, *The Philokalia*

War

If a war is to be just three things are needed. It must be waged by the due authorities, for those who may lawfully use the sword to defend the commonwealth against criminals disturbing it from within may also use the sword of war to protect it from enemies without. But the cause must be just (those whom we attack must have done some wrong which deserves attack), and those waging war must intend to promote good and avoid evil.

—Thomas Aquinas, *Summa Theologica*

War is the ruin of civilization and the return to barbarism. Even if the need to resist violence with force, the defense of security or of essential liberty, makes it seem inevitable, war must always be the last resource.

—Pope John XXIII, *letter to French President Vincent Auriol, Dec. 30, 1950*

Peace is the end sought for by war. For every man seeks peace by waging war, but no man seeks war by waging peace. For even they who intentionally interrupt the peace in which they are living have no hatred of peace, but only wish to change it into a peace which suits them better. They do not, therefore, wish to have no peace, but only one more to their mind.

—Augustine, *The City of God*

Better, I say, is war with the hope of peace everlasting than captivity without any thought of deliverance.

—Augustine, *The City of God*

For David had also put on armor beforehand but, since he was so heavy and awkward in it that he could hardly walk, he removed it at once, signifying that the weapons of this world are vain and superfluous things and that the person who chooses to involve himself in them will have no unimpeded road to heaven, since he will be too heavy and encumbered to walk. At the same time this teaches us that victory is not to be hoped for from arms alone but is to be prayed for in the name of the Savior.

—Maximus of Turin, *sermon*

For although the enemy's weapons may be powerful, nonetheless these weapons of the Savior are stronger. If anyone is armed with them, even though he appear defenseless in the eyes of human beings, he is nonetheless adequately armed because the most high Divinity is guarding him.

—Maximus of Turin, *sermon*

The one who prepares a defense for a city in the name of the Lord is the one who truly makes its citizens secure.

—Maximus of Turin, *sermon*

Peace is the fruit of having conquered war, and the life of man upon this earth—as we read in Sacred Scripture—is a warfare.

—Josemaría Escrivá, *The Forge*

Wealth

see MONEY AND WEALTH

Wickedness

see EVIL

Widowhood

For in a certain manner the inculcation of virginity is strengthened by the example of widows. They who have preserved their marriage bed undefiled are a testimony to virgins that chastity is to be preserved for God.

—Ambrose, *Concerning Widowhood*

Not that old age alone makes the widow, but that the merits of the widow are the duties of old age. For she certainly is the more noble who represses the heat of youth, and the impetuous ardor of youthful age, desiring neither the tenderness of a husband, nor the abundant delights of children, rather than one who, now worn out in body, cold in age, of ripe years, can neither grow warm with pleasures nor hope for offspring.

—Ambrose, *Concerning Widowhood*

For a virgin, though in her also character rather than the body has the first claim, puts away calumny by the integrity of her body, a widow who has lost the assistance of being able to prove her virginity undergoes the inquiry as to her chastity not according to the word of a midwife, but according to her manner of life.

—Ambrose, *Concerning Widowhood*

Let a widow, then, be temperate, pure in the first place from wine, that she may be pure from adultery. He will tempt you in vain, if wine tempts you not.

—Ambrose, *Concerning Widowhood*

Widowhood is, then, good, which is so often praised by the judgment of the apostles, for it is a teacher of the faith and a teacher of chastity.

—Ambrose, *Concerning Widowhood*

It is said that the turtledove, once separated from her mate, does not contract a new union, but remains in widowhood, in remembrance of her first alliance. Listen, O women! What veneration for widowhood, even in these creatures devoid of reason, how they prefer it to an unbecoming multiplicity of marriages.

—Basil the Great, *homily on the Hexaemeron*

Those who are in widowhood should have a courageous chastity, which cannot only despise present and future objects, but can resist the imaginations which may be produced in their minds by the past delights of marriage, which render them all the more liable to the wiles of impurity.

—Francis de Sales, *The Devout Life*

Will

The ardent desire to be in eternal peace is good and holy. But it is necessary to moderate it by a complete resignation to the divine will. It is better to do the divine will on earth than to enjoy heaven.

—Padre Pio, *Counsels*

The demon has only one door by which to enter into our soul: the will; there are no secret doors. No sin is a sin if not committed with the will. When there is no action of the will, there is no sin, but only human weakness.

—Padre Pio, *Spiritual Maxims*

Each man is a law unto himself, when he sets up his will against the universal law, perversely striving to rival his Creator, to be wholly independent, making his will his only law. What a heavy and burdensome yoke upon all the sons of Adam, bowing down our necks, so that life draweth nigh unto hell.

—Bernard of Clairvaux, *On Loving God*

The eternal law of righteousness ordains that he who will not submit to God's sweet rule shall suffer the bitter tyranny of self: but he who wears the easy yoke and light burden of love will escape the intolerable weight of his own self-will.

—Bernard of Clairvaux, *On Loving God*

The will lies between reason and our emotional capacity, and can be set in motion by either. In self-disciplined men it is controlled by reason, in men without discipline by desire.

—Thomas Aquinas, *Summa Theologica*

To have a good will man must have as his ultimate goal the ultimate good that God wills.

—Thomas Aquinas, *Summa Theologica*

The will cannot always stop desire arising, but it can always refuse to consent to it.

—Thomas Aquinas, *Summa Theologica*

God has power to move the human will, but not by force; for then there would be no willing involved and the movement would not be in the will but against it.

—Thomas Aquinas, *Summa Theologica*

Willing and choosing are actions of the same power: the ability to will and the ability to choose are one and the same ability.

—Thomas Aquinas, *Summa Theologica*

To give one's will to God is to give all.

—Thomas Aquinas, *On the Perfection of the Spiritual Life*

So when whatever the will wants is accomplished, the effect of the will is conformed to the will. And thus, our will conforms to the divine will whenever we will what God wants us to will.

—Thomas Aquinas, *On Truth*

Everyone is obliged to conform his will to God's.

—Thomas Aquinas, *On Truth*

If you are faithful to do the Will of God in time, yours shall be accomplished throughout eternity.

—Margaret Mary Alacoque, *Life and Writings of St. Margaret Mary*

No one can resist the Will of God, which will always be accomplished whether we will or no.

—Margaret Mary Alacoque, *Life and Writings of St. Margaret Mary*

It is only necessary to say energetically "I will" and all will go well.

—Margaret Mary Alacoque, *Life and Writings of St. Margaret Mary*

Give up your own will and submit your judgment whenever you have the opportunity of so doing, for I think that this is very pleasing to God.

—Margaret Mary Alacoque, *Life and Writings of St. Margaret Mary*

You know that it is not the noise we make in our lives, or the things we see, that count, but the love with which we do the will of God.

—Pope John XXIII, *Daily Papal Messages*

Let us be resigned to the divine will, and we shall thus render our crosses light, and shall gain great treasures of merits for eternal life.

—Alphonsus Liguori, *sermon*

He that gives his will to God, gives him all he has.

—Alphonsus Liguori, *sermon*

What happens will be what God desires. We are in the power of God, not in our own power.

—Perpetua, *The Passion of Saints Perpetua and Felicity*

All God wants is our heart. God is more pleased when we value our uselessness and weakness out of love and reverence for the Lord's will than when we do violence to ourselves and perform great works of penance.

—Jane Frances de Chantal, *letter to a priest, 1634*

May the most just, the most high, the most amiable will of God ever be loved, adored and accomplished.

—Elizabeth Seton, *Collected Writings*

"Thy will be done!"—What a comfort and support those four little words are to my soul. I have repeated them until they softened to the sweetest harmony.

—Elizabeth Seton, *Collected Writings*

The soul awaits Thy will in certain hope, pressing forward to eternity, reaching out for the things ahead, looking steadfastly upward. How sure, how real, its happiness; resigned in affliction, it finds no bitterness in sorrow unmixed with sin. Keep me only from such sorrow, dearest Lord, and for every other be glory to Thee forever.

—Elizabeth Seton, *conversion journal*

I am nourished by Your will, O Mighty One! Your will is the goal of my existence.

—Faustina Kowalska, *Divine Mercy in My Soul*

To receive God's light and recognize what God wants of us and yet not do it is a great offense against the majesty of God. Such a soul deserves to be completely forsaken by God. It resembles Lucifer, who had great light, but did not do God's will.

—Faustina Kowalska, *Divine Mercy in My Soul*

Let the will of the Lord be thy only delight and joy. Let neither thy desires draw thee on, nor thy fears dishearten thee.

—Mary of Agreda, *The Mystical City of God*

So great is the impetus of the river of God's goodness overflowing on mankind, that only the free will of man, which He has given to him in order to receive its benefits, can raise a dam against it; and whenever, through this free will, man resists the influence and force of the divine Goodness, he (according to thy mode of understanding), violates and grieves this immense love to its very essence. But if creatures would place no obstacle and permit its operations, the whole soul would be inundated and satiated with participation in its divine essence and attributes.

—Mary of Agreda, *The Mystical City of God*

The freedom of the divine will is extremely strong and in no wise can fail or be inclined toward evil.

—Robert Bellarmine, *The Mind's Ascent to God by the Ladder of Created Things*

Only God's will is capable of the infinite love.

—Robert Bellarmine, *The Mind's Ascent to God by the Ladder of Created Things*

Nothing happens to us except by God's will and permission—death or life, sickness or health, riches or poverty, even the wrongs done us by friends or relatives or anyone else. Not a leaf falls from a tree without his consent.

—Catherine of Siena, *letter to a senator's wife, c. 1374–75*

For neither the devil nor anyone else can force me to commit a single deadly sin against my will. We can never be overcome unless we give up this armor and turn it over to the devil by our willing consent.

—Catherine of Siena, *letter to a senator, c. 1375*

When we are stripped of our every wish and clothed in God's will, we are very pleasing to God. Like an untethered horse we run swiftly from grace to grace, from virtue to virtue. There is no tether to restrain us from running because we have cut ourselves loose from every disordered appetite and desire for our own will, which are the tethers and ties that keep the souls of spiritual persons from running free.

—Catherine of Siena, *letter to the Mantellate in Siena, c. 1375*

Whatsoever a man suffers contrary to his own will, he ought not to attribute to the will of men, or of angels, or of any created spirit, but rather to His will who gives power to wills.

—Augustine, *The City of God*

It will happen when God wills.

—Augustine, *The City of God*

Do not be conformed to this world but be transformed by the renewal of your mind, that you may prove what is the will of God, what is good and acceptable and perfect.

—Paul, *Romans 12:2*

A sure way for a Christian to grow rapidly in holiness is a conscientious effort to carry out God's will in all circumstances and at all times.

—Vincent de Paul, *Common Rules or Constitutions of the Congregation of the Mission*

For what man can know the designs of God, or can discover what is his will?

—Louis de Montfort, *The Love of Eternal Wisdom*

To do all things he has only to will them.

—Louis de Montfort, *Treatise on True Devotion to the Blessed Virgin*

For it is unworthy of God, either that He should not will what is good, or that He should be unable to do it.

—Gregory of Nyssa, *The Great Catechism*

For He who made man for the participation of His own peculiar good, and incorporated in him the instincts for all that was excellent, in order that his desire might be carried forward by a corresponding movement in each case to its like, would never have deprived him of that most excellent and precious of all goods; I mean the gift implied in being his own master, and having a free will.

—Gregory of Nyssa, *The Great Catechism*

Moses showed that by free will, human nature rushes towards evil and returns to the good so that God's splendor may once more illumine our human existence.

—Gregory of Nyssa, *Commentary on the Inscriptions of the Psalms*

The soul's exalted and royal nature is shown to be far removed from submissiveness by the fact that it is free and independent and acknowledges no master; it has been provided with its own unchallenged power of choice.

—Gregory of Nyssa, *The Creation of Man*

I will never complain, but resign myself to God's will, for He arranges everything for my good, even making use of poverty, humiliations and the contempt of others for this end.

—Anthony Mary Claret, *autobiography*

Thou seest my heart: I wish to labor not according to my own ideas, but according to Thy will. Deign to make known to me what Thou wishest of me, and how and where Thou wishest.

—Joseph Cafasso, *saying*

God exalts those who carry out his will in the very things in which he humbled them.

—Josemaría Escrivá, *The Way*

Because as God wills everything that happens to us, and as we will all that God wills, nothing can happen except what we will. Nobody can oblige me to do what I do not want to do because I desire to do all that God wishes.

—Claude de la Colombière, *sermon*

How can we have a single moment of repose if we do our own will? How can we live, even if all we do be holy, if we do not know if what we do be pleasing to God?

—Claude de la Colombière, *letter*

We are free and the masters of our fate. Just because we can grow evil from lack of efforts or virtuous by striving, he [God] uses the medicine of the fear of punishment to correct our course and the attraction of the hope of heaven to steer us toward wisdom.

—John Chrysostom, *homily on divine love*

It is always of greater value by far to do what we are made to do (I mean, of course, only in that which is not contrary to God and does not offend him) than to do what we choose to do ourselves.

—Francis de Sales, *Oeuvres*

It is worth knowing, then, that the appetite is the mouth of the will. It is opened wide when it is not encumbered or occupied with any mouthful of pleasure. When the appetite is centered on something, it becomes narrowed by this very fact, since outside of God everything is narrow. That the soul have its success in journeying to God and being joined to him, it must have the mouth of its will opened only to God himself, empty and dispossessed of every morsel of appetite, so God may fill it with his love and sweetness; and it must remain with this hunger and thirst for God alone, without desiring to be satisfied by any other thing, since here below it cannot enjoy God as he is in himself. And what is enjoyable—if there is a desire for it, as I say—impedes this union.

—John of the Cross, *letter*

Since the things of the world cannot enter the soul, they are not in themselves an encumbrance or harm to it; rather, it is the will and appetite dwelling within that cause the damage when set on these things.

—John of the Cross, *The Ascent of Mount Carmel*

Clearly, for a soul to reach union with God through its will and love, it must first be freed from every appetite, however slight. That is, one must not give consent of the will inadvertently and knowingly to an imperfection, and one must have the power and freedom to be able, upon advertence, to refuse this consent.

—John of the Cross, *The Ascent of Mount Carmel*

The strength of the soul comprises the faculties, passions, and appetites. All this strength is ruled by the will. When the will directs these faculties, passions and appetites toward God, turning away from all that is not God, the soul preserves its strength for God, and comes to love him with all its might.

—John of the Cross, *The Ascent of Mount Carmel*

Avoid an excessive desire to change your surroundings or the attitudes either of the brothers or of the fathers in your own regard, because anything that does not depend on your will is surely something permitted by God and it is he—not the others—who wishes that you should experience this.

—Maximilian M. Kolbe, *letter to friars in Japan, 1941*

Every day and every moment the help and grace of God are very necessary to the will.

—John Cassian, *Conferences*

Whoever has free will in his own hands ought to fear and truly understand that nothing so easily leads to eternal punishment as one's own will without a leader.

—Bridget of Sweden, *Book of Questions*

For the person eats of the tree of knowledge of good who appropriates to himself his own will and thus exalts himself over the good things which the Lord says and does in him; and thus, through the suggestion of the devil and the transgression of the command, what he eats becomes for him the fruit of the knowledge of evil.

—Francis of Assisi, *saying*

The will must be fully occupied in loving, but does not understand how it loves. If it understands, it does not understand how it understands, or at least, cannot comprehend anything of what it understands. I do not think that it understands at all, because, as I have said, it does not understand itself. Nor can I myself understand this.

—Teresa of Ávila, *Life*

Actually the soul and the will make better food for people than even bread is. But food eventually stops working in people. The work of the will, however, continues to work in person right up to the time that the person dies and the soul is separated from the body.

—Hildegard of Bingen, *Scivias*

Every praiseworthy or blameworthy act derives its good or bad qualities solely from the will. For from the will comes the root and source of those acts that lie within our power; and even if we cannot fulfill our aim, yet each one will be judged before God according to his intention. So do not look so much at your deeds as at your intention. Every act performed with a right, that is an upright, intention is good; and one performed with an evil intention is not good.

—Anselm, *letter, c. 1095*

In heaven the good God will do all I wish, because I have never done my own will upon earth.

—Thérèse of Liseux, *Counsels and Reminisces*

Wisdom

Propriety is fitting for a life dedicated to the cultivation of wisdom.

—Gregory of Nyssa, *letter*

Even a white head has to be taught, for old age, it seems to me, is no proof of wisdom.

—Gregory of Nazianzus, *letter to the Prefect of Olympios*

There are many sciences dealing with different areas of reality, but only one wisdom. Structurally wisdom is itself a science, drawing conclusions from premises; but what is peculiar to wisdom is its power to judge about everything, including its own premises. So it is a more perfect virtue than science.

—Thomas Aquinas, *Summa Theologica*

If any man is wise, let him show his wisdom by good deeds, not by words; and if he is modest, let him leave others to speak of his modesty, instead of proclaiming it himself.

—Clement of Rome, *first epistle to the Corinthians*

Wisdom is a kindly spirit, and easy of access to those who call upon him.

—Bernard of Clairvaux, sermon on the *Song of Songs*

Oh Word, your wisdom is like that bush you deigned to show to Moses; it burns but it doesn't burn out.

—Maria Maddalena de' Pazzi, *The Dialogues*

If we allow ourselves to become spiritual through our awe of God, we shall also begin to revere our God by ourselves. We shall go through life in wisdom and accomplish good and just works.

—Hildegard of Bingen, *Book of Divine Works*

The just embrace wisdom, and wisdom is in the midst of that form of reason that knows what is living and what is dead and thus learns the right path.

—Hildegard of Bingen, *Book of Divine Works*

Wisdom overcomes all evil deeds caused by the Devil's tricks and places them in chains.

—Hildegard of Bingen, *Book of Divine Works*

If you love wisdom, you must not listen on any question to what the law of the flesh dictates or what the senses judge good or what the world approves or your relatives urge, much less to what flatterers propose. Turn a deaf ear to all these and give your attention to the will of the Lord your God alone.

—Robert Bellarmine, *The Mind's Ascent to God by the Ladder of Created Things*

If you would be wise, recognize that you were created for God's glory and your own eternal salvation, that this is your end, this is the center of your soul, this the treasure of your heart. If you reach this end, you will be happy. If you fall short of it, you will be wretched.

—Robert Bellarmine, *The Mind's Ascent to God by the Ladder of Created Things*

By one unique intuition which always goes on in him and remains unchanged God knows perfectly himself and all other things. Therefore, only the wisdom of God ought to be called more noble and high.

—Robert Bellarmine, *The Mind's Ascent to God by the Ladder of Created Things*

The abundance of one's wisdom does not profit the soul toward eternal salvation unless the soul also shines with a good life. On the contrary, it is more useful to have less knowledge and a better life. Therefore, each person has been given a measure of rationality by means of which he can obtain heaven if he lives piously.

—Bridget of Sweden, *Book of Questions*

Wisdom of soul is a thing of such magnitude, being superior to everything, and to all auspicious and sorrowful events. For neither does it become puffed up by the former, nor cast down and humiliated by the latter, but retains its equilibrium through all events, demonstrating its peculiar strength and power.

—John Chrysostom, *homily*

In the general sense of the term wisdom means a delectable knowledge, a taste for God and his truth.

—Louis de Montfort, *The Love of Eternal Wisdom*

Wisdom is God himself—such is his glorious origin.

—Louis de Montfort, *The Love of Eternal Wisdom*

God himself has his Wisdom, the one and only true Wisdom which we should love and seek as a great treasure. The corrupt world also has its wisdom which must be condemned and detested, for it is evil and destructive. Philosophers also have their wisdom which must be spurned as useless for it can often endanger our salvation.

—Louis de Montfort, *The Love of Eternal Wisdom*

Wisdom gives man not only light to know the truth but also a remarkable power to impart it to others.

—Louis de Montfort, *The Love of Eternal Wisdom*

A blind unmeaning occurrence can never be the work of God; for if it is the property of God, as the Scripture says, to "make all things in wisdom."

—Gregory of Nyssa, *On Infants' Early Death*

Wisdom, when combined with justice, then absolutely becomes a virtue.

—Gregory of Nyssa, *The Great Catechism*

For fear and understanding are the poles of wisdom: fear makes [us] avoid evil and saves [us] from punishment, while understanding is conducive to the deifying ways of virtue.

—Theoleptos of Philadelphia, *letter*

Women

Woman naturally seeks to embrace that which is *living, personal, and whole.* To cherish, guard, protect, nourish and advance growth is her natural, maternal yearning.

—Edith Stein, *Essays on Woman*

The deepest longing of woman's heart is to give herself lovingly, to belong to another, and to possess this other being completely.

—Edith Stein, *Essays on Woman*

Woman can achieve perfect development of her personality only by activating her spiritual powers.

—Edith Stein, *Essays on Woman*

Words

Impure words fall on a weak heart like oil on cloth, spreading all around, and may fill it with evil thoughts and defile it. As bodily poison enters in by the mouth, so that of the heart enters by the ear, and the tongue that utters it is a murderer.

—Francis de Sales, *The Devout Life*

If unholy words are used secretly and with deliberate intention, they are infinitely more poisonous; for just as in proportion to its sharpness and point a dart enters easily into the body, so the more pointed a bad word, the further it penetrates the heart.

—Francis de Sales, *The Devout Life*

If any foolish person speaks to you in unbecoming language, show that your ears are offended, either by turning away from him, or by whatever means may be most discreet at the time.

—Francis de Sales, *The Devout Life*

A spirit of mockery is one of the worst imperfections of the mind, and displeases God greatly, so that he has often punished it most severely. Nothing is more hurtful to charity, and still more to devotion, than contempt and derision of our neighbor, and such is inevitably found in mockery.

—Francis de Sales, *The Devout Life*

Above all, you must be exceedingly exact in what you say; your tongue when you speak of your neighbor is as a knife in the hand of the surgeon who is going to cut between the nerves and tendons. Your stroke must be accurate, and neither deeper nor slighter than what is needed; and while you blame the sin, always spare the sinner as much as possible.

—Francis de Sales, *The Devout Life*

Nothing offends so much as cutting words spoken with contempt for those to whom we speak, particularly if they are spoken by persons of distinction and authority. We have seen men die of sorrow and grief because contemptuous words were spoken to them by their princes, even though they may have been said through the impulse or surprise of some passion.

—Francis de Sales, *Oeuvres*

To speak with a good intention is a merit; to speak uselessly or to a bad end is a sin.

—Ignatius of Loyola, *Spiritual Exercises*

Insult, derision, and words with suchlike tendency belong also to sins of the tongue.

—Ignatius of Loyola, *Spiritual Exercises*

Words are truly the images of the soul.

—Basil the Great, *letter*

The ideas of God, the words by means of which we desire to express the divine realities, are like a glass of water painted on a wall. It can faithfully represent the reality but it does not quench the thirst.

—Marcarius of Egypt, *homily*

God has given you the tongue, not to offend him, but to praise him.

—Alphonsus Liguori, *sermon*

For those who train themselves in the perfection of brotherly love should not speak as they please, letting the tongue follow the mind, since we shall all be called to account not just for harmful words but also for words that are idle. Therefore we should train ourselves not to speak too much, but to say only what is necessary.

—Columban, *sermon*

However wise we may be, we give less offense when we speak less than when we speak more, for when someone lies, curses, criticizes, then they cut their own throat with their sword.

—Columban, *sermon*

Wherefore the remedy against evil words—and not only against these, but against deeds, thoughts, and desires also—is to think beforehand about what we are about to do or speak or desire. And this is the character of men: not to do anything rashly, but to consider what is to be done, and if it agrees with sound reason, to do it; but if not, then not to do it.

—Robert Bellarmine, *The Art of Dying Well*

When the tongue is restrained by reason from uttering evil words, nothing can injure the sense of hearing.

—Robert Bellarmine, *The Art of Dying Well*

I want my tongue to praise God without cease. Great are the faults committed by the tongue. The soul will not attain sanctity if it does not keep watch over its tongue.

—Faustina Kowalska, *Divine Mercy in My Soul*

The tongue is a small member, but it does big things.

—Faustina Kowalska, *Divine Mercy in My Soul*

A talkative soul is empty inside.

—Faustina Kowalska, *Divine Mercy in My Soul*

Keeping silent when one ought to speak is an imperfection and sometimes a sin.

—Faustina Kowalska, *Divine Mercy in My Soul*

Dearly beloved, among all the vices which harass the life of man on earth, the Prophet bestows special castigation on insolence of the tongue. It is not unprofitable for him to do this. He was necessarily aware that sometimes poisons are concocted by the bitter zeal of the mouth, and hatreds stirred up by the excessive facility of the lips.

—Valerian, *homily*

The blow inflicted by the tongue is incurable. The tongue strikes lightly, but it always stirs up deep sighs in the chest through the sorrow it causes. . . . When the ears take in any injury, they transmit it instantly to the depths of the heart, and, if it has once entered there, it dos not come out unless by the exit of death.

—Valerian, *homily*

A wound arising from words is unbearable.

—Valerian, *homily*

The man who broods upon the words of a contentious adversary injures himself.

—Valerian, *homily*

The speech of the proud is accelerated and facile, full of scorn and packed with insults. It is never uttered without a wound, never hurled without pain. Its blow is incurable and its stain indelible.

—Valerian, *homily*

But the seed of the word readily germinates, when the loving-kindness of the preacher waters it in the hearer's breast.

—Gregory the Great, *The Book of Pastoral Rule*

The Deity cannot be expressed in words. And this is proved to us, not only by argument, but by the wisest and most ancient of the Hebrews, so far as they have given us reason for conjecture. For they appropriated certain characters to the honor of the Deity, and would not even allow the name of anything inferior to God to be written with the same letters as that of God, because to their minds it was improper that the Deity should even to that extent admit any of His creatures to a share with Himself.

—Gregory of Nazianzus, *theological oration*

Words should inspire action; otherwise, words are merely rhetoric camouflaging nothingness, concealing merely empty or illusory feelings and opinions.

—Edith Stein, *Essays on Woman*

Let us avoid being pompous or long-winded, or too hasty or too slow. Let us not talk for too long nor use too many words.

—Clement of Alexandria, *The Teacher*

Above all we should strive not to be ignorant of the way we use language. We should make sure that we are not aggressive in how we ask questions and give our replies without seeking to show off. We should not interrupt when someone has something useful to say, nor be eager to make an ostentatious contribution, but rather try to observe a due measure both in listening and in speaking.

—Basil the Great, *letter to Gregory of Nyssa*

Anyone who is going to speak in public should do so only after they have given careful consideration to what they are going to say.

—Basil the Great, *letter to Gregory of Nyssa*

Work

It is most important that you choose your career with care, so that you may really follow the vocation that God has destined for you. No day should pass without some prayer to this end. Often repeat with St. Paul: "Lord, what will you have me do?"

—John Bosco, *Companion of Youth*

To be perfect in our vocation is nothing else than to fulfill the duties which our state of life obliges us to perform, and to accomplish them well, and only for the honor and love of God.

—Francis de Sales, *Introduction to The Devout Life*

We must do it ungrudgingly and in the company of the most Blessed Virgin while she was doing the same work or some saint to whom we have devotion.

—Marguerite Bourgeoys, *Autographic Writings*

Oh, the torment of working without love! It is beyond belief. Love gives a sweet flavor to every viand. If it is bad it makes good, and if it is good it makes it better.

—Catherine of Genoa, *Life and Doctrine*

All work becomes supremely great when it is done in the spirit of our Lord.

—Pope John XXIII, *Daily Papal Messages*

Work, which is the immediate expression of a human personality, must always be rated higher than the possession of external good which of their very nature are merely instrumental.

—Pope John Paul XXIII, *Mater et Magistra*

Never undertake any work or any action without first raising your mind to God and directing to him with a pure intention the action you are about to perform.

—Padre Pio, *letter, 1914*

If you pray before you work, the passage into the soul will not be open to sin.

—Ephraem, *sermon*

Hell is full of desires, whereas Heaven is full of workers.

—Maria Maddalena de' Pazzi, *The Dialogues*

Three are the things that should compel us to work: God's honor, our salvation, and the condemnation and abhorrence of every lie.

—Maria Maddalena de' Pazzi, *The Dialogues*

God is gained either by activity and work, or by the art of invoking the Name of Jesus.

—Theophan the Recluse, *letter*

When we humans work in accord with the strivings of our soul, all our deeds turn out well. But our deeds turn out ill if we follow the flesh.

—Hildegard of Bingen, *Book of Divine Works*

Just as a bee forms honey in its comb, we do our work as if it were honey.

—Hildegard of Bingen, *Book of Divine Works*

I will not allow myself to be so absorbed in the whirlwind of work as to forget about God.

—Faustina Kowalska, *Divine Mercy in My Soul*

Eternal rest is incompatible with the shame of not having duly labored for its attainment.

—Mary of Agreda, *The Mystical City of God*

If you sow sparingly, you shall harvest poorly. But if you sow lavishly, you shall harvest in abundance.

—Henry Suso, *letter*

Our work, suffering and above all our prayer will produce abundant fruits.

—Maximilian M. Kolbe, *letter to friars in Japan, 1937*

Those who do not labor in good works in this world will labor in evil ones in hell.

—Vincent Ferrer, *sermon*

Let those who do not know how to work learn, not from desire to receive wages, but for example and to avoid idleness.

—Francis of Assisi, *The Testament*

Moreover, souls are called with child, when of divine love they conceive an understanding of the Word, so that, if they come to their full time, they may bring forth their conceived intelligence in the shewing forth of work.

—Gregory the Great, *The Book of Pastoral Rule*

For in truth he who does not strenuously execute the good things he has begun imitates in the slackness of his negligence the hand of the destroyer.

—Gregory the Great, *The Book of Pastoral Rule*

I am planted in Christ and am Christ's daily toil.

—Paulinus of Nola, *letter*

Don't put off your work until tomorrow.

—Josemaría Escrivá, *The Way*

We are under an obligation to work, and to work conscientiously, with a sense of responsibility, with love and perseverance, without any shirking or frivolity. Because work is a command from God, and God is to be obeyed, as the psalmist says, *in laetitia*, joyfully!

—Josemaría Escrivá, *The Forge*

If we really want to sanctify our work, we have inescapably to fulfill the first condition: that of working, and working well, with human and supernatural seriousness.

—Josemaría Escrivá, *The Forge*

A person's attitude toward his or her profession clearly helps determine the results achieved in it. Whoever regards his work as a mere source of income or as a pastime will perform differently from the person who feels that his profession is an authentic vocation.

—Edith Stein, *Essays on Woman*

There is no profession that cannot be practiced by a woman.

—Edith Stein, *Essays on Woman*

Exterior employment is no obstacle to solitude of heart when the mind is calm and leaves everything in God's hands.

—Claude de la Colombière, *letter*

Works

see DEEDS

World

You will finally discover that the world was not conceived by chance and without reason, but for a useful end and for the great advantage of all beings, since it is really the school where reasonable souls exercise themselves, the training ground where they learn to know God; since by the sight of visible and sensible things the mind is led, as by a hand, to the contemplation of invisible things.

—Basil the Great, *homily on the Hexaemeron*

Worry

When your heart has fallen raise it gently, humbling yourself greatly before God, and acknowledging your fault, but without marveling at your fall; since it is no marvel that infirmity should be infirm, weakness weak, and frailty frail. But nevertheless heartily detest the offense of which you have been guilty in God's sight, and with hearty courage and confidence in his mercy, begin once more to seek that virtue from which you have fallen away.

—Francis de Sales, *The Devout Life*

Do not undertake your affairs with disquietude, anxiety and worry, and do not hurry and excite yourself about them, for all excitement hinders reason and judgment, and prevents us from doing well that very thing about which we are excited.

—Francis de Sales, *The Devout Life*

When you feel disposed to worry, commend yourself to God, and resolve in no way to gratify your desire until your anxiety is entirely allayed: unless it concerns something that cannot be deferred, in which case you must gently and quietly restrain the course of your desire, softening and moderating it as much as possible, and above all, acting not in accordance with your inclination, but with reason.

—Francis de Sales, *The Devout Life*

If you can disclose your anxiety to the guide of your soul, or at least some pious and trustworthy friend, doubt not that you will be speedily relieved; for sympathy in the sufferings of the heart has the same effect upon the soul as bleeding upon the body of one laboring under grievous fever; it is the most effectual remedy.

—Francis de Sales, *The Devout Life*

Let your one worry be that you never fall away from his grace and that you try to please him alone, always and everywhere.

—Robert Bellarmine, *The Mind's Ascent to God by the Ladder of Created Things*

Worry? Never! For to do so is to lose one's peace.

—Josemaría Escrivá, *The Way*

Worthiness

And that we may be worthy to obtain what we long for, let us strive to live in such a way that we may not be unworthy of so great a Father.

—Bede the Venerable, *homily on the Gospels*

APPENDIX: THE SAINTS

Abbots Agatho, Allois, Anthony, Arsenius, Daniel, Hyperichius, John, John of Short Stature, Macarius, Mathois, Pastor, Pimenion, Poemon, Silvanus, Sisois, Syncletica Monks quoted in the *Sayings of the Desert Fathers*, a compilation of comments and writings on the virtues, as expressed and exemplified by early monastics. *Sayings* probably was compiled around the end of the fifth century.

Aelred of Rievaulx (d. c. 67) *Born in:* Hexham, England. Abbot.
As a child Aelred served as a page to King David. He entered the Cistercian monastery in Yorkshire, and became abbot of Rielvaux in 1146. He then was elevated to superior of all Cistercians in England. Aelred was involved with several monarchs during the course of his life. He wrote treatises, sermons and homilies and much later was called the "Bernard of England" for his eloquence. His best-known work is *The Mirror of Charity*, which sets forth his mystical theology. Other major works are *On the Soul* and *Spiritual Friendship*, in which he discusses his own relationships as well as the nature of love and friendship in general.

Albertus Magnus (c. 1206–1280) *Born in:* Swabia, Germany.
Doctor of the Church, theologian, bishop, and philosopher. Noble-born and well-educated, Albertus Magnus was attracted to the Dominicans in his teens, and became first a mendicant friar, and then a scholar and professor in Paris. His most famous pupil was St. THOMAS AQUINAS. Albertus set the standards for study at all Dominican universities. He initiated what Aquinas later perfected: Scholasticism, the application of Aristotelian methods and principles to the study of revealed doctrine, or the reconciliation of reason and orthodoxy. Albertus was a prodigious writer, thinker, and experimenter and was considered a leading authority on physics, geography, astronomy, mineralogy,

chemistry, and biology. He became an expert in alchemy. *Canonized:* 1931.

Aloysius Gonzaga (1568–1591) *Born in:* Lombardy, Italy.
Scholar and patron of youth. Noble-born Aloysius Gonzaga was sent to military school and then at age 11 to the court of the duke of Mantua. The excesses there repelled him, and he practiced austerities. He renounced his inheritance and entered the Jesuit order in 1585. Sickly himself from childhood, Aloysius devoted his life to caring for the sick. His confessor was St. ROBERT BELLARMINE. Pope Benedict XIII named him the patron of young students in 1729, and Pope Pius XI later designated him the patron of all Christian youth. *Canonized:* 1726.

Alphonsus Marie Liguori (1696–1787) *Born in:* Marianella near Naples, Italy.
Bishop, founder of the Redemptorist Congregation, moral theologian, mystic, and Doctor of the Church. A quick student, Alphonsus Marie Liguori was practicing law by age 19, and excelled as one of Naples's top lawyers by age 27. But the loss of a major case due to his own carelessness caused him to retire in humiliation. A visionary experience guided him to join the Fathers of the Oratory. In 1732 he helped to found a new order, the Congregation of the Most Holy Savior (Savior later was replaced by Redemptorist) and became its director and then superior general. Alphonsus endured years of political upheavals that affected the order, as well as poor health. In later years he turned to writing, completing 110 books and pamphlets, among them *Moral Theology* and *Victories of the Martyrs*. Many of his sermons survive. *Canonized:* 1839.

Ambrose (c. 339–397) *Born in:* Trier (Treves).
Bishop of Milan; Latin Father and Doctor of the Church. The son of the prefect of Gaul, Ambrose studied law, literature, philosophy, and Greek in Rome. He was appointed to various governmental posts in Milan and became bishop of the city in 374. He fought the Arian heresy. Among his works are his famous treatise, *De Fide ad Gratianum Augustum,* or "To Gratian Concerning the Faith," and numerous sermons, homilies, mystical writings, commentaries, hymns, and chants.

Ammonas the Hermit (d. c. 350) *Born in:* Egypt, probably in or near Alexandria.
At age 22 he was forced to marry, but convinced his wife to take a vow of chastity. The two of them set up religious communities for men and women in the desert of Nitria near Alexandria. The one for men had 5,000 hermits at its peak and was called "The City of God" by St. JEROME. Ammonas was widely revered for his sanctity and wisdom.

Anselm (c. 1033–1109) *Born in:* the Piedmont region of Italy.
Archbishop of Canterbury; Doctor of the Church. Noble-born Anselm was sent to a strict monastery school by age five. As a youth he traveled in France, and in 1060 was admitted to the Benedictine order at Bec Abbey. He later became prior and served for 15 years. In 1070 he became abbot and traveled to England. In 1093 Anselm was named archbishop of Canterbury. His most famous work is *Cur Deus Homo*, ("Why God Became Man"), in which he argued that Jesus' incarnation was to satisfy humankind's fall. Other well-known works are *Monologium* and

Proslogium. The latter presents an ontological argument of the existence of God by showing that the mere fact that even nonbelievers understand the uniqueness of God as a perfect being validates His presence. Anselm's arguments influenced great thinkers of his day, such as St. THOMAS AQUINAS (who disagreed) and later philosophers such as Hegel, Kant, and Descartes.

Anthony (251–356) *Born in:* Coma (or Koman), Egypt.
An early founder of monasticism. At age 20 Anthony inherited a large estate, and was inspired by hearing the Gospel to give it away and enter a life of solitude. He is known for the torments and temptations he endured during his time in the Libyan desert. He spent most of his life in isolation.

Anthony of Padua (1195–1231) *Born in:* Lisbon, Portugal.
Doctor of the Church in Evangelism. A popular preacher and teacher, Anthony of Padua was appointed by St. FRANCIS OF ASSISI as lector, or teacher, of theology to the Franciscans—the first member of the order to fill that position. He especially preached against heresy. *Canonized:* 1232.

Anthony Mary Claret (1807–1870) *Born in:* Sallent, Catalonia, northeast Spain.
Archbishop and founder of the Claretians. Anthony intended to be a weaver like his father, but instead decided on a religious life. The Jesuits refused him because of his health, so he became a secular priest in the diocese of Vich at age 28. He was assigned to Sallent. He became a missionary and traveled through Catalonia, the Canary Islands, and parts of Spain, working in the style of the apostles. In 1849 Anthony founded the Missionary Sons of the Immaculate Heart of Mary, which became known as the Claretians. He also was named archbishop of Santiago, Cuba, where he spent the next six years. In 1857 he returned to the court of Queen Isabella as her confessor. He endured political persecution and accompanied the queen into exile to France in 1868 for a year. He then participated in the first Vatican Council in 1869 and 1870, still enduring persecution. Anthony returned to France and died on October 24, 1870, in the Cistercian monastery of Fontfroide in southern France. He had preached 25,000 sermons, written 144 works, and performed many miracles. *Canonized:* 1950.

Arsenius (c. 355–c. 450) Roman deacon, confessor, monk, and hermit; sometimes called Arsenius the Great. Arsenius was appointed tutor to the children of the emperors Theodosius the Great, Arcadius, and Honorius in Constantinople on the recommendation of Pope St. Damascus, He held the position for about a decade and then left to live with monks in Alexandria. When Theodosius died, he retired to the wilderness of Skete, where he practiced great austeries and was tutored by St. John the Dwarf. He inherited a fortune from a rich relative but turned it away. Barbarians raids on Skete forced him out around 434, and he went to the rock of Troe in Memphis, Egypt, and then the island of Canopus, near Alexandria. He returned to Troe and died there.

Athanasius (d. 373) *Born in:* Alexandria, Egypt.
Bishop, Father of the Church, and Doctor of the Church. Born to Christian parents,

Athanasius was well educated, and in 315 went to the desert to study in retreat with St. ANTHONY. In 318 Athanasius was ordained a deacon and became archdeacon and secretary to Alexander, the archbishop. He succeeded Alexander in 326. Athanasius was a vigorous opponent of the Arian heresy. In 335 Arians had him deposed and exiled to Germany. Upon his return in 338, he was deposed again, then vindicated. But back in Alexandria in 345, he was attacked and vilified again. He retreated to the desert for six years to live as a hermit and write. He underwent two more returns and exiles, finally achieving restoration to his Alexandria see. He spent a total of 17 years in exile. Among his most important works are *Apology to Constantius; Apology for His Flight; Letter to the Monks;* and *History of the Arians,* written during his years as a hermit; *On the Incarnation of God*, written during his early years; and *Contra Gentes.*

Augustine (354–470) *Born in:* Tagaste, North Africa.
One of the greatest figures in the Christian Church, named both Western Father of the Church and Doctor of the Church, whose philosophical and theological thought influenced Christianity for at least 1,000 years. Augustine's early years were spent in sin, which he later chronicled in *Confessions.* He often is acknowledged to be second only to St. Paul in influence on Christianity. His writings established the theological foundation for medieval Christianity, and much later influenced the dualistic philosophy of René Descartes. His *The City of God* defends Christian doctrine against pagan thought.

Barsanouphios and John (c. sixth century) *Born in:* Egypt.
Barsanouphios became a monk in the community of Abba Serid near Gaza. He lived as a hermit in silence, communicating only by writing. He had mystical flights to the seventh heaven and was famous for his wisdom. Little is known about John. He lived in Barsanouphios's first cell, practicing silence for 18 years until his death. Both Barsanouphios and John had the gift of clairvoyance and made accurate predictions and prophecies.

Basil the Great (c. 329–379) *Born in:* Caesarea, Cappadocia (now Turkey).
One of the greatest Doctors of the Church; Father of the Church; Bishop of Caesarea. Basil the Great was born to a Christian family. His father, St. Basil the Elder, was a teacher, and his mother, Emmelia, became a martyr. His sister, Macrina, and brothers, GREGORY OF NYSSA and Peter of Sebaste, became saints. Basil, Gregory of Nyssa, and Basil's friend, St. GREGORY OF NAZIANZUS the Younger, became known as the "Three Cappadocians," of whom Basil earned the highest esteem. Basil received religious instruction in the tradition of St. GREGORY THAUMATURGUS from his grandmother, St. Macrina the Elder. He studied abroad and in 356 founded his own monastery. In 362 he was ordained, and in 370 he was named bishop of Caesarea. He was an excellent leader and statesman, and vigorously opposed the Arian heresy. Basil wrote important works on dogma, especially defending the Divinity of the Three Persons of the Trinity; commentaries on the Scriptures; treatises on morals and monastic rules; and sermons. Three hundred and sixty-six of his letters survive. He either composed a liturgy or reformed an existing one; several Eastern liturgies have been attributed to him.

Bede the Venerable (672 or 673–735) *Born in:* The area of Wearmouth-Jarrow, Northumberland, England.
Doctor of the Church and historian. At age seven, Bede was taken by his relatives to the monastery of Sts. Peter and Paul, where he spent the rest of his life. He studied under St. Benedict Biscop. He was ordained deacon at age 19 and priest at age 30. Bede's life was peaceful, spent studying and writing. His most important work, *Ecclesiastical History of the English People*, completed in 729, has remained one of the most authoritative sources of that time period. Bede also wrote chronological treatises, biographies, a description of Jerusalem and other holy places, a martyrology, works on science, numerous commentaries on books of the Bible, verse, and chant music. He is credited with initiating the custom of marking dates from the Incarnation with the term *anno domini*, or A.D. Bede was declared a Doctor of the Church in 1899.

Benedict (c. 480–c. 547) *Born in:* Nursia, Sabine.
Father of Western monasticism and founder of the Benedictines, the oldest Christian religious order in the West, which greatly influenced the spread of civilization in the Middle Ages. The only source for documenting Benedict's life is *The Dialogues* by Pope St. GREGORY THE GREAT. Benedict composed the *Regula Monachorum*, called the Rule (also Benedict's Rule or the Benedictine Rule), a monastic rule that became the standard for monastic living throughout the Western world. The Benedictine Rule is still one of the most important documents of Christian religious practice, and has been interpreted for, and applied to, the lay life as well as to the monastic life.

Bernadine of Siena (1380–1444) *Born in:* Siena, Italy.
Franciscan missionary and preacher called "the second Paul." A charismastic figure, Bernadine traveled extensively throughout central and northern Italy on foot, preaching against immorality for hours at a time, several times a day. He also stressed punishment for sin, reward for virtue, the mercy of Jesus, and the love of Mary. His special devotion was to the Holy Name of Jesus. He became the foremost missionary in Italy, and also healed people, especially lepers.

Bernard of Clairvaux (1090–1153) *Born in:* Fontaines, France.
Cistercian abbot and Doctor of the Church, famous for the spiritual sweetness of his teachings. Bernard's many works on ascetical theology were inspired by his interior life of deep contemplation and prayer. He was renowned as a superb speaker and writer. Among Bernard's works on ascetical theology are *De Gratia et Libero Arbitrio* ("On Grace and Free Will") and *De Gradibus Humilitatus et Superbiae* ("On the Steps of Humility and Pride"), *De Dilgendo Deo* ("On Loving God"), *De Consideratione* ("On Meditation"), written for his pupil who became Pope Eugene III, and *Sermones super Cantica Canticorum* ("Sermons on the Song of Songs"). In addition, he composed more than 300 sermons and 500 letters, which demonstrate his deep devotion to Mary and the infant Jesus. *Canonized:* 1174.

Bonaventure (1221–1274) *Born in:* Bagnorea, Italy.
Cardinal-Bishop, Minister General of the Friars Minor, Doctor of the Church. Bonaventure is considered one of the great theologians of the Church along with his contemporary, St. THOMAS AQUINAS. He wrote extensively on theology and philosophy; some of his works are mystical in nature. He joined the Order of Friars Minor and became their minister general in 1257. In 1264 he took over direction of the Poor Clares and founded the Society of the Gonfalone in honor of the Blessed Virgin Mary. Pope Gregory X named him cardinal-bishop of Albano in 1273. Bonaventure's greatest work is *Commentary on the Sentences*, a sweeping treatment of the entire of Scholastic theology, which is summarized in another of his works, *Brevoliquium*. Like Aquinas, he defended Aristotle. His most exemplary mystical work is *De Triplici Via*, which explores perfection. In addition, he wrote numerous treatises and exegeses. Nearly 500 of his sermons have survived. *Canonized:* 1482.

Bridget of Sweden (1303–1373) *Born in:* Upland, Sweden.
Wife, mystic, and founder of the Brigittines monastic order; patron of Sweden. Bridget became known for her prophetic dreams and visions, many of them concerning politics and affairs of state. At the time, the church was in upheaval; the pope resided in Avignon, not Rome. From her visions, Bridget believed herself charged with a mission to restore the papacy to Rome and reform what she considered to be lax morals in the church. She followed the guidance of her visions, traveling to Rome, undertaking pilgrimages, and offering outspoken opinions. *Canonized:* 1391.

Brother André, Bl. (1845–1937) *Born in:* Montreal, Canada.
Brother of the Holy Cross Brothers, renowned healer and founder of St. Joseph's Oratory on Mount Royal, Montreal. Sickly and uneducated, Brother André spent his life as a doorkeeper at Notre Dame College, Mount Royal. He belonged to the Congregation of the Holy Cross, a religious order dedicated to the teaching profession. Brother André gained recognition as a miracle healer. *Beatified:* 1987.

Catherine dei Ricci (1522–1590) *Born in:* Florence, Italy.
Dominican mystic and stigmatist. Of wealthy birth, she entered the Dominican Convent of San Vicenzo in Prato, Tuscany, at age 14. Her reputation for sanctity and prudence, severe austeries and mortifications, as well as her astonishing mystical life, attracted visits by numerous bishops, cardinals, and princes, among them three future popes: Clement VIII, Marcellus II, and Leo XI . Catherine corresponded with St. Charles Borromeo and Pope Pius V and had mystical visits with SS. PHILIP NERI and MARIA MADDALENA DE' PAZZI. Catherine experienced many visions, raptures, and stigmata. She also experienced a mystical marriage with Christ. In 1542 she began to experience weekly, 28-hour-long ecstasies in which she relived the Passion, including stigmata. These ecstasies went on for 12 years. *Canonized:* 1746.

Catherine of Genoa (1447–1510) *Born in:* Genoa, Italy.

Extraordinary mystic. At age 16 Catherine was married against her will to an abusive man. Around 1473 she had a life-changing mystical experience during confession, in which she felt herself pierced by a burning ray of divine love that swept her into an ecstasy. She felt united with God and purged of her miseries. She experienced visions for the rest of her life. She withdrew as much as possible from the world, but volunteered to help the worst of the poor and sick. She is especially known for two respected mystical works, *Spiritual Dialogue Between the Soul, the Body, Self-Love, the Spirit, Humanity and the Lord God* and *Treatise on Purgatory*.

Catherine of Siena (1347–1380) *Born in:* Siena, Italy.
Doctor of the Church and second woman to be so named; one of the Church's greatest mystics; Dominican tertiary; and papal adviser. Catherine experienced religious visions from an early age. In 1370 she went into a prolonged trance, a kind of mystical death, in which she had a vision of hell, purgatory, and heaven, and heard a divine command to leave her cell and enter the public life of the world. From this trance, she produced her great mystical work, *The Dialogue of the Seraphic Virgin Catherine of Siena*. She advised heads of state, nobility, and the papacy, and helped to reconcile Pope Urban VI to Rome in the Great Schism. In 1375 she received the stigmata while praying. *Canonized:* 1461.

Clare of Assisi (1194–1253) *Born in:* Assisi, Italy.
Founder of the Franciscan Poor Clares. In 1212 Clare heard Francis of Assisi preach, and was inspired to imitate him. She ran away from home. Francis gave her a Franciscan habit, and she entered a Benedictine convent. Later she was joined by her sister, Agnes, and mother, Beatrice. Clare became the superior of the Poor Clares, who lived under a rule of absolute poverty. Clare established other convents in Europe. She was sought for her wisdom by high-ranking clergy and secular officials. *Canonized:* 1255.

Claude de la Colombière, Bl. (1641-1682) *Born in:* Saint-Symphorizen d'Orzen, near Lyons, France.
Jesuit preacher. Claude joined the Jesuits in 1659 and quickly became famous as a preacher. In 1675 he was named superior of Paray-le-Monial College. A year later he was sent to England to serve as chaplain to the duchess of York. He was falsely accused of participating in a plot to assassinate King Charles II, was imprisoned, and then banished. His health was permanently ruined, and he died shortly after returning to Paray-le-Monial. Claude was one of the main supporters and confessor of St. MARGARET MARY ALOCOQUE and her Sacred Heart devotion. Numerous of his letters, retreat notes and sermons survive. *Beatified:* 1929.

Clement of Alexandria (d. c. 215) *Born in:* probably Athens. Greek theologian and Father of the Church. Clement of Alexandria was converted and traveled about in search of religious instruction. He settled in Alexandria and studied under Pantaenus, head of the catechetical school of Alexandria. He succeeded Pantaenus in about 190. In 202, he left Alexandria because of Christian persecutions and went to Caesarea in Cappadocia (now part of Turkey), where he met his friend and former pupil, Bishop Alexander, who was converting people from prison. He was succeeded in Alexandria by Origen. Clement probably died in Cappadocia. He left a large body of writings. Some of his doctrines were found to be erroneous or suspect. Nonetheless, his name was entered in the martyrologies, and he was venerated as a saint into the 17th century, when Pope Clement VIII dropped him from the list. Clement's works have found new favor in modern times.

Clement of Rome (1st–2nd centuries.) Fourth bishop of Rome, Clement was credited with writing an important epistle addressing unrest in the Church of Corinth. He is called one of the "Apostolic Fathers."

Columban (c. 543–615) *Born in:* Leinster, Ireland.
Irish abbot in France. Noble by birth, Columban (also Columbanus) decided at a young age to become a religious, and studied with St. Comgall. He was ordained in 590. He took a band of followers to England and France. In France they established monasteries, but were exiled after Columban criticized the king of Burgundy for keeping mistresses. In his travels, Columban evangelized elsewhere in France, and in parts of Germany and Switzerland.

Cyprian of Carthage (c. 200–258) *Born in:* Carthage.
Bishop of Carthage; Father of the Church; martyr. Cyprian was a wealthy man who converted to Christianity and was baptized around 246. He sold his property, including his gardens at Carthage, and gave most of his revenues to the poor. He was elected Bishop of Carthage in 248 or 249. He was martyred during the persecutions of Emperor Valerian.

Cyril of Jerusalem (c. 315–c. 386) *Born in:* Jerusalem.
Bishop of Jerusalem, Father of the Church and Doctor of the Church. Cyril probably was raised a Christian. He became a priest around 345–47, and was ordained by St. MAXIMUS OF TURIN. Cyril became the bishop or patriarch or Jerusalem, succeeding Maximus after the latter died. He dealt with the Arian heresy, and three times was exiled as a result of the politics. He attended the Council of Constantinople in 381 with St. GREGORY OF NYSSA. Of Cyril's valued body of work, the most famous is his theological masterpiece, *Catecheses*, a collection of 18 instructional addresses for baptismal candidates during Lent and five—known as the *Mystagogi* —for the recently baptized at Easter. He composed numerous catechetical lectures and sermons.

Edith Stein (1891-1942) *Born in:* Breslau, Germany (now Wroclaw, Poland).
Martyr. Edith was born to a Jewish family, but lost interest in Judaism as a teenager. She entered the University of Breslau in 1911, where she was drawn to philosophy, women's issues, and suffrage. She graduated from the University of Göttingen 1915. During World War I she worked as a field nurse, earning a medal of valor. She obtained her doctorate in philosophy in 1917, summa cum laude, at the University of Freiburg. Drawn to Catholicism, she was baptized in 1922. She worked as a teacher, and then in 1933 joined the Discalced Carmelite cloister in Cologne, taking the name Teresa Benedicta of the Cross. In 1942 she and her sister Rosa, also a

convert to Christianity, were arrested by the Nazis and sent to Auschwitz, where they died in a gas chamber. She wrote several philosophical books of importance, most notably *Finite and Being*, and was a champion of women's rights. *Canonized:* 1998.

Elisabeth of Schönau (1129–1165) *Born in:* Schönau, Germany.
Benedictine abbess and mystic. Born to a well-to-do family, Elizabeth became a Benedictine nun at age 12 and was mentored by St. HILDEGARD OF BINGEN. Her visionary life began in 1152 during a deep depression. Throughout her life she had numerous visions, ecstasies, trances, and diabolical visitations. She made prophecies. Her visionary experiences were recorded and translated by her brother and secretary, Ekbert. Her *First, Second* and *Third Book of Visions* chronicle her early visionary and prophetic life. *The Book of the Ways of God* comprises 10 sermons based on a vision of a mountain with 10 paths leading to the summit. *The Resurrection of the Blessed Virgin* is her vision of the death and assumption of Mary, and *The Book of Revelations About the Sacred Company of the Virgins of Cologne* is about the martyrdom of St. Ursula, and Elizabeth's conversations with the martyred virgins. Some of her letters also survive. Despite her importance as one of the medieval Rhineland mystics, Elisabeth's cult was never formalized. However, she is included in the Roman Martyrology.

Elizabeth Seton (1774–1821) *Born in:* New York City.
Founder of the Daughters of Charity of St. Joseph and the American parochial school system; first native-born American saint. In 1794 Elizabeth married William Magee Seton, a first-generation American and heir to a wealthy shipping firm. They had five children. Elizabeth became a philanthropist with her sister Rebecca and helped found the Society for the Relief of Poor Widows with Small Children. After the Napoleonic Wars, the shipping business failed and William died. Elizabeth converted to Catholicism and founded her new order in Emmitsburg, Maryland, in 1812. The order established free schools, orphanages, and hospitals in addition to the parochial schools. The Daughters of Charity were incorporated into the full Sisters of Charity of St. Vincent de Paul in 1850. *Canonized:* 1975.

Ephraem (c. 306–373) *Born in:* Nisibis, Mesopotamia (now in Turkey).
Doctor of the Church. Ephraem's father was a pagan priest, but Ephraem was raised in the Christian mysteries by St. James, bishop of Nisibis, and was baptized either at age 18 or 28. After attending the Council of Nicea in 325, he helped James give religious instruction in Nisibis. When the Romans lost the city to the Persians in 363, Ephraem joined the fleeing Christians and became a hermit in Edessa, where he spent the last 10 years of his life. A prolific writer, he composed commentaries on the Scriptures, most of which have been lost or survive in fragments. He wrote sermons and exhortations, mostly in verse, and composed hymns. He is credited with introducing hymns to the public.

Faustina Kowalska (1905–1938) *Born in:* Glogowiec, Poland.
Nun and mystic; originator of the Divine Mercy movement. Faustina decided on the

religious life by age seven. She was 20, and working as a housemaid, when she had her first vision, of Jesus in his Passion. He ordered her to join a convent. She joined the Congregation of the Sisters of Our Lady of Mercy in Warsaw. She was especially devoted to Mary Immaculate and the Eucharist. She had frequent visions and stigmata, which she recorded in a diary, eventually published as *Divine Mercy in My Soul.* Jesus instructed her to spread a message of Divine Mercy throughout the world and to live her entire life in imitation of Jesus' as a sacrifice. According to his instruction, Faustina commissioned a now-famous painting of Jesus with red and white rays of light emanating from his Sacret Heart, with the inscription, "Jesus, I Trust in You." *Canonized:* 2000.

Francis of Assisi (1181?–1226) *Born in:* Assisi, Italy.
Often called the most Christ-like of all the saints, Francis of Assisi is known for his love of animals, and for his stigmata, said to be given to him by an angel. He is considered to be the founder of all Franciscan orders. As a wealthy youth, he was dissolute. He joined the Crusades, but illness and a visionary experience caused him to leave and dedicate himself to God. He took a vow of absolute poverty, composed a rule, attracted followers, and traveled about as a preacher. In 1224 he received the stigmata while praying. His poem "Canticle of Brother Sun" remains popular today. *Canonized:* 1228.

Francis de Sales (1567–1622) *Born in:* Thorens, France.
Bishop of Geneva, Doctor of the Church, founder and popular preacher. Of noble birth, Francis was well schooled and became a lawyer. He refused an arranged marriage and instead entered the religious life as provost of the Chapter of Geneva, a position under the patronage of the pope. Francis became a well-liked, eloquent preacher and evangelist, converting people on his extensive travels. In 1607 he founded the Institute of the Visitation of the Blessed Virgin Mary for young girls and widows. His best-known works are *Philothea*, or *An Introduction to the Devout Life*, which lays out the requirements for a devout life of prayer and virtuous living; *Controversies*, which addresses the fundamentals of Catholic faith; *Treatise on the Love of God*, a 12–book examination of the history and theory of Divine love; *Spiritual Conferences*, conversations on religious virtues, which Francis wrote for the sisters of the Visitation; and *Defense of the Standard of the Cross*, a discussion of Catholic doctrine on the veneration of the cross. Many of his sermons and letters also survive. *Canonized:* 1665.

Francis Xavier (1506–1522) *Born in:* the castle of Xavier near Sanguesa, Navarre, Spain.
First Jesuit missionary. Educated in Paris, Francis began his career as a teacher of Aristotelian philosophy at the University of Paris. There he met St. IGNATIUS OF LOYOLA, then a student, and joined with his group of seven to study spiritual practice. The group took a vow of chastity in 1536. After his ordination as priest, Francis joined Ignatius's new order, the Society of Jesus. Francis spent much of his life as a missionary abroad. In 1541 he was sent to India and then to the western Pacific and Japan. He died in China. Francis is considered one of the greatest missionaries

since Paul. He converted thousands, and reportedly performed many miracles. Numerous of his letters survive. *Canonized:* 1622.

Gertrude the Great (c. 1256–1302) *Born:* near Eisleben, Saxony, Germany.
Benedictine abbess and mystic who is the forerunner of St. MARGARET MARY ALACOQUE in devotion to the Sacred Heart. Gertrude is the only woman saint to be called "Great." Gertrude began her visionary life in 1281. The best-known of her surviving mystical works is *Spiritual Exercises*, a collection of prayers, meditations, chants and devotions for baptism through preparation for death. *Canonized:* 1678.

Gregory the Great (540–604) *Born in:* Rome.
Pope; Father of the Church; Doctor of the Church. A patrician by birth, Gregory was the first monk to become pope. His reign is distinguished by his statesmanship, his writings, and his encouragement of the monasteries, as well as his miracles. He is considered one of the four great Latin Fathers of the Church. Little is known of his early years. He was drawn to the religious life and spent long hours meditating on the Scriptures. In 573 he became the prefect of Rome, but a year later abandoned the job to become a monk. He turned his home into a monastery under the patronage of St. Andrew, and turned his six Sicilian estates into monasteries. He served as ambassador to the court of Byzantium in Constantinople, and then as adviser to Pope Pelagius II in Rome. He became pope in 590. Among his important works are the *Liber Regulae Pastoralis* ("Book of Pastoral Rule"), guidelines of religious practice; four *Dialogues*, collections of saints' lives and their miracles; and the *Magna Moralis*, a mystical commentary on the Book of Job; and homilies. Of his letters, 850 are extant. He is credited with creating Gregorian chant.

Gregory VII (c. 1021–1085) *Born in:* Ravaco, near Saona, in Tuscany, Italy.
Pope. Baptized Hildebrand, Gregory joined the Benedictines. Pope Gratian named him secretary in 1045, but a few months later he was deposed, and Gregory followed him into exile. After Gratian died in 1047, Gregory resumed the monastic life. In 1049 Pope Leo IX brought him to Rome to be a cardinal-subdeacon and administrator of the Patrimony of St. Peter's. He held other posts, and his success led to service for Popes Victor II, Stephen, Nicholas II, and Alexander II. Gregory was elected pope in 1073. He undertook substantial reforms. *Canonized:* 1606.

Gregory of Nazianzus (c. 325–389 or 390) *Born in:* Arianzus, Asia Minor.
Father of the Church; Doctor of the Church; called one of the three "Cappadocian Fathers" with SS. BASIL THE GREAT and GREGORY OF NYSSA; brother of Ss. Caesarius of Nazianzus and Gorgonia. Gregory was born to a wealthy family of Christian converts; his father was bishop of Nazianzus. He was educated in Caesarea, Palestine; Alexandria; and Athens. He leaned toward a career in law or rhetoric but was persuaded by his father to be ordained priest. He helped Basil compile his rule, served as the first bishop of Sasima, and withdrew to a monastic life. Gregory emerged to fight the Arian heresy, producing some of his greatest oratorical works, including his five *Theological*

Discourses. He composed numerous epistles, sermons, orations, and thousands of verses of poetry.

Gregory of Nyssa (d. c. after 385 or 386) *Born in:* Caesaria, Cappadocia (modern Turkey). Bishop of Nyssa; Father of the Church; brother of SS. BASIL THE GREAT, Macrina the Younger, and Peter of Sebaste; called one of the three "Cappadocian Fathers" with Basil and St. GREGORY OF NAZIANZUS. Gregory studied for a career in rhetoric. He married, but after his appointment as bishop of Nyssa in 371, he was chaste. He was deposed by enemies in 376 and restored in 378. He became bishop of Sebaste in 380. He was known for his orthodoxy and opposition to the Arian heresy. Among his works are numerous treatises on the Scriptures, theology, and the ascetical life; a *Catechesis* that defends Catholic teaching; and *De anima et ressurectione* ("Life and Resurrection"), a dialogue between Gregory and his dead sister, Macrina, about death and resurrection.

Gregory Palamas (c. 1296–1359) *Born in:* probably Constantiople.
Athonite monk and Archbishop of Thessalonica. After his father died, Gregory entered a monastery on Mt. Athos and followed the Rule of St. Basil, living in solitude for most of 20 years. In the 1330s he began to defend the controversial practice of hesychasm, centered on a method of prayer used by monks in Byzantine monasticism that involved controlled breathing and posture to induce a vision of light. The defense became known as Palamism; it was officially adopted by the Orthodox Church in 1341. Gregory was excommunicated in 1344, but in 1347 was consecrated bishop of Thessalonika. Among his writings are numerous homilies and treatises.

Gregory of Sinai (d. after 450) *Born in:* Koukoulon, Asia Minor.
Gregory and his family were taken prisoner by Turks and stripped of their wealth. Grateful for their survival and release, Gregory became a monk on Cyprus. He then went to the Monastery of St. Catherine at Mt.Sinai, where he learned the spiritual practice of hesychasm. He left the monastery to tour the Holy Land, then went on to Crete to continue perfecting his practice of hesychasm, studying under the famous mystic St. Arsenios. He spent time at Mt. Athos and Constantinople before settling in Thrace for the remainder of his life. He wrote prolifically about hesychasm, establishing guidelines followed by St. GREGORY PALAMAS and others.

Gregory Thaumaturgus (213–270 or 275) *Born in:* Neocaesarea, Pontus (also Pontos), now in modern Turkey.
Bishop of Neocaesarea; Father of the Church. Born to a distinguished pagan family, Gregory studied under Origen and was converted by him. He was elected bishop of Neocaesarea in about 238 or 239. He was an inspired preacher reputed to have miraculous powers (Thamaturgus means "wonder-worker"). Among Gregory's important writings are *Oratio Panegyrica*, an enthusiastic and admiring homage to Origen; *Exposition of the Faith*, in which he asserts his orthodox views about the Trinity; *Epostola Canonica;* and a dissertation addressed to Theopompus concerning the passibility and impassibility of God.

Henry Suso, Bl. (c. 1295–1366) *Born in:* Constance, Swabia.
Dominican mystic, preacher, poet, and author. Noble-born, Henry had a mystical experience at age 18 that propelled him to give up the ways of the outer world and become "the Servant of the Eternal Wisdom." He initiated a life-long practice of severe austerities and mortifications. He had frequent visions and ecstasies. He studied under Meister Eckhardt and began his apostolic career in 1334. He was esteemed throughout Europe as a preacher. His early works, heavily influenced by Eckhart, were *The Little Book of Truth* and *The Little Book of Eternal Wisdom*. Henry influenced Thomas à Kempis, who wrote *The Imitation of Christ. Beatified:* 1831.

Hesychius of Sinai (d. c.432–433) *Born in:* Jerusalem.
Monk and priest. As a youth Hesychius was a student of St. Gregory the Theologian. After Gregory's death, Hesychius spent the rest of his life as a hermit in Palestine, studying and writing. In 412 the archbishop of Jerusalem ordained him as priest. He preached and gained fame as a teacher. He is renowned for his biblical scholarship and explanations of the Scriptures.

Hilary of Poitiers (c. 315–368) *Born in:* Poitiers, Aquitane (now part of France).
Bishop of Poitiers; Father of the Church and Doctor of the Church. Noble-born Hilary was middle-aged and married when he converted. After his election as bishop of Poitiers in 350, he and his wife remained married but were celibate. He defended the faith against the Arian heresy. His most celebrated work is *De Trinitate*, 12 books arguing the consubstantiality of the Father, Son, and Holy Spirit. He wrote numerous hymns and treatises.

Hildegard of Bingen (1098–1179) *Born in:* Bickelheim (or Bockelheim), Germany.
Benedictine abbess and acclaimed prophet, mystic, theologian, writer, poet, composer, and early feminist, although never officially canonized. The first major German mystic, Hildegard of Bingen is best known for a series of mystical illuminations, or visions, which she experienced and chronicled in mid-life, and which were far in advance of the religious outlooks of her day. Her power and influence made her one of the most important women of her time. Her work has enjoyed renewed, serious interest in contemporary times. She was a visionary from childhood. Her works, still popular today, are *Scivias*, illuminations on prophecy, denunciation of vice, and the universe as egg or sphere; *The Book of Life's Merits* or *The Book of the Rewards of Life*, a juxtaposition of virtues and sins, and *Book of Divine Works*, a complex cosmology on the origin of life, the nature of heaven, and the history of salvation. She also wrote *Physical Things*, about nature; *Causes and Cures*, about medicine; *Answers to Thirty-eight Questions; Ordo Vitutum*, a morality play set to music (included in *Scivias*); a commentary on theology and Scriptures, more than 70 poems; 50 allegorical homilies; and 300 letters.

Ignatius of Antioch (c. 50–c. 107) *Born:* probably in Syria.
Bishop of Antioch, martyr. Ignatius was named bishop of Antioch during formative years of Christianity. He was a great orator and a prolific writer. He longed to become a martyr and was granted his wish under the Roman emperor Trajan, who had him

thrown to lions. Among his most famous writings are a series of pastoral letters in the last months of his life. In them, he was the first to use the term "the Catholic Church." Ignatius is called one of the "Apostolic Fathers."

Ignatius of Loyola (1491–1556) *Born in:* Loyola Castle near Azpeitia, in the Basque province of Guipúzcoa, Spain.
Founder of the Society of Jesus, known as the Jesuits. Ignatius led a dissolute life in his youth. In 1521 a war injury brought about a spiritual turning point. He retired to a cave, where he spent 10 months in prayer and visionary experience, which later resulted in his famous work, *Spiritual Exercises.* He was ordained a priest in 1534, the same year he and his followers (including St. FRANCIS XAVIER) founded what became the Jesuits. Ignatius also established several foundations, including one for Jewish converts to Catholicism and another for loose women who were anxious to reform but felt no call to the religious life. Many of his sermons survive. *Canonized:* 1622.

Irenaeus (c. 130–202) *Born in:* Asia Minor.
Bishop of Lyons; Father of the Church. As a young man, Irenaeus joined the priesthood and became a missionary. He spent most of his life as bishop of Lyons. His writings rank him among the greatest of the fathers of the church; he is considered the first great Christian theologian. His work helped to defeat the Gnostic heresy and laid the foundations of Christian theology. His best-known work is *Adversus haereses*, an exposition of the Gnostic heresy as well as other heretical philosophies. *Proof of the Apostolic Preaching* expounds on the Gospels as interpreted through Old Testament prophecies. He wrote numerous other treatises, and letters.

Isaac of Nineveh (seventh century)
Mystic, bishop of Nineveh. Isaac was consecrated bishop of Nineveh sometime between 660 and 680. After five months, he resigned to become an anchorite in Bet Huzaje. Later, he went to the monastery of Rabban Shabur in Iran. His intense studying rendered him blind, and he dictated many of his writings. His *Ascetical Discourses* influenced Byzantine spiritual literature.

Jane Frances de Chantal (1572–1641)
Born in: Dijon, France.
Founder of the Order of the Visitation of the Virgin Mary. Jane's father was president of the Burgundian parliament. At age 20 she married the baron de Chantal and had six children. Her husband was killed in a hunting accident in 1601, forcing Jane to live under the domination of her cruel father-in-law. In 1604 she heard St. FRANCIS DE SALES preach, and became one of his disciples. In 1610 she took the veil and founded the Order of the Visitation of the Virgin Mary. The order accepted widows and others who for health or other reasons could not enter more traditional orders. The order grew to 86 convents; Jane assumed full governance of them after Francis's death in 1622. Numerous of her letters survive. *Canonized:*1767.

Jerome (347–419) *Born in:* Stridonium near Aquileia, Italy.
Scholar, Doctor of the Church, and translator of the Latin Vulgate Bible. Jerome

was one of the greatest thinkers of the early church, and also one of the most controversial. He enjoyed an affluent upbringing and became a respected pagan scholar. In 374, during a severe illness, a dream or visionary experience convinced him he was displeasing God and he must convert to Christianity. He spent four years as a hermit in the desert, and then resumed his scholarly career, studying under St. GREGORY OF NAZIANZUS. He traveled with St. Paula; they founded monasteries and convents. Jerome's ecclesiastical writings include a continuation of the *Historia Ecclesiastica* of Eusebius of Caesarea, to 378, and *De Viris Illustribus* (392), about leading ecclesiastical writers. He also translated Origen and wrote controversial treatises. A large number of his letters survive. His greatest accomplishment was his translation of the Bible, including the Apochrypha, from Greek and Hebrew into Latin. The Latin Vulgate Bible was the primary authority until about the mid-20th century.

John XXIII, Bl. (1881–1963) *Born in:* Sotto il Monte, near Bergamo, Italy.
Pope. Baptized Angelo Giuseppe Roncalli, John was ordained priest in 1904 in Rome after studying at the Apollinaire Seminary. He served in the Italian army during World War I. In 1917 Pope Benedict XV called him to Rome to reorganize the Congregation for the Propagation of the Faith. In 1925 Pope Pius XI made him an archbishop, Apostolic Visitor to Bulgaria, and then Apostolic Delegate to Greece and Turkey. He was elected pope in 1958. An excellent diplomat, John promoted social reforms and interfaith communication and convened the liberalizing Second Vatican Council. *Beatified:* 2000.

John the Baptist (first century)
Prophet, martyr and Precursor or Forerunner of the Lord, called "the man sent from God." According to the Gospel of Luke, John was born to the elderly Zechariah and Elizabeth after a visit by the angel Gabriel. Nothing of his early years is known. He was probably about 32 when he began his spiritual mission by withdrawing into the desert to fast and pray. He then started preaching and baptizing people in the river Jordan. He baptized Jesus. John was arrested by King Herod Atipas, who was tricked by his daughter, Salome, into ordering John to be beheaded.

John Baptiste Marie Vianney (1786–1869) *Born in:* Dardilly, France.
Preacher and the Curé d'Ars. At age 20, barely educated, John enrolled in a new ecclesiastical school in Ecully. He struggled in his studies, and was drafted into the army. He deserted and was saved from arrest by his brother, who took his place. John returned to school, and then was named curé, or parish priest, of Ars, a village about 20 miles north of Lyons. He spent the rest of his life there, inspiring thousands who traveled to hear his fiery sermons, many of which survive. *Canonized:* 1925.

John Bosco (1815–1888) *Born in:* Becchi, Piedmont, Italy.
Founder of the Society of St. FRANCIS DE SALES, known as the Salesians. At age nine, John had the first of many lucid, visionary dreams that shaped his religious career. At age 16 he began studying for the priesthood and was ordained at age 26. He went to Turin and began a Sunday catechism for poor boys. The success of

this led to construction of a church under the patronage of his favorite saint, Francis de Sales. In 1859 John's work became the Society of St. Francis de Sales. In 1872 he established an order of women called Daughters of Our Lady, Help of Christians. Pope Pius IX instructed John to record his unusual dreams for him. More than 150 were collected; many were prophetic and concerned his boys and the Salesian Order. His dreams inspired many talks and sermons. John was mentor to St. Dominic Savio. *Canonized:* 1934.

John de Brébeuf (1593–1649) *Born in:* Condé-sur-Vire, Normandy, France.
Jesuit martyr. Ordained a Jesuit priest, John volunteered as a missionary to Ontario. He was in an advanced state of tuberculosis when he arrived in Ontario, but he endured for 25 years there under brutal and hostile conditions. He won converts among the Huron Indians, but not among the Iroquois. He helped to compose a catechism for the Indians. In 1649 he and a group of companions were captured at Sault Ste. Marie by the Iroquois, enemies of the Hurons. They were subjected to cruel tortures, including necklaces of red-hot lance blades, belts of burning bark, and the crushing of their bones. John continued to preach through the tortures. The Indians tore their victims' faces to pieces and then killed them by plunging them into boiling water in a mock baptism. John's valor so impressed his killers that they drank his blood. John's letters describe his missionary experiences. *Canonized:* 1930.

John Cassian (c. 360–433) Abbot; Father of the Church.
Little is known about John until 380, when he became a monk in Bethlehem. He spent several years traveling in Egypt and Asia Minor, visiting monasteries and keeping detailed records of the monastic practices he observed. In Rome, he was ordained priest. From his journeys, he wrote a 12–volume work, *Remedies for the Eight Deadly Sins*, which describes the rules and organization of communities in Egypt and Palestine, and of the means used by the monks in their spiritual combat of the eight chief hindrances to a monk's perfection. Another work, *Conferences on the Egyptian Monks*, relates discussions had with the monks. About 430, John was commissioned by the future Pope St. Leo to write a seven-volume critique of the Nestorian heresy, *On the Incarnation of the Lord.* After his death, *Conferences* was declared apocryphal, and John was condemned by a church council.

John Chrysostom (c. 347–407) *Born in:* Antioch.
Doctor of the Church, Greek Father of the Church, Bishop of Constantinople, theologian. John's surname is not known; Chrysostom means "golden-mouthed." John is considered to be the greatest of the Greek fathers of the church, and one of the greatest and most eloquent of all preachers of the faith. More writings of his are extant than of any other doctor of the church. Well-educated, he entered the religious life, spent time in a cave near Antioch, and in 386 was ordained a priest. Until 397, John enjoyed the golden age of his life. He was a prolific writer and a popular, charismatic preacher. His fame spread through the Byzantine Empire. In 397 he was sent to Constantinople, but he was unable to manage the stormy politics

there. He was exiled twice. The second time, he was marched to the Caucasus Mountains and died en route. His most famous work is *On the Priesthood*, a dialogue between himself and St. BASIL THE GREAT. Twenty-one sermons survive; they are full of moral, dogmatic, and historical knowledge. He wrote hundreds of homilies on the scriptures. Some 238 of his letters survive; most are from his days in exile. John was declared a Doctor of the Church in 451.

John Climacus (c. 570–c. 649) *Born in:* Syria.
Abbot of Sinai; mystic; Father of the Church. At age 16, John withdrew to the famous monastery at Mount Sinai, and received his tonsure within three to four years. After the death of his mentor, Abba Martyrius, John entered a cave at Tholas at the foot of the mountain. There he spent 20 years in near isolation, studying the lives of the saints and practicing severe austerities. He visited monks in Egypt. In 600 he became abbot of the Sinai monastery and attracted many pilgrims. While abbot, he composed his important work, *The Ladder of Divine Ascent*, from which he earned his surname, Climacus, which means "ladder." The 30 chapters correspond to the first 30 years of Jesus' life and provide steps in the spiritual ladder of ascent to God.

John Damascene (c. 676–c.754 to 787) *Born in:* Damascus.
Patriarch of Jerusalem; last Eastern Father of the Church; Doctor of the Church; poet. John's tutoring by a monk influenced him to abandon his father's judicial profession in 719 and join the monastery of St. Sabas near Jerusalem. He became involved in the Iconoclast heresy; his *On Holy Images* defends the veneration of icons. His most famous work, *The Fountain of Wisdom*, was the first summary of connected theological opinions and basic truths of the faith, drawing on the woks of eminent church fathers. John also wrote more than 150 works on philosophy, religious education, theology and hagiographies, numerous sermons and treatises, a defense of the Blessed Virgin Mary's title as Theotokos (God-bearer), and three great hymns or canons. He was a gifted orator. He was declared a Doctor of the Church in 1890.

John Eudes (1601–1670) *Born in:* Ri, Normandy, France.
Initiator of the devotion to the Sacred Heart with St. MARGARET MARY ALACOQUE. After attending the Jesuit college at Caen, John joined the Congregation of the Oratory of France in 1623. He worked as a preacher and missionary. Resigning in 1643, he founded the Congregation of Jesus and Mary (the Eudists) at Caen, composed of secular priests. He founded seminaries, but was unable to get papal approval of the order. He did get approval of his new order of the Sisters of Our Lady of Charity of the Refuge. With St. Mary Margaret Alacoque, John initiated devotion to the Sacred Heart of Jesus (he composed the Mass for the Sacred Heart in 1668) and the Holy Heart of Mary. *Canonized:* 1925.

John of Ávila (1499–1569) *Born in:* Almodóvar del Campo, Castile, Spain.
Priest and missionary. John studied law at the University of Salamanca and theology at Alcala, and then became a hermit. After his ordination, he gained fame for his

oratorical skills. His popularity as a fiery preacher attracted the attention of the Spanish Inquisition, which arrested and imprisoned him. Released, he traveled through Andalusia as a missionary. John served as the spiritual advisor to SS. TERESA OF ÁVILA, PETER OF ALCÁNTARA, JOHN OF THE CROSS, and Francis Borgia. His writings include numerous sermons, letters, and treatises. *Canonized:* 1970.

John of the Cross (1542–1591) *Born in:* Fontiveros, Old Castile, Spain.
Spanish mystic, Renaissance poet, a founder of the Discalced Carmelite Order, and Doctor of the Church. John was educated by Jesuits. At age 21, he entered the Carmelite monastery of Medina del Campo, and was given the name of John of St. Matthias. He was sent to the Carmelite monastery near the University of Salamanca, and was ordained a priest at age 25. He met and became friends with St. TERESA OF ÁVILA. Both were unhappy with the laxity they saw in the order and founded the reformed Discalced Carmelites. In 1577 John was kidnapped by Carmelite opponents and imprisoned in a nearly lightless cell in Toledo. For nine months he was beaten and starved. He finally escaped, reportedly with the help of an apparition of Mary. John wrote his mystical work, *The Spiritual Canticle*, while in prison. Shortly after his escape, he wrote *The Ascent of Mount Carmel*, *The Living Flame of Love*, and his most famous work, *The Dark Night of the Soul*, a continuation of *The Ascent of Mount Carmel*. These works describe the soul's mystical journey toward God, and detail the stages of mystical union. Numerous of his letters also survive. He was declared a Doctor of the Church in 1926. *Canonized:* 1726.

Josemaría Escrivá (1902–1975) *Born in:* Barbastro, Aragón, Spain.
Founder of the Opus Dei and the Priestly Society of the Holy Cross. Josemaría was ordained a priest at the Logrono seminary in 1925. He studied law in Madrid. In 1928 he was inspired to found Opus Dei ("the work of God"), an evangelist order. In 1943 he founded the Priestly Society of the Holy Cross as a complement to Opus Dei. In 1946 Josemaría moved to Rome. There he obtained a doctorate in theology from the Lateran University and was appointed to positions in the Vatican. He traveled throughout the world to develop Opus Dei. Josemaría wrote books on theology and spirituality, among them *The Way, The Furrow,* and *The Forge*. *Beatified:* 1992. *Canonized:* October 2002.

Joseph Cafasso (1811–1860) *Born in:* Castelnuovo D'Asti, Piedmont, Italy.
Ascetic and confessor. Joseph was ordained in 1833 and then became professor and rector of the ecclesiastical college of Turin. He was renowned for his piety and became a close friend of St. JOHN BOSCO. *Canonized:* 1947.

Julian of Norwich (1342 or 1343–c. 1423).
Mystic. Little is known about Julian's life. She was a solitary anchoress in a cell adjoining the Church of St. Julian in Conisford, Norwich. This church belonged to the Benedictines of Carrow, so she may have been a Benedictine nun. She was well educated. By her own account, she prayed to God for a life-threatening condition in her 30th year in order to purify herself. This occurred, and Julian nearly died. While on her deathbed, she had a mystical experience in which God gave her a series

of 16 showings, or revelations. She recovered and spent the rest of her life contemplating her experience. Her account exists in two versions, *Revelations of Divine Love*, and a shorter version, *Showings*.

Lawrence of Brindisi (1559–1619) *Born in:* Brindisi, Italy.
Capuchin Friar; Doctor of the Church. In 1575 Lawrence joined the Capuchin Friars Minor, a strict offshoot of the Franciscans. He studied at the University of Padua, and then preached and evangelized throughout Europe. He held all the offices in his order. In 1601 Lawrence was made chaplain of Emperor Rudolf II's army, which was fighting the Turks. In 1605 he was sent to evangelize Germany, where he served as papal nuncio to the court of Bavaria. Lawrence's writings include hundreds of sermons, commentaries on books of the Bible (he is especially noted for his commentary on Genesis), various treatises, and religious polemics. He was declared a Doctor of the Church in 1959. *Canonized:* 1881.

Louis de Montfort (1673–1716) *Born in:* Montfort, France.
Confessor and founder of the Sisters of Divine Wisdom. In 1685 Louis entered the Jesuit College of St. Thomas Becket in Rennes. In 1692 he went to Paris to undertake training at the Seminary of St. Sulpice. He was ordained a priest in 1700 and desired to do missionary work in Canada, but he was sent instead to Nantes, and then became chaplain of the hospital in Poitiers. There he founded his Daughters of Divine Wisdom congregation from the women administrators of the poorhouse. He then went to Paris and worked at a poorhouse. A fiery man filled with apostolic zeal, Louis had difficulty in his relations with people, and he was often invited to leave. Criticism of him, his sermons, and his congregation mounted. He went to Rome and was appointed a missionary apostolic by Pope Clement XI. From 1706 until his death he traveled to some 200 parishes to preach. Louis was especially devoted to Mary, and in 1715 founded the Missionaries of the Company of Mary. He also founded the Brothers of St. Gabriel congregation. Some of his writings are mystical in nature. Among his best-known works are *True Devotion to the Blessed Virgin* and *The Love of Eternal Wisdom*. Numerous of his sermons, letters, and hymns also survive. *Canonized:* 1947.

Louise de Marillac (1591–1660) *Born in:* Probably Ferrières-en-Brie, France.
Social worker, founder and partner in social work with St. VINCENT DE PAUL. Well-born to a powerful family, Louise de Marillac gave up her early ambition to be a Capuchin nun, and married at age 22. She lost her husband to illness 12 years later, and then decided to devote her life to God. Around 1624–25 she met St. VINCENT DE PAUL, who was organizing his Confraternities of Charity. He gave her direction of the Ladies of Charity. In 1633 she began to train social workers in her home, and founded the Sisters or Daughters of Charity of St. Paul. Louise and Vincent kept up a close correspondence. Louise's surviving letters to him and her sisters number 740. *Canonized:* 1934.

Maria Maddalena de' Pazzi (1566–1607) *Born in:* Florence, Italy.
Carmelite nun and mystic. Born to a noble, deeply religious family, Maria Maddalena was educated by Jesuits and

learned to meditate at an early age. At age 16 she entered the convent Santa Maria degli Angeli and took the veil the following year. Soon after entering the convent, she began having intense mystical experiences and fell severely ill, nearly dying. After her recovery, she began to have daily visions of, and conversations with, the Trinity and Christ, whom she called the Word. She believed Christ wanted her to summon his being through her voice. Her raptures were recorded by her sisters, who kept them secret except for a few immediate male superiors. Maria Maddalena's entire mystical career never left the convent, not even most of the letters she wrote to the pope, bishops, and priests. Her visions, which ended at age 41, were preserved in several manuscripts, most notable of which are *The Forty Days, The Dialogues,* and *Probation*. *Canonized:* 1660.

Marcarius of Egypt (c. 300– c. 390) Coptic monk, priest, and spiritual father who lived in the desert of Sketis. Marcarius—also called Marcarius the Great—figures prominently in the *Sayings of the Desert Fathers*. He also is credited with the authorship of homilies known as the *Markarian Homilies,* but this authorship is in doubt.

Margaret Mary Alacoque (1647–1690) *Born in:* L'Hautecour, France.
Mystic and leader of the devotion to the Sacred Heart of Jesus. A devout child, Margaret Mary began mortifying herself at a young age and consecrated herself to a religious life at age 15. In 1671 she entered the Visitation Convent at Paray. In 1672 she had the first of a series of revelations that would last a year and a half. In these visions Christ told her that he had chosen her to spread devotion to his Sacred Heart, and to establish a Feast of the Sacred Heart. It was not until 1686 that she was able to win approval for this from her superiors. St. CLAUDE DE LA COLOMBIÈRE was one of her early supporters, and she also was aided by St. JOHN EUDES. Her autobiography and letters are sources of spiritual inspiration. *Canonized:* 1920.

Marguerite Bourgeoys (1620–1700) *Born in:* Troyes, France.
Founder of the Sisters of Notre Dame. Refused by the Carmelites and Poor Clares at age 19, Marguerite joined an uncloistered community. Unhappy there, she was recruited as a teacher for Ville-Marie, New France, now Montreal, Canada. She arrived in 1653, and began teaching and caring for the sick. In 1672 she founded the Sisters of Notre Dame. The order established missions for the Indians, and won the right to teach throughout Canada. Many hardships were endured in the wars between the settlers and the Indians. Marguerite made several trips back and forth across the Atlantic. In 1889 the order was established in America. Marguerite's writings include her autobiography and letters. *Canonized:* 1982.

Mary of Agreda, Ven. (1602–1665) *Born in:* Agreda, Spain.
Abbess; mystic. Mary entered the Convent of the Immaculate Conception for discalced nuns in Agreda, founded by her parents, and became abbess at age 25. She experienced numerous ecstasies, levitations, bilocations, lengthy trances and other mystical phenomena. She bilocated and traveled mystically throughout Spain and Portugal. From 1620–1631, she made

more than 500 visits—as many as four a day—to America to teach the Indians, who called her the Lady in Blue. Her significant written work is *The Mystical City of God*, dictated by the Blessed Virgin Mary. She burned the manuscript upon instructions from her confessor, only to have Mary instruct her to write it again. The book is a four-volume, 2,676–page account of the Blessed Virgin's life, the hidden life of Jesus, the creation of the world, the Apocalypse, heaven and hell, and other Christian topics.

Matrona (d. 307) *Also known as:* Matrona of Thessalonica. Martyr. Little is known of the life of Matrona until the year of her martyrdom. She may have been an orphan. As a girl or young woman she was sold as a slave to a wealthy Jewish woman. According to lore, when her mistress discovered she was a Christian, she had Matrona beaten to death. Some sources give the year of her death as 350.

Maximilian Kolbe (1894–1941) *Born in:* Zdunska-Wola, Poland.
Founder of the Knights of the Immaculata; Franciscan martyr of World War II. In 1910 Maximilian took the habit in the Conventual Franciscans. Sent to Rome, he earned a doctorate in philosophy and later a doctorate in theology. In 1917 he founded the Knights of the Immaculata to counteract religious indifference. He contracted tuberculosis in 1920, but continued to work to develop his order. During World War II, he was arrested twice by the Nazis, in 1939 and 1941. The second time, he was sent to Auschwitz. When 10 people in his cell block were selected to be executed, Maximilian substituted himself for one of them. The Nazis attempted to starve the 10 to death, but lost patience when four remained alive, including Maximilian. He and the others were killed by lethal injection. Maximilian wrote numerous articles and letters. *Canonized:* 1982.

Maximus of Turin (d. 408–423)
First bishop of Turin. Little is known of his life. His ministry was from c. 390 to 408–423; Gennadius of Marseilles fixes his death sometime during the 15-year span of the joint reigns of Honorius and Theodosius the younger. Maximus was considered a capable preacher. Numerous of his sermons survive.

Maximus the Confessor (580–662) *Born in:* Constantinople.
Abbot, mystic, theologian, and Father of the Church. Noble-born, Maximus was well educated. As a young man, he was appointed the first secretary to Emperor Heraclius. He resigned after three years to enter the monastery at Chrysopolis (now Scutari), and soon became abbot there. After a few years he was transferred (perhaps for political reasons) to the monastery of St. George at Cyzicus (now Erdek). He became embroiled in the politics over the Monothelitism heresy and helped to develop the doctrine of the two wills of Christ. In 653 he was charged with treason by Emperor Constans II, a defender of Monothelitism, was tried, and exiled to Perberis. In 661–62 he and two companions were returned to Constantinople, interrogated, and severely mutilated: their tongues were cut out and their right hands cut off. He was exiled to Lazica on the Black Sea, where he remained the rest of his life. He is called "the Confessor" for his sufferings

for the faith. He wrote more than 90 works on dogma, theology and mysticism. Most notable among them are *Mystagogia, Chapters on Knowledge, Centuries on Charity, Ambigua,* and *Short Theological and Polemical Treatises.*

Mechtilde of Magdeburg (c. 1207–1297) *Born in:* Magdeburg, Thuringia, Lower Saxony. Beguine mystic. Born probably to a noble family, Mechtilde began experiencing visions at age 12. She had daily visitations for 30 years, but kept them secret until she was 43. At age 23 she left home and joined the Beguines, a community of lay women who wished to be in religious service but not take permanent vows or be cloistered. Mechtilde spent 40 years as a Beguine, ministering to the sick and poor, and practiced an ascetic life and contemplation. She suffered much illness. She recorded her visions, and her confessor—Heinrich of Halle, a Dominican—arranged them into six books. Some of her writings were circulated during her lifetime. She had many critics, in part because the Beguines were not popular with the clergy. At age 63, she took refuge in a Cistercian convent in Helfta. There she was left blind by illness and wondered how she could repay the nuns. At their urging, she dictated a seventh book as a gift to them. Her works, well known in the 14th century, sank into obscurity and were rediscovered in the 19th century. Among them is *The Flowing Light of the Godhead.*

Methodius (d. c. 311) *Also known as:* Methodius of Olympus. Bishop, perhaps of Olympus in Lycia (now part of Turkey), and Tyre, or of Patara in Lycia. Methodius was famous for his preaching and scholarship, authoring treatises. He was martyred in Chalcis, Greece.

Nilus (d. c. 430) *Also known as:* Nilus the Elder. Bishop and friend of St. John Chrysostom. Nilus gave up his family and a comfortable life at court in Constantinople to become a monk on Mount Sinai. His son was kidnapped by Arabs, and he left the mountain to search for him. He was successful, and the two were ordained and went to Mount Sinai together. Nilus became bishop of Ancyra. He is noted for his ascetical treatises and letters.

Padre Pio (1887–1968) *Born in:* Pietrelcina, Italy.
Capuchin friar; stigmatist; miracleworker. Born Francesco Forgione, he became a Capuchin novice at age 16 in Morcone and took the habit in 1902 or 1903 as Padre Pio. He contracted tuberculosis and suffered from poor health for the rest of his life. He was drafted into the army in 1915, but was forced to leave in 1916 due to his health. He went to the monastery of San Giovanni Rotondo, where he stayed for the rest of his life. In 1910 he had his first stigmata experience affecting his hands, and in 1918 had a transverberation, or mystical wounding, during a vision. About a month later, he experienced stigmata again, this time all five wounds. The wounds remained and bled throughout his remaining life. The stigmata and Padre Pio's miracles of healing caused people to flock to see him, and in response the Church in 1923 forbade him to preach or write letters. In 1940 he established the Home for the Relief of Suffering. Padre Pio's miracles include bilocation. He is one of the most popular saints of modern times. *Canonized:* 2002.

Patrick (c. 389–461) *Born in:* Bannaventa or Bannavem Taberniae, Britain.
Archbishop of Armagh, Apostle of Ireland, one of the three great patron saints of Ireland with Brigid and Columba. Patrick was born to Christian Roman parents. At age 16 he was kidnapped into slavery. According to lore he spent six years in slavery. One night he had a dream in which he was told that his ship was ready. He escaped to a cargo ship and had adventures in different lands, returning to Britain between 412 and 415. A dream instructed him to go to Ireland to spread Christianity. He spent several years studying theology in Gaul and was ordained deacon. In 432 he went to Ireland. In 441 he was made archbishop. Many legends are told about Patrick; the most famous is that he drove all the snakes out of Ireland. *Letter to the Soldiers of Coroticus* is one of three manuscripts attributed to Patrick. He also wrote the *Confessio* or *Confession,* justifying his life and work and apologizing for a sin committed in his youth. The *Lorica* is a mystical poem.

Paul (d. c. 67) *Born in:* Tarsus.
Apostle to the Gentiles, mystic, martyr, theologian, and missionary, one of the most influential figures in the establishment of the Christian religion. A Roman citizen and a strict Jew, Saul—his given name—was a well-to-do tentmaker. He supported the Pharisees and persecuted Christians. Around 36, he had a mystical experience while traveling on the road to Damascus, in which he was temporarily blinded and encountered the risen Christ. Converted, he became Paul, the greatest missionary of Christianity, evangelizing throughout the Mediterranean and Asia Minor. He was arrested twice and jailed. He was martyred when Nero had him beheaded. Paul developed his ideas about Christianity in his epistles, of which 14 are included in the New Testament.

Paulinus of Nola (c.355–431). *Born in:* Aquitania.
Monk who influenced development of Gallic monastic life. In his twenties, Paulinus served as governor of Campagnia. He returned to private life, married, and enjoyed a wealthy lifestyle near Bordeaux. In 389 he was baptized and entered a monastery in Spain. He established a monastery in Nola in 395, remaining there until his death. His letters have historical importance for the information they contain about monastic life during a critical period of the collapse of the Roman Empire.

Pelagia the Penitent (d. 284) *Born in:* Antioch, Syria.
Penitent woman. According to legend, Pelagia was born to a wealthy family. A beauty, she spent her early life in dissipation and pleasure-seeking. She happened to hear a sermon by a famous bishop, Nonnos, and decided to repent. After her baptism she gave away her possessions and went into the desert, disguised as a monk. There she sought to cleanse herself by living an ascetic life and studying religion and philosophy. She went to Jerusalem, where she lived for three years in the Garden of Gethsemane. She left there as a model of piety and lived for another 58 years.

Perpetua (d. 203) *Born in:* Probably Carthage.
Martyr. According to legend, Perpetua was a young married noblewoman who

converted to Christianity. She was arrested and refused to renounce her faith. She was condemned to death with other Christians, and died in an arena under attack by wild animals and a swordsman. Prior to her death, Perpetua had a vision; her story and vision were recorded.

Peter of Alcántara (1499–1562) *Born in:* Alcántara, Estremadura, Spain.
Penitent and mystic. After studying law in Salamanca, Peter joined the Observant Franciscans at Manjaretes. In 1521 he founded a friary in Badajoz. He served as superior of missions in Spain and Portugal, and was chaplain to the court of King John III of Portugal. In 1538 he was elected provincial for Saint Gabriel in Estremadura. Discouraged over politics, he resigned and spent two years as a hermit. In about 1556 he founded the Reformed Friars Minor of Spain (usually called the Alcatrine Franciscans); by the time of his death the order was absorbed into another order, the Conventuals and the Observants. In 1560 he met St. TERESA OF ÁVILA and served as her father and confessor. Peter wrote several works of mysticism, the most important of which is a *Treatise on Prayer and Meditation. Canonized:* 1669.

Peter Canisius (1521–1597) *Born in:* Nimwegen, Germany (now in the Netherlands).
Jesuit theologian; Doctor of the Church. In 1546, after university studies, Peter joined the Jesuits in Mainz. He founded the first German house of the order in Cologne, and lectured and taught at the university. He was a brilliant preacher and inspired many. In 1547 Peter attended the Council of Trent as procurator for the bishop of Augsburg. He became deeply involved in the politics of the Reformation and Counter-Reformation. While teaching at the University of Vienna, he wrote his greatest work, his Catechism, a model for catechisms to follow. In 1556 Peter was named provincial of southern Germany. He established colleges for boys, traveled and preached, and responded to the needs of the papacy. He founded a school in Fribourg and sodalities of the Blessed Virgin for citizens and for women and students. His other major works are *The History of John the Baptist*, *The Incomparable Virgin Mary*, and *Centuries of Magdeburg*. Also surviving are numerous treatises, letters, and sermons on Catholic dogma and teachings. *Canonized and declared Doctor of the Church:* 1925.

Peter Chrysologus (c. 400–c. 450) *Born in:* Imola, Emilia, now in Italy.
Bishop of Ravena; Doctor of the Church; Father of the Church. Little is known of his life. Peter converted to Christianity as an adult. According to tradition, he was made bishop of Ravenna in 433 by Pope St. Sixtus III in consequence of a vision. He campaigned against paganism and was an eloquent preacher. He was declared Doctor of the Church in 1729.

Peter Damian (1007–1072) *Born in:* Ravenna, Italy.
Cardinal; reformer; Doctor of the Church. By age 25, noble-born Peter was famous as a university teacher. Dissatisfied with academic life, he left his profession and became a hermit in Fonte-Avellana, practicing severe austerities. He founded several hermitages and became prior. Peter became deeply involved in the politics and schisms of the Church and became renowned as a reformer. Pope Stephen X

named him a cardinal, and he also served Popes Nicholas II and Alexander II. Peter was a prolific writer, authoring numerous sermons, treatises, and letters. He was declared a Doctor of the Church in 1828.

Philip Neri (1515–1595) *Born in:* Florence, Italy.
Missionary and founder of the Congregation of the Oratory. In 1533 Philip decided to devote his life to God, and went to Rome with no money. He earned a living tutoring, and gave most of his money to the poor. He did charitable work in hospitals. He lived nearly like a hermit and practiced severe austerities. In 1544 he met St. IGNATIUS LOYOLA; the same year he had a momentous mystical experience in which he was infused with the Holy Spirit. In 1548 he founded a confraternity of laymen to spread the devotion of the Forty Hours and help pilgrims. After his ordination in 1851, Philip founded the Congregation of the Oratory order and later co-founded the Confraternity of the Most Holy Trinity, devoted to assisting pilgrims and convalescents. Philip's oratorical powers earned him the name of "Apostle of Rome." He was an effective proselytizer and motivator, and his skill at reading the thoughts of others was legendary. Unfortunately, Philip burned most of his writings prior to his death. *Canonized:* 1622.

Placid Riccardi (1844–1915) *Born in:* Trevi, Italy.
Monk and spiritual adviser. The son of a businessman, Placid (born Thomas) went to Rome intending to study for a legal career. He changed his mind and in 1866 entered the monastery of St.-Paul's-Outside-the-Walls. He was ordained in 1871. In 1884 he was sent as chaplain to the Benedictine nuns of Amelia. He then went to Sanfiano, where he lived in solitude for 17 years and gave spiritual counsel to nuns and the local people. In 1915 he became gravely ill, and returned to the monastery to die. Many of his letters survive.

Polycarp of Smyrna (d. c.155?)
Martyred Bishop of Smyrna and Greek Father of the Church. Little is known of Polycarp's life. He is said to have been converted at age 10 by St. John the Evangelist and became his disciple. At about age 26 he was consecrated bishop of Smyrna by John the Beloved. He was arrested in an anti-Christian campaign and sentenced to die by being burned alive. According to tradition, his body refused to burn, and he was then stabbed to death.

Robert Bellarmine (1542–1621) *Born in:* Montepulciano, Tuscany, Italy.
Cardinal; theologian; Doctor of the Church. Of noble birth, Robert joined the Jesuits in 1560. He studied Thomistic theology in Rome and Padua, and became the first Jesuit professor at the University of Louvain. Robert held important posts at the College of Rome and then became provincial of Naples. In 1597 Pope Clement VIII appointed him his own theologian and also examiner of bishops and consultor of the Holy Office. In 1599 Clement made him a cardinal. Twice Robert was a candidate for the papacy, but lost. He remained as a member of the Holy Office and became involved in Church disputes and campaigns against heresies. He became head of the Vatican Library in 1605. It was his duty to accuse Galileo of

heresy for his heliocentric theory. Robert was a brilliant and prolific writer. His greatest work is *Controversies of the Christian Faith Against the Heretics of This Time*, which examines Catholic and Protestant theological arguments. He also wrote two catechisms, one for children and one for teachers, both of which remain popular, as well as numerous catechetical and spiritual treatises, commentaries on the Scriptures, and other works. He was declared a Doctor of the Church in 1923. *Canonized:* 1930.

Robert Southwell (c. 1561-1595) *Born in:* Norfolk, England.
Jesuit, poet, and martyr. After studying in Douay and Paris, Robert joined the Jesuits in 1578 and was ordained in 1584. In 1586 he was sent to England, where a year later he became chaplain to Countess Anne of Arundel, whose husband, Bl. Thomas Philip, was imprisoned in the Tower of London. Robert was betrayed and arrested in 1592. He was cruelly tortured, including being racked nine times, and then was cast into a dungeon, where he languished for three years. He was executed at Tyburn. *Canonized:* 1970, one of the Forty Martyrs of England and Wales.

Sebastian Valfrè, Bl. (1629–1710) *Born in:* Verduno, Piedmont, Italy.
Preacher, prophet, and charity worker. Born to a poor family, Sebastian joined the Congregation of the Oratory in Turin in 1651 and was ordained the following year. He rose to master of novices and superior of the house, but declined the archbishopric of Turin, preferring instead to work directly with the poor. He was a skilled preacher. Sebastian's writings include his letters, prophecies, and visionary insights.

Symeon the New Theologian (949 or 957–1022) *Born in:* Galatine, Paphlagonia.
Abbot and theologian. A bright student, Symeon was sent to Constantinople at age 14 to live with an uncle. He visited the Monastery of Studios and was so impressed he wanted to become a novice there. He was denied twice, and was finally admitted at age 27 in 984, after years of religious study. Symeon was sent to the monastery of St. Mamas, where he was ordained at age 30, and took the name of Symeon, after a monk he met on his first visit to the Studios monastery. He became abbot and initiated strict reforms. After six years, his opponents succeeded in having him exiled. He wandered, and then established his own monastery, where, in his private chapel, he composed hymns and wrote theological works, including catechisms. He declined an invitation to return to Constantinople. Among his notable works are *Catechetical Discourses, Ethical Discourses,* and *Hymns of Divine Love.*

Teresa of Ávila (1515–1582) *Born in:* the area near Ávila in Castile, Spain.
Mystic, Carmelite nun, a founder of the Discalced Carmelite Order, and Doctor of the Church. At age 15 Teresa was sent to an Augustinian convent and decided to become a nun. At age 20 or 21 she entered the Incarnation of the Carmelite nuns in Ávila. She began to suffer from severe ill health, through which she discovered the power of prayer. She healed herself on her deathbed. After her recovery she began to have mystical experiences, including raptures and flights out of the body. She spent long periods alone in the prayer of quiet and the prayer of union, during which she often fell into a trance.

In 1559 she experienced a transverberation, a "striking through," in which an angel pierced her heart with an arrow of love. In 1562 Teresa established the reformed Discalced Carmelite order with stricter rules. At age 53 she met John de Ypes y Álvarez, who became St. JOHN OF THE CROSS; the two maintained a close friendship carried on by correspondence. John established Discalced Carmelite monasteries. Teresa's written works remain spiritual classics: her autobiography, *Life*, and *The Interior Castle* and *The Way of Perfection*. Teresa was the first woman to be declared a Doctor of the Church, in 1970. *Canonized:* 1662.

Theoleptos of Philadelphia (c. 1250–1322) *Born in:* Nicaea. Metropolitan of Philadelphia.
Of humble birth, Theoleptos married and became a deacon. He became involved in anti-unionist politics, which forced him to flee into the desert in 1275. There he became a monk and practiced contemplation and an ascetical life. Summoned to Constantinople, he defied the ruler, Mark VIII, and was imprisoned. In jail he met Nikophoros the Hesychast, who taught him the hesychast method of prayer. He became one of Nikophoros's disciples. Theoleptos was released from prison and returned to Nicaea, but elected to live as a hermit, despite the entreaties of his wife. His holiness attracted pilgrims. He took a spiritual companion, an Italian monk named Neilos. Neilos died and came to him in a dream, offering him a drink of miraculous water. Thereafter, Theoleptos became a writer of Orthodox spiritual works. In 1283 he was named metropolitan of Philadelphia, a post he held until his death. He was an able administrator, and defended the city against invading Turks in 1311. He initiated St. GREGORY PALAMAS into hesychasm. Some of his inspired works are included in *The Philokalia*, such as *On Inner Work in Christ and the Monastic Profession*.

Theophan the Recluse (1815–1894)
Russian bishop who translated *The Philokalia* into Russian from the Slavonic translation of the original Greek and Latin texts. Theophan's work was published in five volumes by the Monastery of St. Panteleimon on Mount Athos between 1877 and 1913, and became the basis for English translations.

Théophane Vénard (1829–1861) *Born in:* St. Loup, Poitiers, France.
Martyr. A sickly child, Théophane had an early ambition to be a priest and martyr. In 1850 he entered the College of the Foreign Missions of Paris and was ordained in 1852. He was sent to Hong Kong and then towestern Tonkin (Vietnam). Persecuted and racked by bad health, Théophane ministered to the Christians there. In 1860 he was arrested and imprisoned for months in a cage, and then beheaded. Throughout his ordeal he maintained courage and sweetness. *Canonized:* 1988.

Thérèse of Lisieux (1873–1897) *Born in:* Alcon, Normandy, France.
Discalced Carmelite nun; mystic; Doctor of the Church. On a pilgrimage to Rome at age 15, Thérèse asked Pope Leo XIII for special permission to become a nun, even though she was not old enough to enter a convent. She soon was admitted to the Carmelites, and took the name Thérèse of the Child Jesus. Thérèse distinguished herself with her exceptional piety; she had mystical experiences. In 1896 she

contracted tuberculosis. During her decline, her conversations and spiritual counsels were recorded. She called her simple doctrine "the little way of spiritual childhood," which involves an infallible trust in, and love of God. Thérèse's autobiography, *The Story of a Soul,* remains one of the most popular Catholic books of all time. She was declared a Doctor of the Church in 1997. *Canonized:* 1925.

Thomas Aquinas (1225–1274) *Born in:* Roccasecca near Aquino, Italy.
Dominican, scholar and Doctor of the Church, regarded as the father of Scholasticism and the chief synthesizer of philosophy and theology for the Catholic Church. At age 18 Thomas joined the Dominicans, and soon became the lecture transcriber for St. Albert the Great in Cologne. He was drawn to the works of Aristotle, who had a profound impact upon his own philosophy. In 1256 Thomas became a teacher, and within a year was teaching theology to Dominicans in Paris. Throughout his life he devoted himself to study and writing. Thomas's complete writings include biblical commentaries, commentaries on Aristotle, and polemical tracts. His most famous works are two enormous treatises covering the whole range of Christian doctrine and its philosophical background: *Summa Contra Gentiles* (On the truth of the Catholic faith against the unbelievers) and *Summa Theologica*, ranging over God, creation, angels, human nature and happiness, grace, virtues, Christ, and sacraments. Begun in 1266, *Summa Theologica* was unfinished at his death; it remains one of the Church's most important theological works. Other notable works are *De Ente et Essentia* (On being and essence); *De Regimine Principium* (On kingship); *Contra Impugnantes Religionem*, defending Mendicant Orders; *De Perfectae Vitae Spiritualis*, on the spiritual life; *De Unitate Intellectus Contra Averroistas*, against the Averroists; *Quaestiones Disputatae* and *Quaestiones Quodlibetales*, debated questions for lecture halls. Thomas was declared a Doctor of the Church and Doctor Angelicus in 1567. *Canonized:* 1323.

Thomas More (1478–1535) *Born in:* London.
Lord Chancellor of England; scholar; martyr. Thomas's father was a lawyer and a judge, and Thomas followed in his footsteps, studying law at Oxford University. He was admitted to the bar in 1501, and joined Parliament in 1504. He married twice (his first wife died). Thomas held various governmental posts and received the favor of King Henry VIII. Henry knighted him and made him speaker of the House of Commons, high steward for the University of Cambridge, and chancellor of the duchy of Lancaster. When Cardinal Thomas Wolsey failed to get Henry a divorce from his wife, Catherine of Aragon, Henry removed him as chancellor of England in 1529 and named Thomas More his successor. Disagreeing with Henry over the divorce, Thomas resigned in 1532. He was arrested in 1534 and charged with treason. He was beheaded in 1534. Thomas's best-known work is *Utopia*, written in 1515–16, a criticism of English society that may have been inspired by his lectures on St. Augustine's *City of God.* Other notable works are *The Four Last Things*, published in 1520, *Dialogue of Comfort Against Tribulation* (1553), and *Dialogue concerning Heresies and Confutation of Tyndale's Answer,* which refuted the Protestant writings of Matthew Tyndale. *Canonized:* 1935.

Valerian (d. c. 460)
Bishop and orator. A monk at the monastery of Lerins, Valerian was named bishop of Cimiez, Gaul. He participated in the Council of Riez in 439 and council of Vaison in 442. Some of his sermons were discovered in the 16th century, attesting to his eloquence as an orator.

Vincent de Paul (c. 1581–1660) *Born in:* Pouy (now called St.-Vincent-de-Paul) near the village of Dax in Gascony.
Apostle of Charity; Friend of the Poor. Founder of the Congregation of the Mission and the Sisters of Charity; Patron of all Charities. After studying at the universities of Toulouse and Saragossa, Spain, Vincent became a Franciscan. In 1605 he was on a boat raided by pirates, and he was sold into slavery in Tunis. He was released in 1607, and returned to Paris in 1609. He became tutor and chaplain to the family of Philip de Gondi, Count of Joigny, and then pastor of the parish church at Châtillon-les-Dombes in eastern France. He founded the first Confraternity of Charity. Around 1623 a wealthy patron gave Vincent an endowment to start a new order, and the Congregation of the Mission was born, to tend the sick and establish seminaries for would-be priests. In 1633, Vincent and St. LOUISE DE MARILLAC cofounded the Sisters (also called the Daughters) of Charity, to establish hospitals and asylums. Vincent remained active in politics and also campaigned against heresies. *Canonized:* 1737.

Vincent Ferrer (1350–1458) *Born in:* Valencia, Spain.
Dominican friar and missionary. At age 17 Vincent became a Dominican, and was sent to Barcelona, where he studied and then taught. He went to Toulouse and worked as papal legate for Cardinal Pedro de Luna. When the cardinal became the antipope Benedict XIII, he appointed Vincent as his confessor and apostolic penitentiary. During a serious illness, Vincent had a vision in which SS. Dominic and FRANCIS OF ASSISI instructed him to go out and preach. He spent 20 years traveling throughout western Europe preaching penance for sin and preparation for judgment. He then returned to Spain, where he spent eight years preaching, working miracles, and converting thousands of Moors. Vincent was popular, and many of his sermons survive. *Canonized:* 1455.

BIBLIOGRAPHY

Aelred of Rievaulx. *The Way of Friendship.* Edited by M. Basil Pennington. Hyde Park, N.Y.: New City Press, 2001.

———. *On the Mysteries.* Translated by Rev. H. de Romestin. Available online at http://www.ewtn.com/library/PATRISTC/PII10-7.TXT. Downloaded Sept. 13, 2001.

———. *Concerning Repentance.* Translated by Rev. H. de Romestin. Available online at http://www.ewtn.com/library/PATRISTC/PII10-8.TXT. Downloaded Sept. 13, 2001.

———. *Concerning Virgins, to Marcellina, His Sister.* Available online at http://www.ewtn.com/library/PATRISTC/PII10-9.TXT. Downloaded Sept. 13, 2001.

Ambrose. *Concerning Widows.* Translated by Rev. H. de Romestin. Available online at http://www.ewtn.com/library/PATRISTC/PII10-10.TXT. Downloaded Sept. 13, 2001.

An Aquinas Reader. Edited by Mary T, Clark. New York: Fordham University Press, 1972.

The Art of Prayer: An Orthodox Anthology. Igumen Chariton of Valamo. Compiled by Kadloubovsky and translated by E. M. Palmer. London: Faber and Faber, 1997.

Aquinas, St. Thomas. *Basic Writings of St. Thomas Aquinas*. Edited by Anton C. Pegis. New York: Random House, 1945.

Athanasius. *On the Incarnation*. Available online at http:listserv.american.edu/catholic/church/fathers/others/ath-inc.txt. Downloaded Sept. 4, 2001.

Augustine. *The City of God*. Translated by Marcus Dods. New York: Modern Library/Random House, 1950.

———. *Confessions.* Translated by John K. Ryan. Garden City, N.Y.: Image/Doubleday Books, 1960.

The Autobiography of Saint Thérèse of Lisieux: The Story of a Soul. Translated by John Beevers. New York: Doubleday, 1990.

Basil the Great. *Gateway to Paradise.* Edited by Oliver Davies and translated by Tim Witherow. London: New City, 1991.

———. *Nine Homilies on the Hexaemeron.* Translated by Rev. Blomfield Jackson.

Available online at http://www.ewtn.com/library/PATRISTC/PII8-2.TXT. Downloaded Sept. 13, 2001.

Bede the Venerable. *Homilies on the Gospels: Book Two, Lent to the Dedication of the Church*. Translated by Lawrence T. Martin and David Hurst. Kalamazoo, Mich.: Cistercian Publications, 1991.

Bernard of Clairvaux. *On the Love of God and other Selected Writings*. Edited by Msgr. Charles J. Dollen. New York: Alba House, 1996.

Birgitta of Sweden. *Life and Selected Revelations*. Translated by Albert Ryle Kezel. Mahwah, N.J.: Paulist Press, 1990.

Bonaventure. *The Soul's Journey into God, The Tree of Life, The Life of St. Francis*. Translated by Ewert Cousins. Mahwah, N.J.: Paulist Press, 1978.

Bowles, Emily. *The Life and Letters of St. Jane Frances Fremyot de Chantal*. London: Burns and Oates, 1872.

Carty, Rev. Charles Mortimer. *Padre Pio the Stigmatist*. Rockford, Ill.: TAN Books and Publishers, 1973.

Celtic Spirituality. Translated by Oliver Davies. Mahwah, N.J.: Paulist Press, 1999.

Chittister, Joan. *The Rule of Benedict: Insights for the Ages*. New York: Crossroad Publishing, 1992.

Clark, Ann L. *Elisabeth of Schönau: A Twelfth-Century Visionary*. Philadelphia: University of Pennsylvania Press, 1992.

Colahan, Clark. *The Visions of Sor Maria de Agreda*. Tucson: University of Arizona Press, 1994.

Coleridge, Henry James. *The Life and Letters of St. Francis Xavier*. Vols. 1 and 2. London: Burns and Oates, 1872.

The Collected Works of St. John of the Cross. Rev. ed. Translated by Kieran Kavanaugh. Washington, D.C.: ICS Publications, 1991.

Coomaraswarmy, Rama. *The Invocation of the Name of Jesus As Practiced in the Western Church*. Louisville, Ky.: Fons Vitae, 1999.

Corrigan, Felicitas. *The Saints Humanly Speaking*. Ann Arbor, Mich.: Servant Publications, 2000.

Cyprian of Carthage. *The Good of Patience*. Available online at http://listserv.http:listserv.american.edu/catholic/church/fathers/cyprian/cyp-pati.txt.

———. *Jealousy and Envy*. Available online at http://listserv.http:listserv.american.edu/catholic/church/fathers/cyprian/cyp-jeal.txt.

———. *Works and Almsgiving*. Available online at http://listserv.http:listserv.american.edu/catholic/church/fathers/cyprian/cyp-work.txt. Downloaded Sept. 4, 2001.

Cyril of Jerusalem. "First Catechetical Lecture." Translated by Edwin Hamilton Gifford. Available online at http://www.ocf.org/OthrodoxPage/reading/St.Pachomius/Greek/Catech/lexr1.html. Downloaded Sept. 4, 2001.

———. "Second Catechetical Lecture." Translated by Edwin Hamilton Gifford. Available online at http://www.ocf.org/OthrodoxPage/reading/St.Pachomius/Greek/Catech/lexr2.html. Downloaded Sept. 4, 2001.

———. "Catechetical Lectures 1–2 with Procatechesis." Translated by Mr. Church; revised translation by Edward Hamilton Gifford. Available online at http://www.ewtn.com/library/PATRISTC/PII7-1.TXT. Downloaded Sept. 13, 2001.

Early Christian Writings: The Apostolic Fathers. Translated by Maxwell

Staniforth; revised translation by Andrew Louth. London: Penguin Books, 1987.

The Confession of Saint Patrick. Translated by John Skinner. New York: Image Books/Doubleday, 1998.

The Dialogue of Saint Catherine of Siena. Translated by Alar Thorold. Rockford, Ill.: TAN Books and Publishers, 1974.

Elisabeth of Schönau. *The Complete Works*. Translated by Anne L. Clark. Mahwah, N.J.: Paulist Press, 2000.

Edith Stein. *Essays on Woman*. 2nd ed. Translated by Freda Mary Oben. Washington, D.C.: ICS Publications, 1996.

The Fathers Speak. Georges Barrios, ed. and trans. Crestwood, N.Y.: St. Vladimir's Seminary Press, 1986.

Francis de Sales. *Introduction to the Devout Life*. Rockford, Ill.: TAN Books and Publishers, 1994.

Francis of Assisi: Early Documents. Vol I: *The Saint*. New York: New City Press, 1999.

Francis and Clare: The Complete Works. Translated by Regis J. Armstrong and Ignatius C. Brady. New York: Paulist Press, 1982.

Gertrude the Great of Helfta. *Spiritual Exercises*. Translated by Gertrud Jaron Lewis and Jack Lewis. Kalamazoo, Mich.: Cistercian Publications, 1989.

Gregory Nazianzen. *Orations 27-32: The Five Theological Orations*. Translated by Charles Gordon Browne. Available online at http://www.ewtn.com/library/PATRISTC/PII7-4.TXT. Downloaded Sept. 13, 2001.

Gregory the Great. *The Dialogues, Book Two*. Indianapolis, Ind.: Bobbs-Merrill, 1967.

———. *The Book of Pastoral Rule*. Translated by Rev. James Barmby. Available online at http://www.ewtn.com/library/PATRISTC/PII2-4.TXT. Downloaded Sept. 5, 2001.

Gregory of Nyssa. *Ascetical Works*. Translated by Virginia Woods Callaban. Washington, D.C.: Catholic University of America Press, 1967.

———. *Commentary on the Inscriptions of the Psalms*. Translated by Casimir McCambley. Brookline, Mass.: Hellenic College Press, n.d.

———. *The Great Catechism*. Translated by Rev. William Moore. Available online at http://www.ewtn.com/library/PATRISTC/PII5-15.TXT. Downloaded Sept. 13, 2001.

———. *On Infants' Early Death*. Translated by Rev. William Moore. Available online at http://www.ewtn.com/library/PATRISTC/PII5-11.TXT. Downloaded Sept. 13, 2001.

———. *On Pilgrimages*. Translated by Rev. William Moore. Available online at http://www.ewtn.com/library/PATRISTC/PII5-12.TXT. Downloaded Sept. 13, 2001.

Gregory Thaumaturgos. *Canonical Epistle*. Available online at http://www.ewtn.com/library/PATRISTC/ANF6-3.TXT. Downloaded Sept. 13, 2001.

Henry Suso. *The Exemplar, with Two German Sermons*. Translated by Frank Tobin. Mahwah, N.J.: Paulist Press, 1989.

Hero, Angela C. *The Life and Letters of Theoleptos of Philadelphia*. Brookline, Mass.: Hellenic College Press, 1994.

Hildegard of Bingen's Book of Divine Works with Letters and Songs. Edited by Matthew Fox. Santa Fe, N.Mex.: Bear & Co., 1987.

Hildegard of Bingen's Scivias. Translated by Bruce Hozeski. Santa Fe, N.Mex.: Bear & Co., 1986.

The Hymns of Saint Hilary of Poitiers in the Codex Aretinus. Translated by Walter Neidig Myers. Phildelphia: Ph.D. thesis for the University of Pennsylvania, 1928.

Jerome. *Select Letters.* Translated by F. A. Wright. Cambridge, Mass.: Harvard University Press, 1999.

Pope John XXIII. *In My Own Words.* Compiled and edited by Anthony F. Chiffolo. Liguori, Mo: Liguori Publications, 1999.

St. John Bosco. *St. Joseph Cafasso: Priest of the Gallows.* Rockford, Ill.: TAN Books and Publishers, 1983.

John Cassian. *Conferences.* Translated by Colm Luibheid. Mahwah, N.J.: Paulist Press, 1985.

John Climacus. *The Ladder of Divine Ascent.* Translated by Colm Luidheid and Norm Russell. Mahwah, N.J.: Paulist Press, 1982.

John of the Cross. *Dark Night of the Soul.* Translated by E. Allison Peers. Garden City, N.Y.: Image/Doubleday, 1959.

Escrivá, Josemaría. *The Forge.* Princeton, N.J.: Scepter Press, 1988.

———. *The Way.* Dublin: Four Courts Press Ltd., 1985.

Julian of Norwich. *Showings.* New York: Paulist Press, 1978.

The Kolbe Reader: The Writings of St. Maxmilian M. Kolbe. Fr. Anselm W. Romb, OFM Conv., ed. Libertyville, Ill.: Franciscan Marytown Press, 1987.

LaFrenière, Bernard. *Brother André According to Witnesses.* Montreal: St. Joseph's Oratory, 1990.

The Letters of Catherine of Siena. Vol. I. Translated by Suzanne Noffke, O.P. Binghamton, N.Y.: Medieval & Renaissance Texts & Studies, 1988.

The Letters of St. Cyprian of Carthage. Vol. 1, *Letters 1–27.* Translated by G. W. Clarke. Ramsey, N.Y.: Newman Press/Paulist Press, 1984.

Letters of St. Paulinus of Nola. Vols. 1 and 2. Translated by P. G. Walsh. London: Longmans, Green, 1966.

de Montfort, Louis. "Fragments of 34 Letters." Available online at http://www.ewtn.com/library/Montfort/34LETTRS.HTM. Downloaded Sept. 5, 2001.

———. "Letter to the People of Montbernage." Available online at http://www.ewtn.com/library/Montfort/LMONTBER.HTM. Downloaded Sept. 5, 2001.

———. *The Love of Eternal Wisdom.* Available online at http://www.ewtn.com/library/Montfort/LEW.HTM. Downloaded Sept. 5, 2001.

Madigan, Shawn, ed. *Mystics, Visionaries and Prophets: A Historical Anthology of Women's Spiritual Writings.* Minneapolis: Fortress Press, 1998.

Maria Maddalena de' Pazzi. *Selected Revelations.* Translated by Armando Maggi. Mahwah, N.J.: Paulist Press, 2000.

Maximus Confessor. *Selected Writings.* Translated by George C. Berthold. Mahwah, N.J.: Paulist Press, 1985.

Mayer, Wendy, and Pauline Allen. *John Chrysostom.* London: Routledge, 2000.

Methodius. *Concerning Free Will.* Translated by Rev. William R. Clark. Available online at http://www.ewtn.com/library/PATRISTC/ANF6-21.TXT. Downloaded Sept. 13, 2001.

Meyedorff, John. *A Study of Gregory Palamas.* London: The Faith Press, 1964.

O Fiaich, Tomas. *Columbanus in His Own Words.* Dublin: Veritas Publications, 1974.

Padre Pio. *In My Own Words*. Compiled and edited by Anthony F. Chiffolo. Liguori, Mo.: Liguori Publications, 2000.

Peter of Alcántara. *Treatise on Prayer & Meditation*. Translated by Dominic Davis, O.F.M. London: Burns, Oats and Washbourne, Ltd., 1926.

Peter Chrysologus. *Selected Sermons*, and Saint Valerian: *Homilies*. Translated by George E. Ganss. Washington, D.C.: Catholic University of America Press, 1965.

The Philokalia. Compiled by St. Kiodimos of the Holy Mountain and Makarios of Corinth, and translated by G. E. H. Palmer, Philip Sherrard, and Kallistos Ware. Vols. 3 and 4. London: Faber & Faber Ltd. 1984, 1995.

Prevot, Andre. *Love, Peace and Joy: Devotion to the Sacred Heart of Jesus According to St. Gertrude*. Rockford, Ill.: TAN Books and Publishers, 1984.

Revelations of St. Bridget on the Life and Passion of Our Lord and the Life of His Blessed Mother. Rockford, Ill.: TAN Books and Publishers, 1984.

Saint Anthony, Herald of the Good News, a Guide and Light for Today: Excerpts from the Sermones *of Saint Anthony.* Translated by Claude M. Jarmak, with Thomas E. Hunt. Ellicott City, Md: Conventual Franciscan Friars, 1995.

The Sermons of St. Maximus of Turin. Translated by Boniface Ramsey. New York: Newman Press, 1989.

Robert Bellarmine. *Live Well, Die Holy: The Art of Being A Saint, Now and Forever.* Manchester, N.H.: Sophia Institute Press, 1998.

———. *Spiritual Writings*. Translated by John Patrick Donnelly, S.J., and Roland J. Teske, S.J. Mahwah, N.J.: Paulist Press, 1989.

Rubenson, Samuel. *The Letters of St. Anthony: Monasticism and the Making of a Saint*. Minneapolis: Fortress Press, 1995.

Select Treatises of St. Athanasius in Controversy with the Arians. Translated by John Henry Cardinal Newman. London: Longmans, Green and Co., 1890.

Sermons of St. Alphonsus Liguori. Rockford, Ill.: TAN Books and Publishers, 1982.

Sister M. Faustina Kowalska. *Divine Mercy in My Soul*. Stockbridge, Mass.: Marian Press, 1987.

The Soul of Elizabeth Seton. New York: Benziger Brothers, 1936.

Spidlik, Thomas. *Drinking from the Hidden Fountain: A Patristic Breviary.* London: New City, 1995.

St. Anselm's Proslogion. Translated by M. J. Charlesworth. Oxford: Oxford University Press, 1965.

St. John Chrysostom on Marriage and Family Life. Translated by Catharine P. Roth and David Anderson. Crestwood: N.Y.: St. Vladimir's Seminary Press, 1986.

St. Lorenzo da Brindisi. *Selected Mariology Sermons*. Translated by Mary Ann Mandym. Series of the Doctors of the Universal Church, 1976.

St. Symeon the New Theologian. *On the Mystical Life: The Ethical Discourses of St. Symeon the New Theologian*. Vol. 2: *On Virtue and Chrisitian Life*. Translated by Alexander Golitzin. Crestwood, N.Y.: St. Vladimir's Seminary Press, 1996.

———. *The Interior Castle*. New York: Paulist Press, 1979.

St Teresa of Ávila. *The Life of Saint Teresa of Avila by Herself.* London: Penguin Books, 1957.

———. *The Way of Perfection*. Translated by E. Allison Peers. New York: Doubleday/Image Books, 1964.

The Spiritual Direction of Saint Claude de la Colombière. Translated by Mother M. Philip. San Francisco: Ignatius Press, 1998.

Thomas Aquinas. *Summa Theologiae*. Edited by Timothy McDermott. Allen, Tex.: Christian Classics, 1989.

Thoughts of Saint Therese. Rockford, Ill.: TAN Books and Publishers, 1988.

Venerable Mary of Agreda. *The Mystical City of God*. Abridgment. Translated by Fiscar Marison. Rockford, Ill.: TAN Books and Publishers, 1978.

St. Vincent Ferrer. *A Christology from the Sermons of St. Vincent Ferrer of the Order of Preachers*. Selected and translated by S.M.C. London: Blackfriars Publications, 1954.

Vincent de Paul and Louise de Marillac. *Rules, Conferences and Writings*. Mahwah, N.J.: Paulist Press, 1995.

The Voice of the Saints. Rockford, Ill.: TAN Books and Publishers, 1986.

INDEX

Boldface page numbers denote main subject categories.

A

B

C

D

E

E

G

I

J

K

L

M

N

O

P

R

S

T

U

V